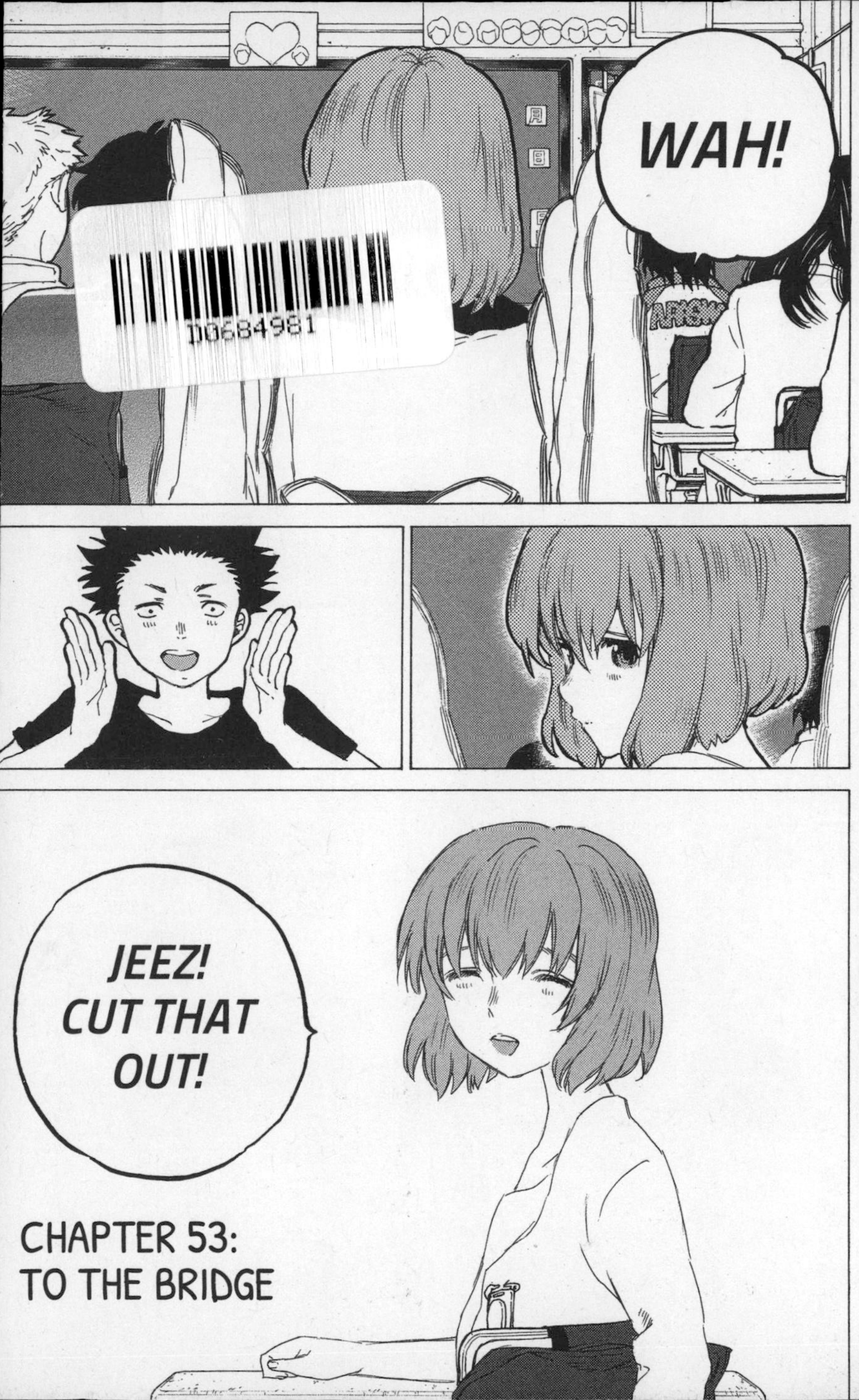
WAH!
JEEZ! CUT THAT OUT!
CHAPTER 53: TO THE BRIDGE

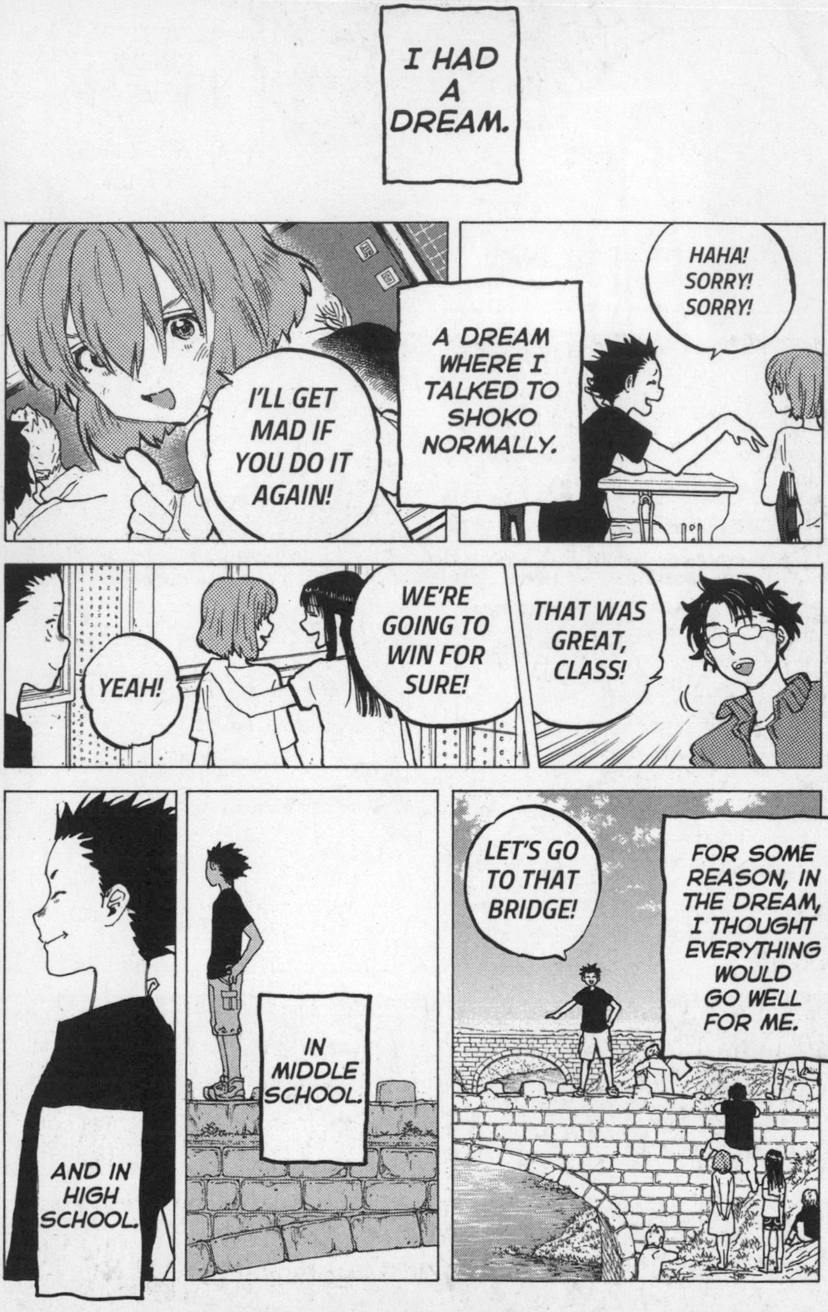
I HAD A DREAM.
HAHA! SORRY! SORRY!
A DREAM WHERE I TALKED TO SHOKO NORMALLY.
I'LL GET MAD IF YOU DO IT AGAIN!
THAT WAS GREAT, CLASS!
WE'RE GOING TO WIN FOR SURE!
YEAH!
FOR SOME REASON, IN THE DREAM, I THOUGHT EVERYTHING WOULD GO WELL FOR ME.
LET'S GO TO THAT BRIDGE!
IN MIDDLE SCHOOL.
AND IN HIGH SCHOOL.

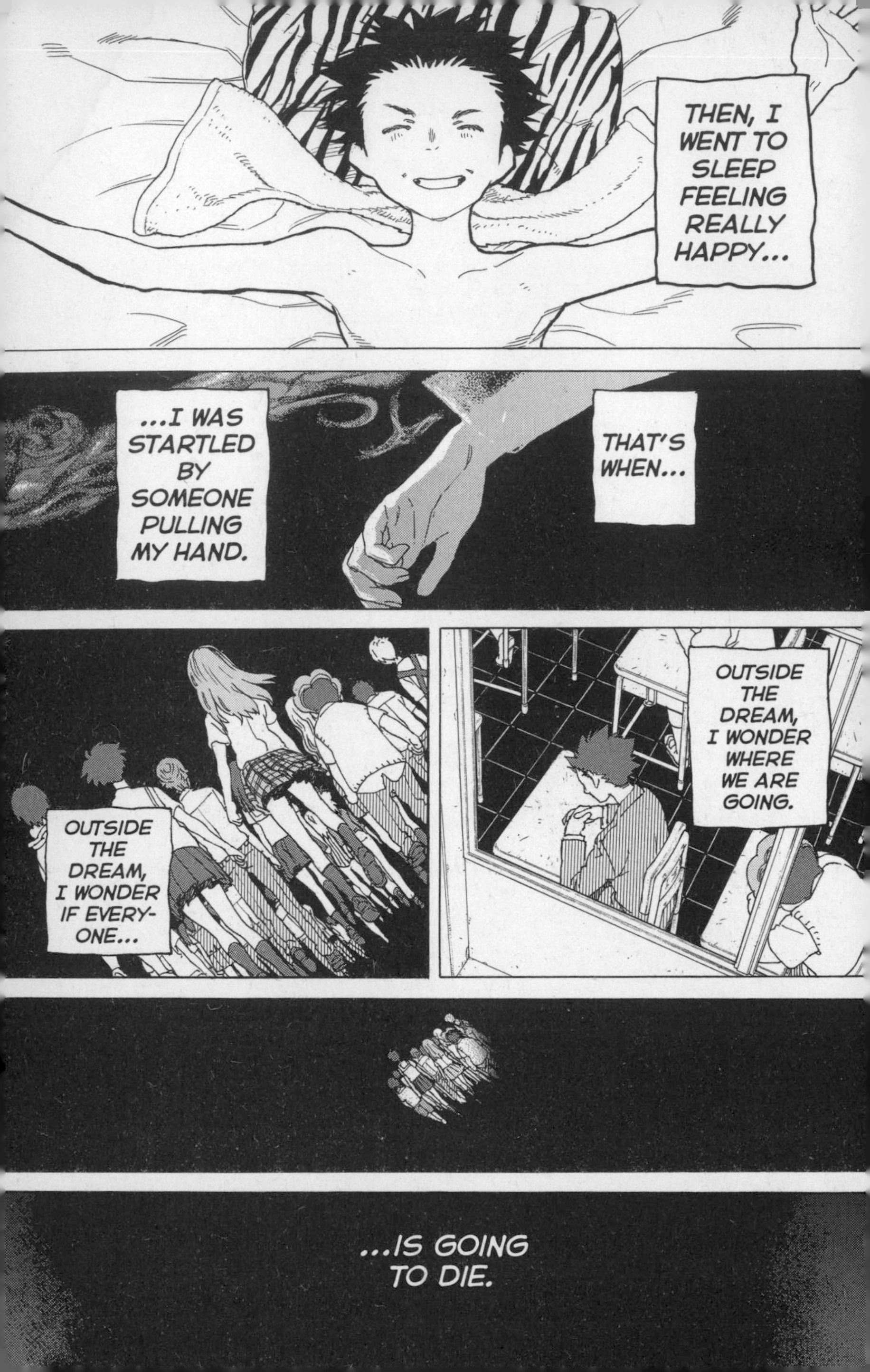
THEN, I WENT TO SLEEP FEELING REALLY HAPPY...
THAT'S WHEN...
...I WAS STARTLED BY SOMEONE PULLING MY HAND.
OUTSIDE THE DREAM, I WONDER WHERE WE ARE GOING.
OUTSIDE THE DREAM, I WONDER IF EVERY-ONE...
...IS GOING TO DIE.

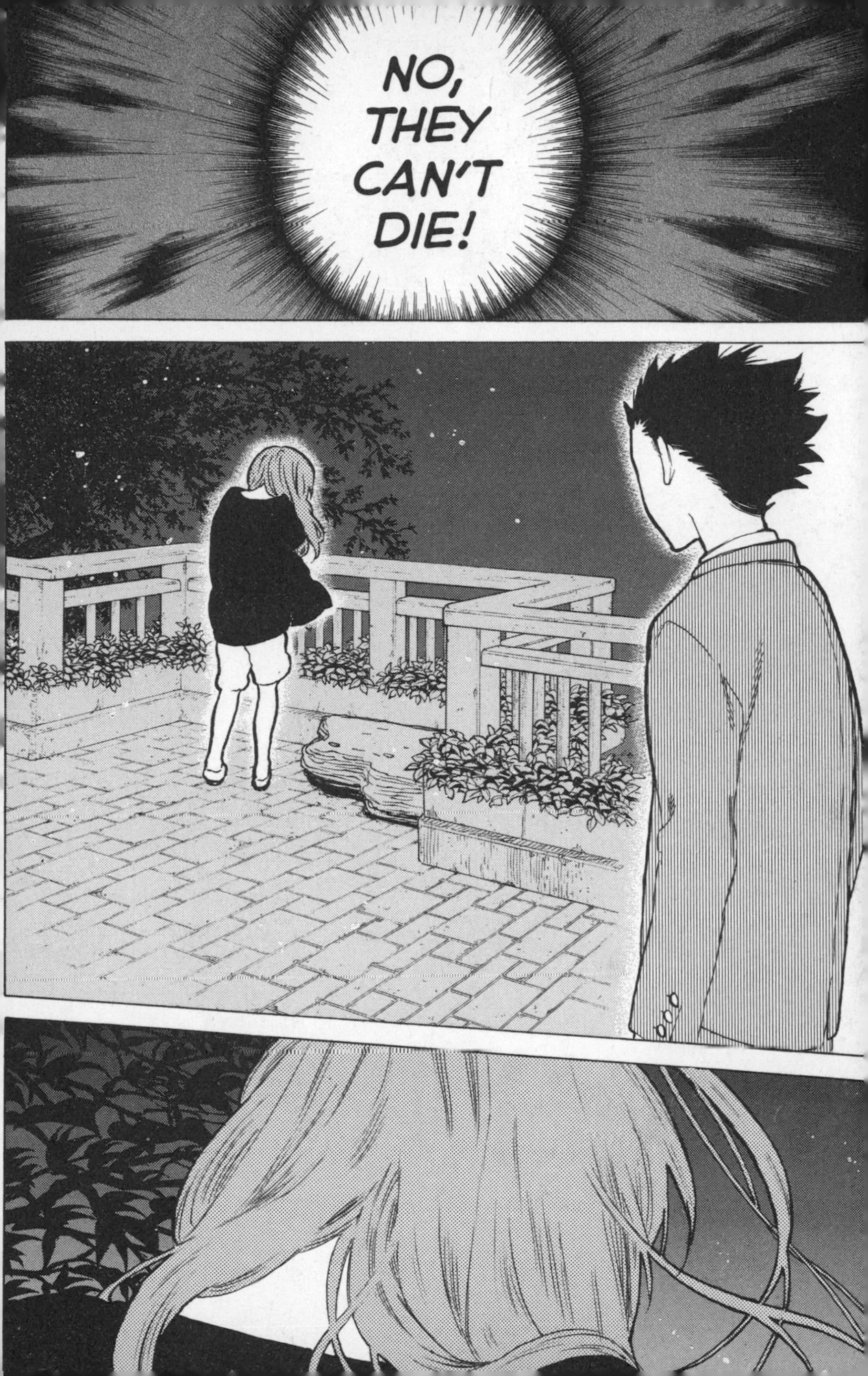
NO, THEY CAN'T DIE!

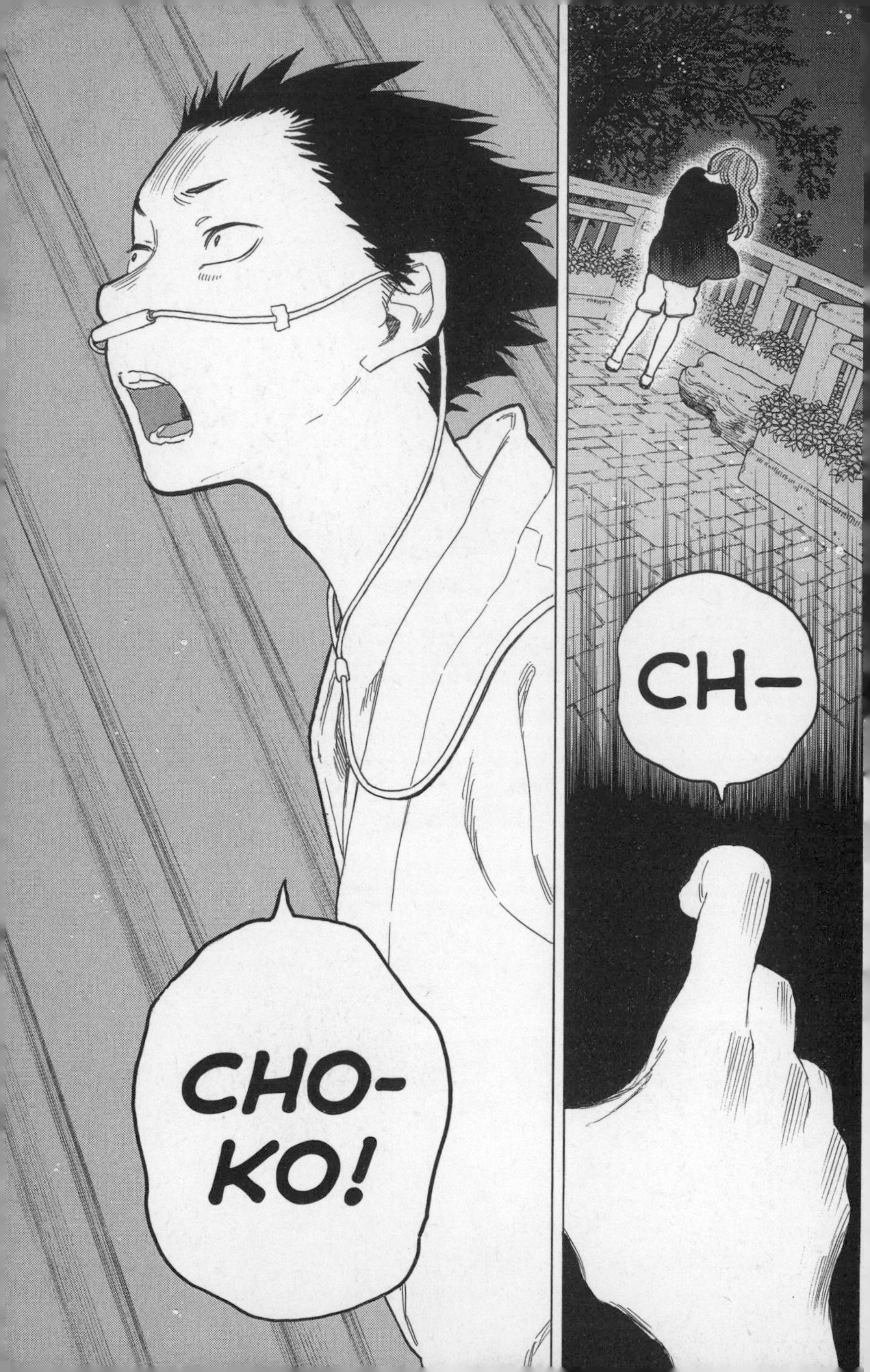
CH-
CHO-KO!

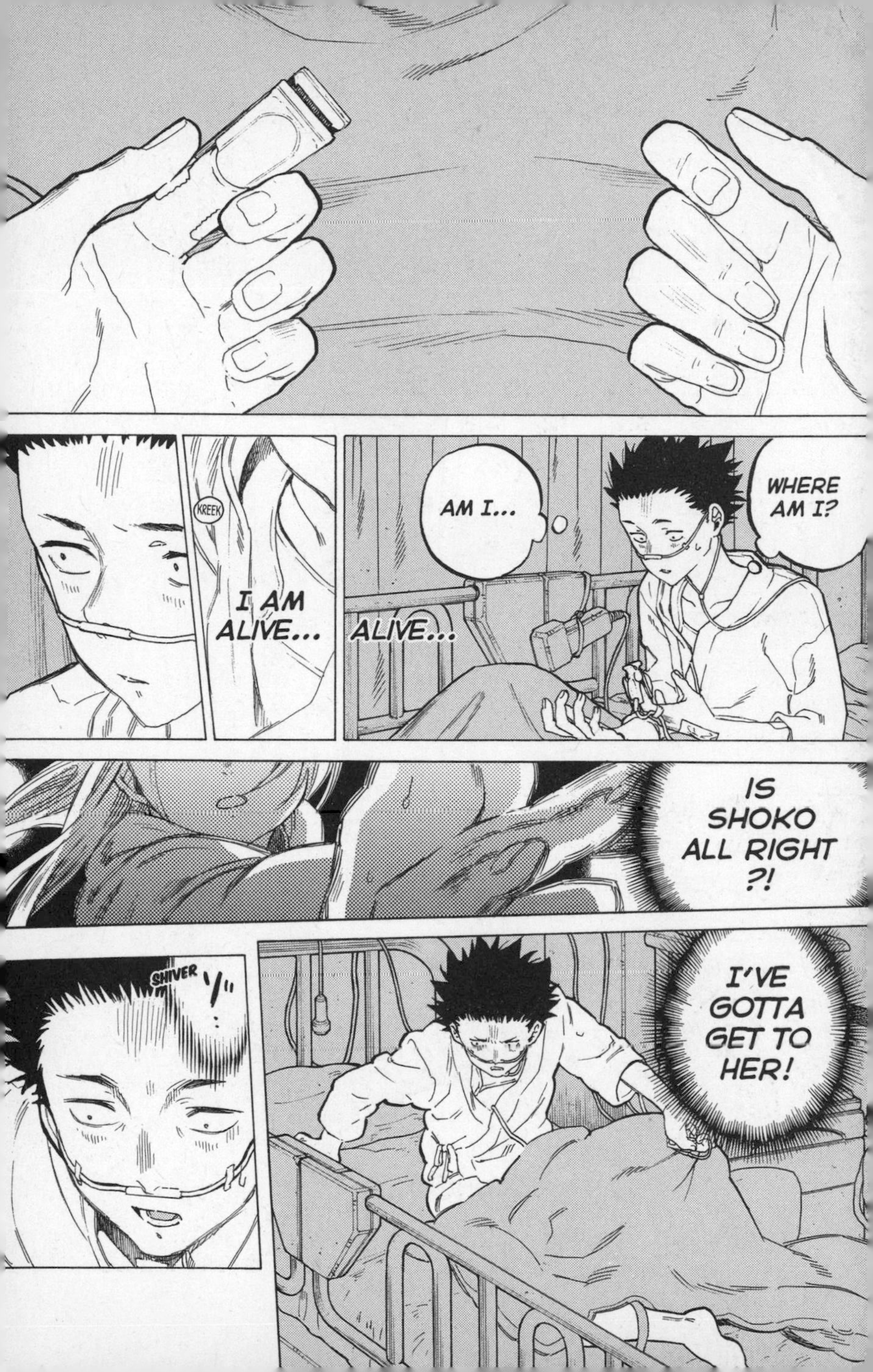
WHERE AM I?
AM I...
ALIVE...
KREEK
I AM ALIVE...
IS SHOKO ALL RIGHT ?!
I'VE GOTTA GET TO HER!
SHIVER

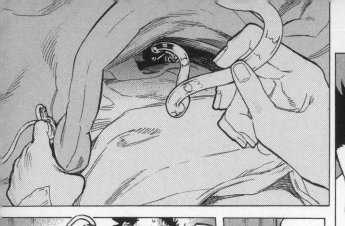

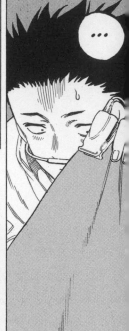

...

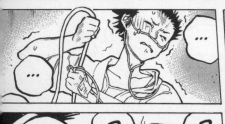

...

WHOA!

WHOA!

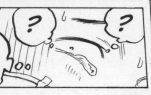

I CAN'T PULL IT OUT?!

?

?

SPROING

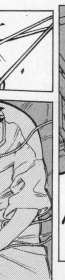

THESE ARE IN THE WAY!

RIP

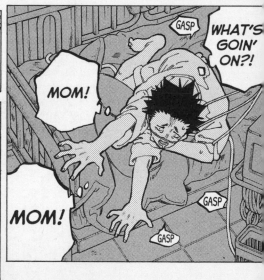

GASP

WHAT'S GOIN' ON?!

MOM!

MOM!

GASP

GASP

9

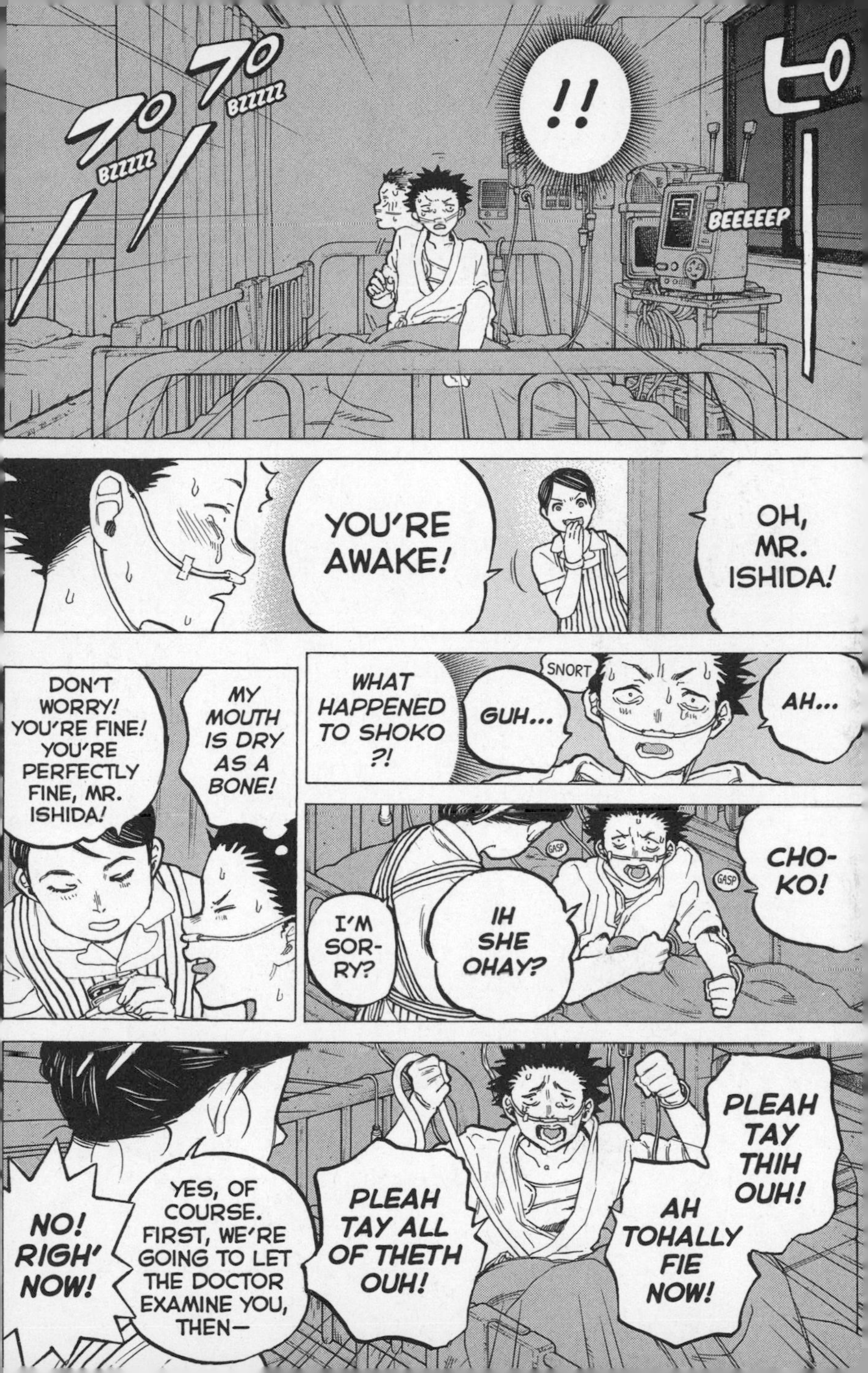

ピー
BEEEEEP
!!
プ
BZZZZZ
プ
BZZZZZ
OH, MR. ISHIDA!
YOU'RE AWAKE!
AH...
SNORT
GUH...
WHAT HAPPENED TO SHOKO?!
CHO-KO!
GASP
GASP
IH SHE OHAY?
I'M SORRY?
MY MOUTH IS DRY AS A BONE!
DON'T WORRY! YOU'RE FINE! YOU'RE PERFECTLY FINE, MR. ISHIDA!
PLEAH TAY THIH OUH!
AH TOHALLY FIE NOW!
PLEAH TAY ALL OF THETH OUH!
YES, OF COURSE. FIRST, WE'RE GOING TO LET THE DOCTOR EXAMINE YOU, THEN—
NO! RIGH' NOW!

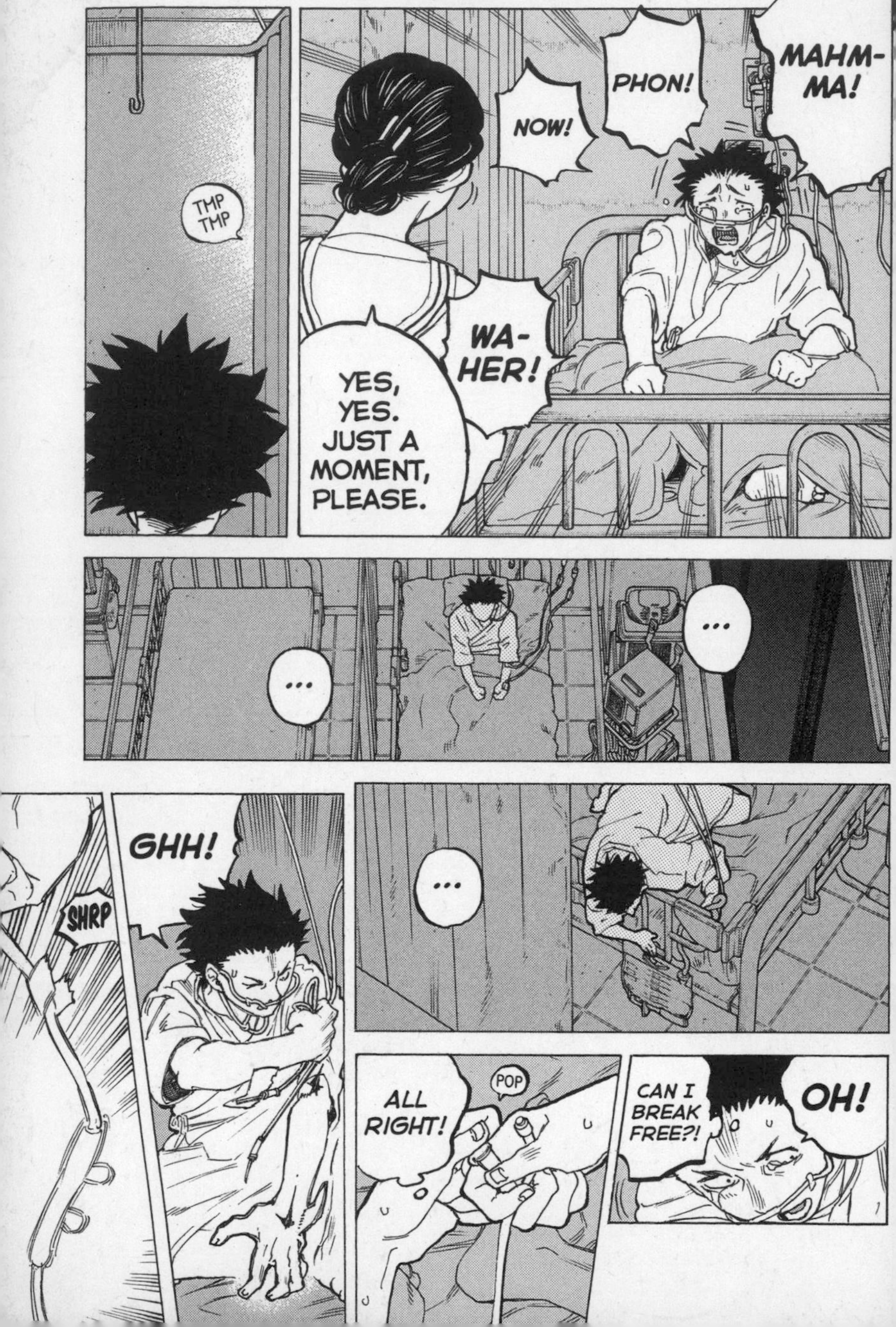
MAHMM-MA!
PHON!
NOW!
WA-HER!
YES, YES. JUST A MOMENT, PLEASE.
TMP TMP
...
...
...
OH!
CAN I BREAK FREE?!
POP
ALL RIGHT!
GHH!
SHRP

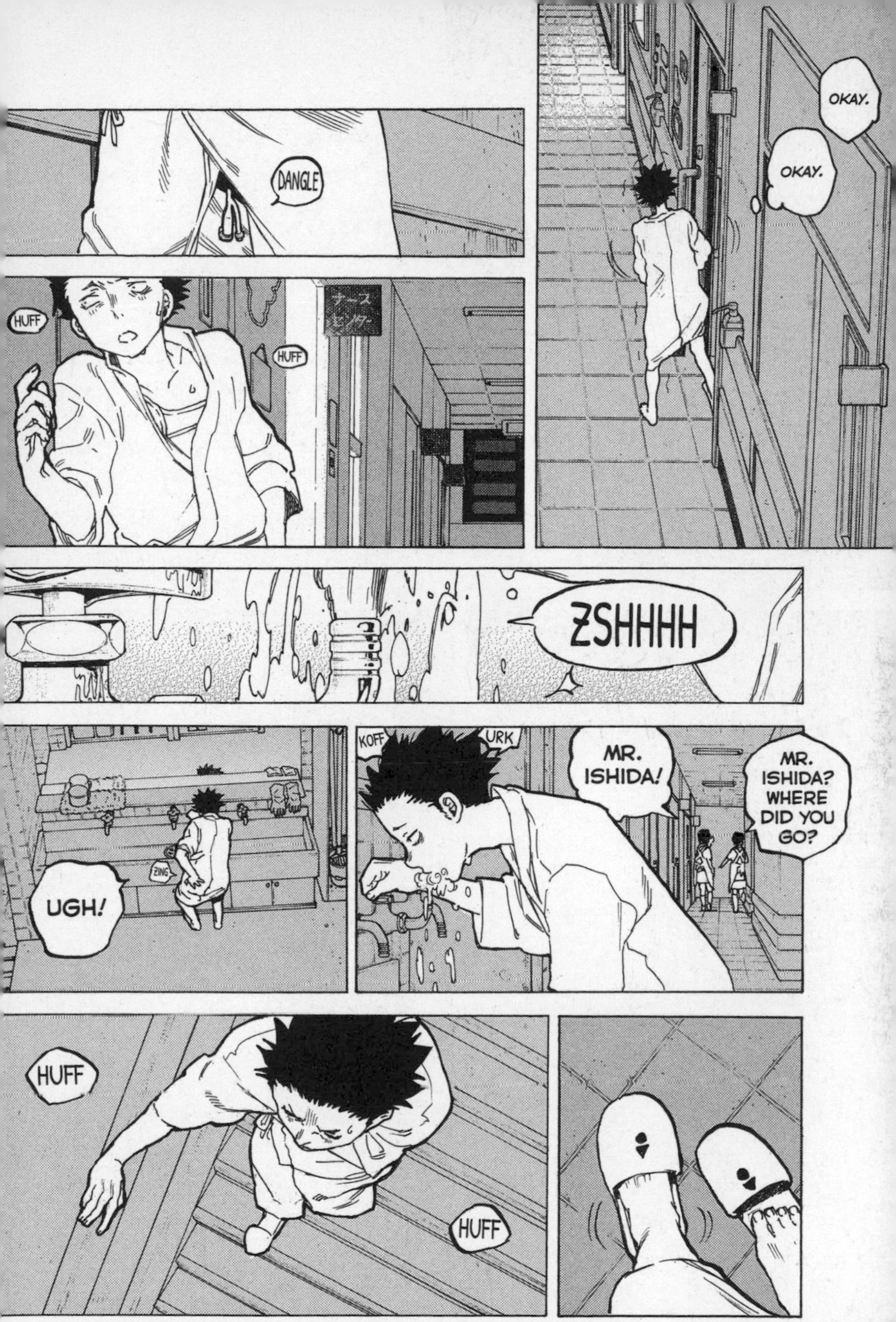
OKAY.
OKAY.
DANGLE
HUFF
HUFF
ZSHHHH
MR. ISHIDA? WHERE DID YOU GO?
MR. ISHIDA!
URK
KOFF
ZING
UGH!
HUFF
HUFF

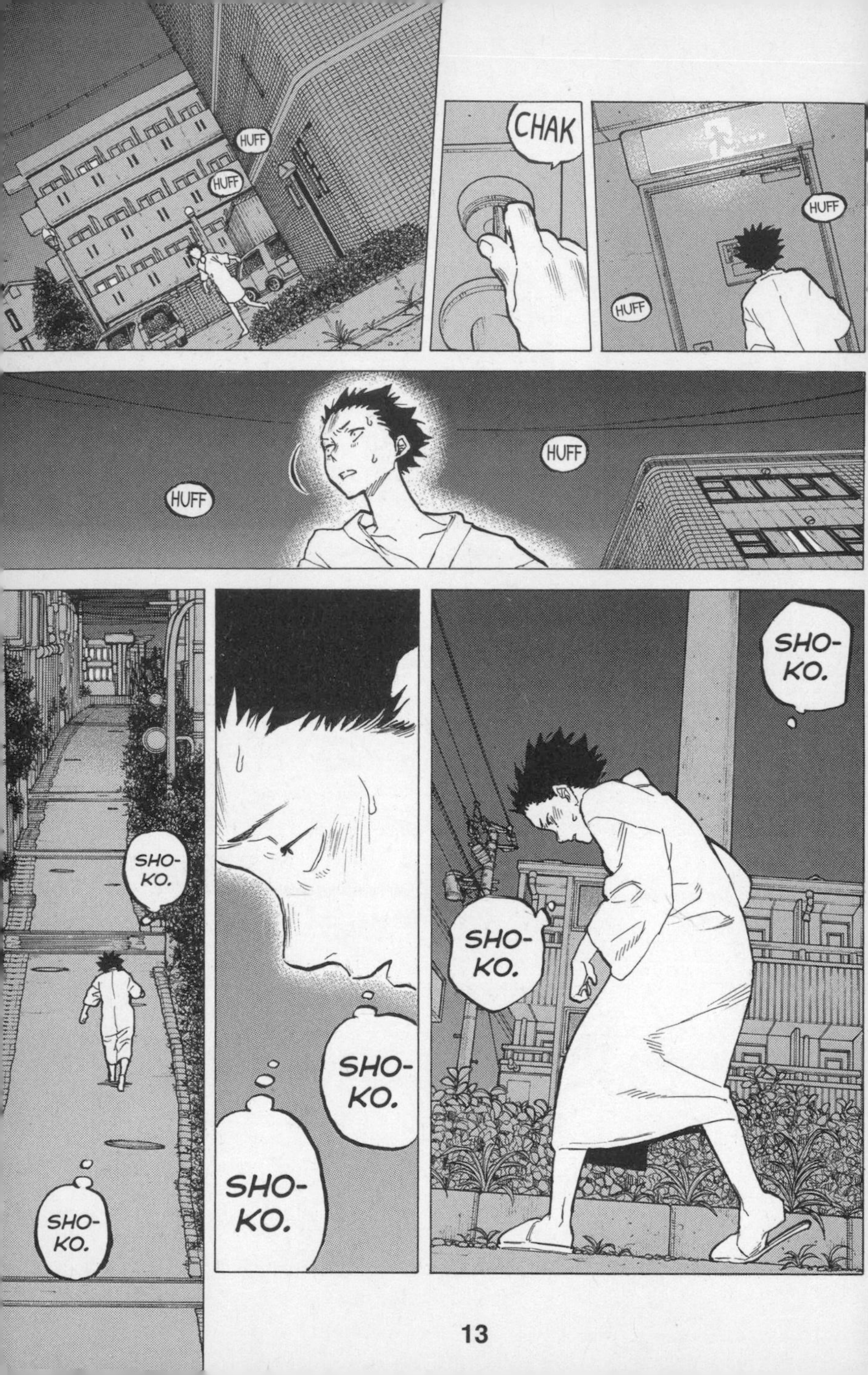
HUFF
HUFF
CHAK
HUFF
HUFF
HUFF
HUFF
SHO-KO.
SHO-KO.
SHO-KO.
SHO-KO.
SHO-KO.
SHO-KO.

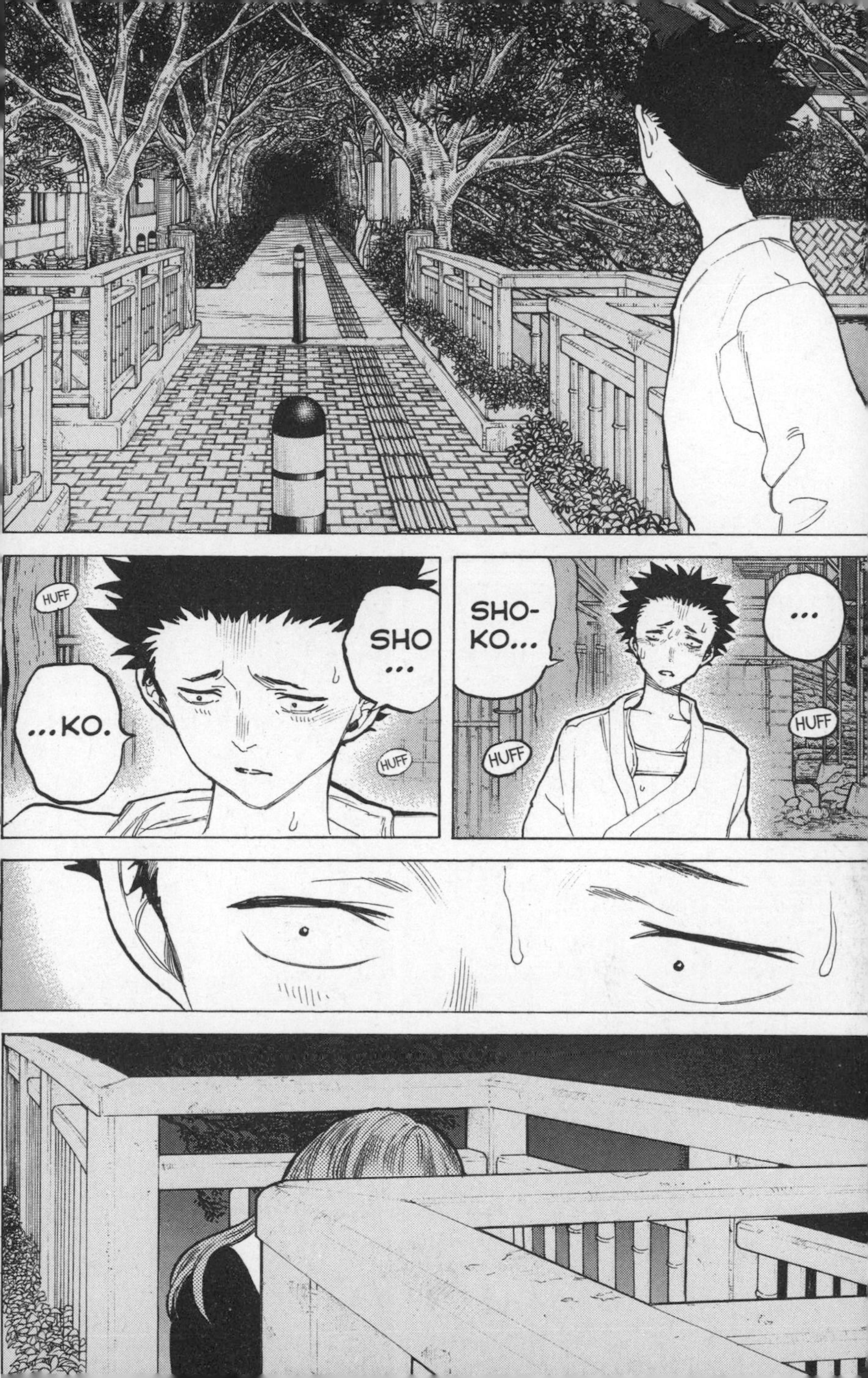
...
SHO-KO...
HUFF
HUFF
SHO
...
HUFF
...KO.
HUFF

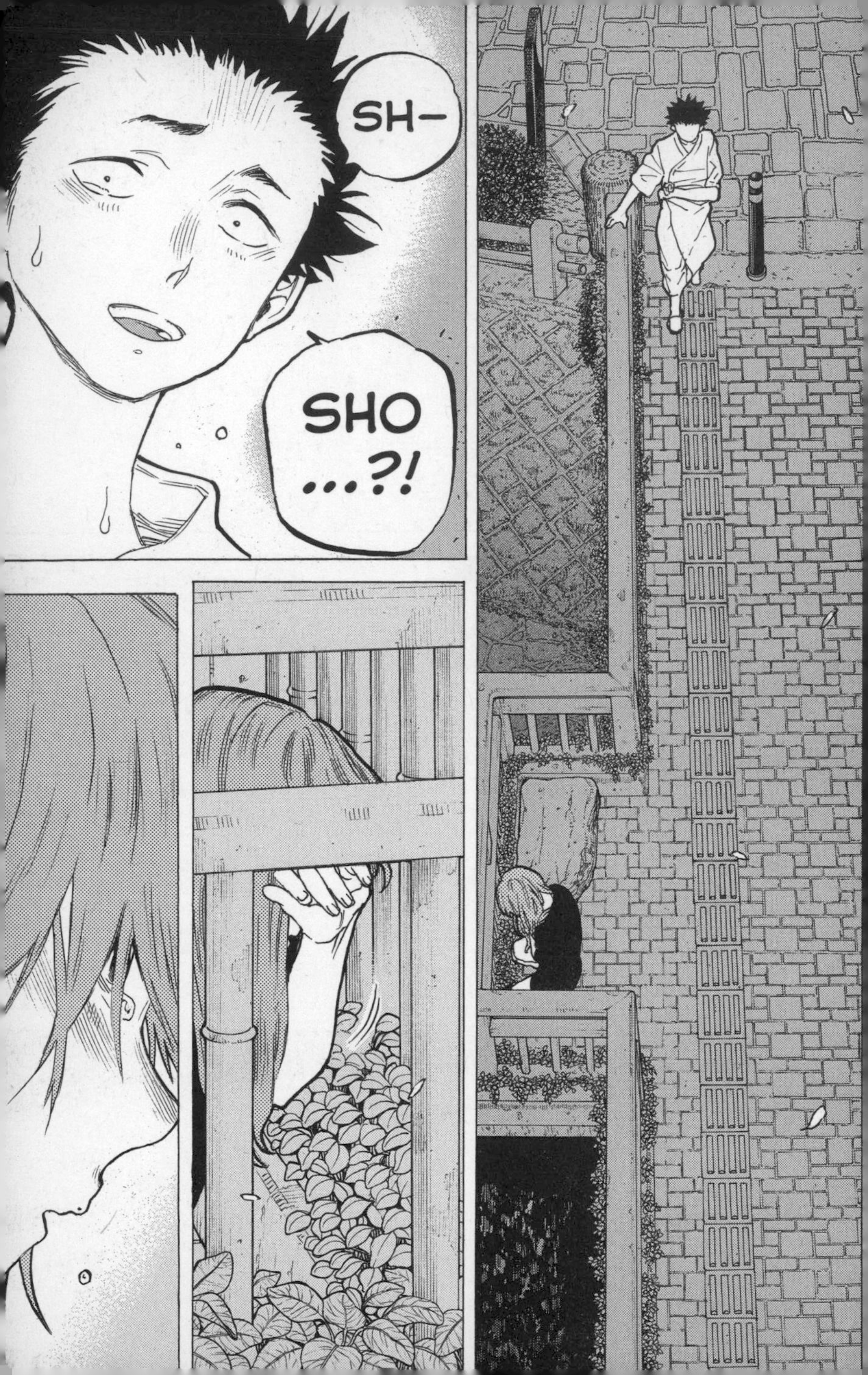
SH-
SHO ...?!

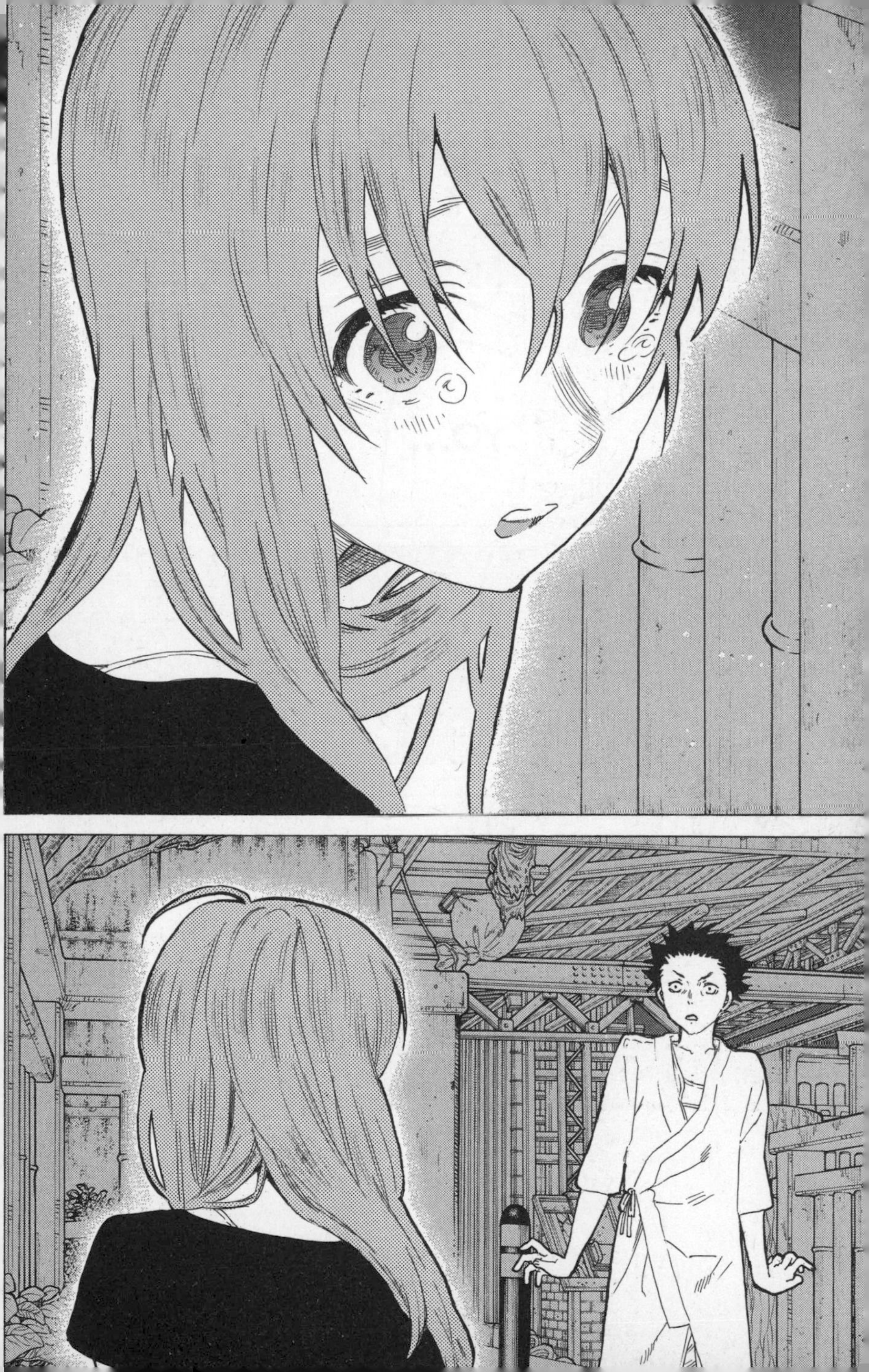

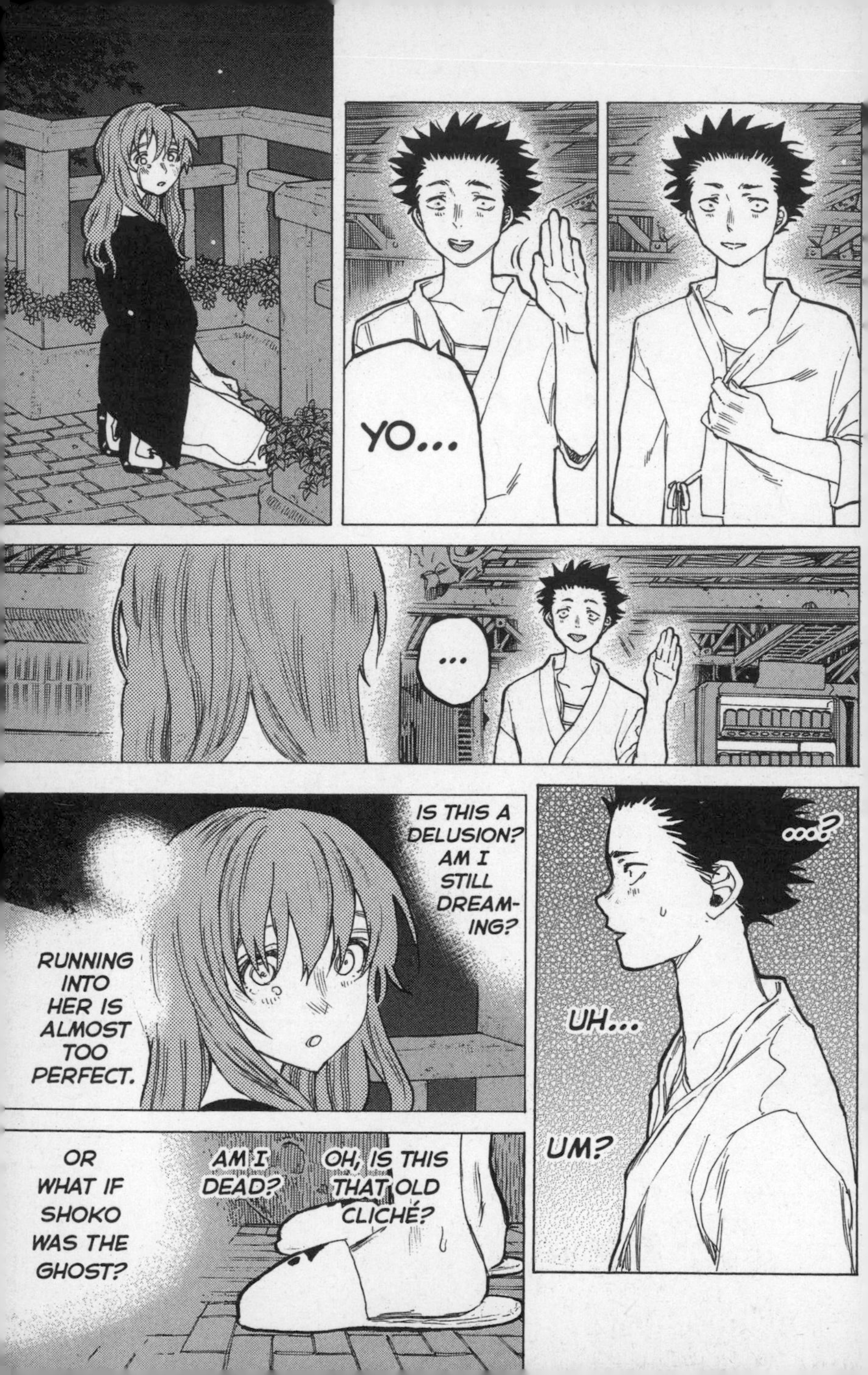
YO...
...
...?
UH...
UM?
IS THIS A DELUSION? AM I STILL DREAMING?
RUNNING INTO HER IS ALMOST TOO PERFECT.
OH, IS THIS THAT OLD CLICHÉ?
AM I DEAD?
OR WHAT IF SHOKO WAS THE GHOST?

SKRUB SKRUB
STARE
FWISH
...
HUH?

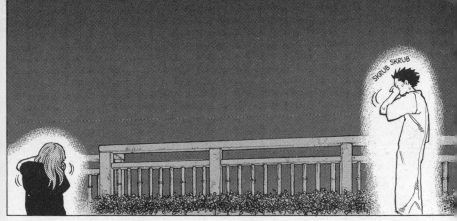

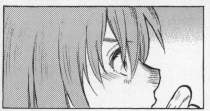

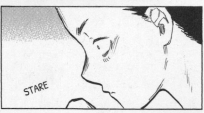

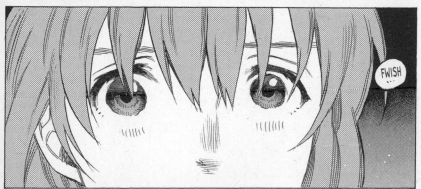

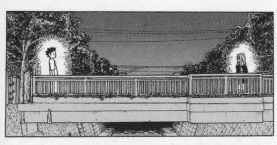

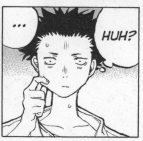

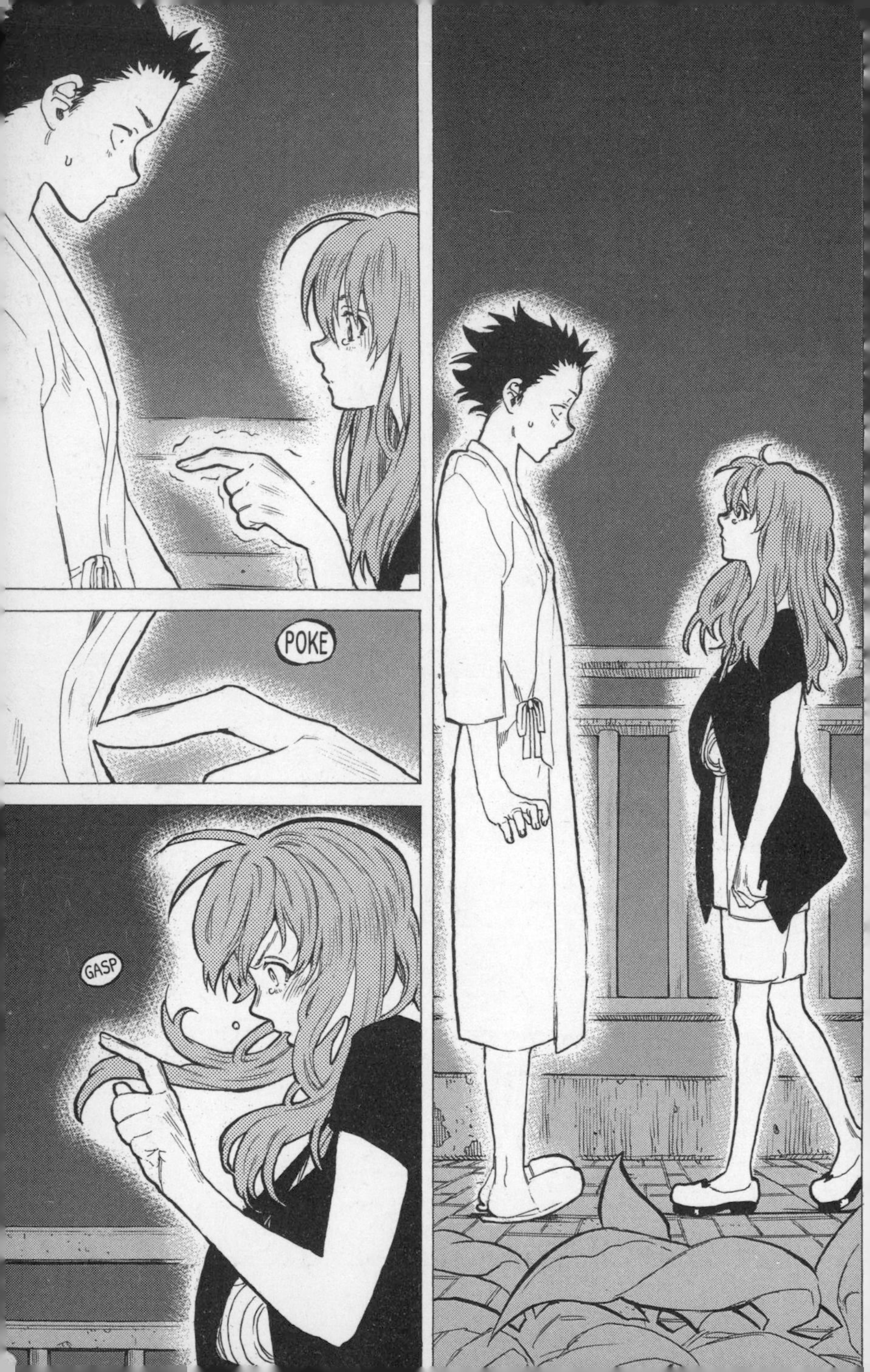
POKE
GASP

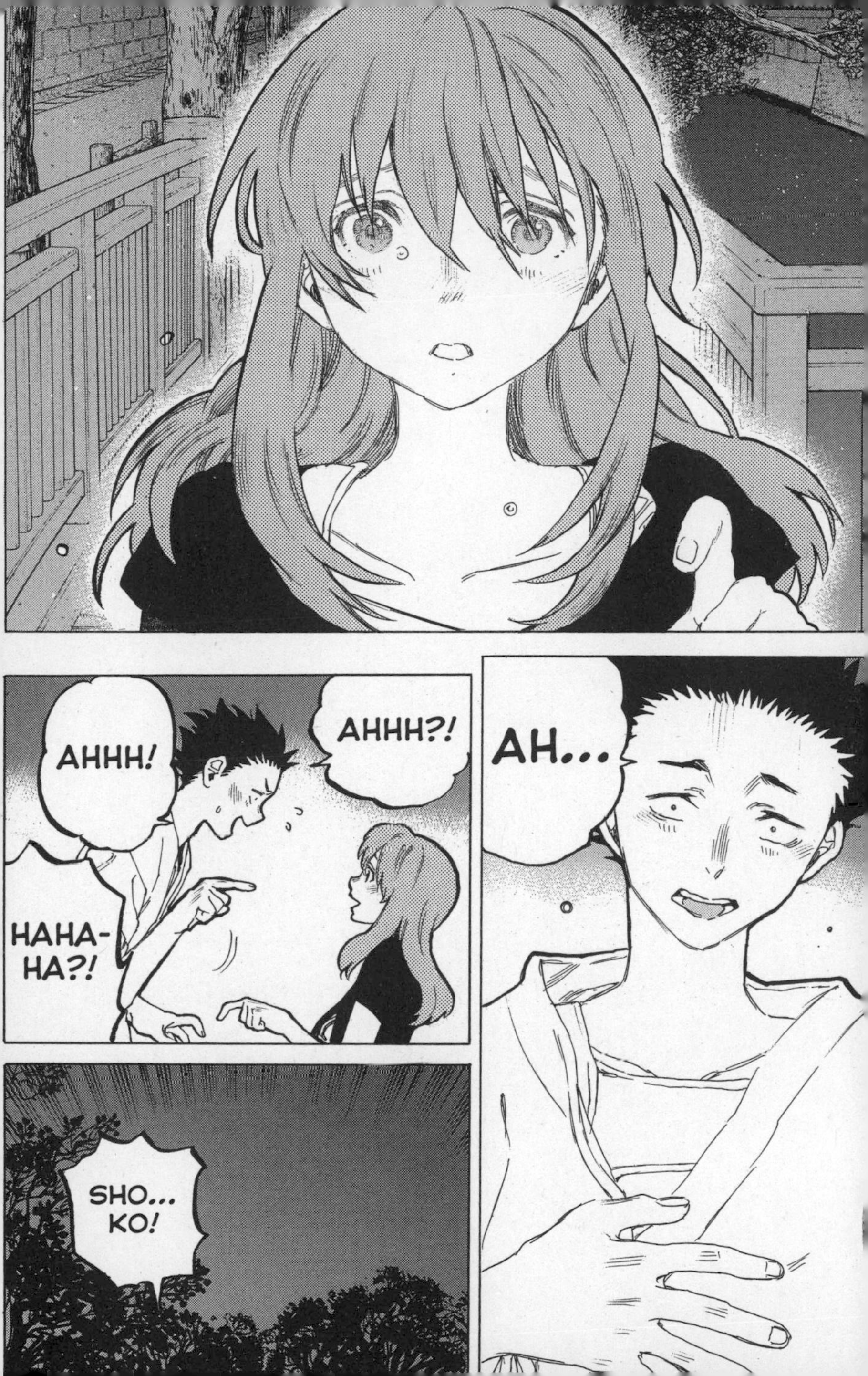
AH...
AHHH?!
AHHH!
HAHA-HA?!
SHO... KO!

a Silent Voice

a Silent Voice

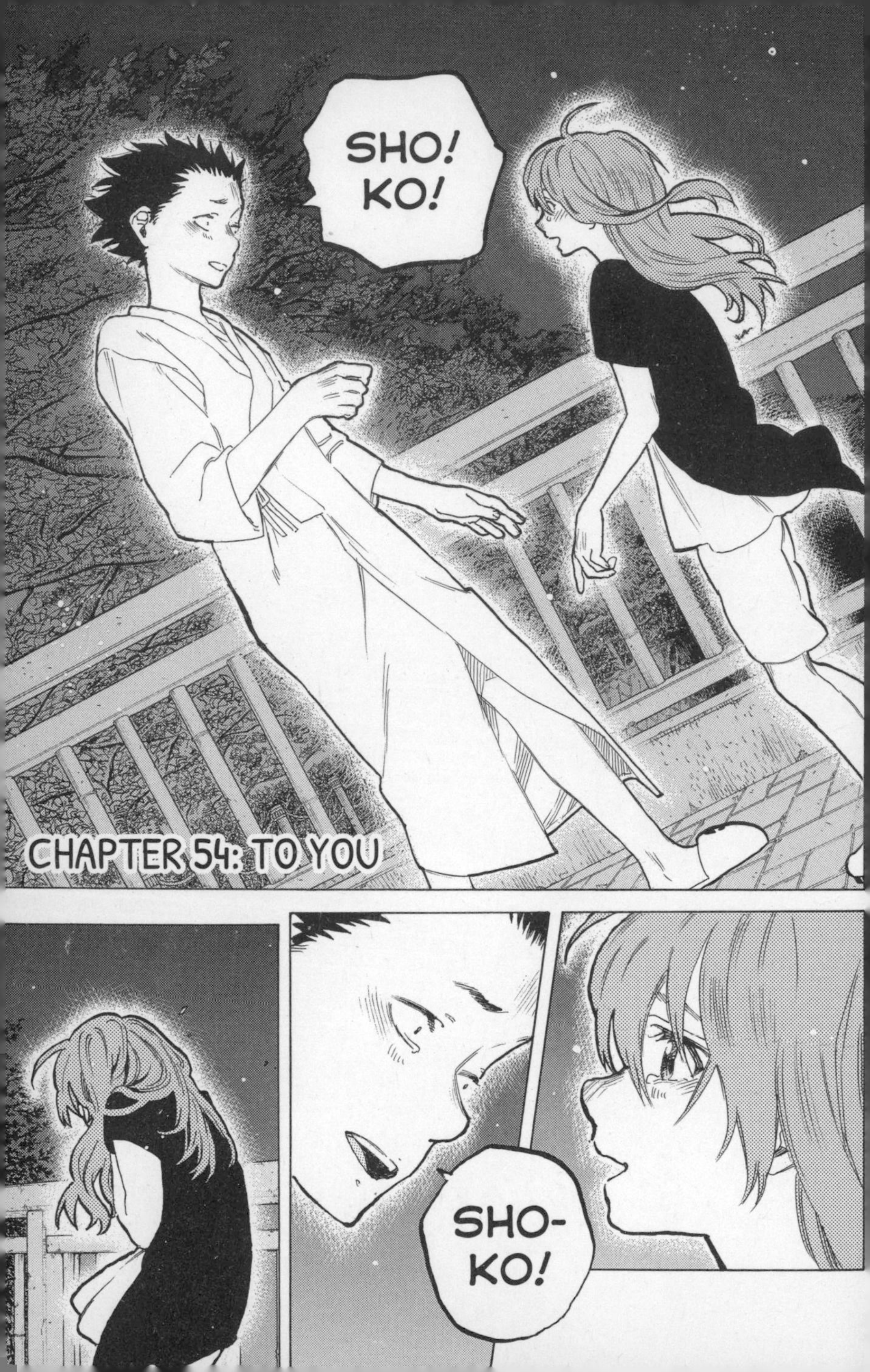
SHO! KO!
CHAPTER 54: TO YOU
SHO- KO!

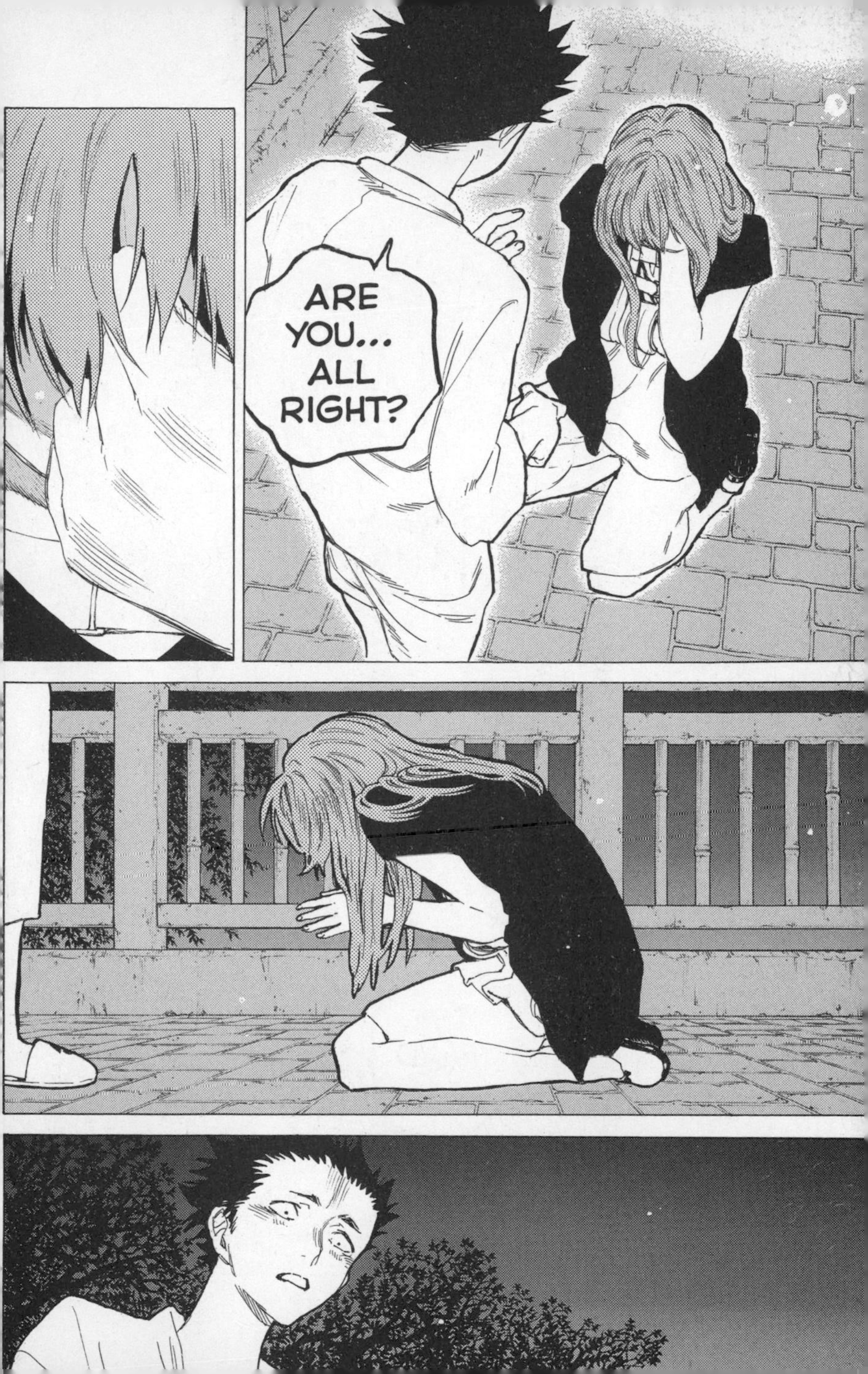
ARE YOU... ALL RIGHT?

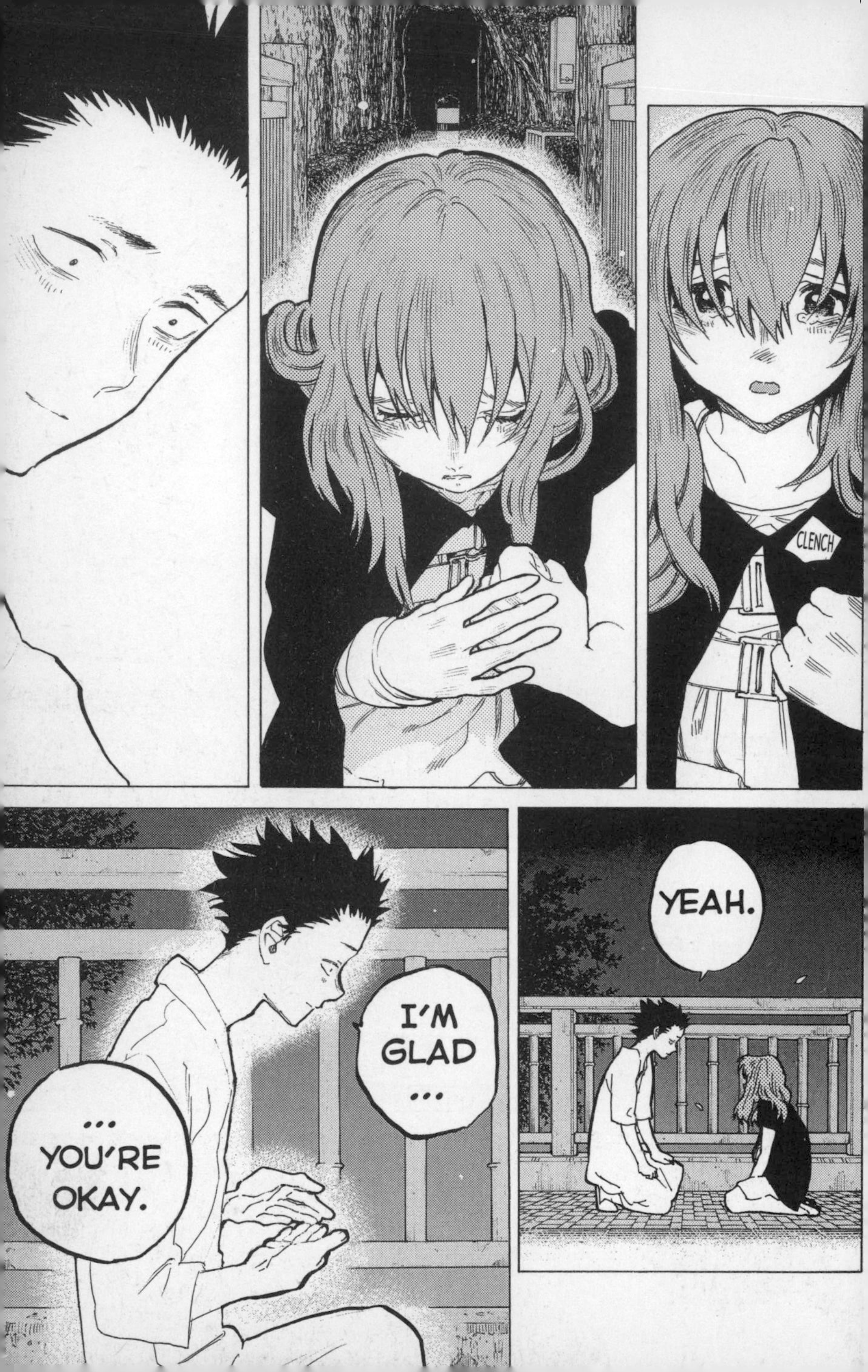
CLENCH
YEAH.
I'M GLAD ...
... YOU'RE OKAY.

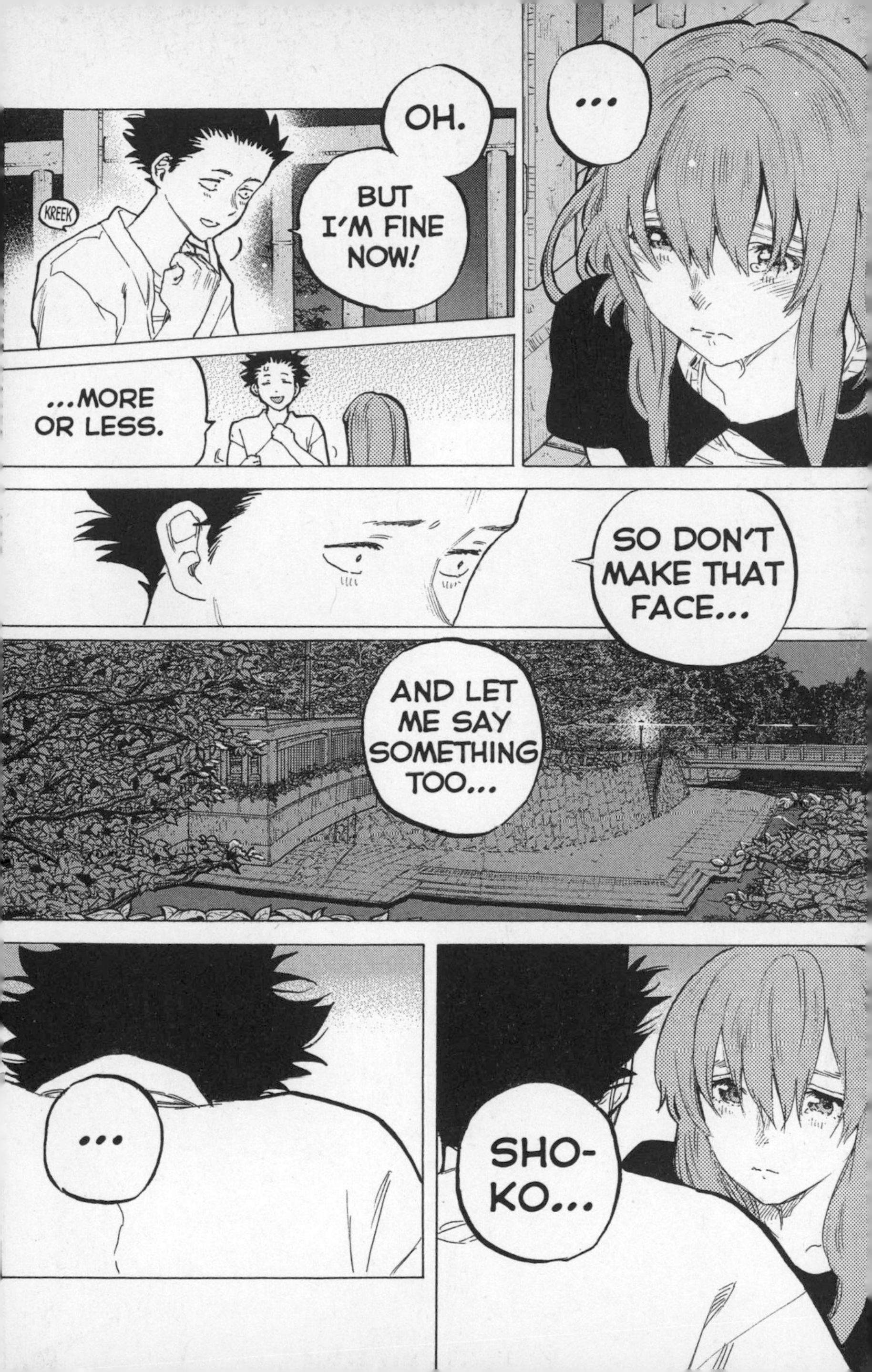
...
OH.
BUT I'M FINE NOW!
KREEK
...MORE OR LESS.
SO DON'T MAKE THAT FACE...
AND LET ME SAY SOMETHING TOO...
SHO-KO...
...

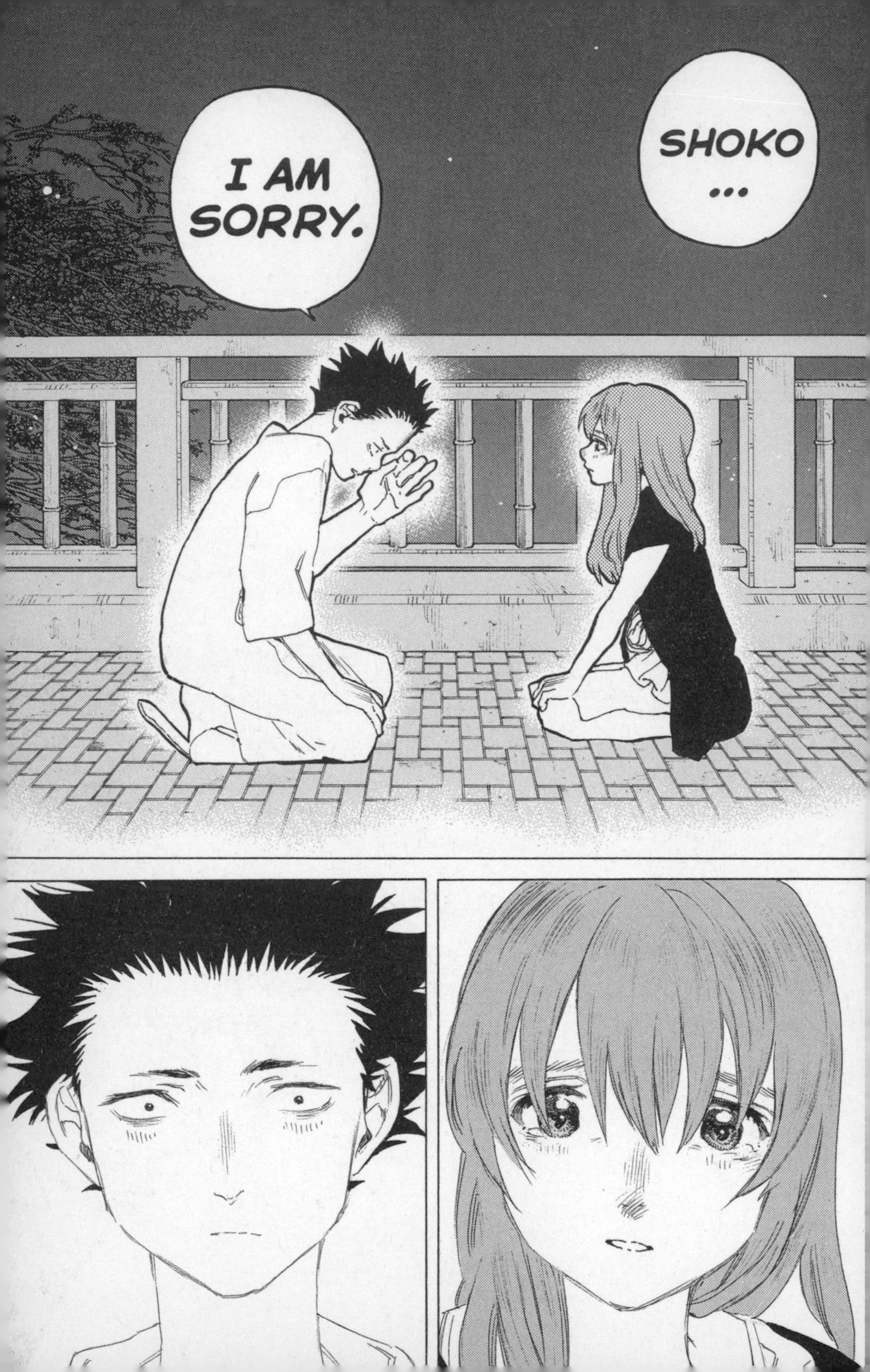
SHOKO ...
I AM SORRY.

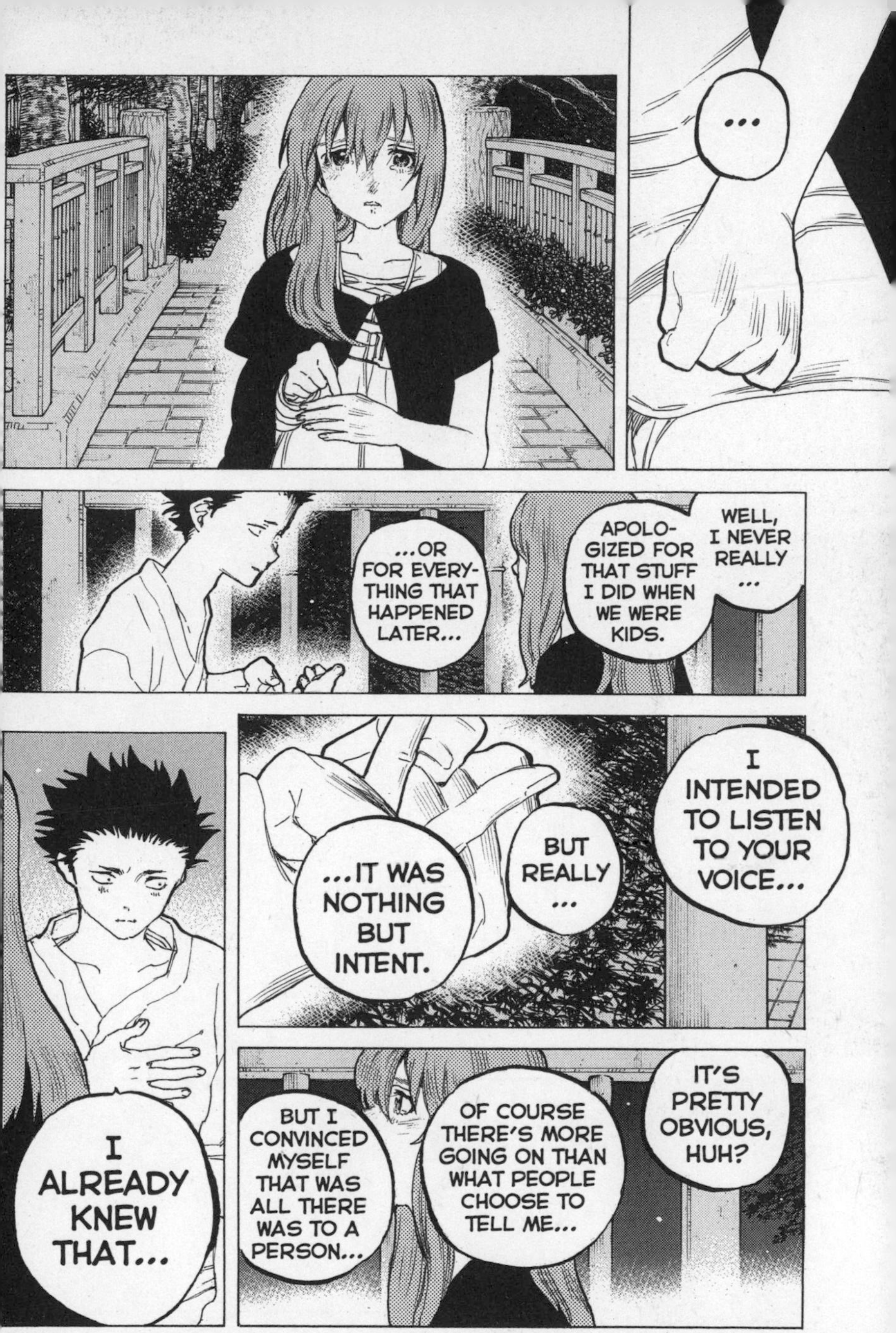
...
WELL, I NEVER REALLY ...
APOLOGIZED FOR THAT STUFF I DID WHEN WE WERE KIDS.
...OR FOR EVERYTHING THAT HAPPENED LATER...
I INTENDED TO LISTEN TO YOUR VOICE...
BUT REALLY ...
...IT WAS NOTHING BUT INTENT.
IT'S PRETTY OBVIOUS, HUH?
OF COURSE THERE'S MORE GOING ON THAN WHAT PEOPLE CHOOSE TO TELL ME...
BUT I CONVINCED MYSELF THAT WAS ALL THERE WAS TO A PERSON...
I ALREADY KNEW THAT...

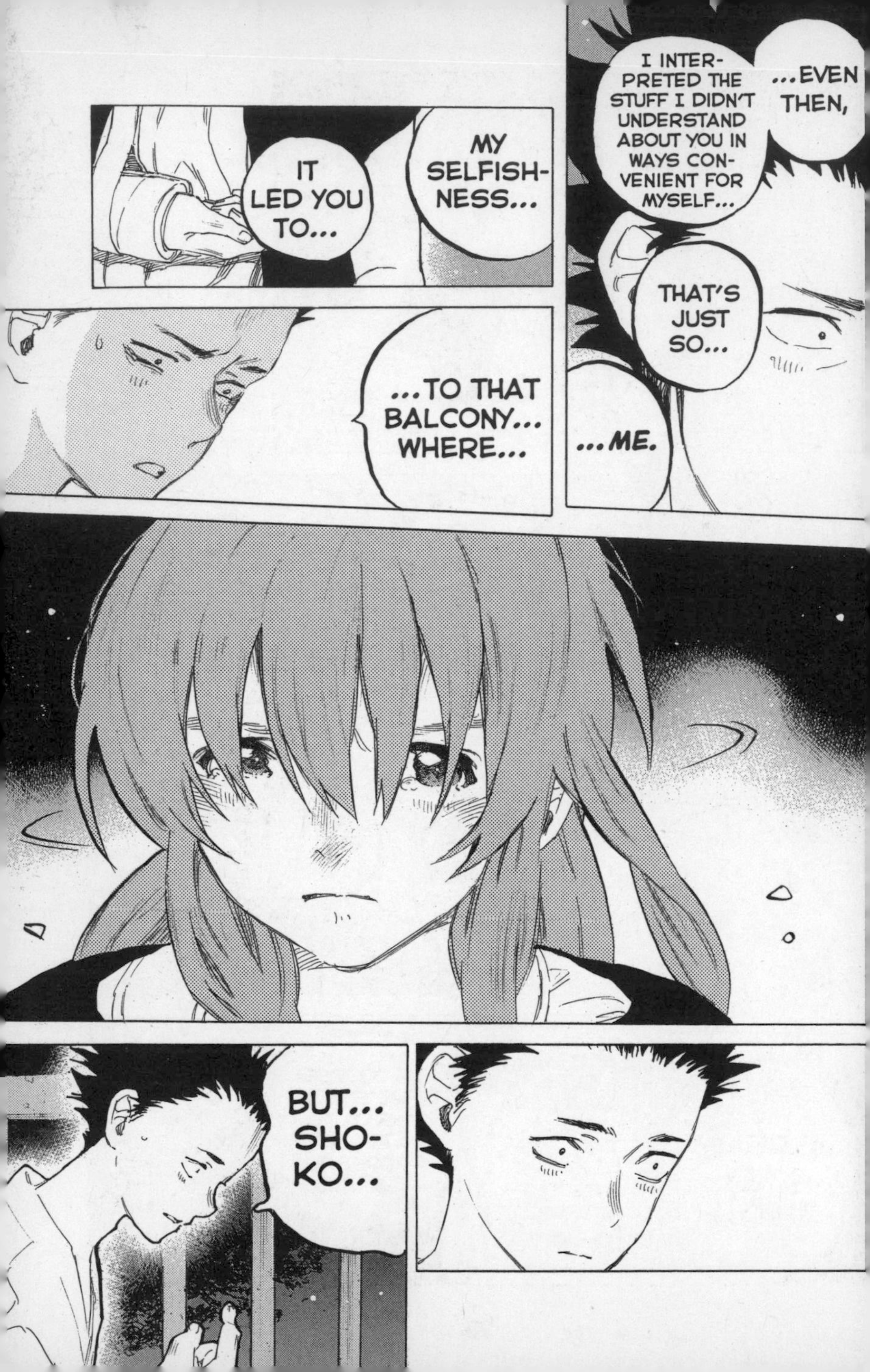
...EVEN THEN,
I INTERPRETED THE STUFF I DIDN'T UNDERSTAND ABOUT YOU IN WAYS CONVENIENT FOR MYSELF...
THAT'S JUST SO...
...ME.
MY SELFISHNESS...
IT LED YOU TO...
...TO THAT BALCONY... WHERE...
BUT... SHOKO...

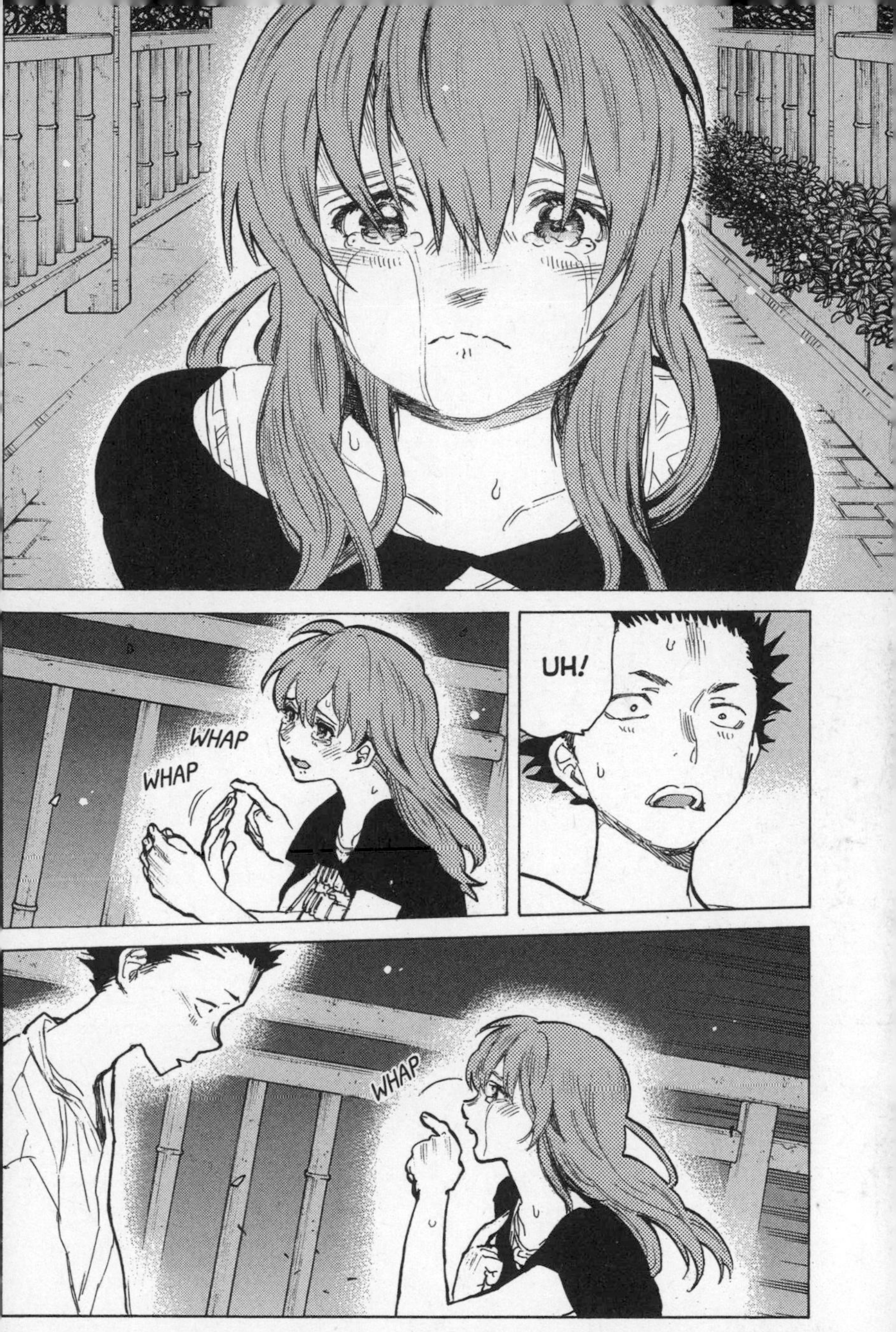
UH!
WHAP
WHAP
WHAP

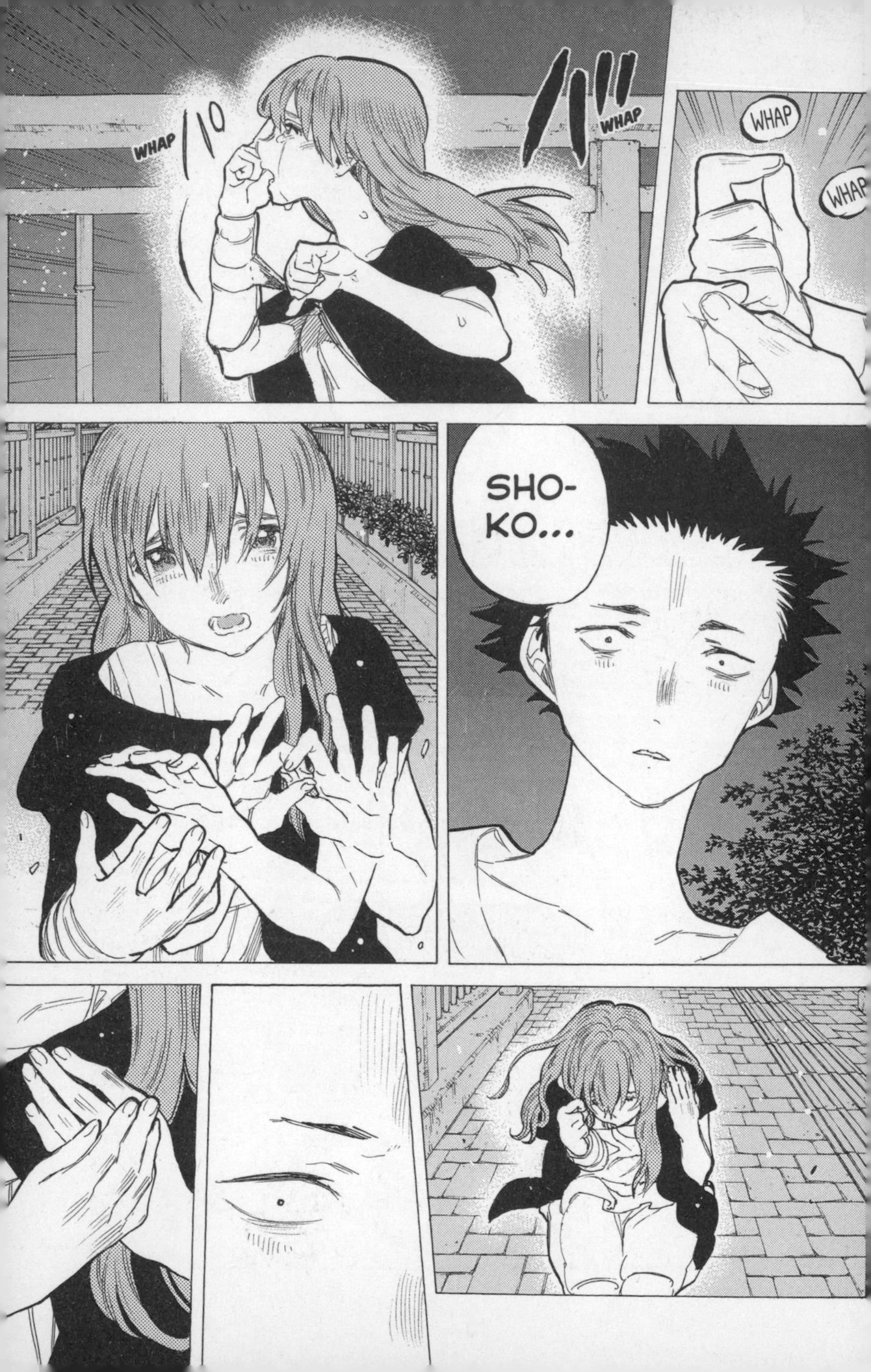
WHAP
WHAP
WHAP
WHAP
SHO-KO...

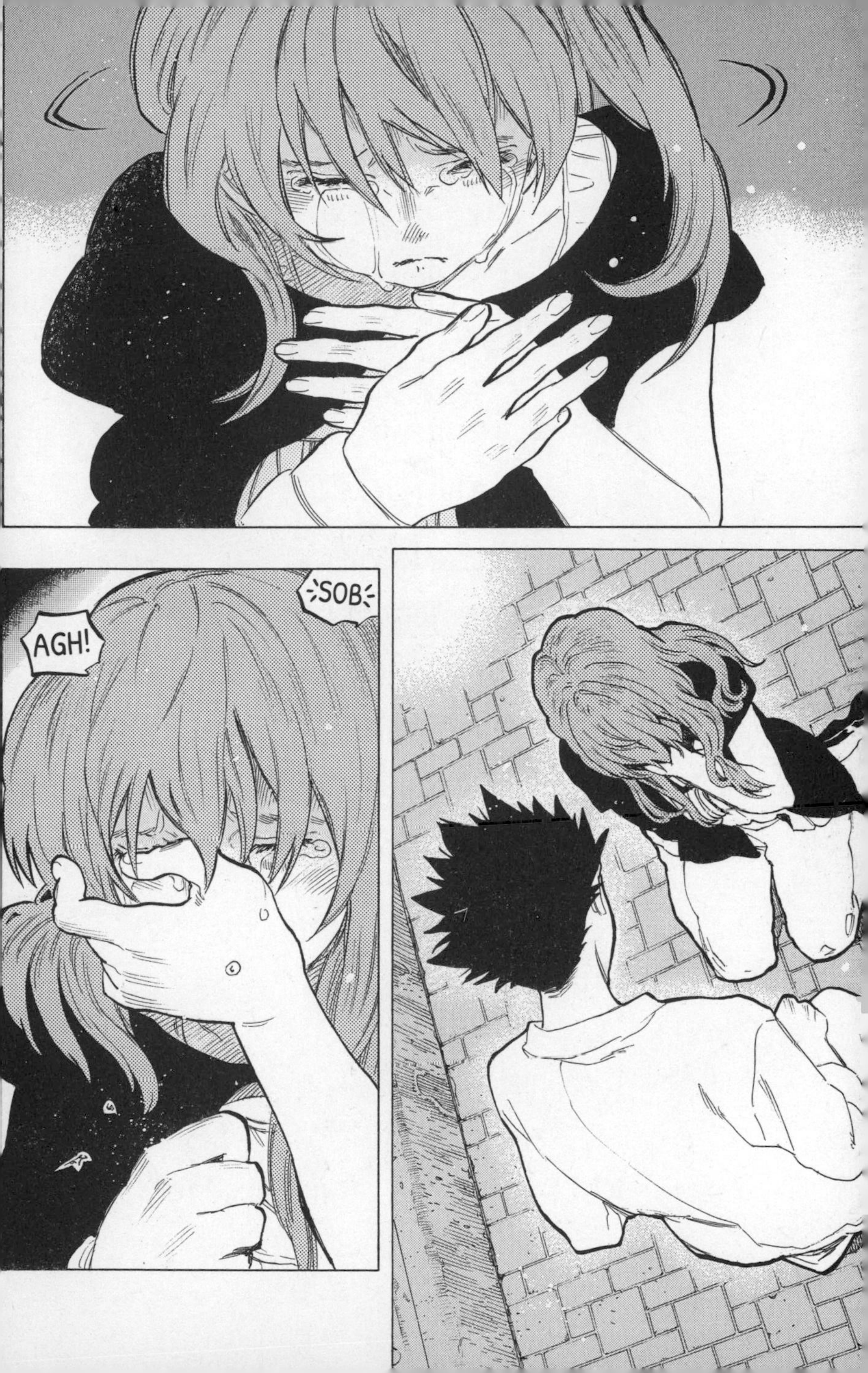
SOB
AGH!

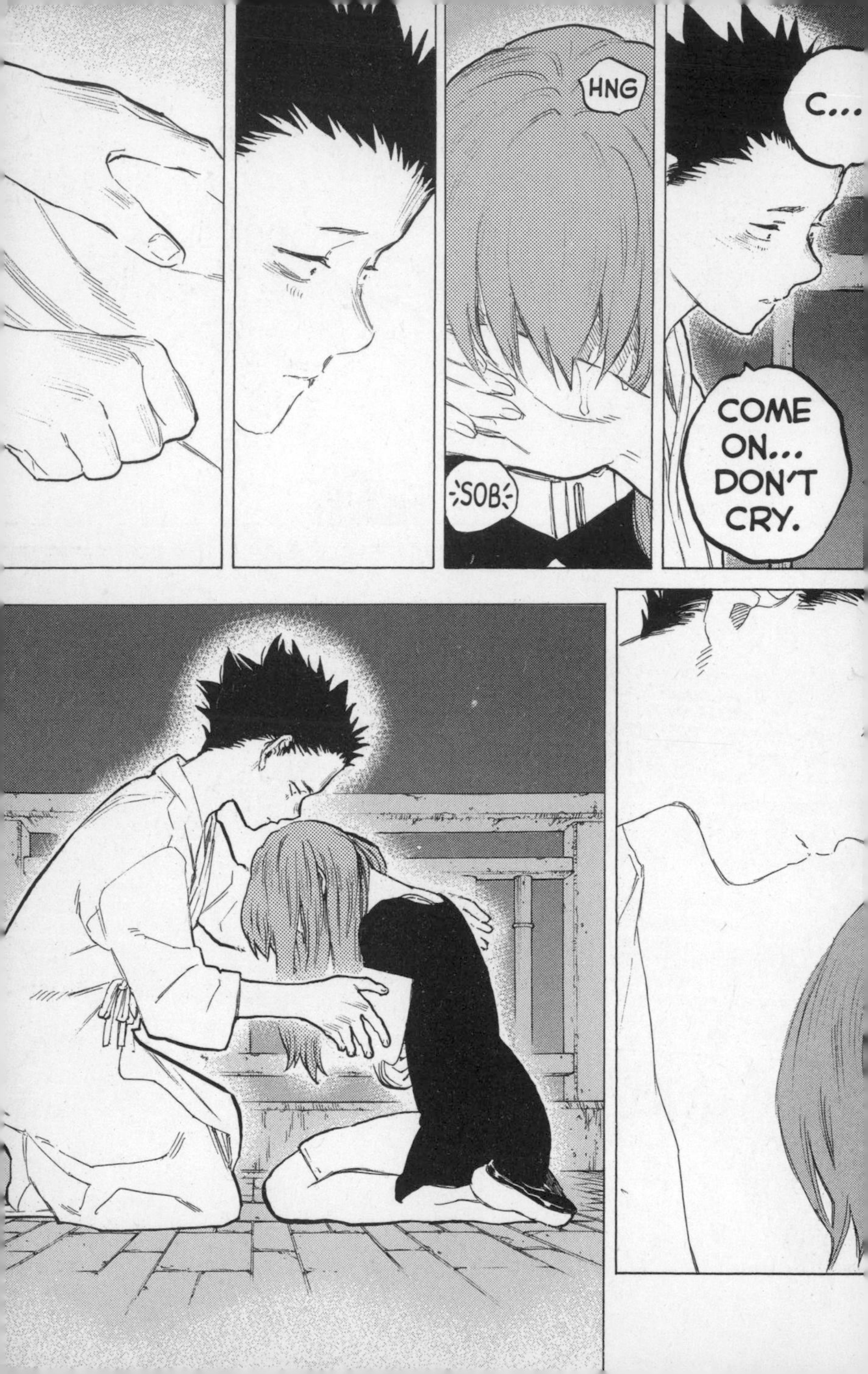
C...
COME ON... DON'T CRY.
HNG
SOB

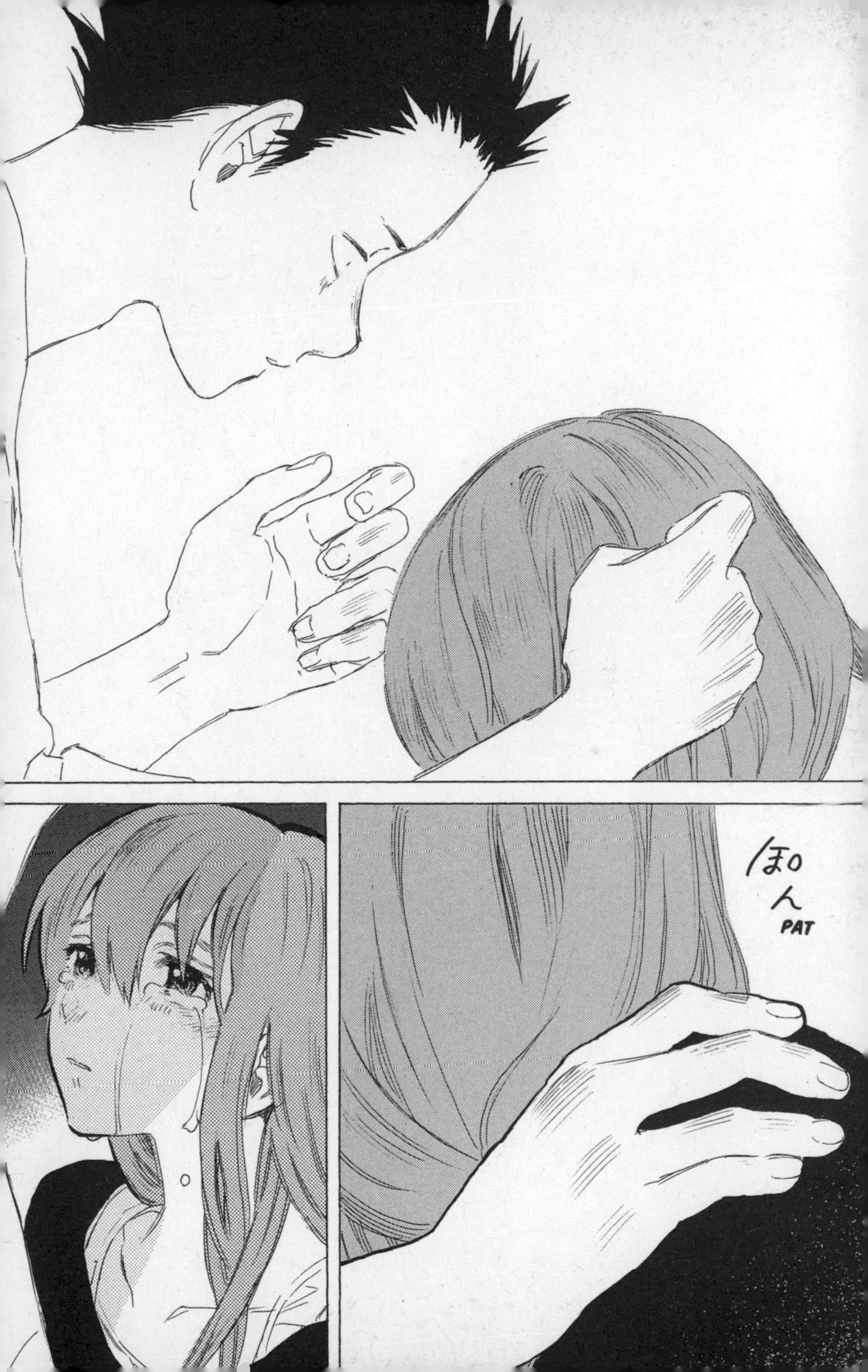
ぽん
PAT

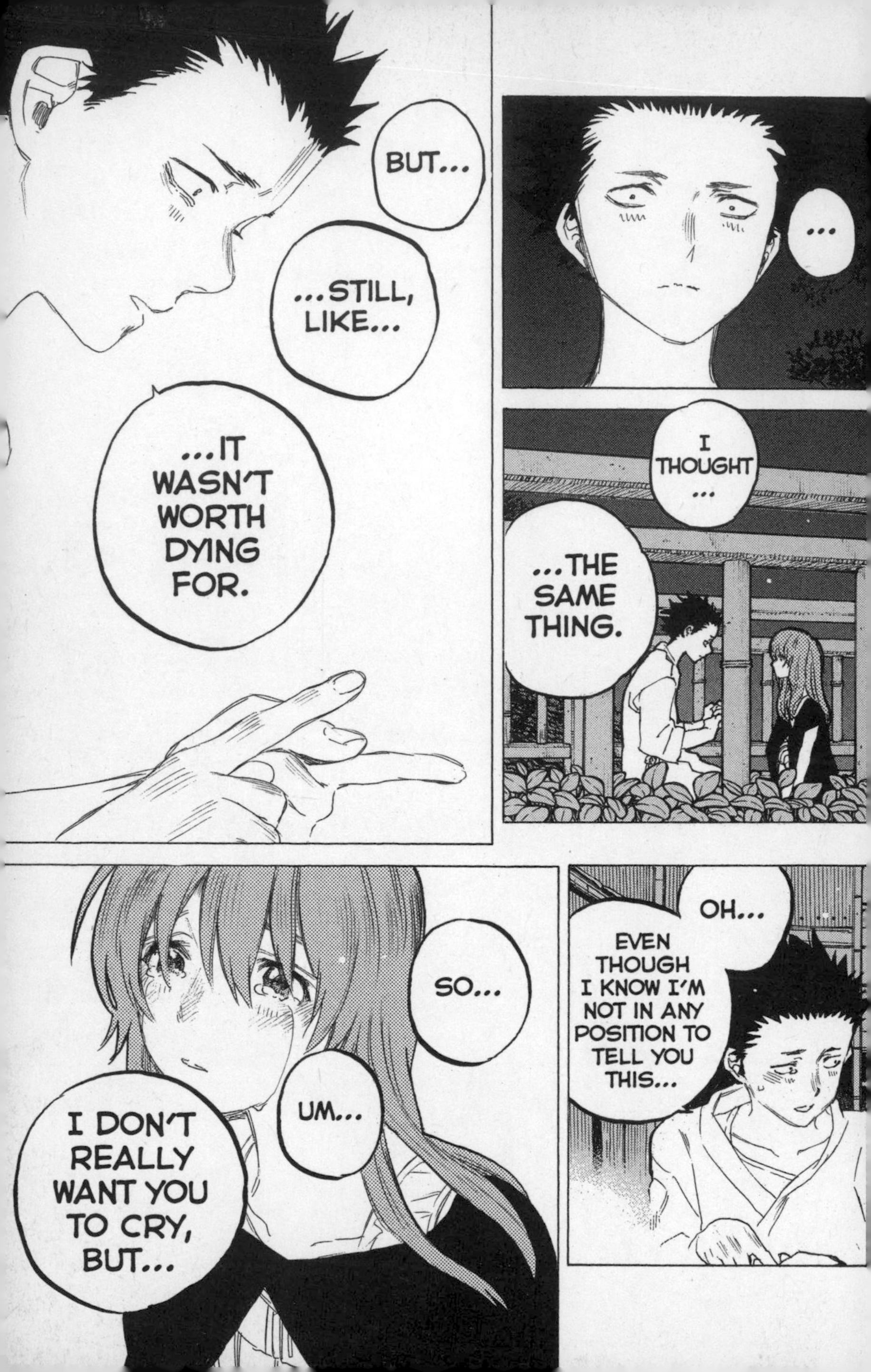
...
I THOUGHT...
...THE SAME THING.
BUT...
...STILL, LIKE...
...IT WASN'T WORTH DYING FOR.
OH...
EVEN THOUGH I KNOW I'M NOT IN ANY POSITION TO TELL YOU THIS...
SO...
UM...
I DON'T REALLY WANT YOU TO CRY, BUT...

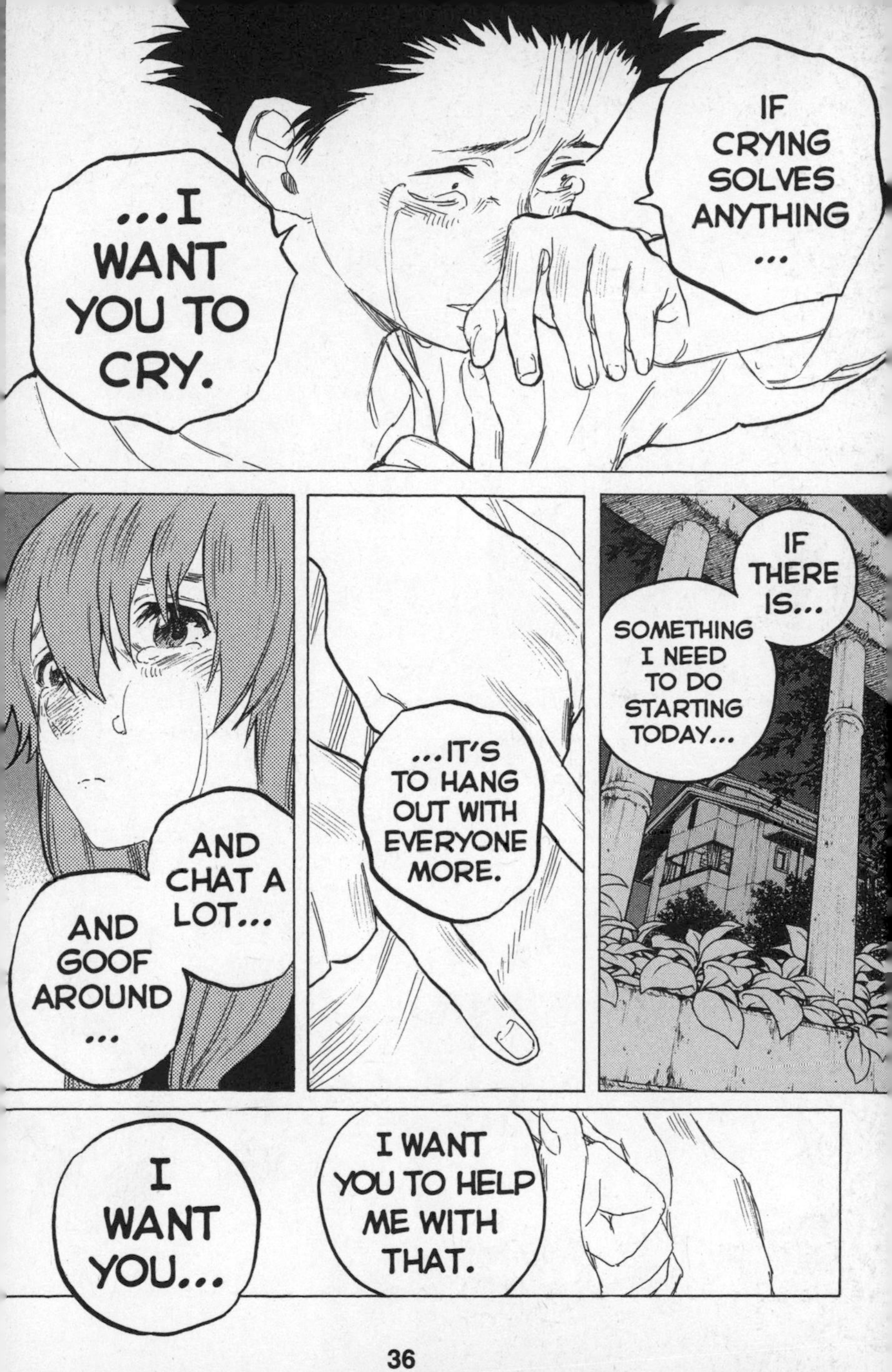
IF CRYING SOLVES ANYTHING ...
...I WANT YOU TO CRY.
IF THERE IS...
SOMETHING I NEED TO DO STARTING TODAY...
...IT'S TO HANG OUT WITH EVERYONE MORE.
AND CHAT A LOT...
AND GOOF AROUND ...
I WANT YOU TO HELP ME WITH THAT.
I WANT YOU...

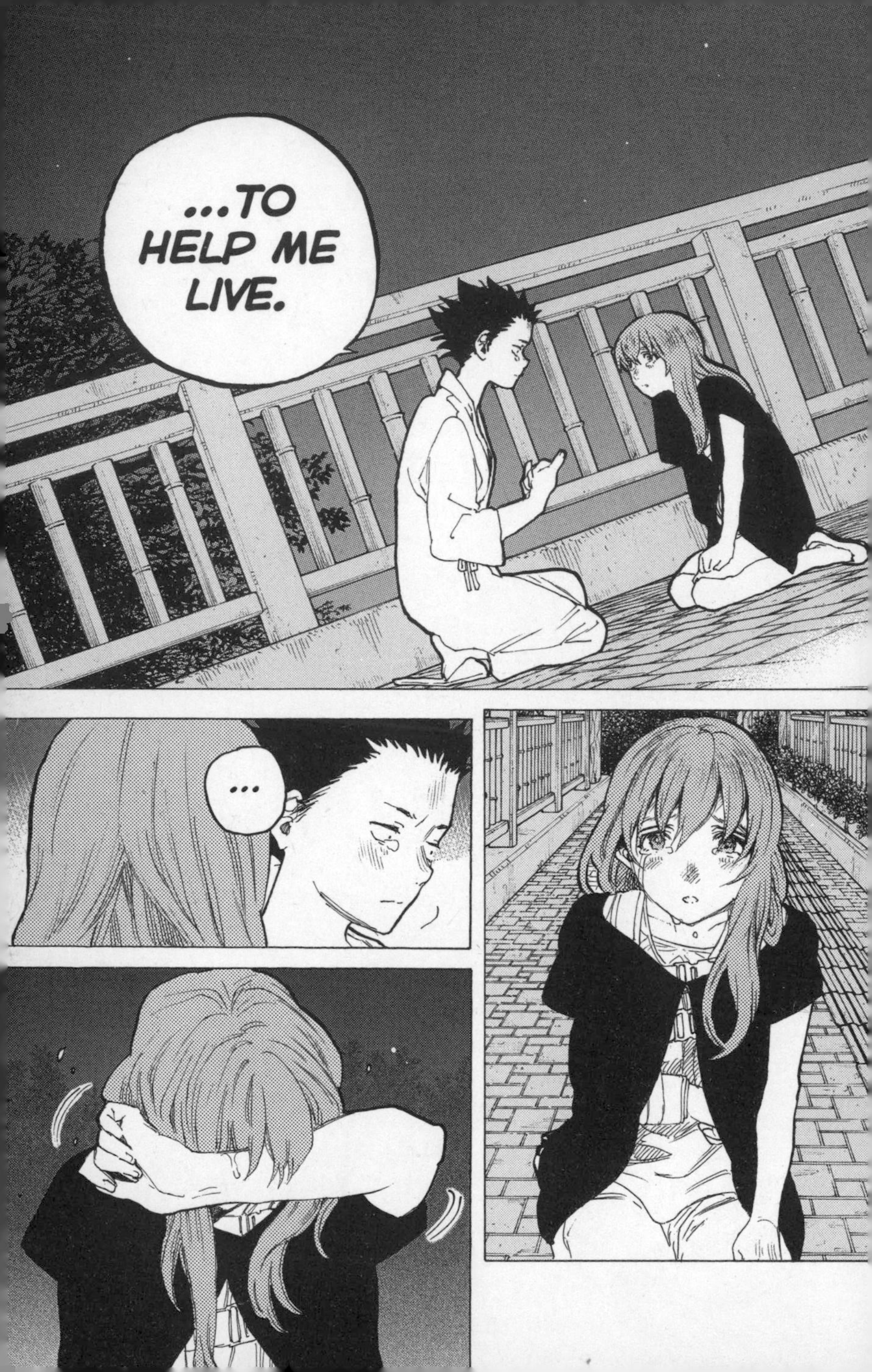
...TO HELP ME LIVE.
...

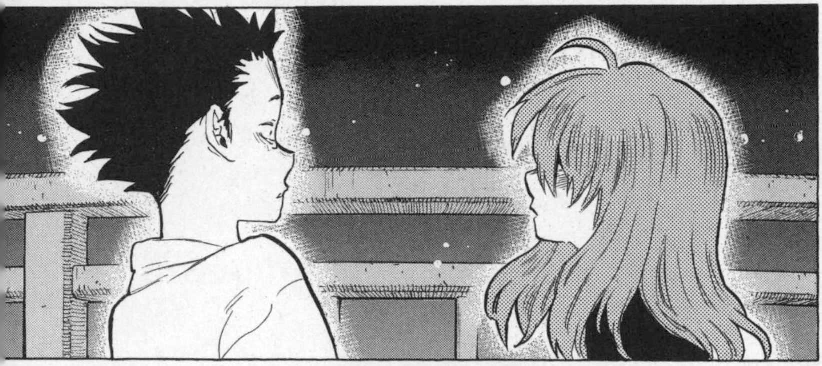
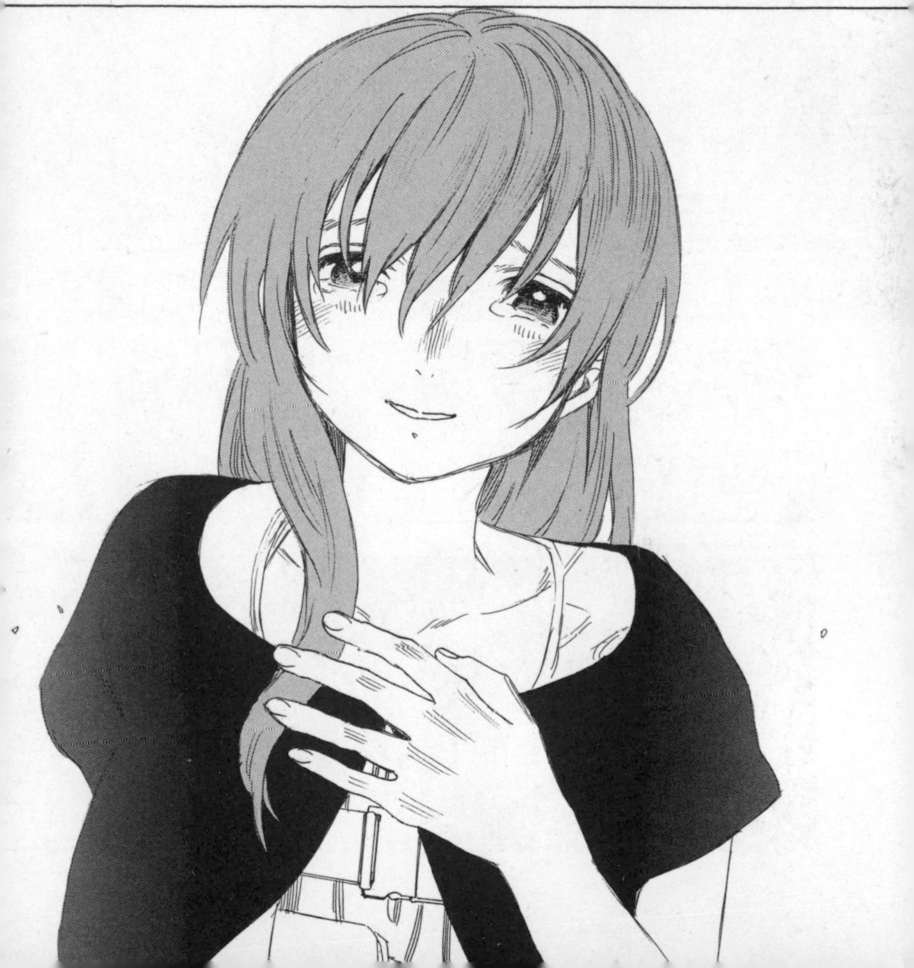

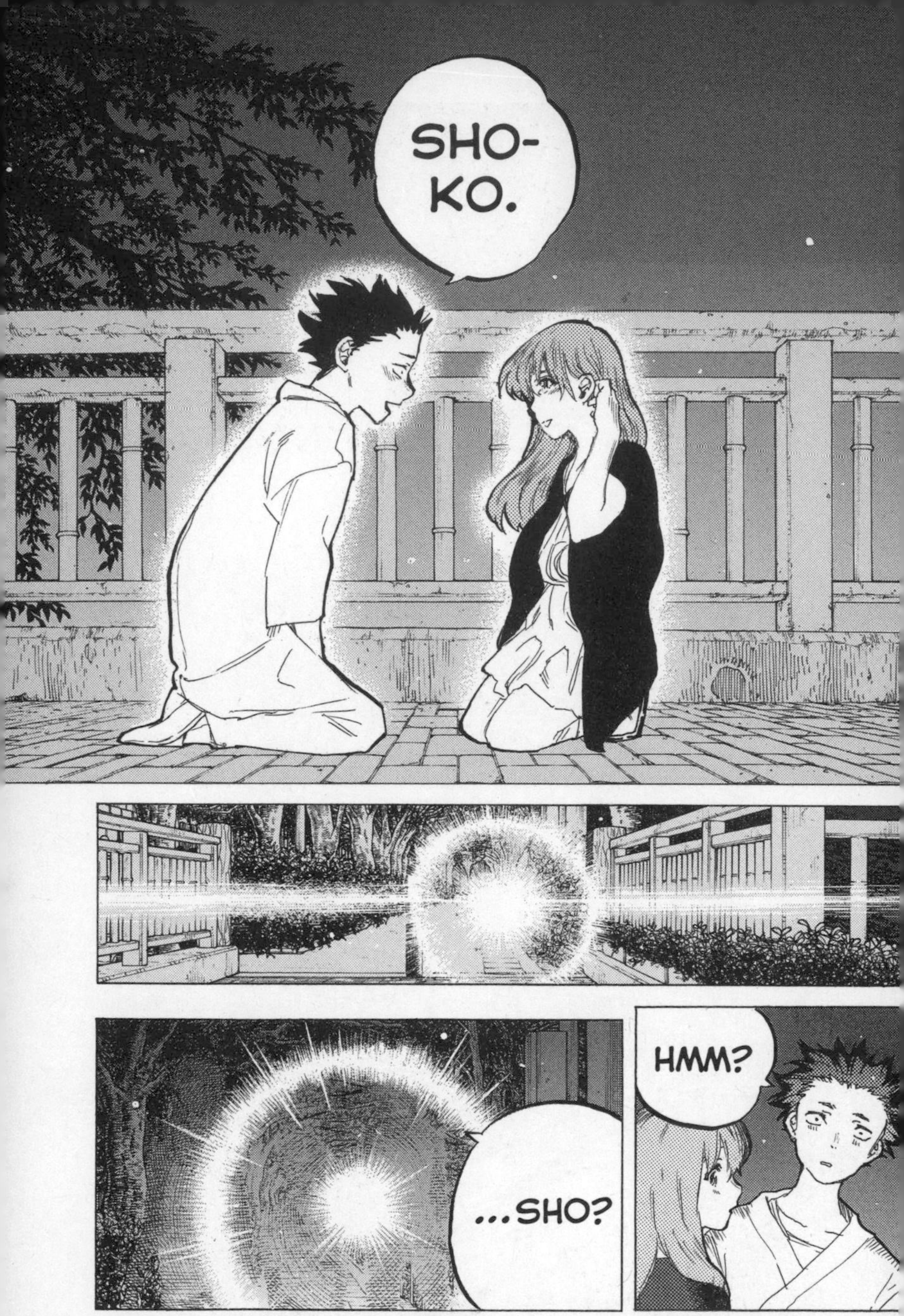
SHO-KO.
HMM?
...SHO?

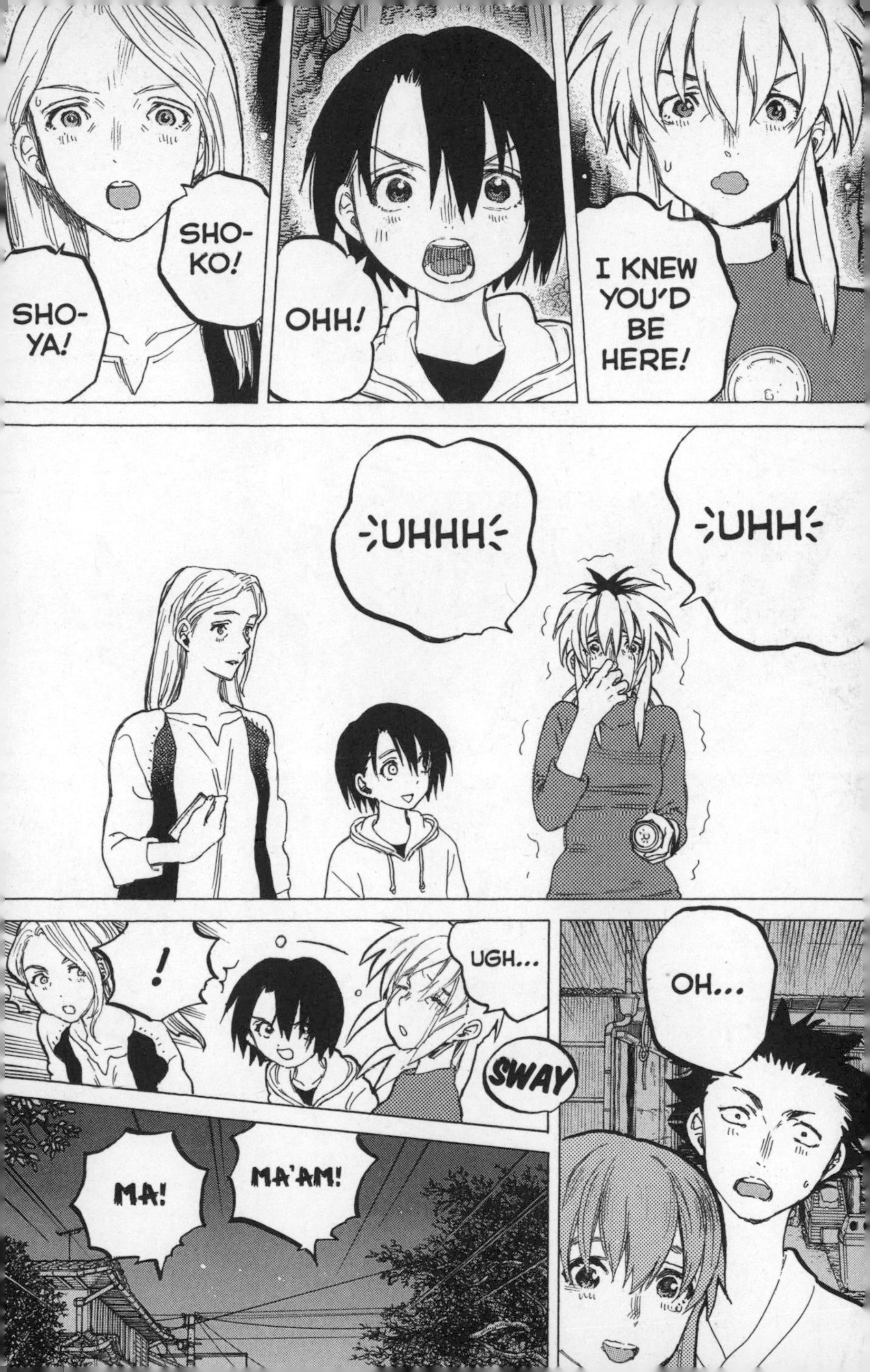
I KNEW YOU'D BE HERE!
OHH!
SHO-KO!
SHO-YA!
-UHH-
-UHHH-
OH...
UGH...
SWAY
!
MA'AM!
MA!

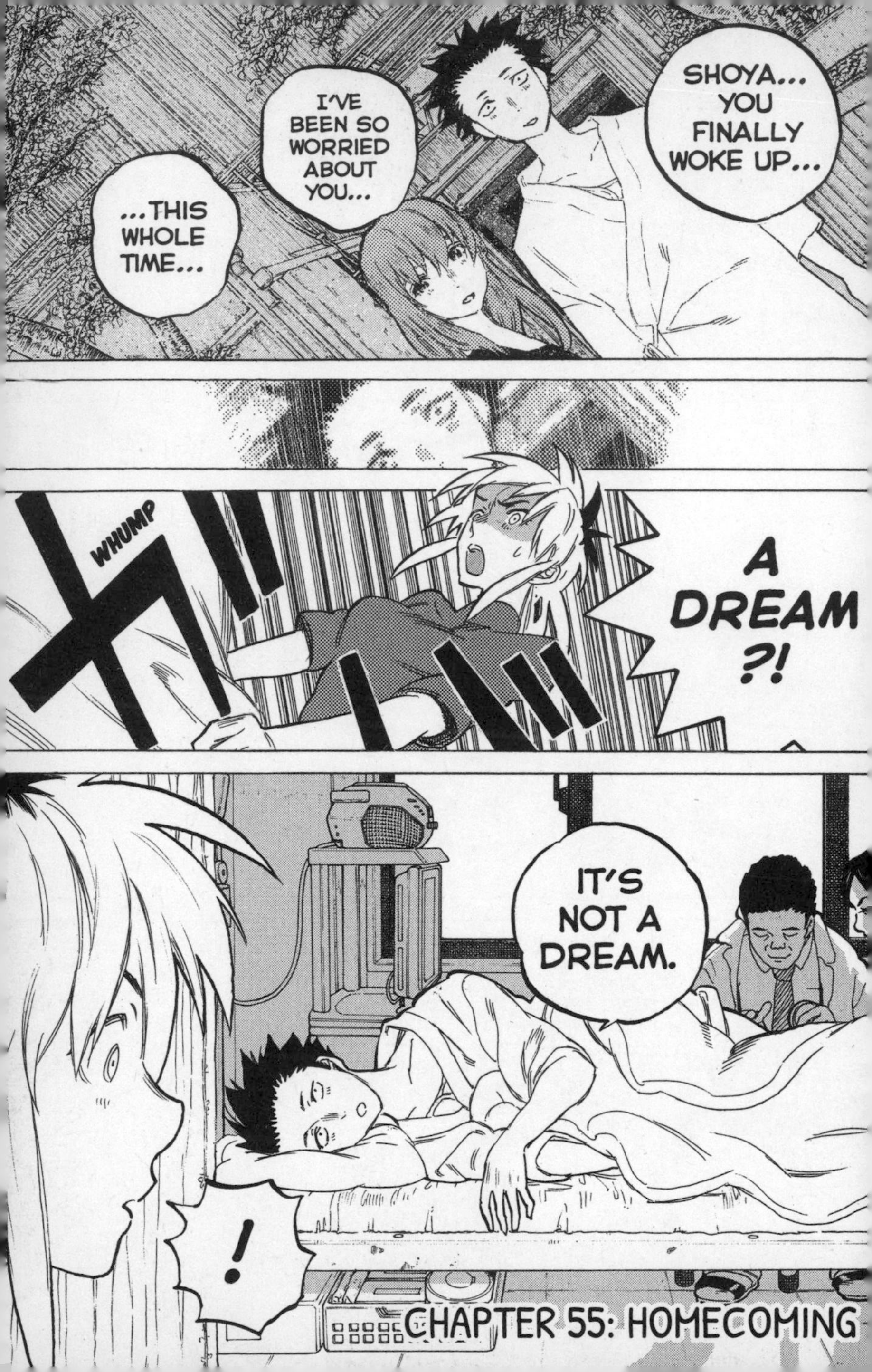
SHOYA... YOU FINALLY WOKE UP...
I'VE BEEN SO WORRIED ABOUT YOU...
...THIS WHOLE TIME...
A DREAM ?!
WHUMP
IT'S NOT A DREAM.
!
CHAPTER 55: HOMECOMING

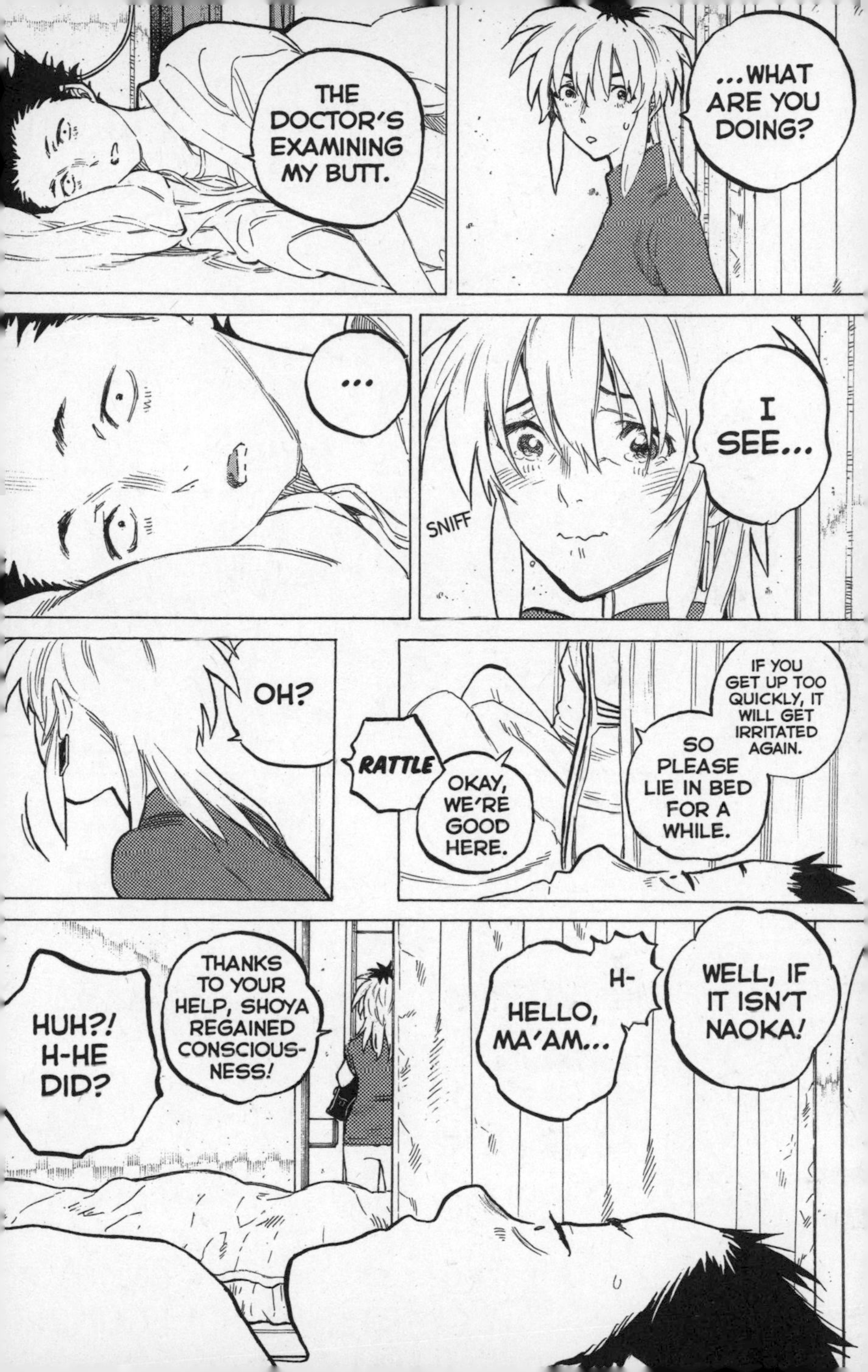
...WHAT ARE YOU DOING?
THE DOCTOR'S EXAMINING MY BUTT.
I SEE...
SNIFF
...
IF YOU GET UP TOO QUICKLY, IT WILL GET IRRITATED AGAIN.
SO PLEASE LIE IN BED FOR A WHILE.
OKAY, WE'RE GOOD HERE.
RATTLE
OH?
WELL, IF IT ISN'T NAOKA!
H-
HELLO, MA'AM...
THANKS TO YOUR HELP, SHOYA REGAINED CONSCIOUS-NESS!
HUH?! H-HE DID?

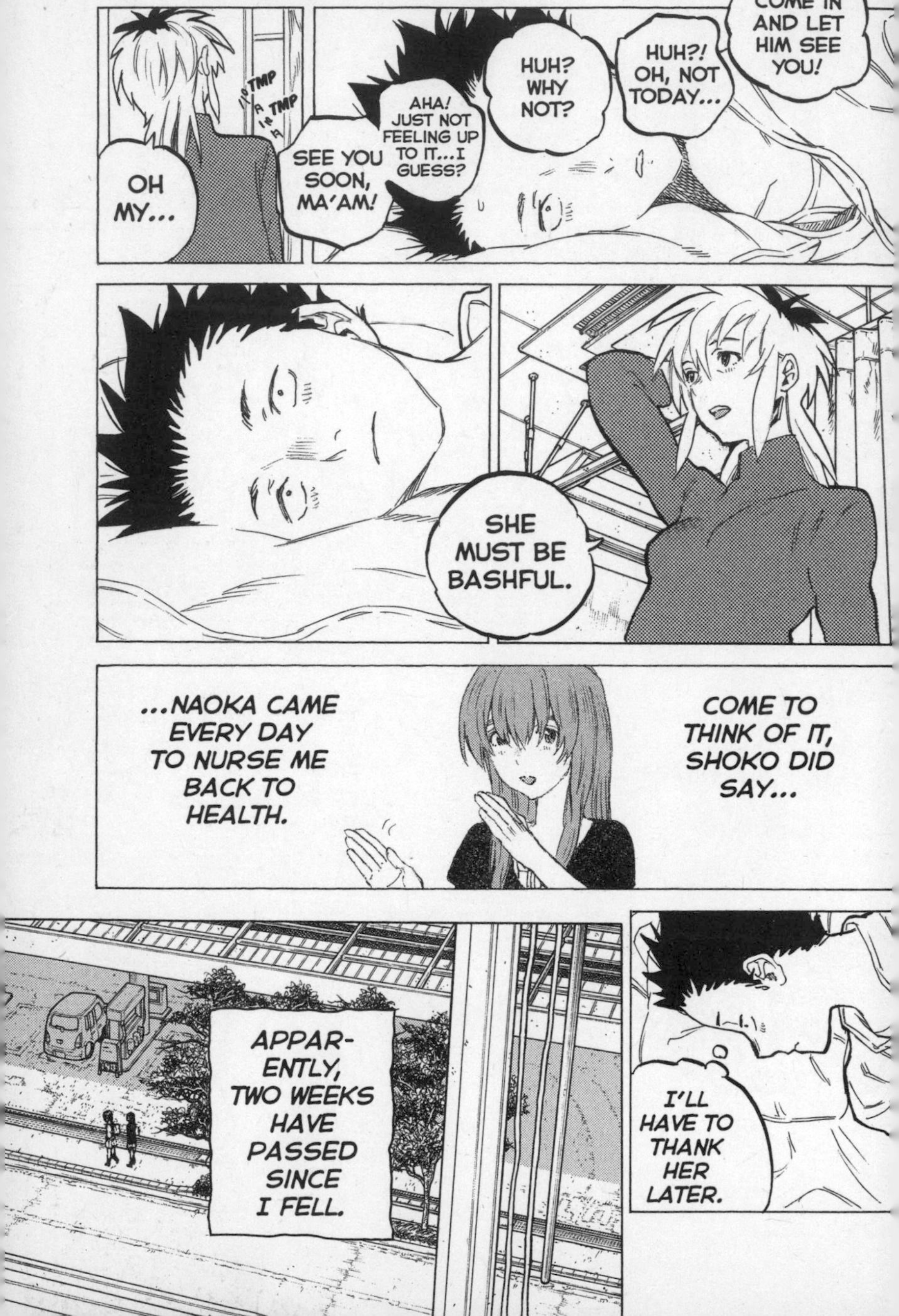
COME IN AND LET HIM SEE YOU!
HUH?! OH, NOT TODAY...
HUH? WHY NOT?
AHA! JUST NOT FEELING UP TO IT...I GUESS?
SEE YOU SOON, MA'AM!
TMP TMP
OH MY...
SHE MUST BE BASHFUL.
COME TO THINK OF IT, SHOKO DID SAY...
...NAOKA CAME EVERY DAY TO NURSE ME BACK TO HEALTH.
I'LL HAVE TO THANK HER LATER.
APPARENTLY, TWO WEEKS HAVE PASSED SINCE I FELL.

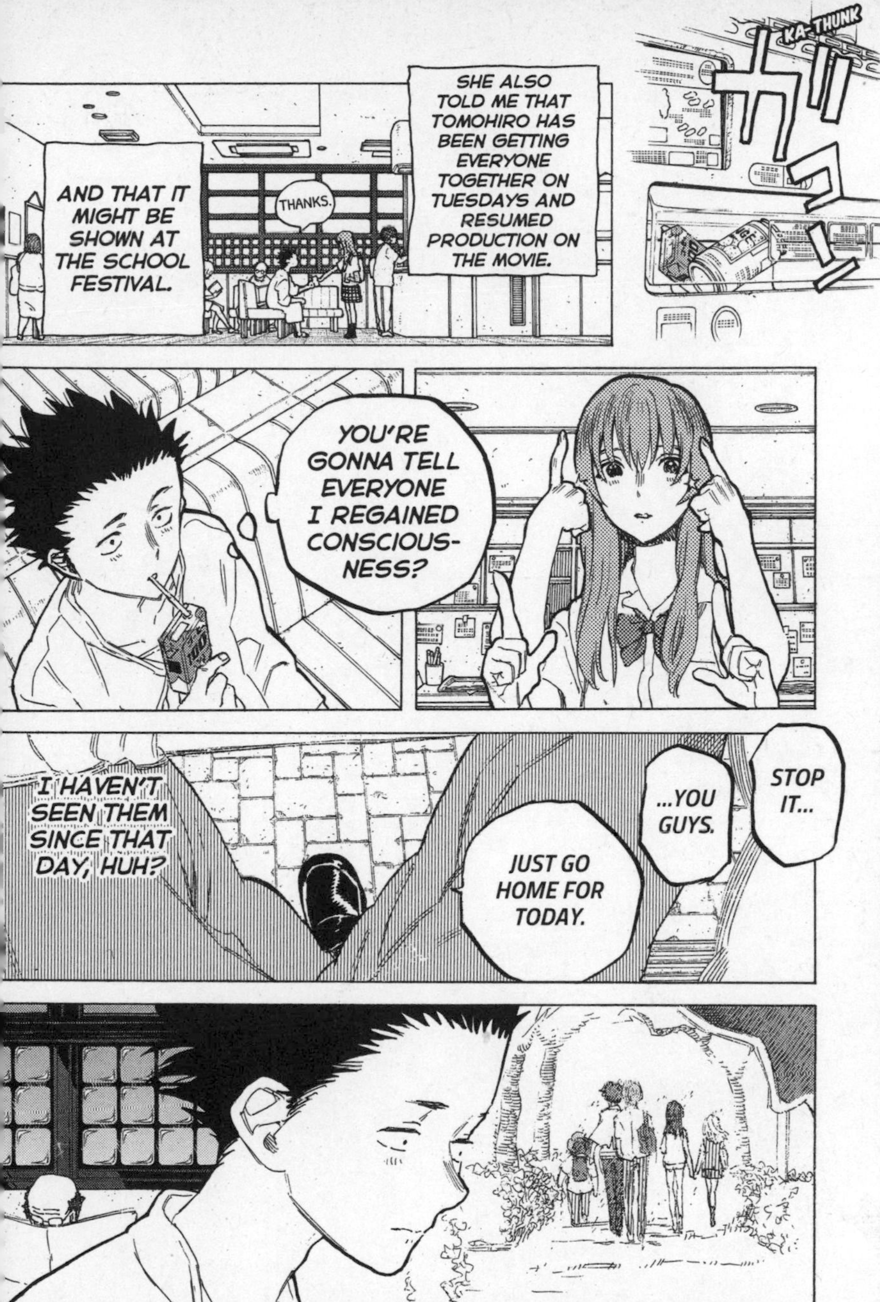
KA-THUNK
SHE ALSO TOLD ME THAT TOMOHIRO HAS BEEN GETTING EVERYONE TOGETHER ON TUESDAYS AND RESUMED PRODUCTION ON THE MOVIE.
THANKS.
AND THAT IT MIGHT BE SHOWN AT THE SCHOOL FESTIVAL.
YOU'RE GONNA TELL EVERYONE I REGAINED CONSCIOUS-NESS?
STOP IT...
...YOU GUYS.
JUST GO HOME FOR TODAY.
I HAVEN'T SEEN THEM SINCE THAT DAY, HUH?

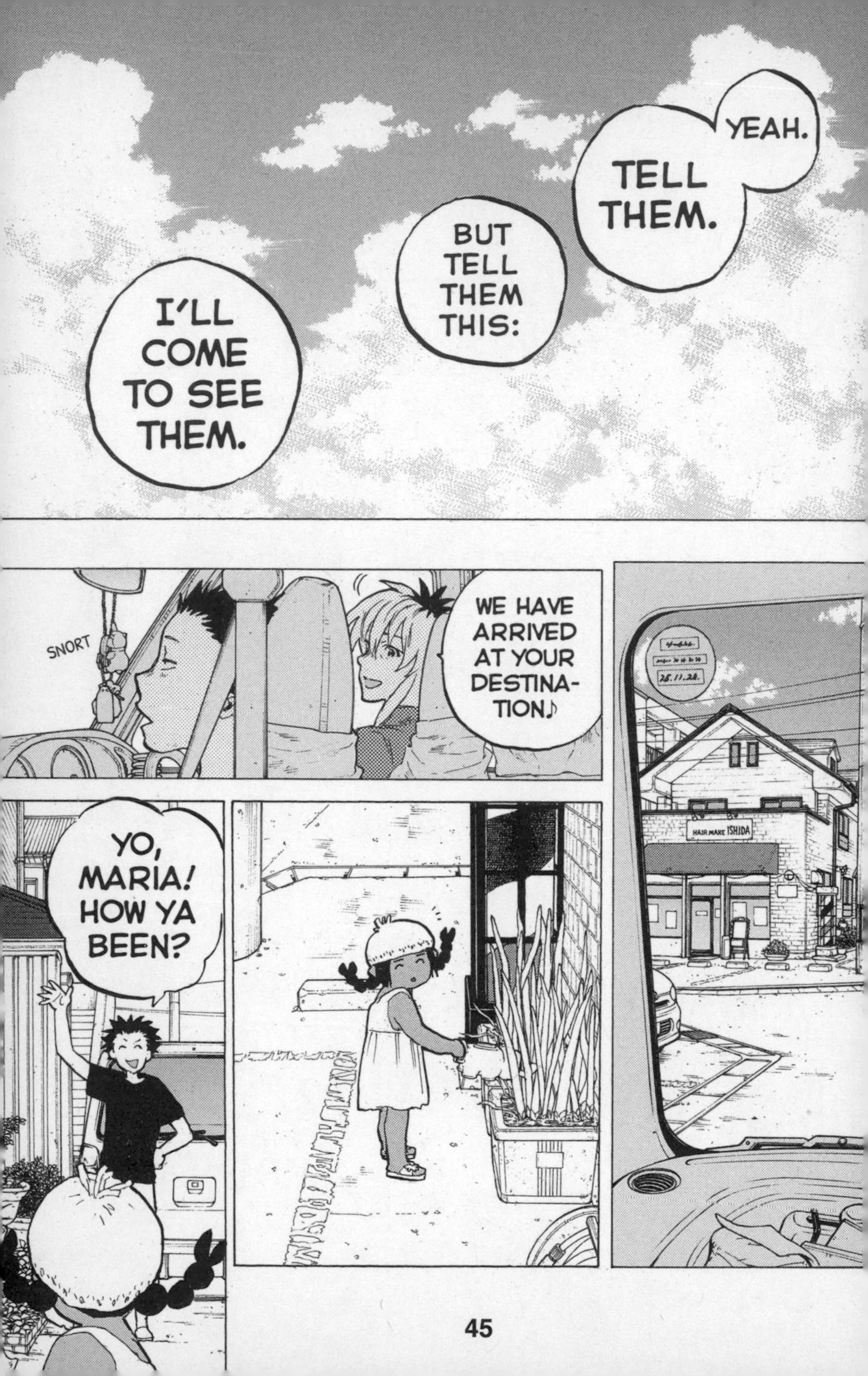
YEAH.
TELL THEM.
BUT TELL THEM THIS:
I'LL COME TO SEE THEM.
HAIR MAKE ISHIDA
WE HAVE ARRIVED AT YOUR DESTINATION♪
SNORT
YO, MARIA! HOW YA BEEN?

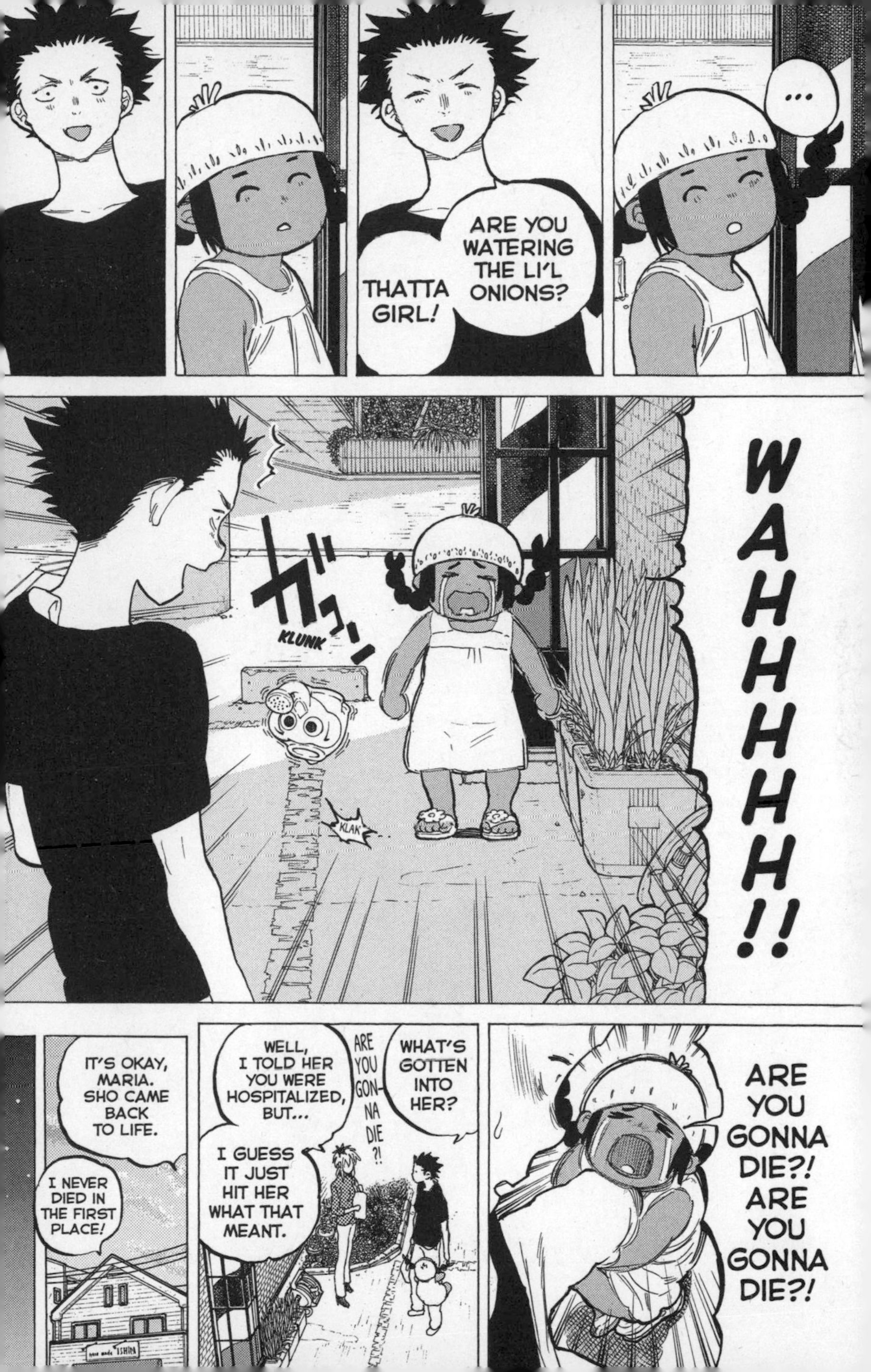
...
ARE YOU WATERING THE LI'L ONIONS?
THATTA GIRL!
WAHHHHHH!!
KLUNK
KLAK
ARE YOU GONNA DIE?! ARE YOU GONNA DIE?!
WHAT'S GOTTEN INTO HER?
ARE YOU GONNA DIE ?!
WELL, I TOLD HER YOU WERE HOSPITALIZED, BUT...
I GUESS IT JUST HIT HER WHAT THAT MEANT.
IT'S OKAY, MARIA. SHO CAME BACK TO LIFE.
I NEVER DIED IN THE FIRST PLACE!

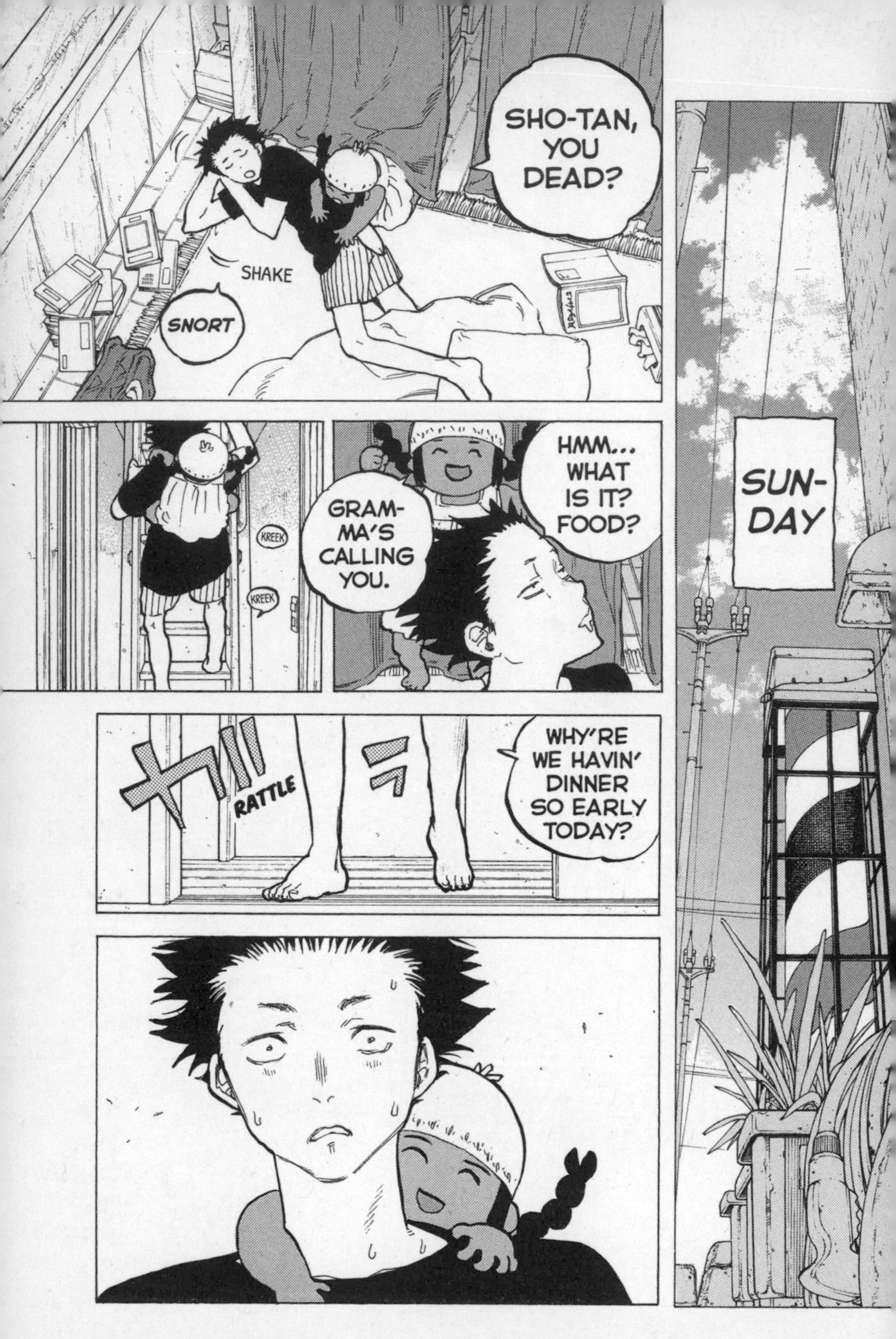
SUN-DAY
SHO-TAN, YOU DEAD?
SHAKE
SNORT
HMM... WHAT IS IT? FOOD?
GRAM-MA'S CALLING YOU.
KREEK
KREEK
WHY'RE WE HAVIN' DINNER SO EARLY TODAY?
RATTLE

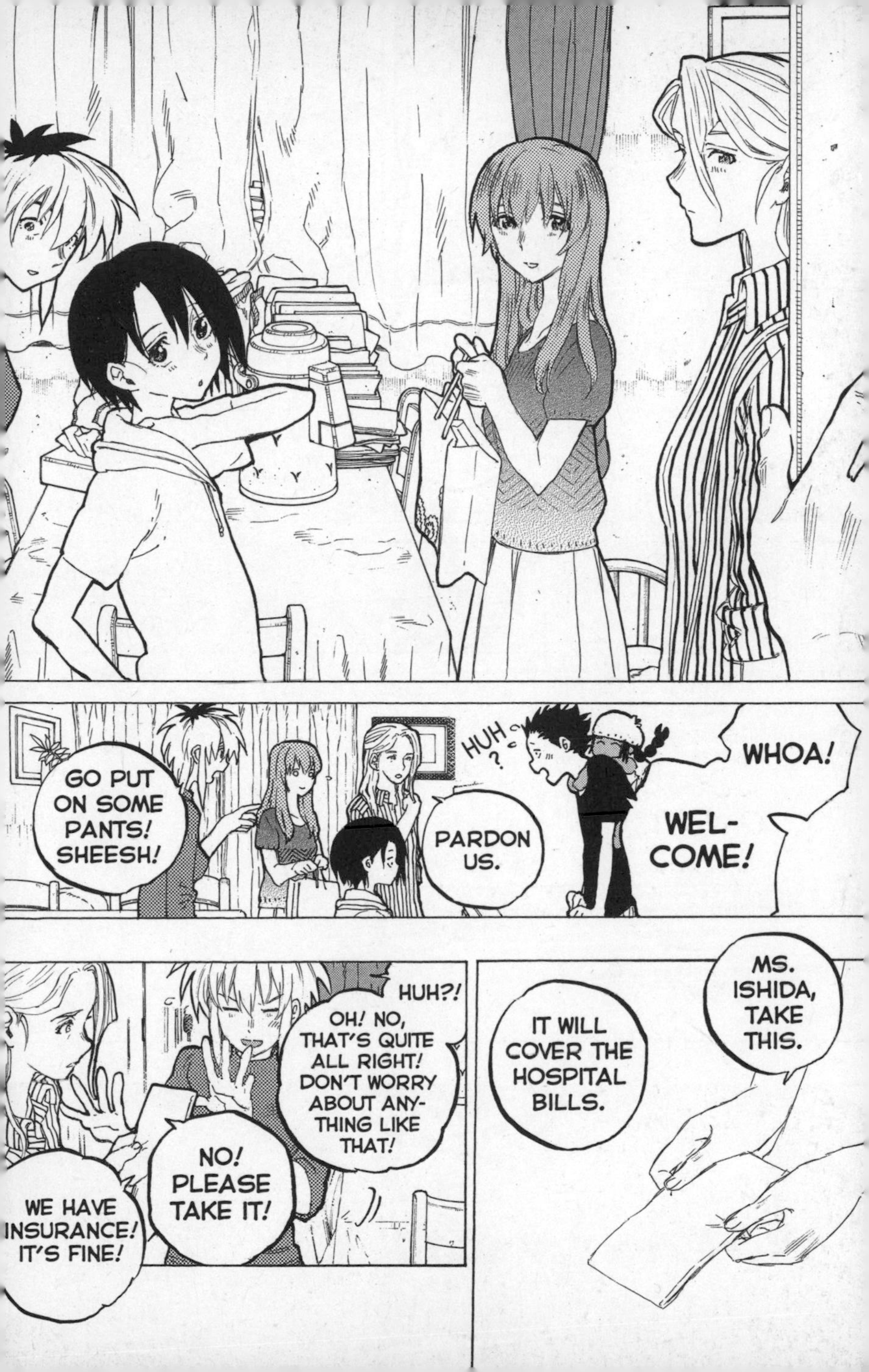
WHOA!
WEL-COME!
HUH ? ?
PARDON US.
GO PUT ON SOME PANTS! SHEESH!
MS. ISHIDA, TAKE THIS.
IT WILL COVER THE HOSPITAL BILLS.
HUH?!
OH! NO, THAT'S QUITE ALL RIGHT! DON'T WORRY ABOUT ANY-THING LIKE THAT!
NO! PLEASE TAKE IT!
WE HAVE INSURANCE! IT'S FINE!

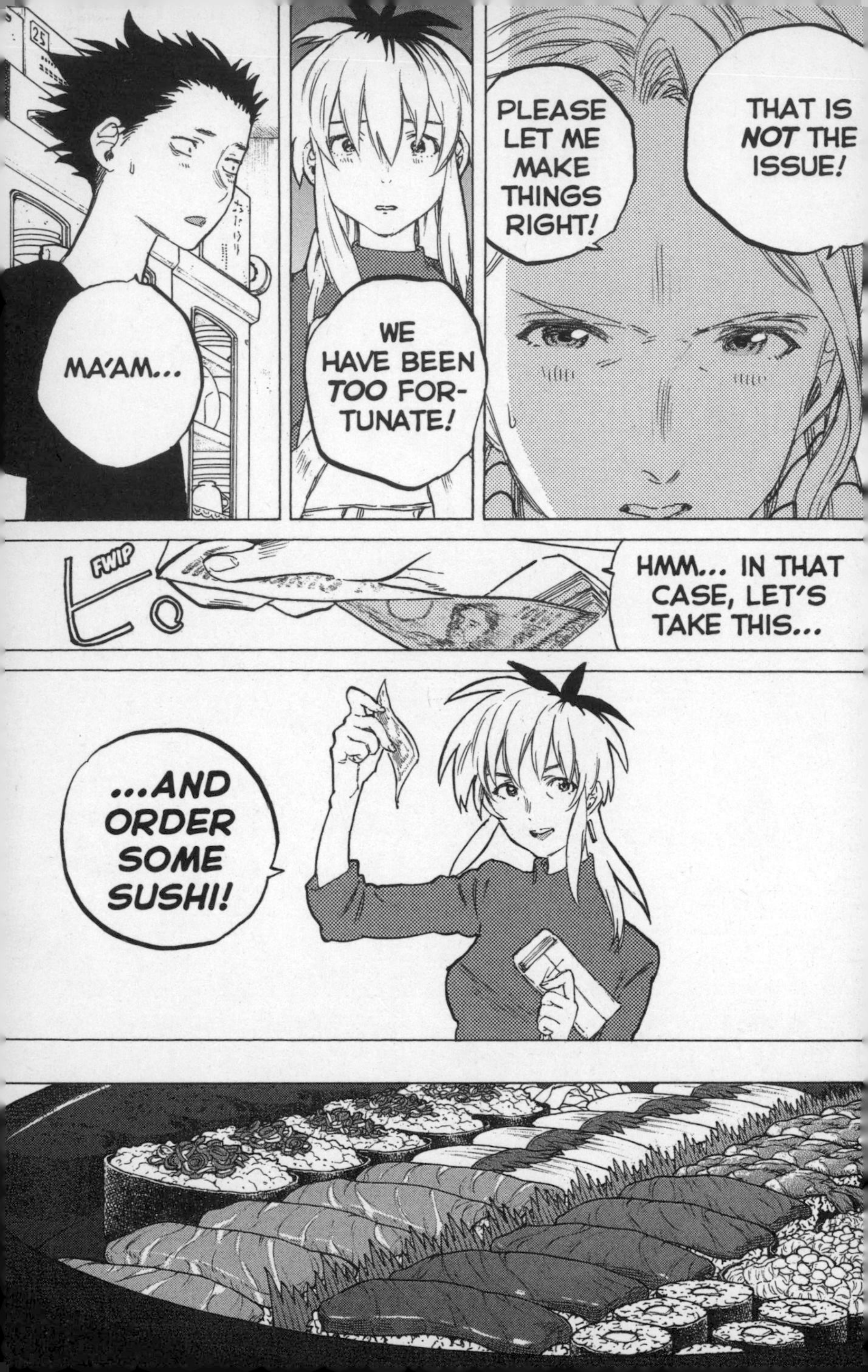
THAT IS NOT THE ISSUE!
PLEASE LET ME MAKE THINGS RIGHT!
WE HAVE BEEN TOO FORTUNATE!
MA'AM...
HMM... IN THAT CASE, LET'S TAKE THIS...
FWIP
...AND ORDER SOME SUSHI!

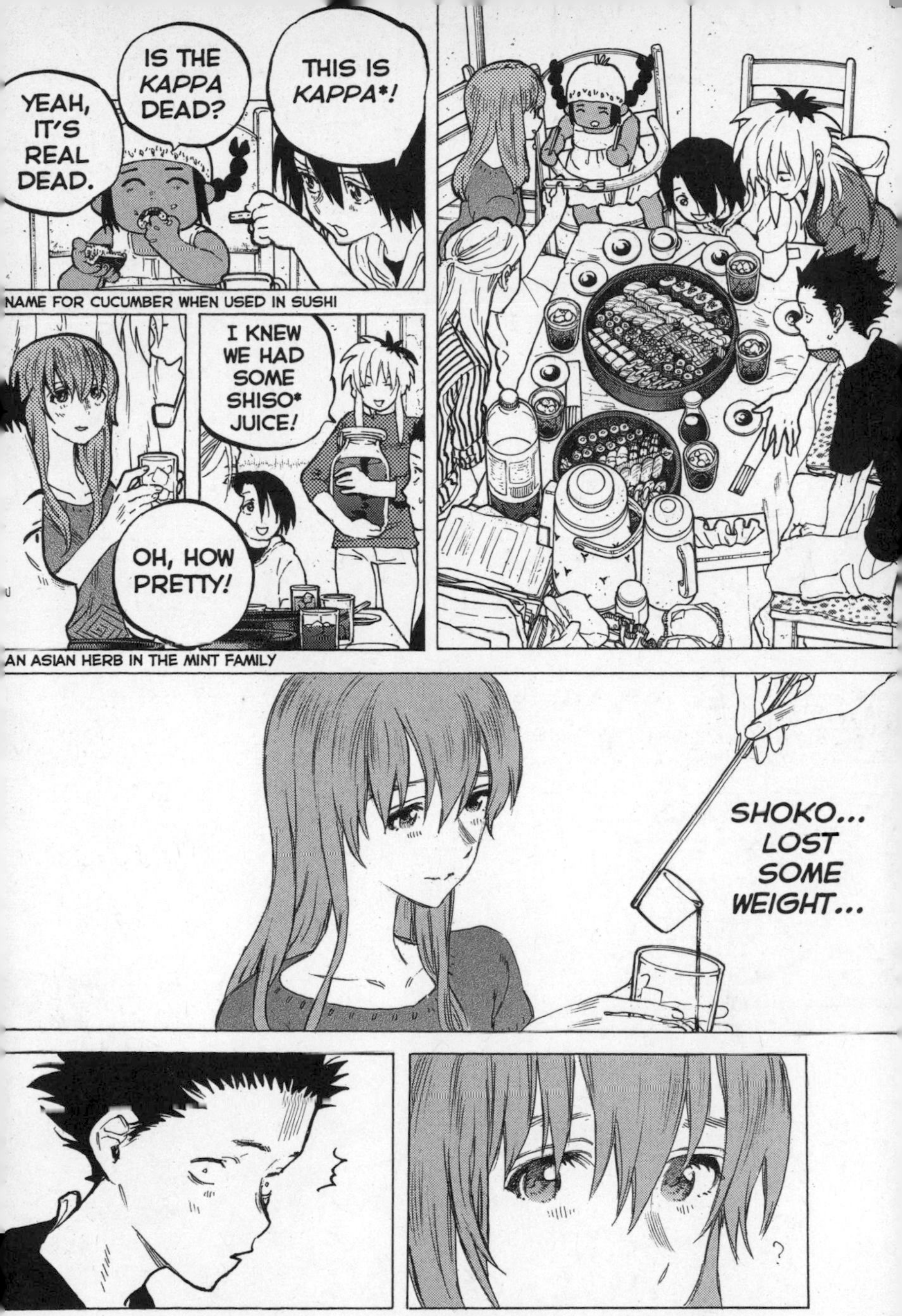
THIS IS KAPPA*!
IS THE KAPPA DEAD?
YEAH, IT'S REAL DEAD.
NAME FOR CUCUMBER WHEN USED IN SUSHI
I KNEW WE HAD SOME SHISO* JUICE!
OH, HOW PRETTY!
AN ASIAN HERB IN THE MINT FAMILY
SHOKO... LOST SOME WEIGHT...

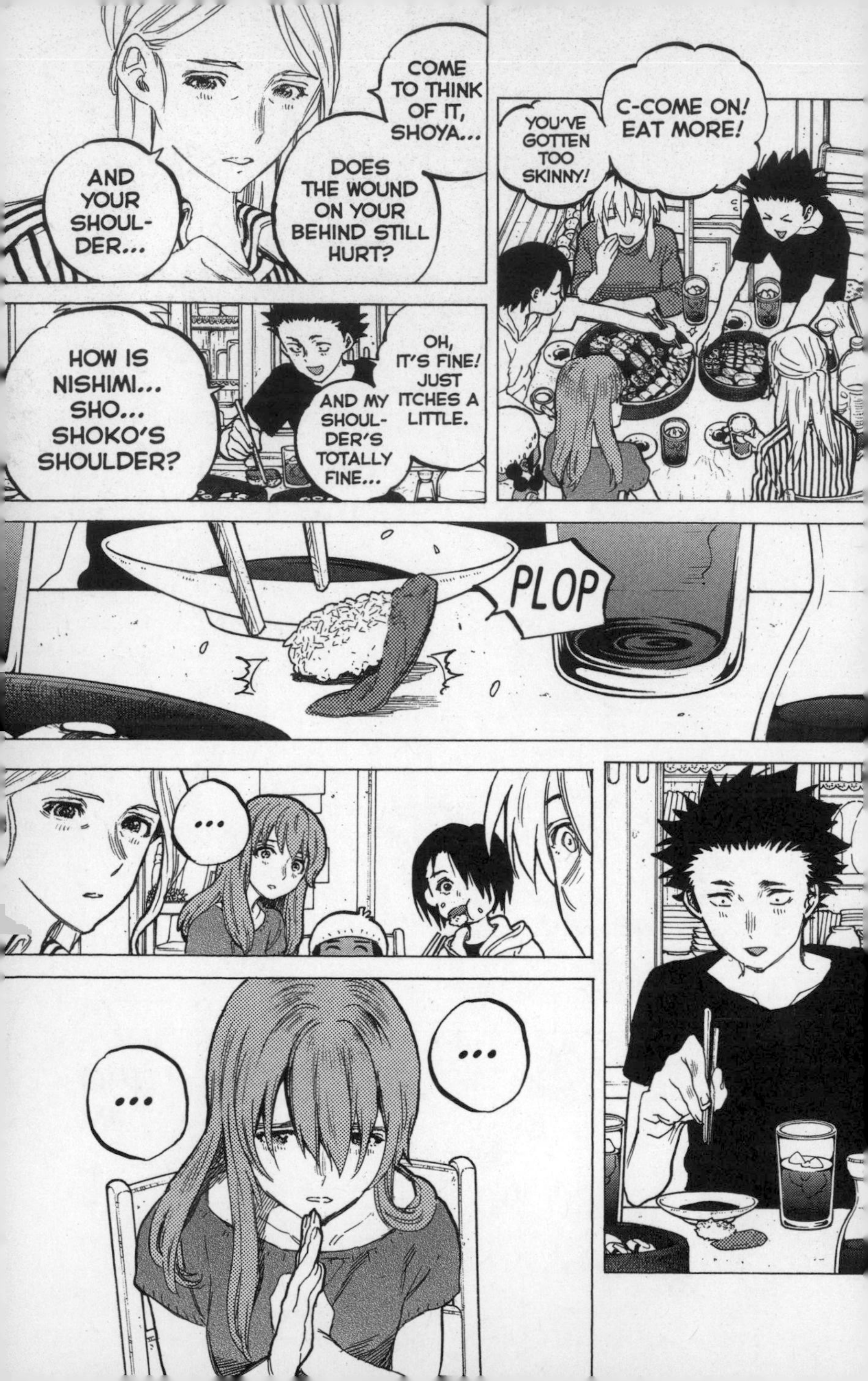
C-COME ON! EAT MORE!
YOU'VE GOTTEN TOO SKINNY!
COME TO THINK OF IT, SHOYA...
DOES THE WOUND ON YOUR BEHIND STILL HURT?
AND YOUR SHOUL-DER...
OH, IT'S FINE! JUST ITCHES A LITTLE.
AND MY SHOUL-DER'S TOTALLY FINE...
HOW IS NISHIMI... SHO... SHOKO'S SHOULDER?
PLOP
...
...
...

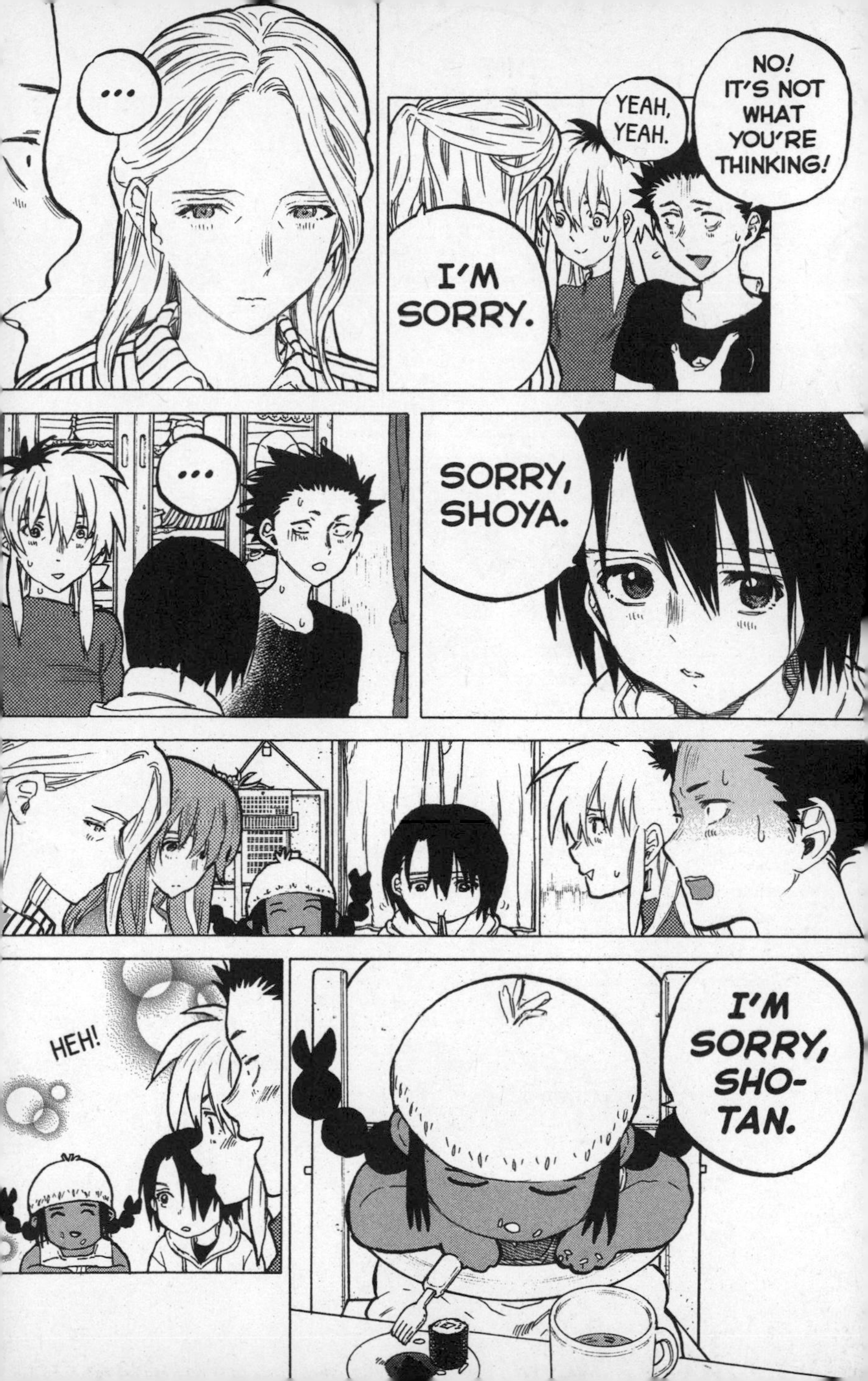
NO! IT'S NOT WHAT YOU'RE THINKING!
YEAH, YEAH.
I'M SORRY.
...
SORRY, SHOYA.
...
I'M SORRY, SHO-TAN.
HEH!

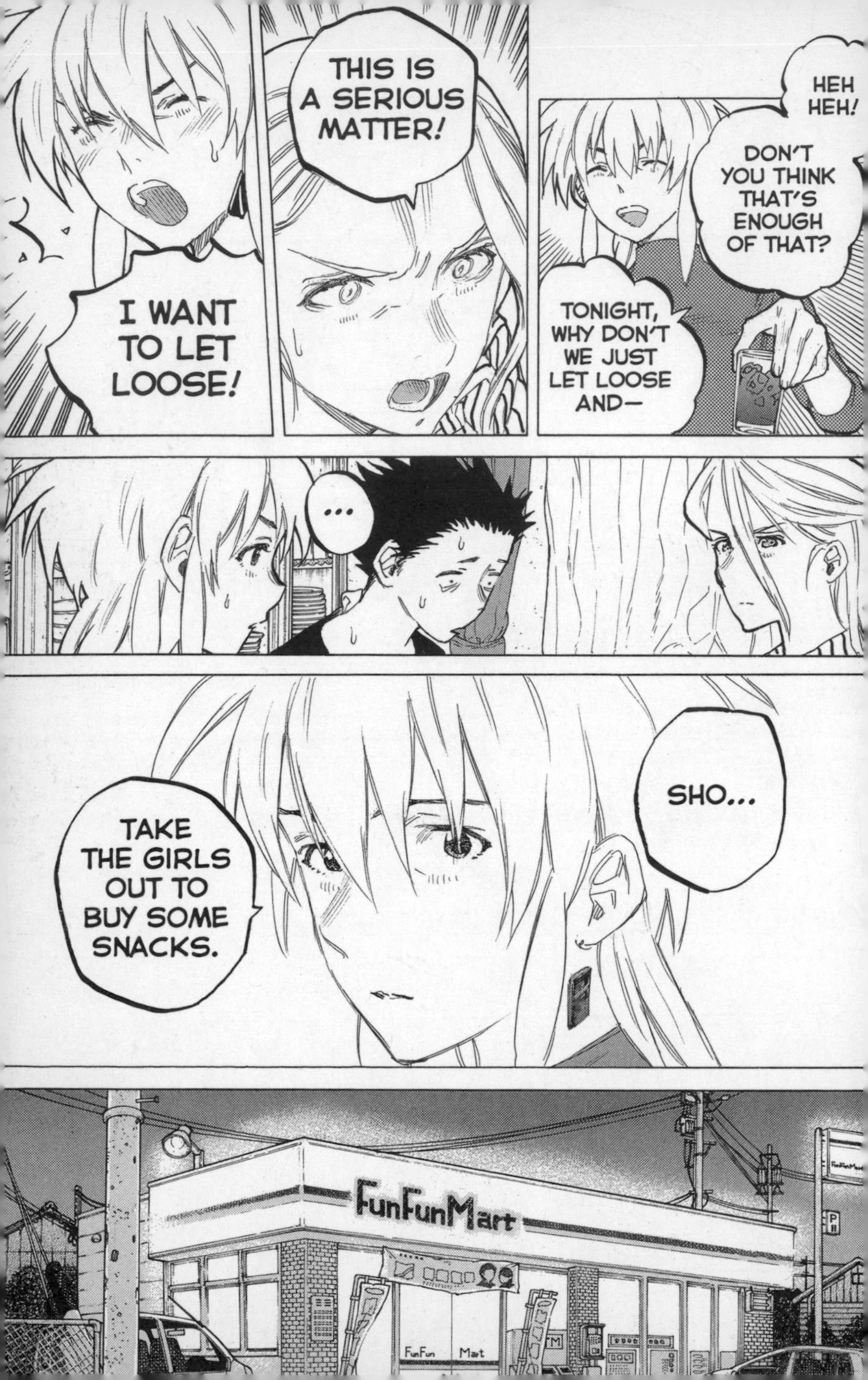
HEH HEH!
DON'T YOU THINK THAT'S ENOUGH OF THAT?
TONIGHT, WHY DON'T WE JUST LET LOOSE AND—
THIS IS A SERIOUS MATTER!
I WANT TO LET LOOSE!
...
SHO...
TAKE THE GIRLS OUT TO BUY SOME SNACKS.
FunFunMart
FunFun Mart

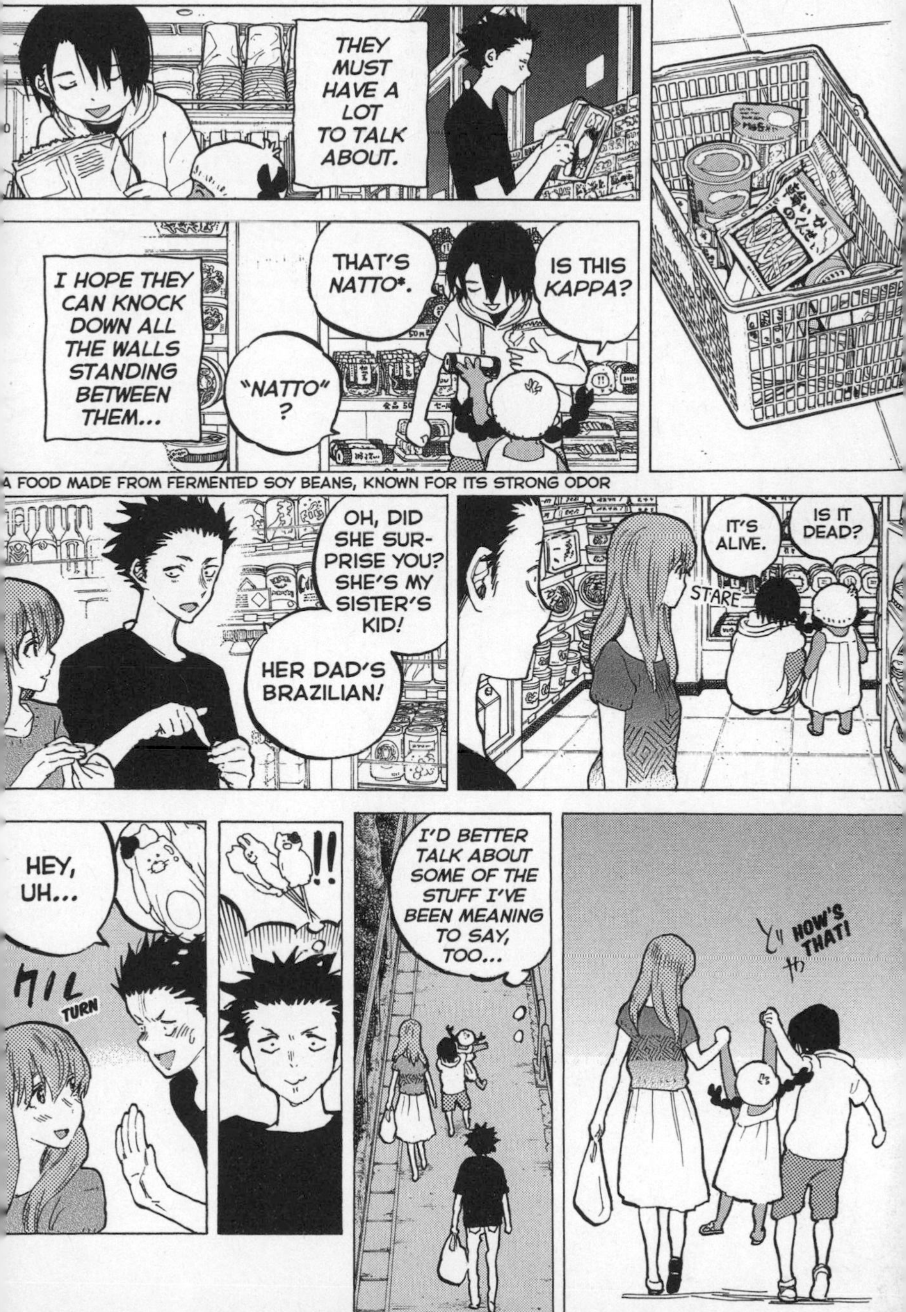
THEY MUST HAVE A LOT TO TALK ABOUT.
IS THIS KAPPA?
THAT'S NATTO*.
"NATTO"?
I HOPE THEY CAN KNOCK DOWN ALL THE WALLS STANDING BETWEEN THEM...
* A FOOD MADE FROM FERMENTED SOY BEANS, KNOWN FOR ITS STRONG ODOR
IS IT DEAD?
IT'S ALIVE.
STARE
OH, DID SHE SURPRISE YOU? SHE'S MY SISTER'S KID!
HER DAD'S BRAZILIAN!
HOW'S THAT!
I'D BETTER TALK ABOUT SOME OF THE STUFF I'VE BEEN MEANING TO SAY, TOO...
!!
HEY, UH...
TURN

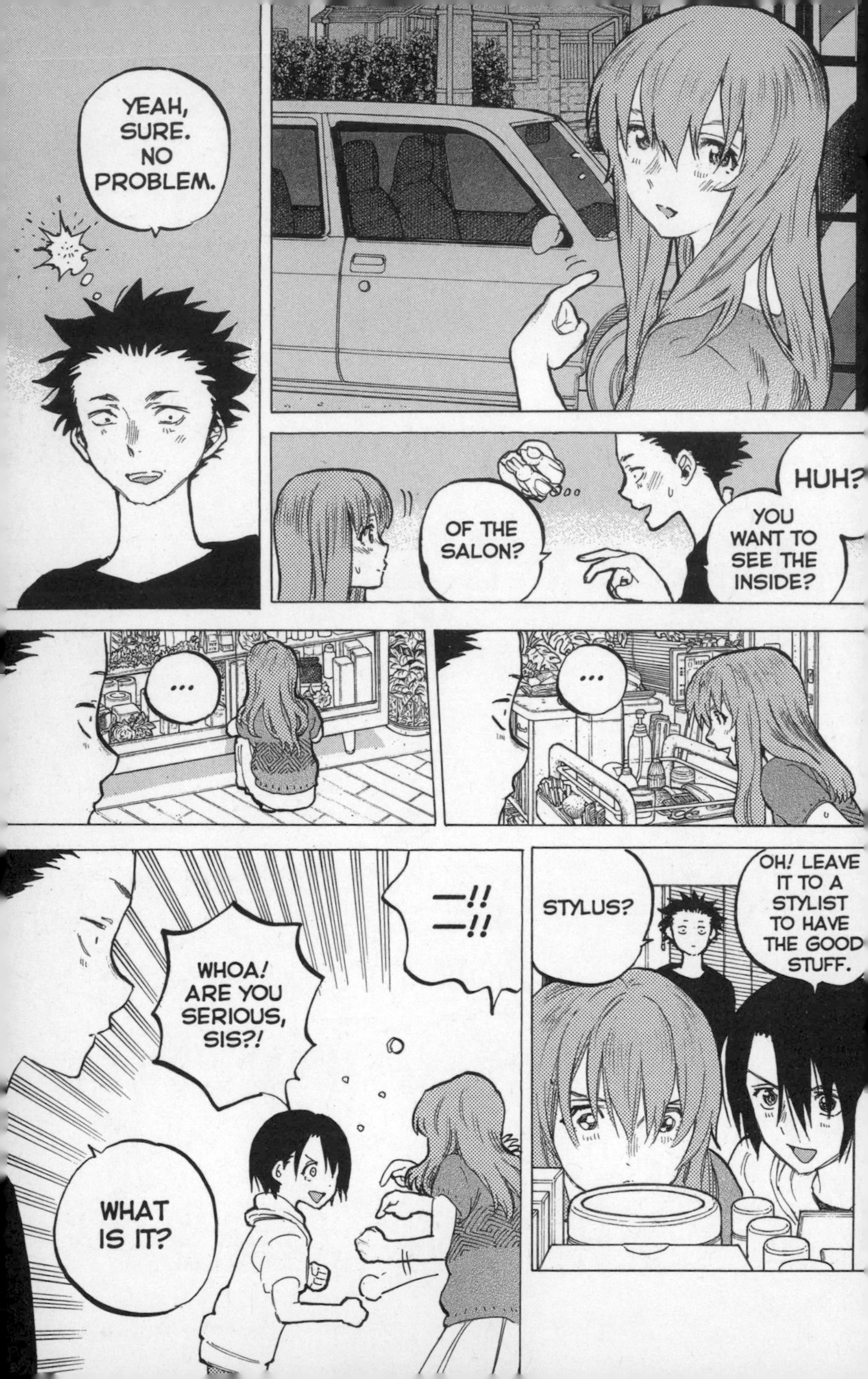
HUH?
YOU WANT TO SEE THE INSIDE?
OF THE SALON?
YEAH, SURE. NO PROBLEM.
...
...
OH! LEAVE IT TO A STYLIST TO HAVE THE GOOD STUFF.
STYLUS?
—!!
—!!
WHOA! ARE YOU SERIOUS, SIS?!
WHAT IS IT?

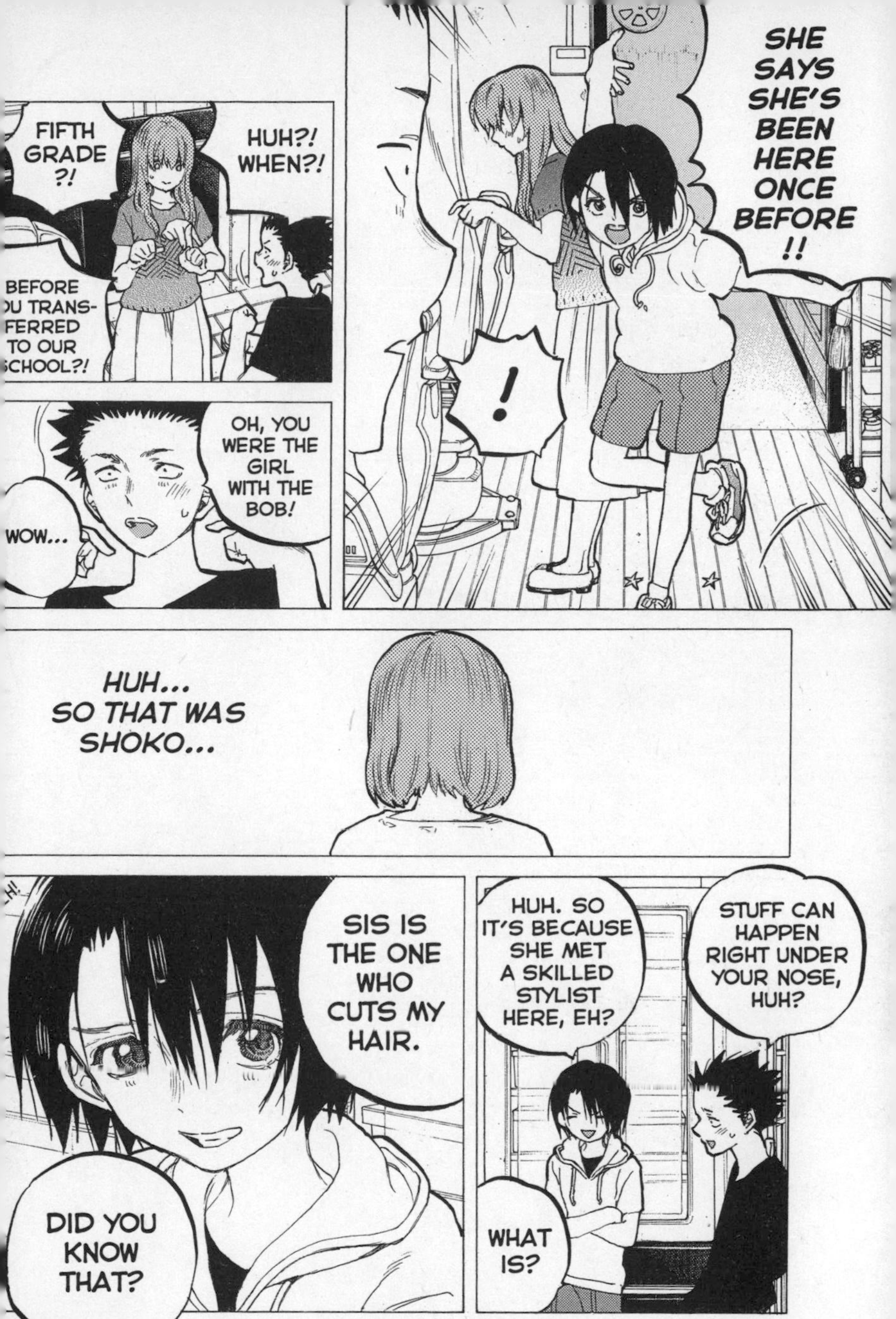
SHE SAYS SHE'S BEEN HERE ONCE BEFORE!!
!
HUH?! WHEN?!
FIFTH GRADE?!
BEFORE OU TRANS-FERRED TO OUR SCHOOL?!
OH, YOU WERE THE GIRL WITH THE BOB!
WOW...
HUH... SO THAT WAS SHOKO...
STUFF CAN HAPPEN RIGHT UNDER YOUR NOSE, HUH?
HUH. SO IT'S BECAUSE SHE MET A SKILLED STYLIST HERE, EH?
WHAT IS?
SIS IS THE ONE WHO CUTS MY HAIR.
DID YOU KNOW THAT?

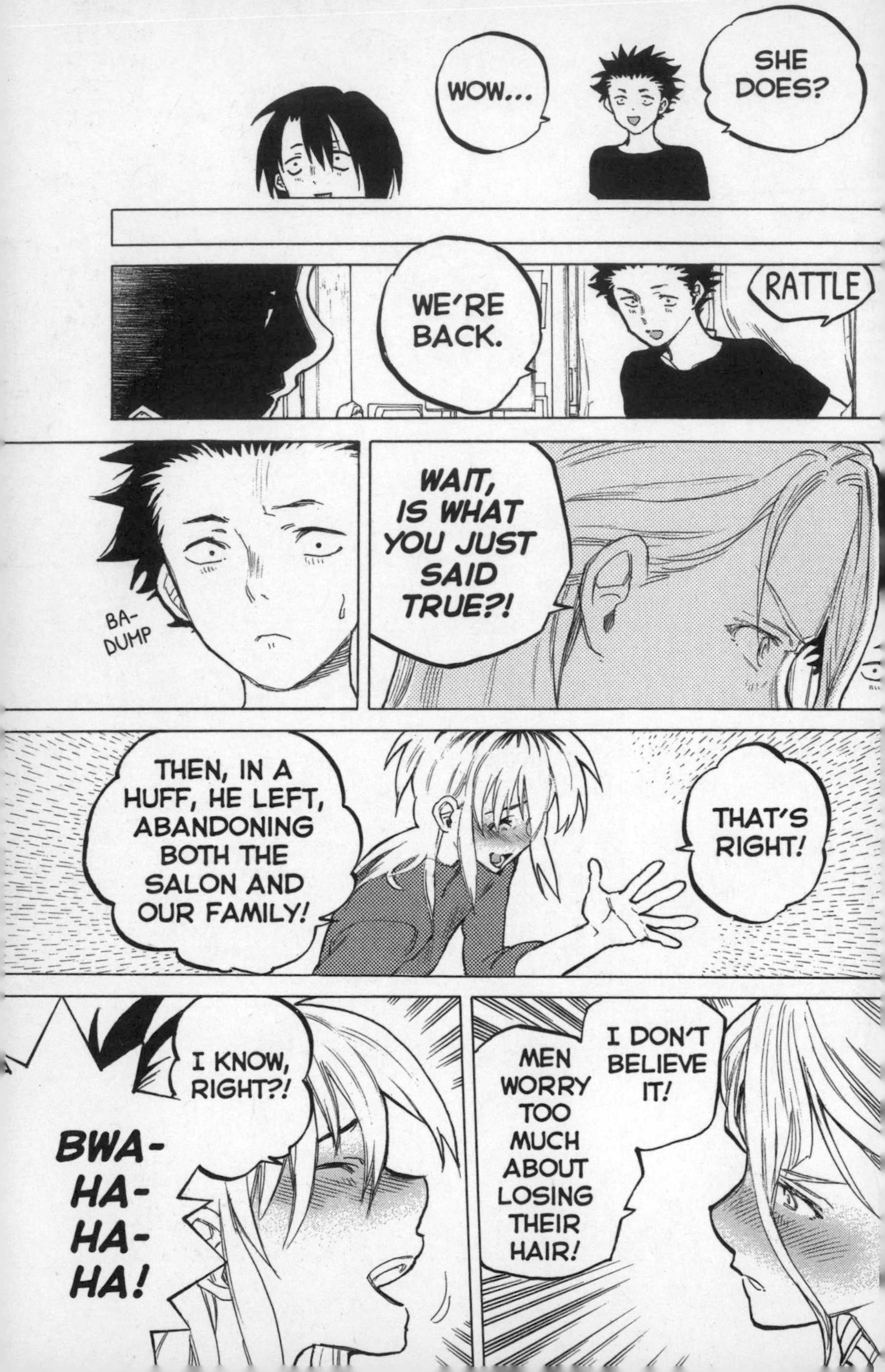
SHE DOES?
WOW...
RATTLE
WE'RE BACK.
WAIT, IS WHAT YOU JUST SAID TRUE?!
BA-DUMP
THAT'S RIGHT!
THEN, IN A HUFF, HE LEFT, ABANDONING BOTH THE SALON AND OUR FAMILY!
I DON'T BELIEVE IT!
MEN WORRY TOO MUCH ABOUT LOSING THEIR HAIR!
I KNOW, RIGHT?!
BWA-HA-HA-HA!

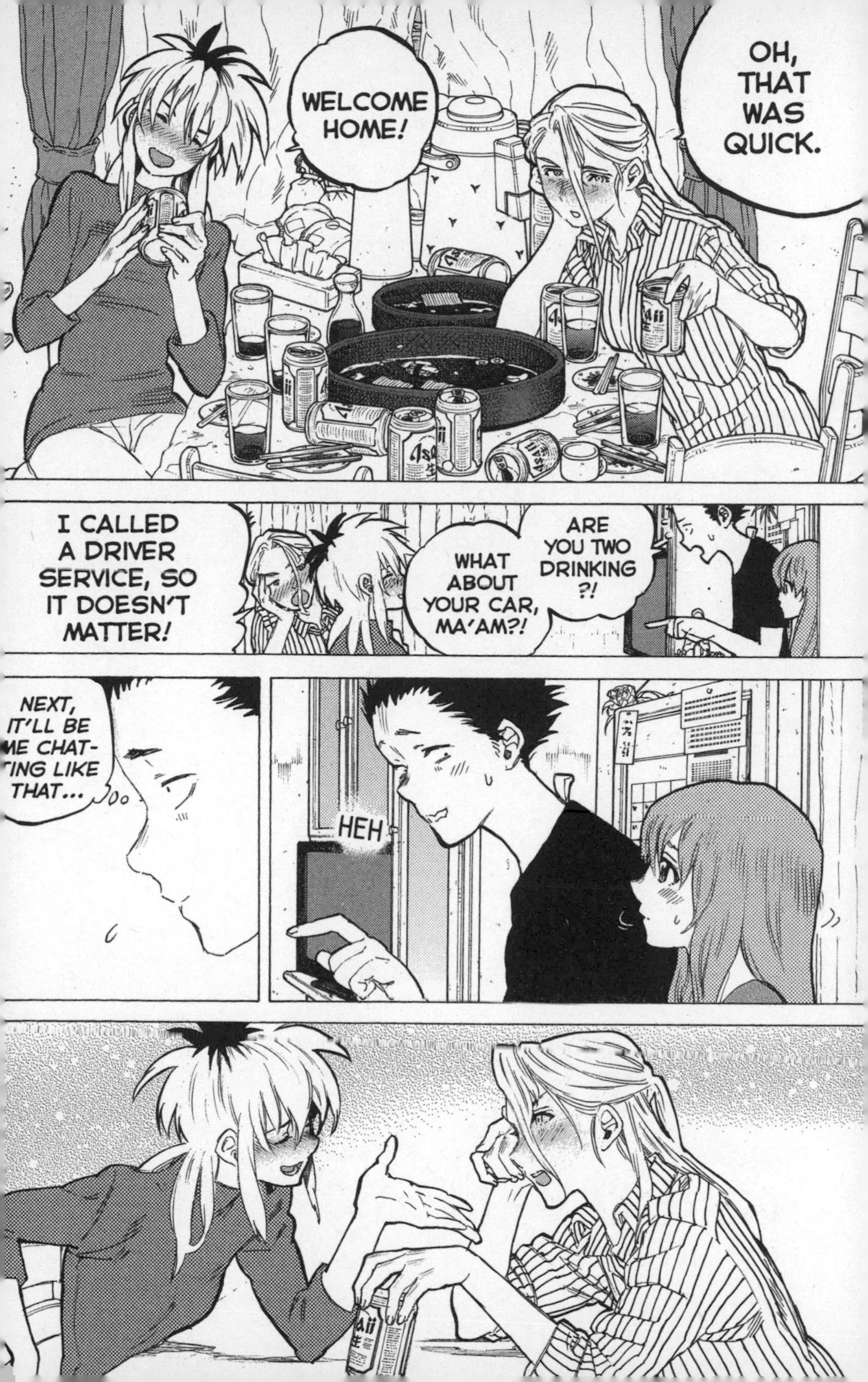
OH, THAT WAS QUICK.
WELCOME HOME!
ARE YOU TWO DRINKING ?!
WHAT ABOUT YOUR CAR, MA'AM?!
I CALLED A DRIVER SERVICE, SO IT DOESN'T MATTER!
HEH
NEXT, IT'LL BE ME CHATTING LIKE THAT...

a Silent Voice

a Silent Voice

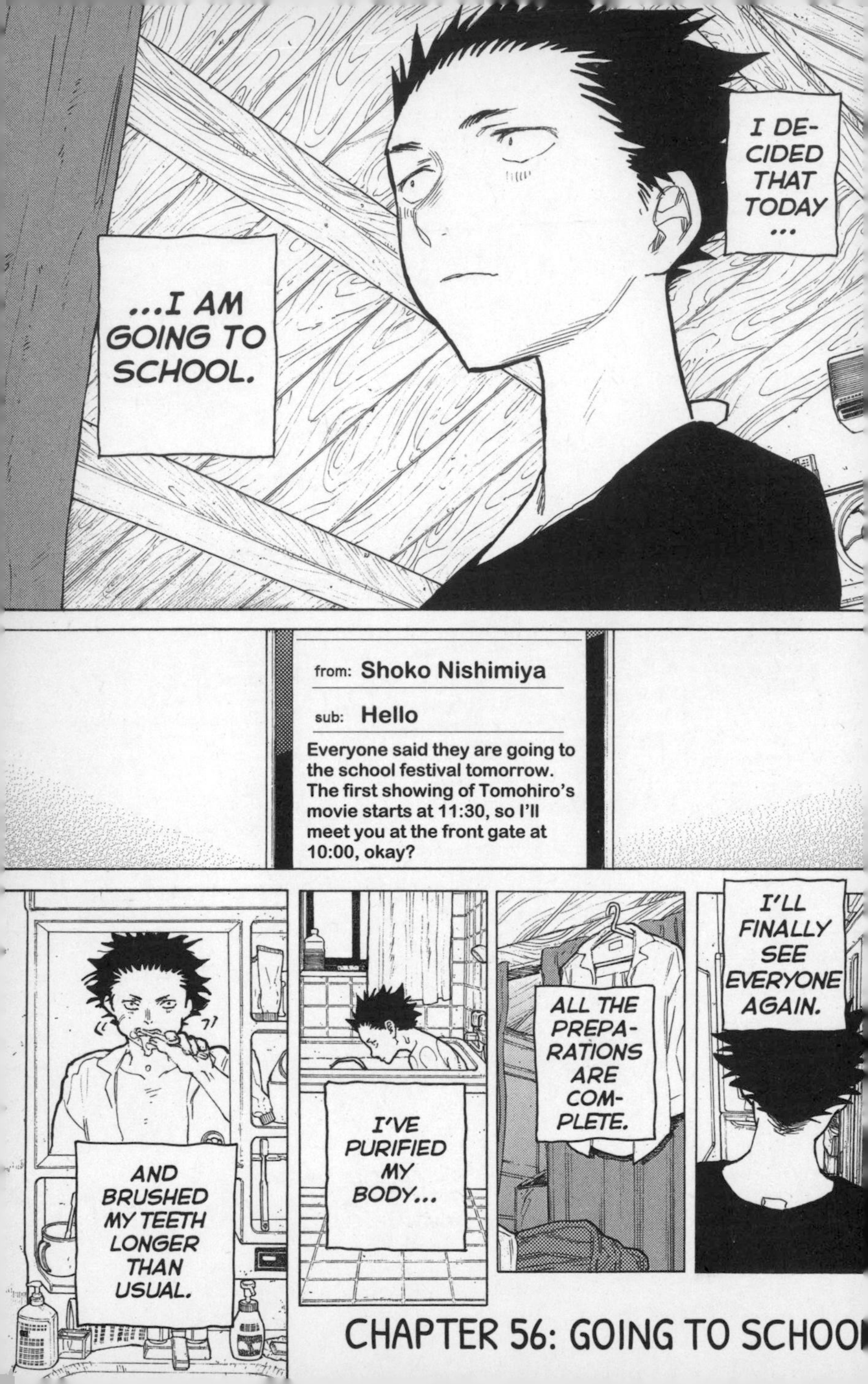
I DE-
CIDED
THAT
TODAY
...
...I AM GOING TO SCHOOL.
from: Shoko Nishimiya
sub: Hello
Everyone said they are going to the school festival tomorrow. The first showing of Tomohiro's movie starts at 11:30, so I'll meet you at the front gate at 10:00, okay?
I'LL FINALLY SEE EVERYONE AGAIN.
ALL THE PREPA-
RATIONS ARE COM-
PLETE.
I'VE PURIFIED MY BODY...
AND BRUSHED MY TEETH LONGER THAN USUAL.
CHAPTER 56: GOING TO SCHOO

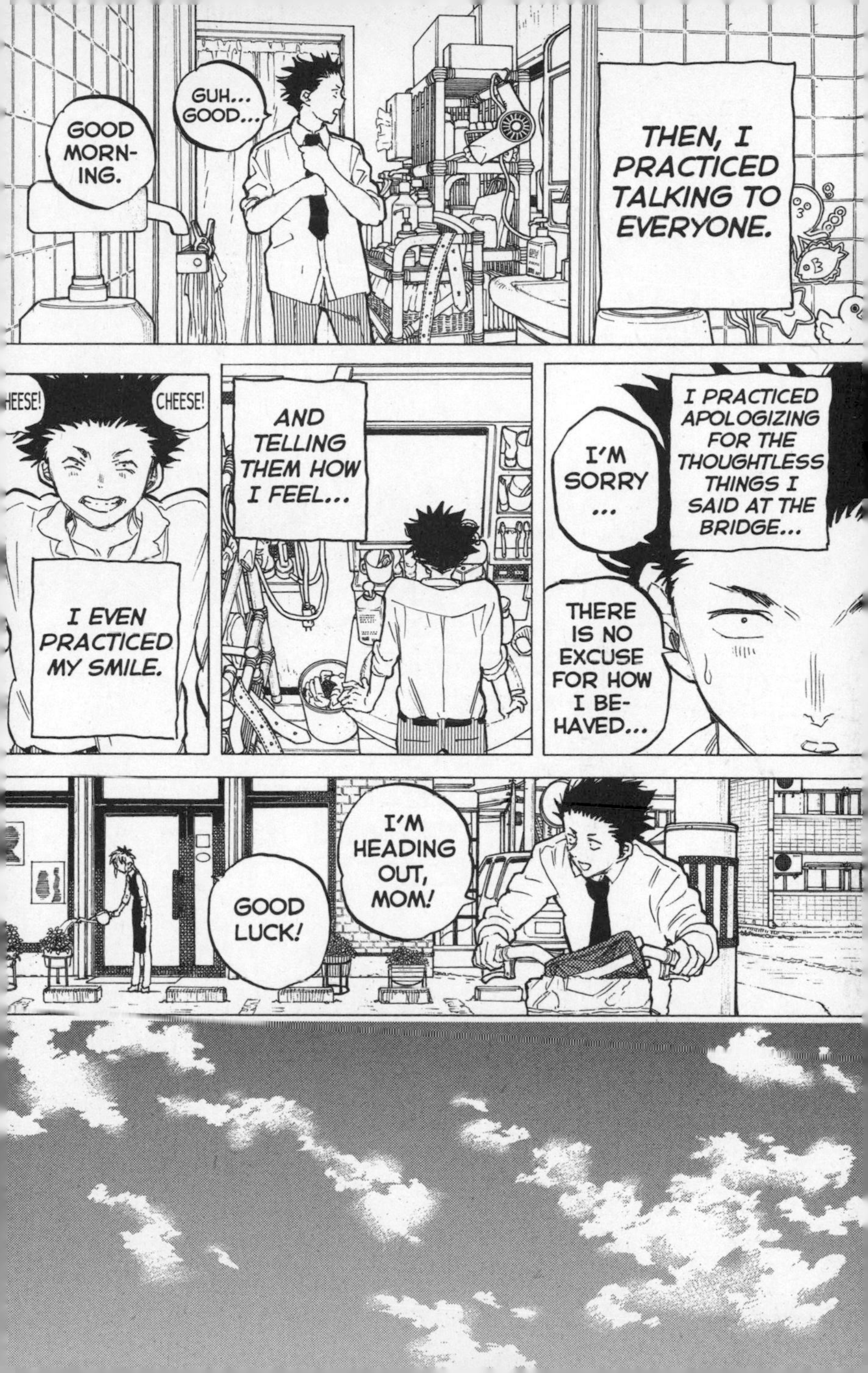

THEN, I PRACTICED TALKING TO EVERYONE.
GUH... GOOD...
GOOD MORN-ING.
I PRACTICED APOLOGIZING FOR THE THOUGHTLESS THINGS I SAID AT THE BRIDGE...
I'M SORRY ...
THERE IS NO EXCUSE FOR HOW I BE-HAVED...
AND TELLING THEM HOW I FEEL...
CHEESE!
HEESE!
I EVEN PRACTICED MY SMILE.
I'M HEADING OUT, MOM!
GOOD LUCK!

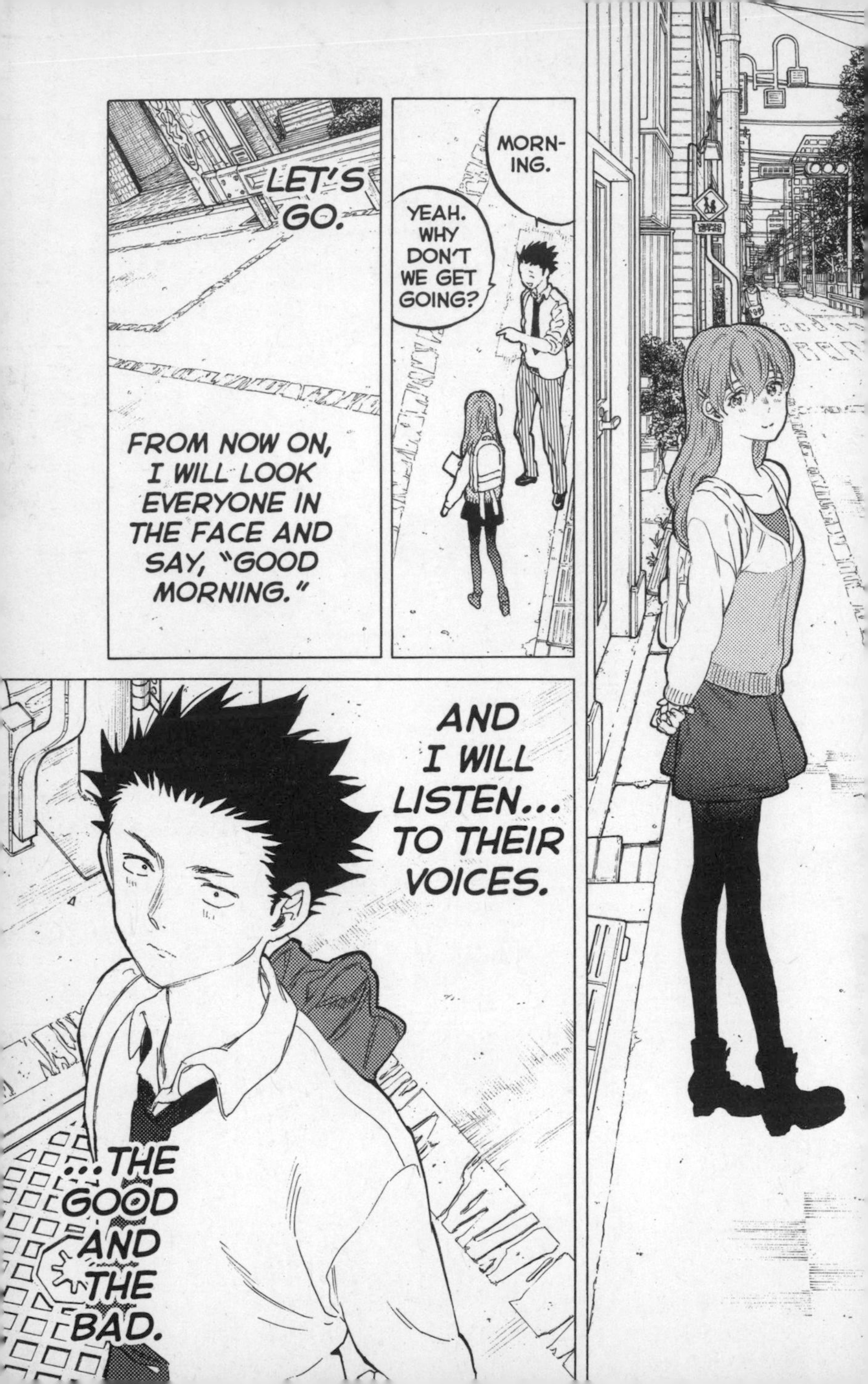
MORNING.
YEAH. WHY DON'T WE GET GOING?
LET'S GO.
FROM NOW ON, I WILL LOOK EVERYONE IN THE FACE AND SAY, "GOOD MORNING."
AND I WILL LISTEN... TO THEIR VOICES.
...THE GOOD AND THE BAD.

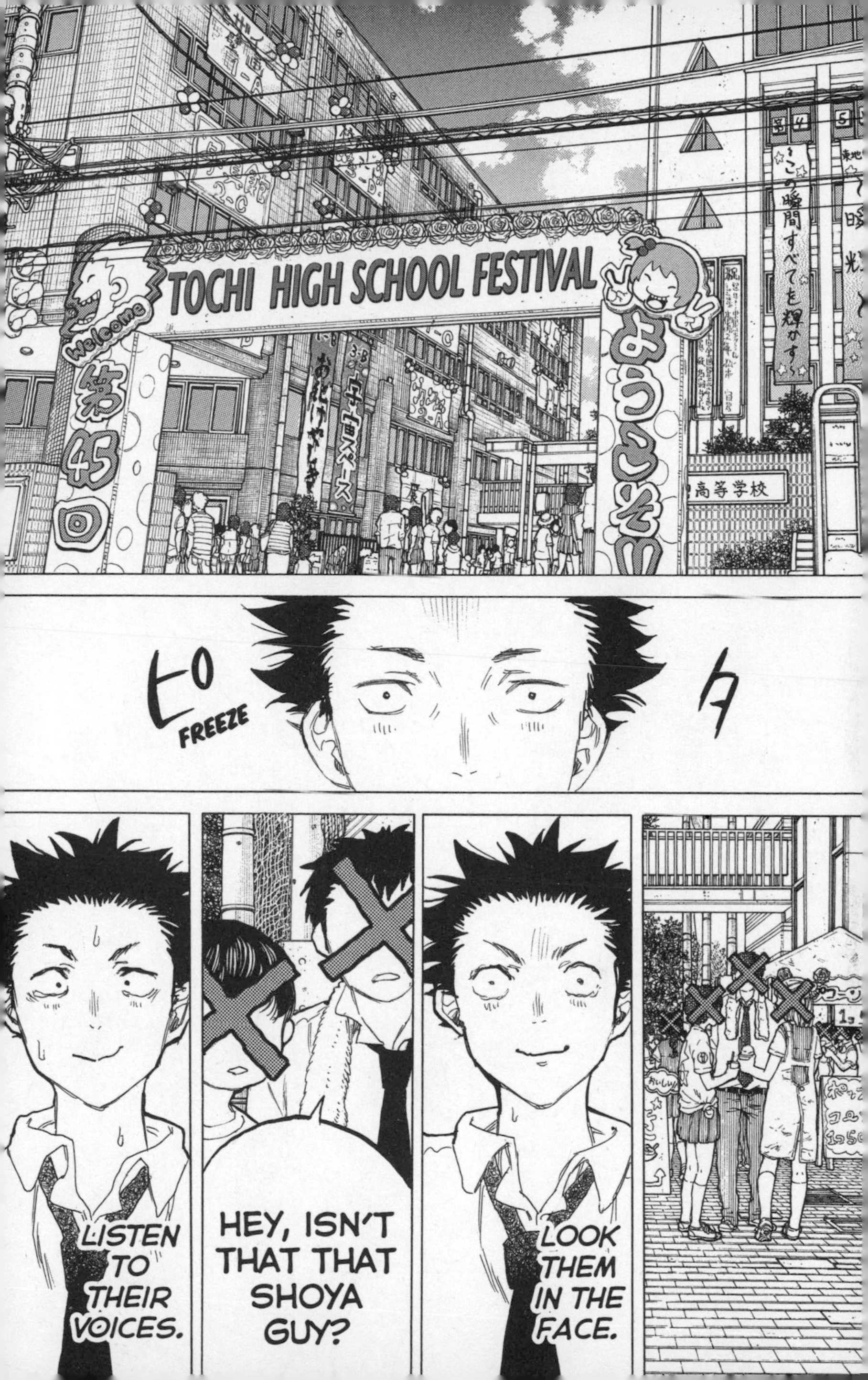
TOCHI HIGH SCHOOL FESTIVAL
Welcome
第45回
ようこそ
高等学校
～この瞬間すべてを輝かす～
ピタ
FREEZE
LOOK THEM IN THE FACE.
HEY, ISN'T THAT THAT SHOYA GUY?
LISTEN TO THEIR VOICES.

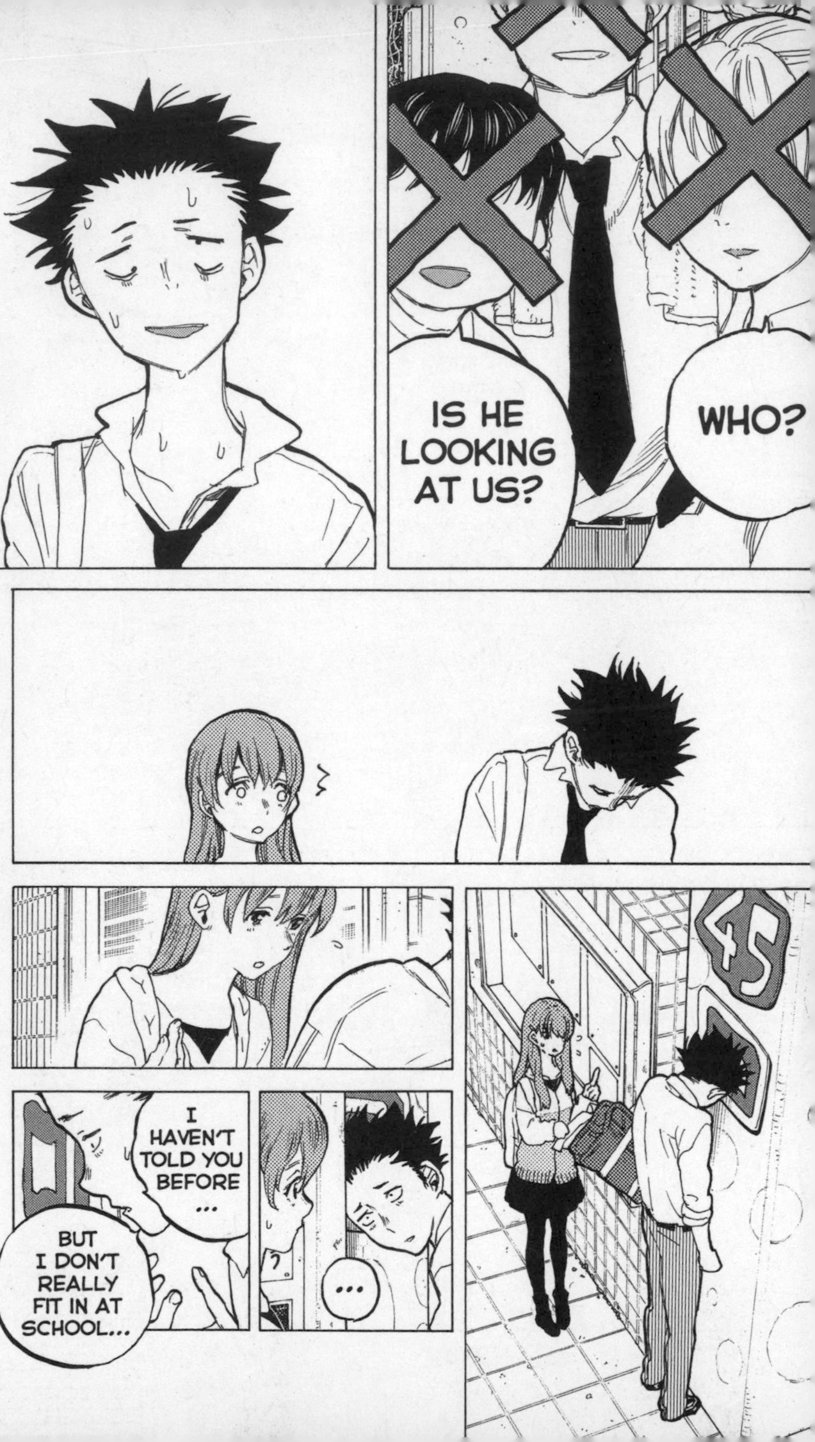
WHO?
IS HE LOOKING AT US?
...
I HAVEN'T TOLD YOU BEFORE ...
BUT I DON'T REALLY FIT IN AT SCHOOL...

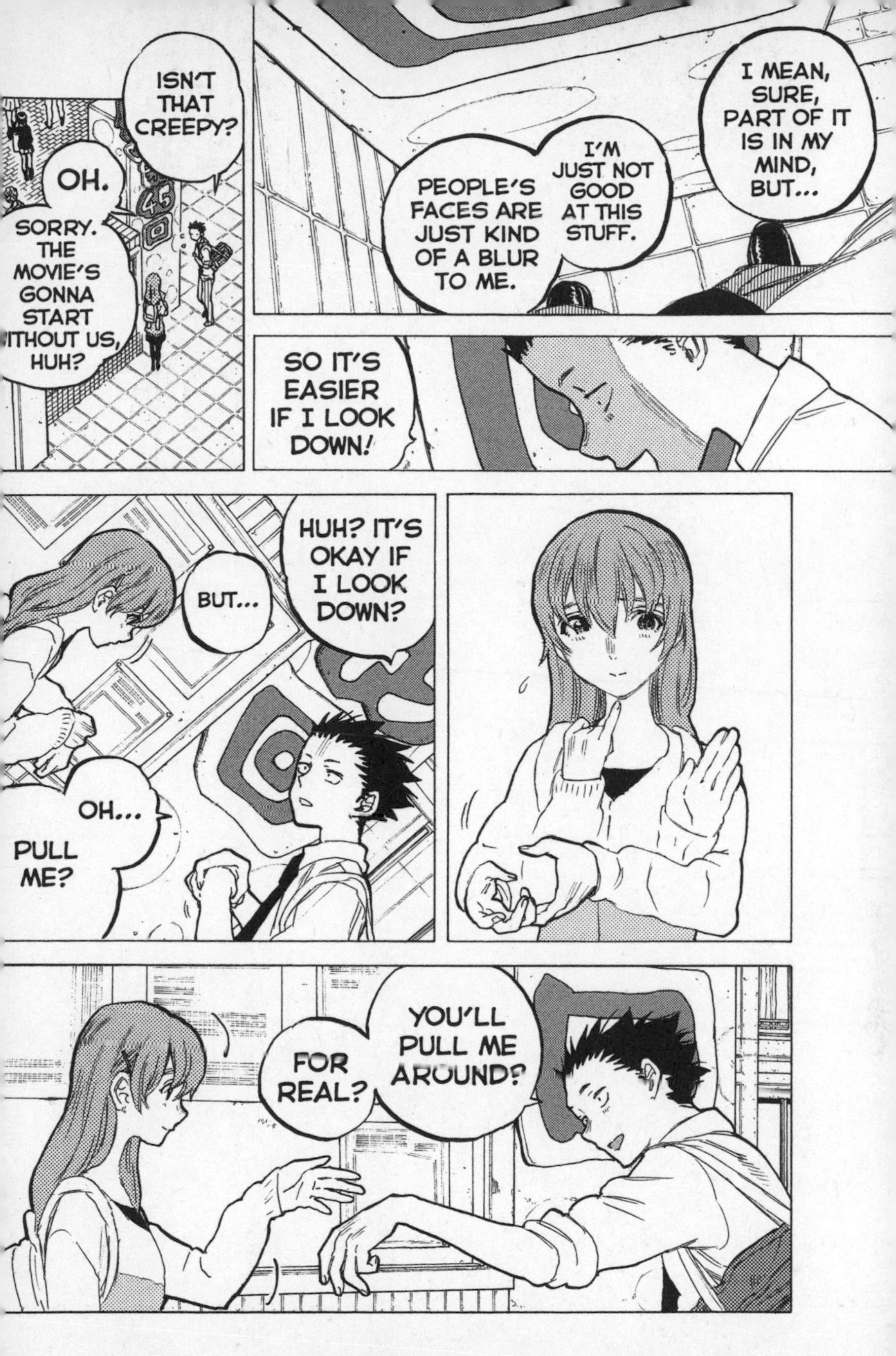
I MEAN, SURE, PART OF IT IS IN MY MIND, BUT...
I'M JUST NOT GOOD AT THIS STUFF.
PEOPLE'S FACES ARE JUST KIND OF A BLUR TO ME.
SO IT'S EASIER IF I LOOK DOWN!
ISN'T THAT CREEPY?
OH.
SORRY. THE MOVIE'S GONNA START ITHOUT US, HUH?
HUH? IT'S OKAY IF I LOOK DOWN?
BUT...
OH...
PULL ME?
YOU'LL PULL ME AROUND?
FOR REAL?

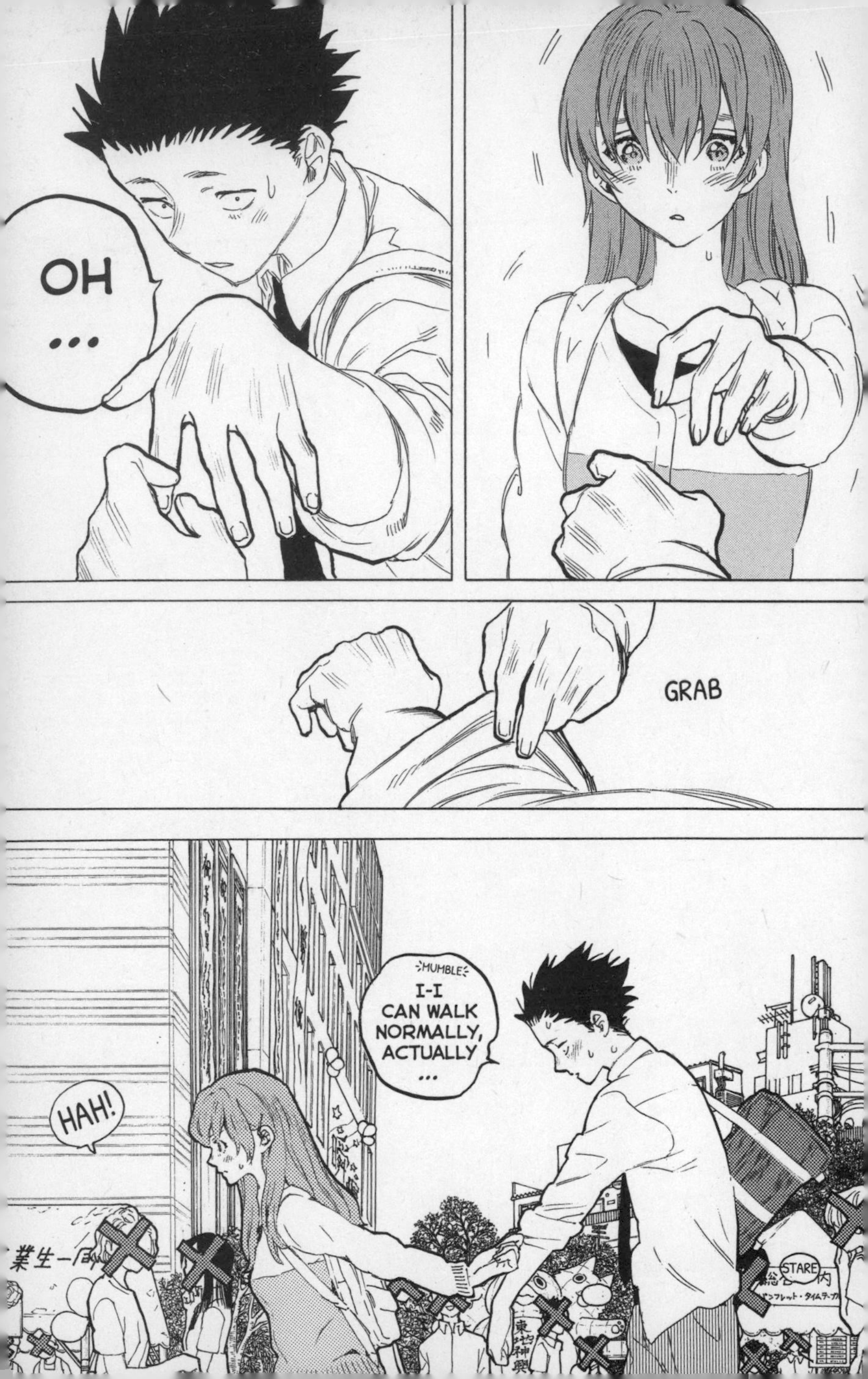
OH ...
GRAB
MUMBLE
I-I CAN WALK NORMALLY, ACTUALLY ...
STARE
HAH!

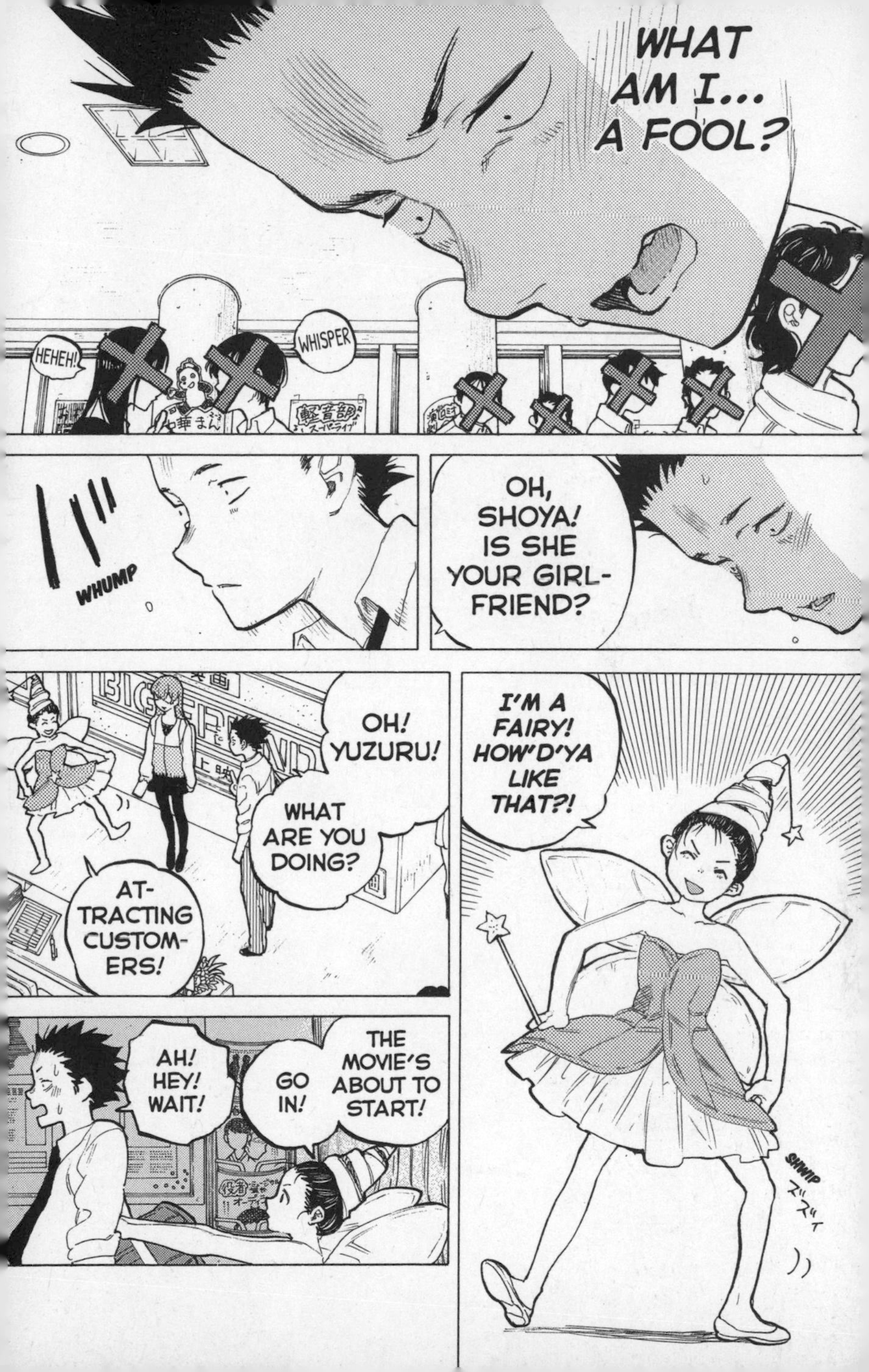
WHAT AM I... A FOOL?
WHISPER
HEHEH!
OH, SHOYA! IS SHE YOUR GIRL-FRIEND?
WHUMP
I'M A FAIRY! HOW'D'YA LIKE THAT?!
SHWIP
OH! YUZURU!
WHAT ARE YOU DOING?
AT-TRACTING CUSTOM-ERS!
THE MOVIE'S ABOUT TO START!
GO IN!
AH! HEY! WAIT!

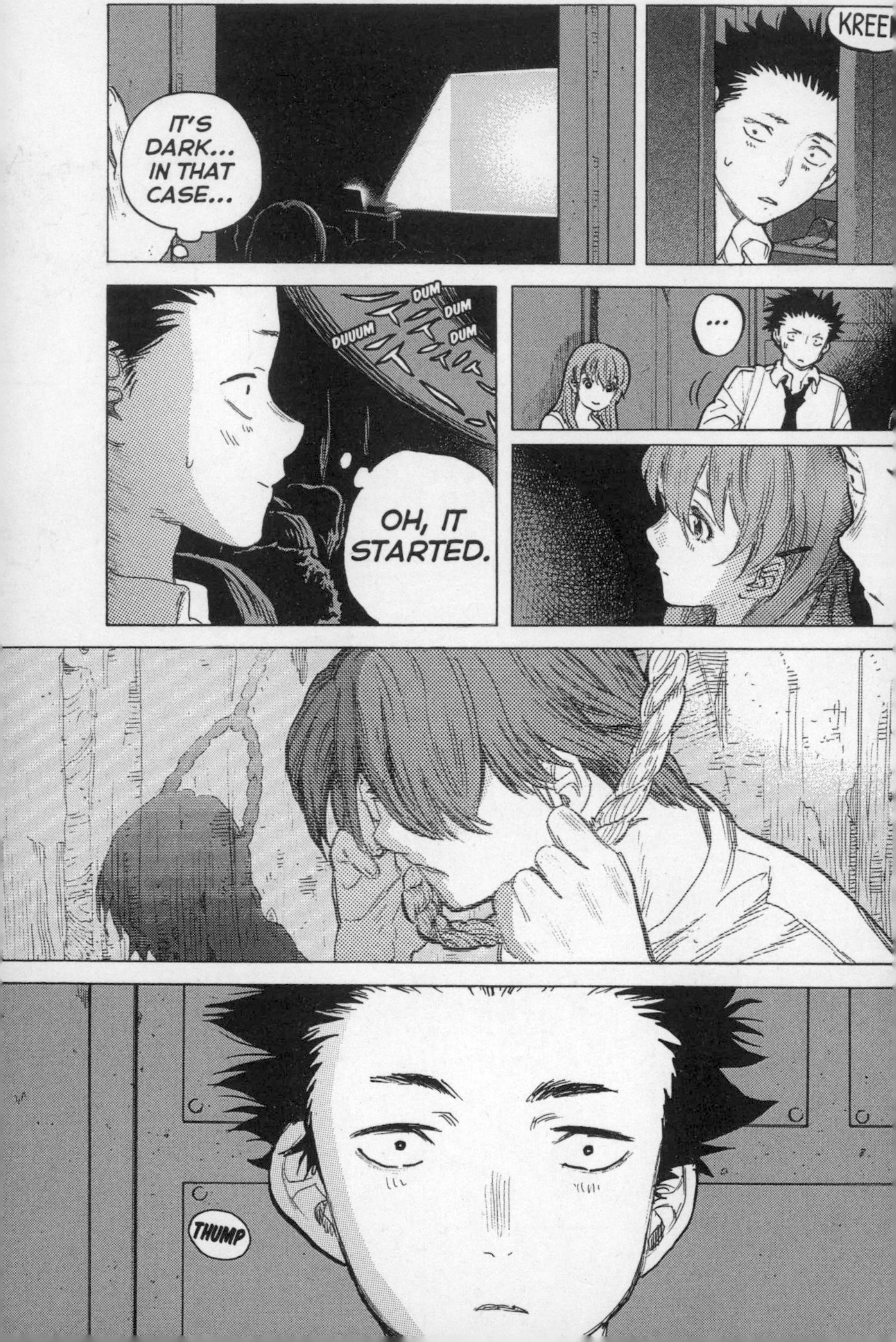
KREE
IT'S DARK... IN THAT CASE...
...
DUM
DUM
DUUUM
DUM
OH, IT STARTED.
THUMP

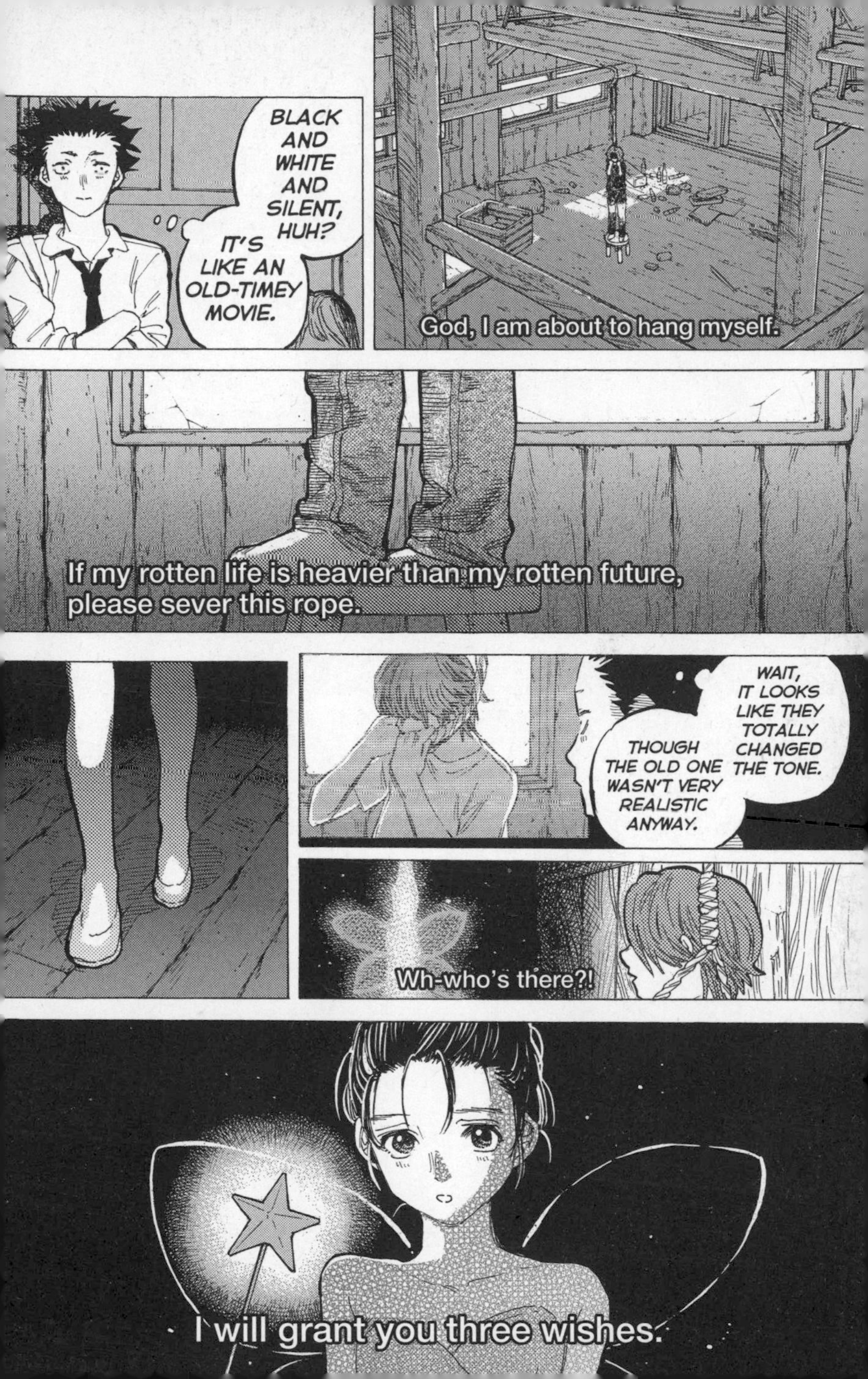
God, I am about to hang myself.
BLACK AND WHITE AND SILENT, HUH?
IT'S LIKE AN OLD-TIMEY MOVIE.
If my rotten life is heavier than my rotten future, please sever this rope.
WAIT, IT LOOKS LIKE THEY TOTALLY CHANGED THE TONE.
THOUGH THE OLD ONE WASN'T VERY REALISTIC ANYWAY.
Wh-who's there?!
I will grant you three wishes.

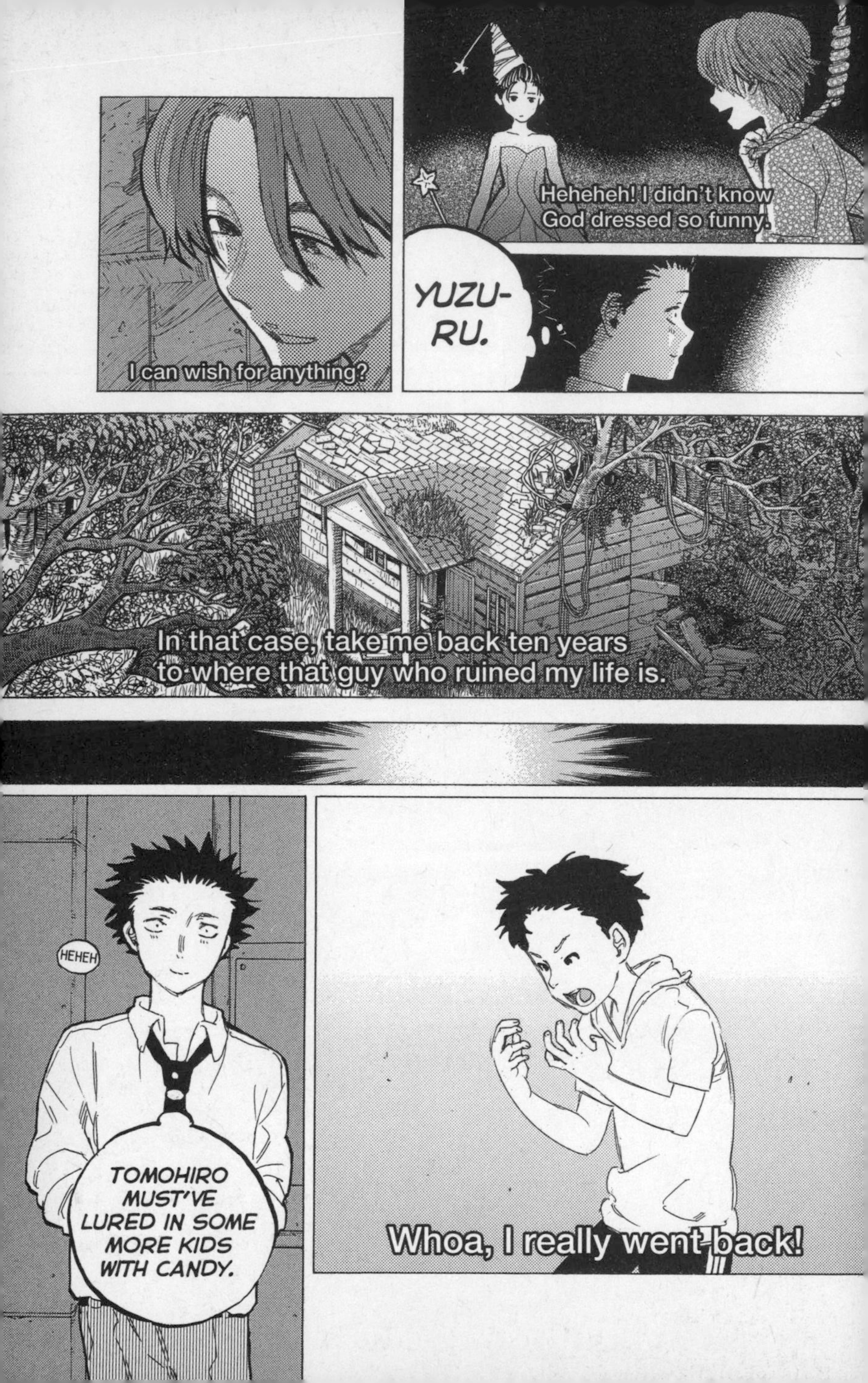
Heheheh! I didn't know God dressed so funny.
YUZU-RU.
I can wish for anything?
In that case, take me back ten years to where that guy who ruined my life is.
Whoa, I really went back!
HEHEH
TOMOHIRO MUST'VE LURED IN SOME MORE KIDS WITH CANDY.

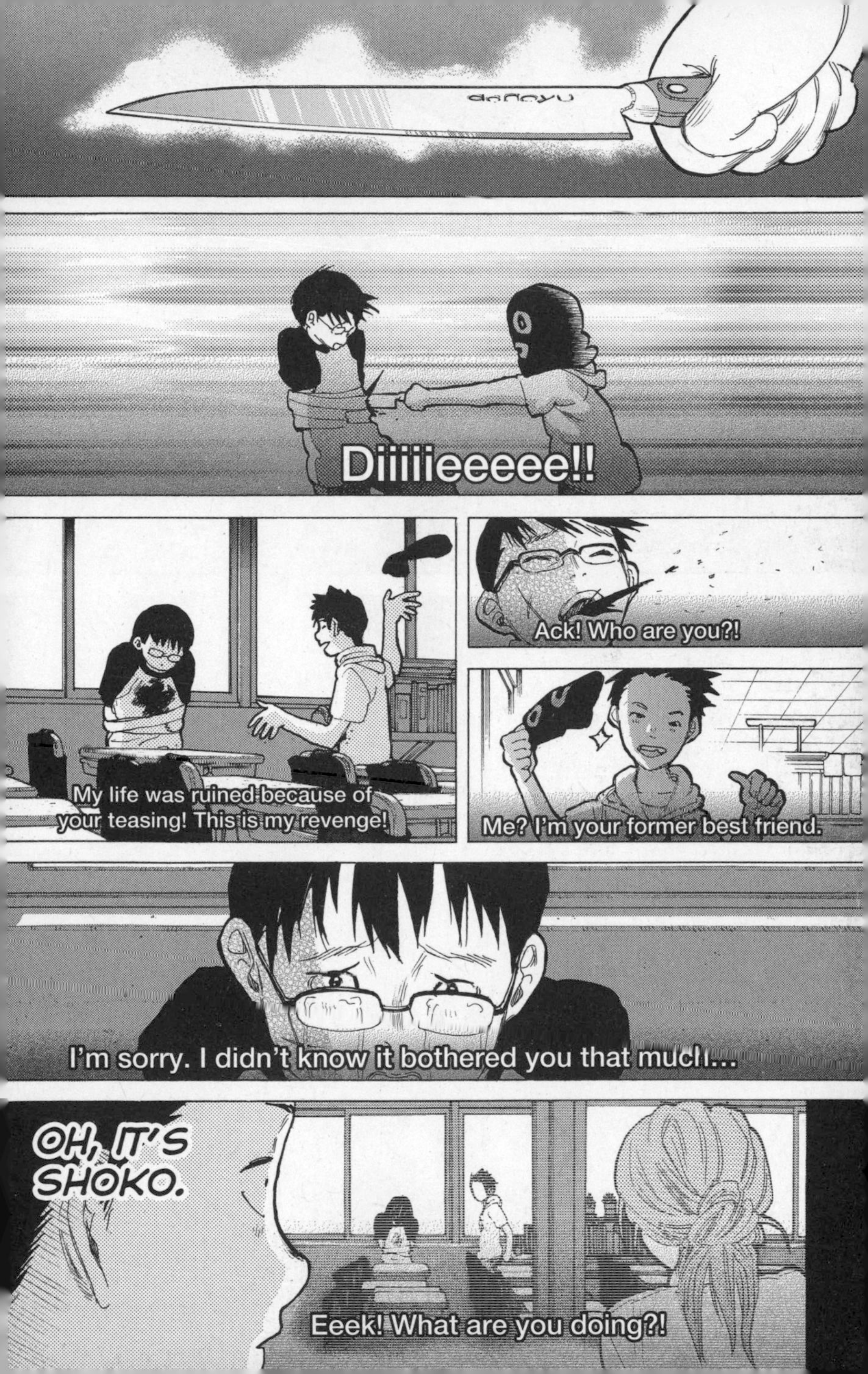
Diiiiieeeee!!
Ack! Who are you?!
Me? I'm your former best friend.
My life was ruined because of your teasing! This is my revenge!
I'm sorry. I didn't know it bothered you that much...
OH, IT'S SHOKO.
Eeek! What are you doing?!

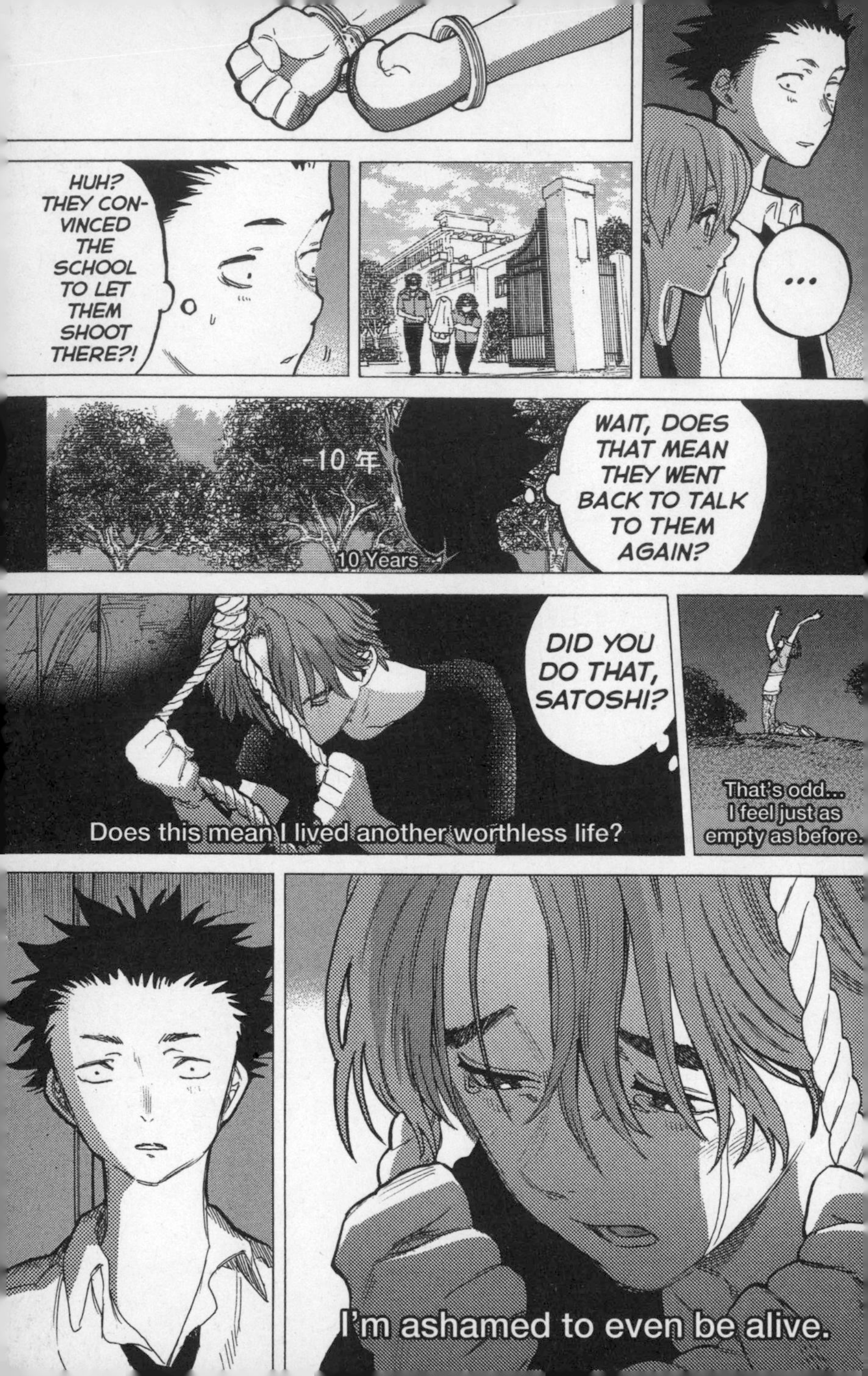
...
HUH? THEY CON-VINCED THE SCHOOL TO LET THEM SHOOT THERE?!
WAIT, DOES THAT MEAN THEY WENT BACK TO TALK TO THEM AGAIN?
-10 年
10 Years
That's odd... I feel just as empty as before.
DID YOU DO THAT, SATOSHI?
Does this mean I lived another worthless life?
I'm ashamed to even be alive.

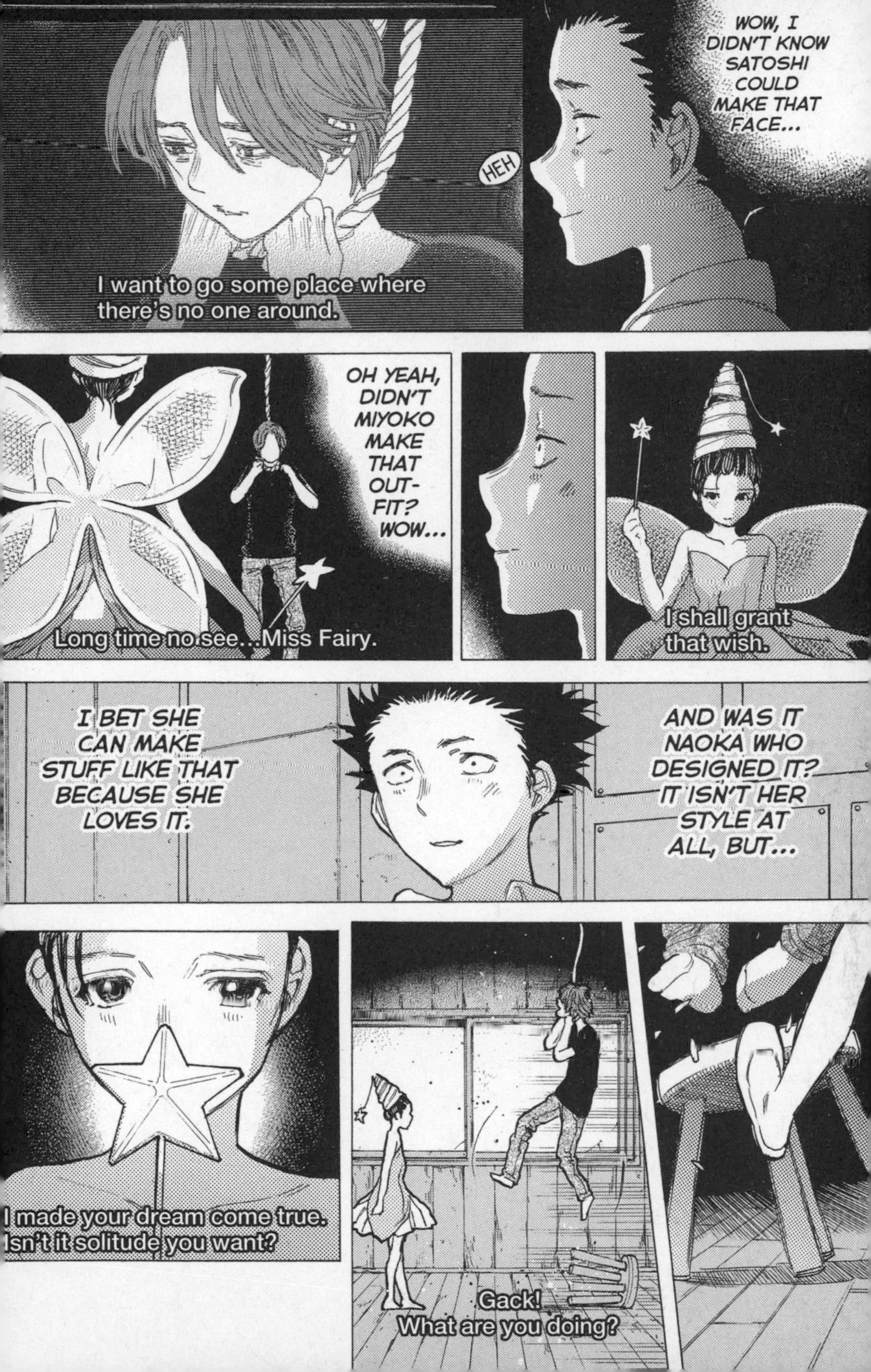
WOW, I DIDN'T KNOW SATOSHI COULD MAKE THAT FACE...
HEH
I want to go some place where there's no one around.
I shall grant that wish.
OH YEAH, DIDN'T MIYOKO MAKE THAT OUT-FIT? WOW...
Long time no see...Miss Fairy.
AND WAS IT NAOKA WHO DESIGNED IT? IT ISN'T HER STYLE AT ALL, BUT...
I BET SHE CAN MAKE STUFF LIKE THAT BECAUSE SHE LOVES IT.
Gack! What are you doing?
I made your dream come true. Isn't it solitude you want?

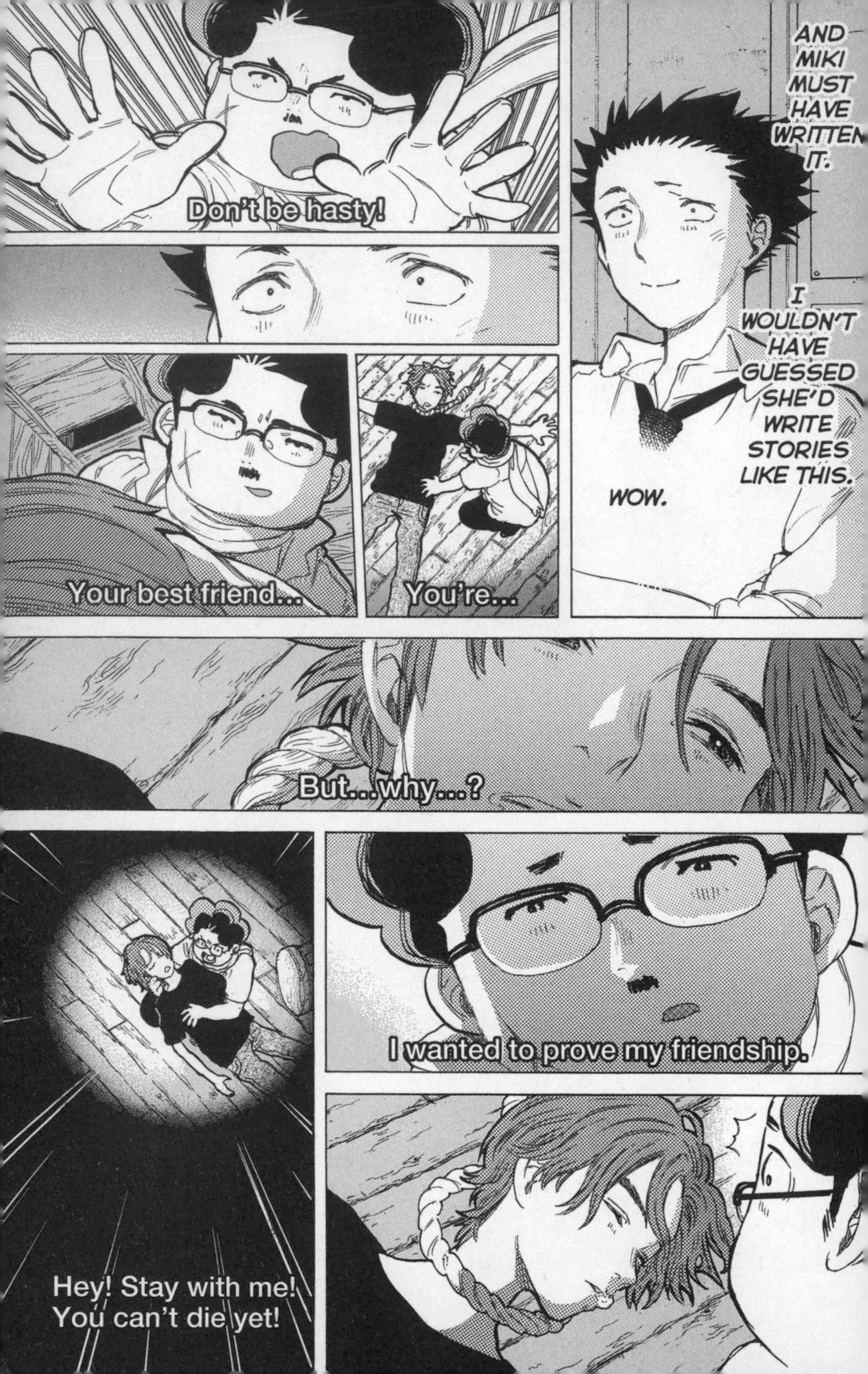
AND MIKI MUST HAVE WRITTEN IT.
I WOULDN'T HAVE GUESSED SHE'D WRITE STORIES LIKE THIS.
WOW.
Don't be hasty!
You're...
Your best friend...
But...why...?
I wanted to prove my friendship.
Hey! Stay with me! You can't die yet!

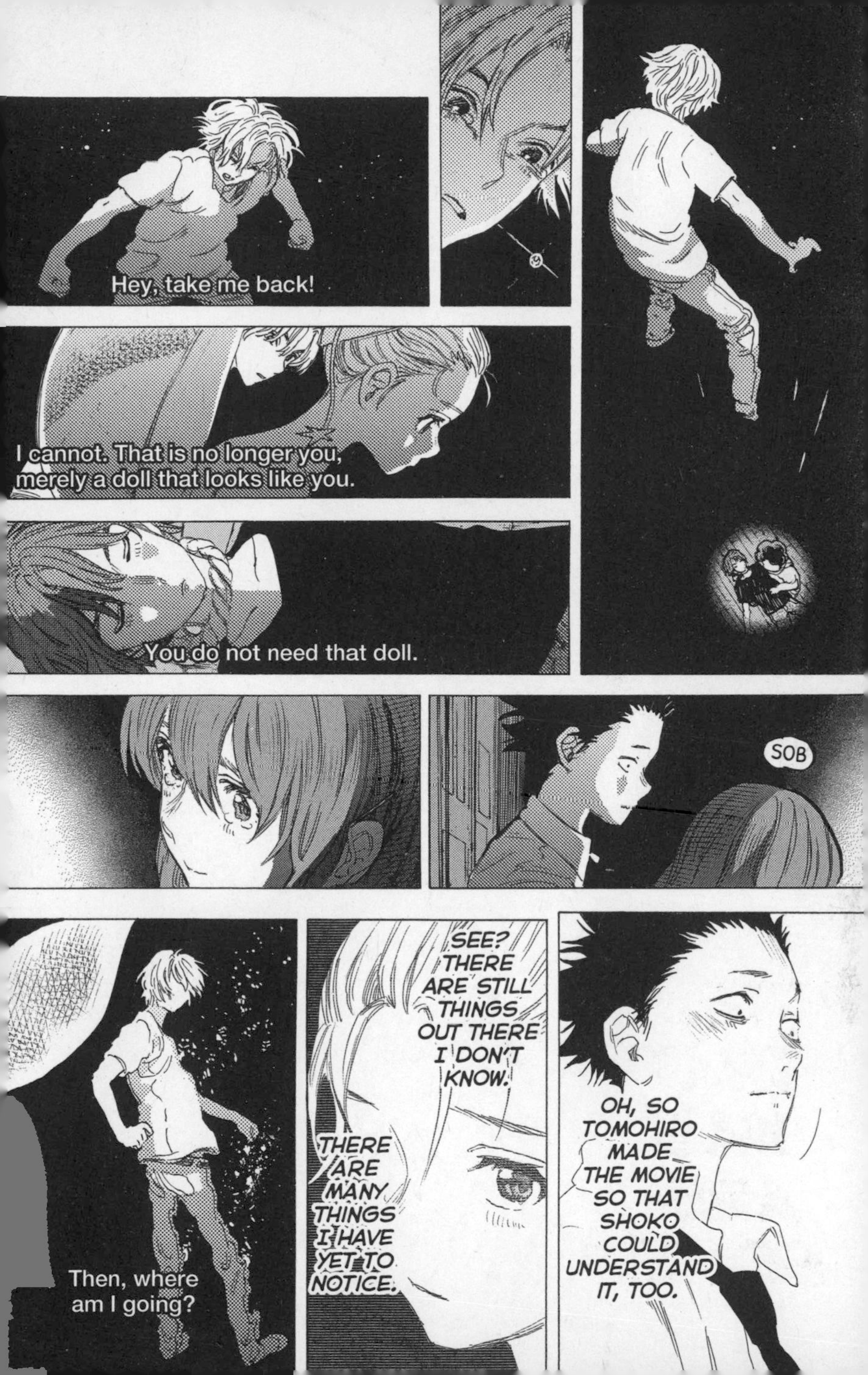

Hey, take me back!
I cannot. That is no longer you, merely a doll that looks like you.
You do not need that doll.
SOB
OH, SO TOMOHIRO MADE THE MOVIE SO THAT SHOKO COULD UNDERSTAND IT, TOO.
SEE? THERE ARE STILL THINGS OUT THERE I DON'T KNOW.
THERE ARE MANY THINGS I HAVE YET TO NOTICE.
Then, where am I going?

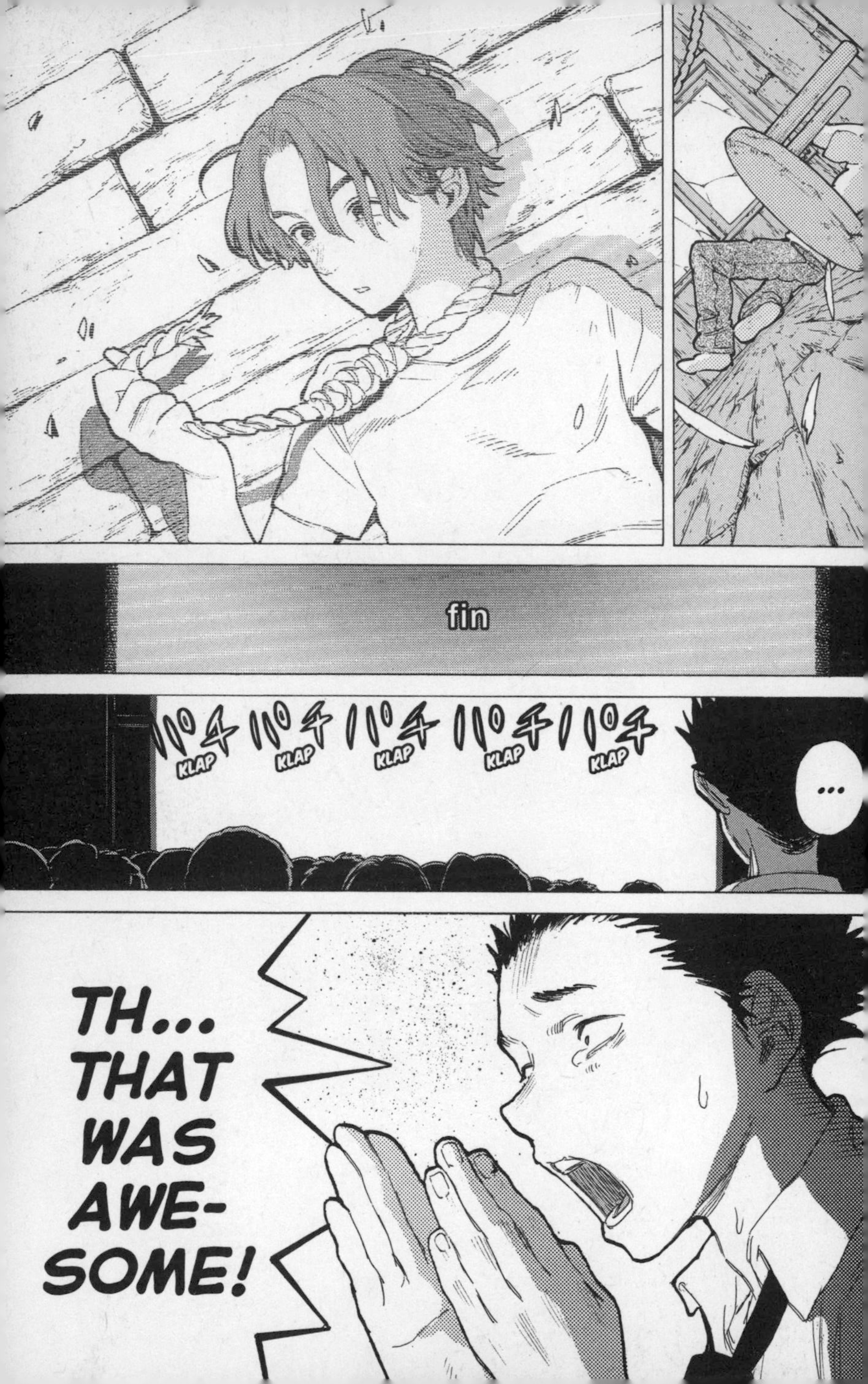
fin
...
パチパチパチパチパチ
KLAP KLAP KLAP KLAP KLAP
TH... THAT WAS AWE-SOME!

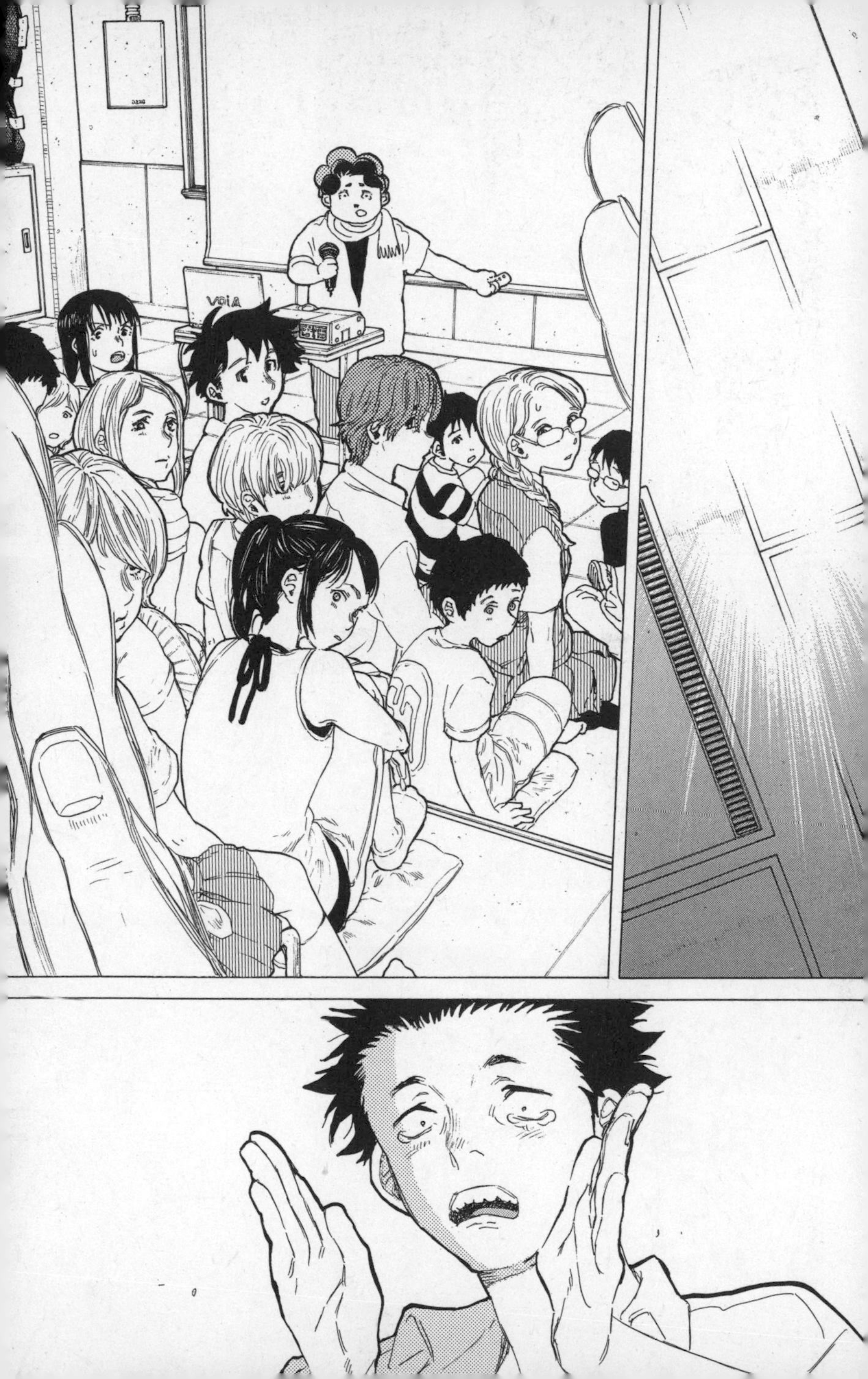

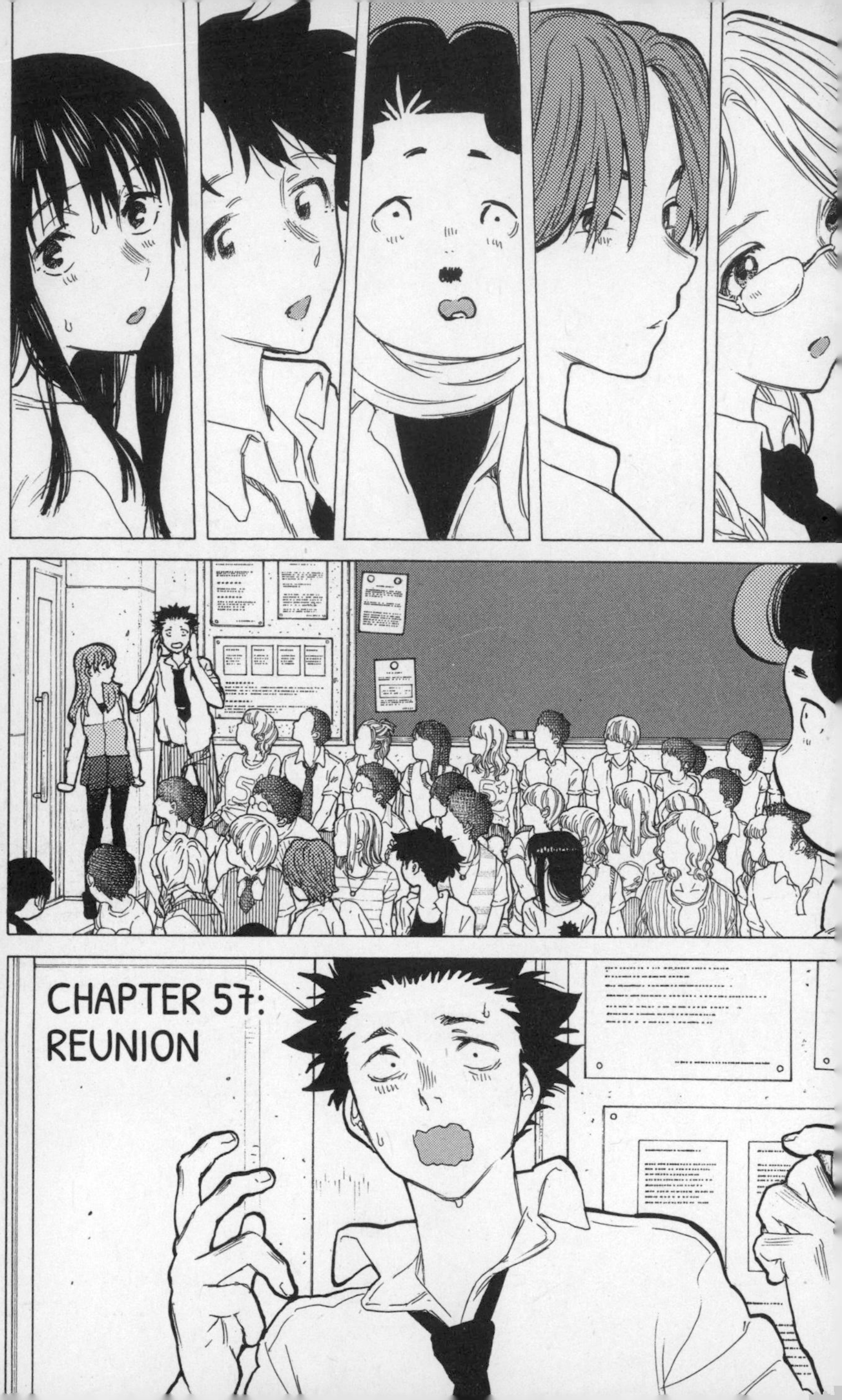
CHAPTER 57:
REUNION

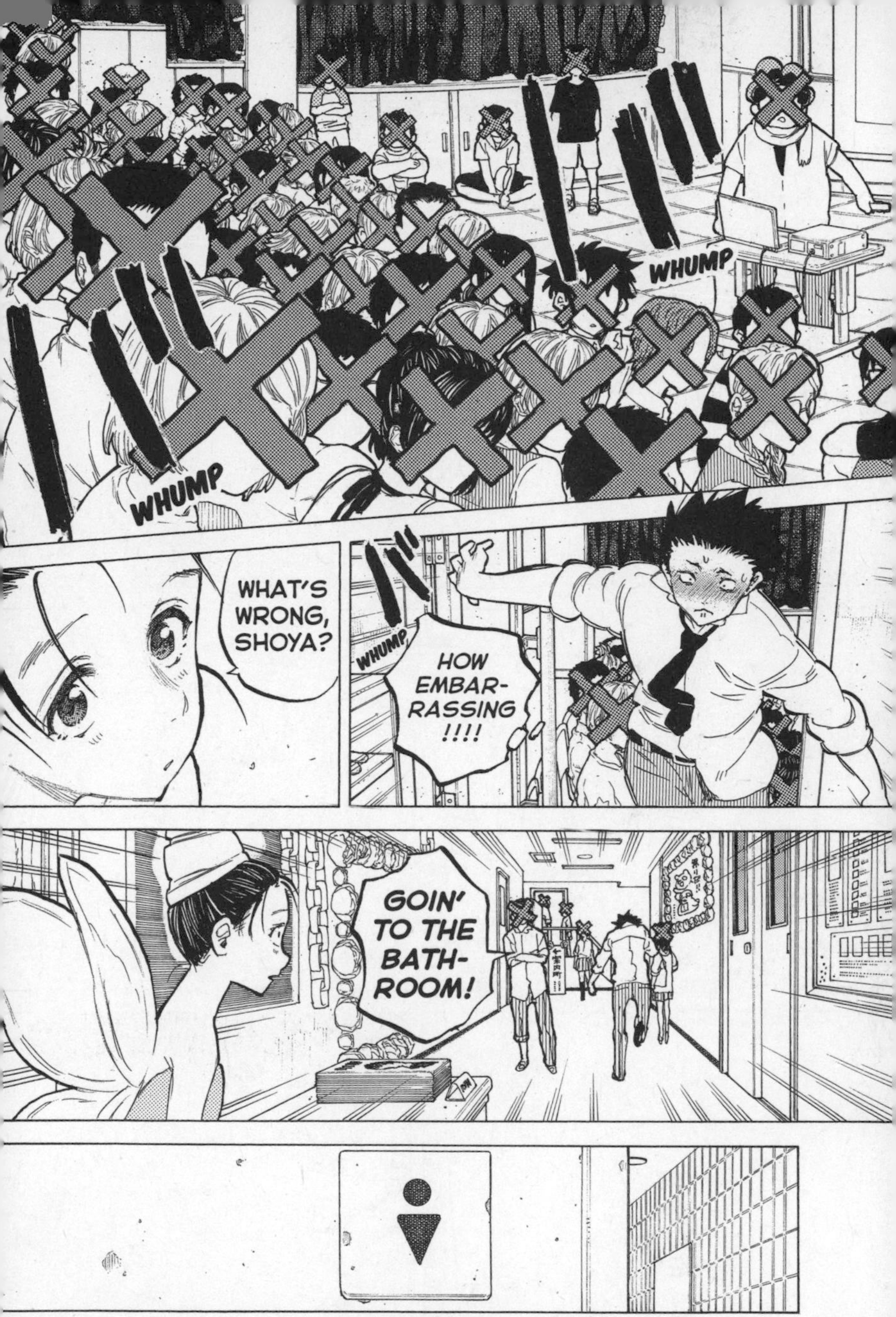
WHUMP
WHUMP
WHUMP
HOW EMBAR-RASSING!!!!
WHAT'S WRONG, SHOYA?
GOIN' TO THE BATH-ROOM!

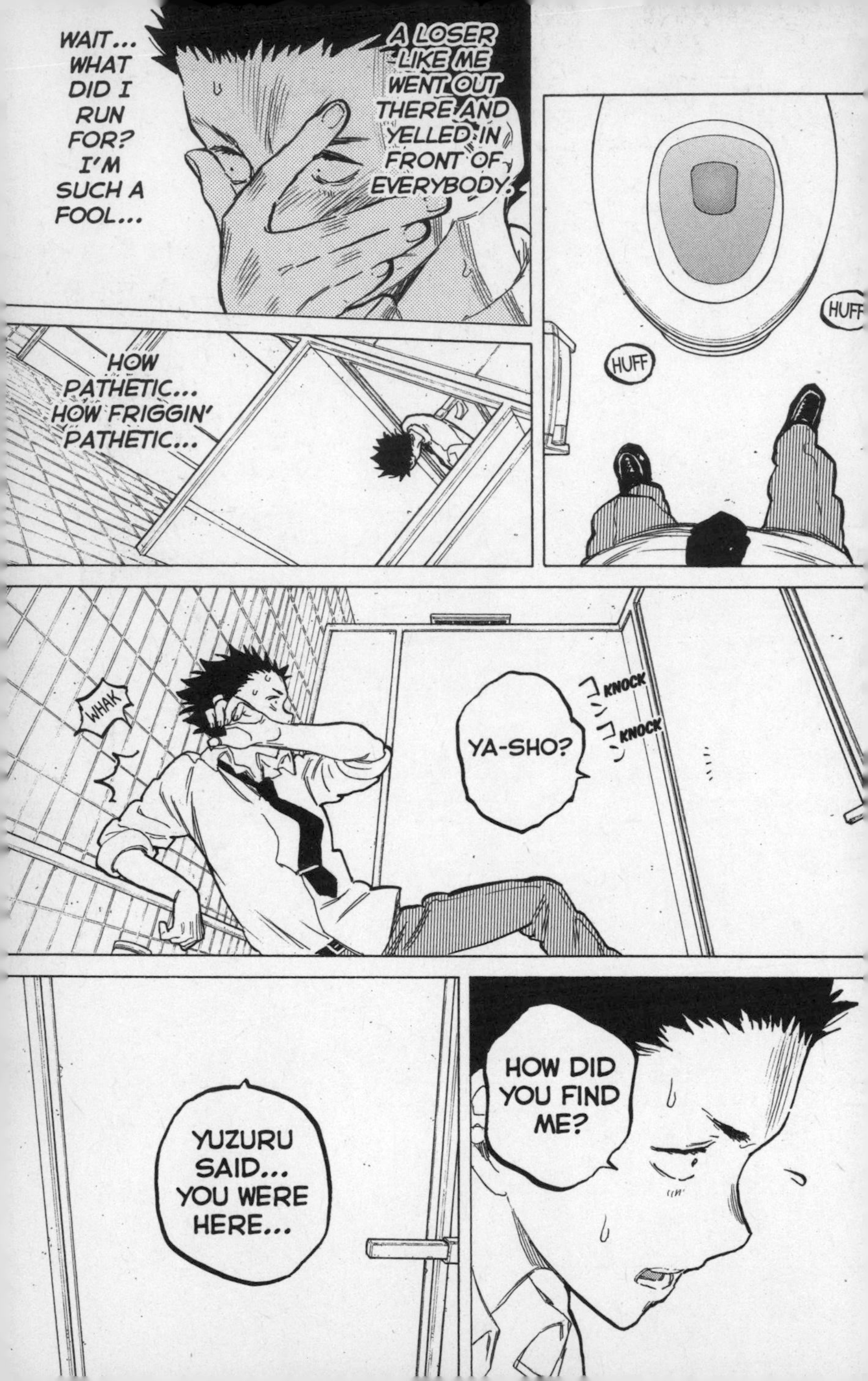
A LOSER LIKE ME WENT OUT THERE AND YELLED IN FRONT OF EVERYBODY.
WAIT... WHAT DID I RUN FOR? I'M SUCH A FOOL...
HUFF
HUFF
HOW PATHETIC... HOW FRIGGIN' PATHETIC...
KNOCK
KNOCK
YA-SHO?
WHAK
HOW DID YOU FIND ME?
YUZURU SAID... YOU WERE HERE...

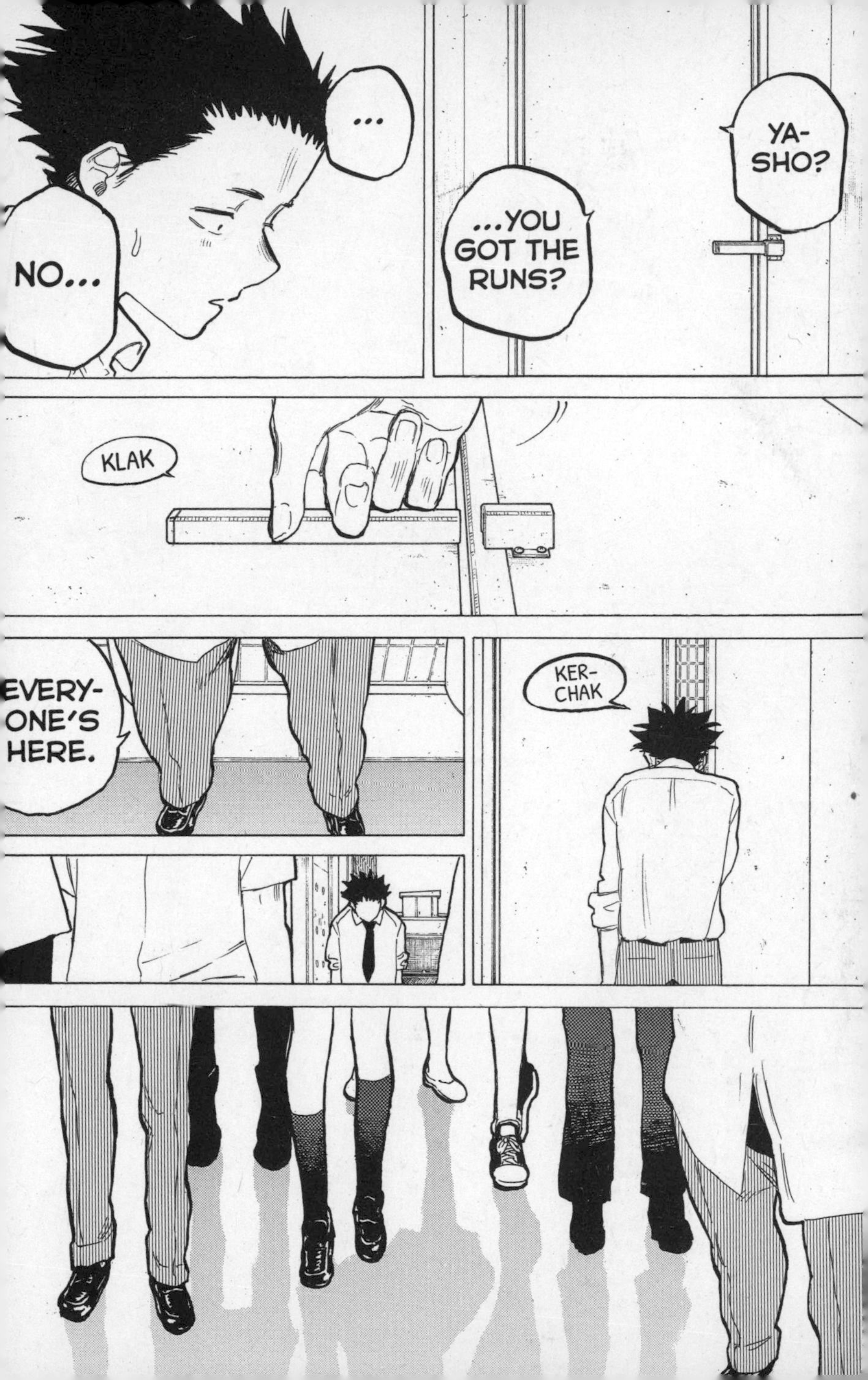
YA-SHO?
...YOU GOT THE RUNS?
...
NO...
KLAK
KER-CHAK
EVERY-ONE'S HERE.

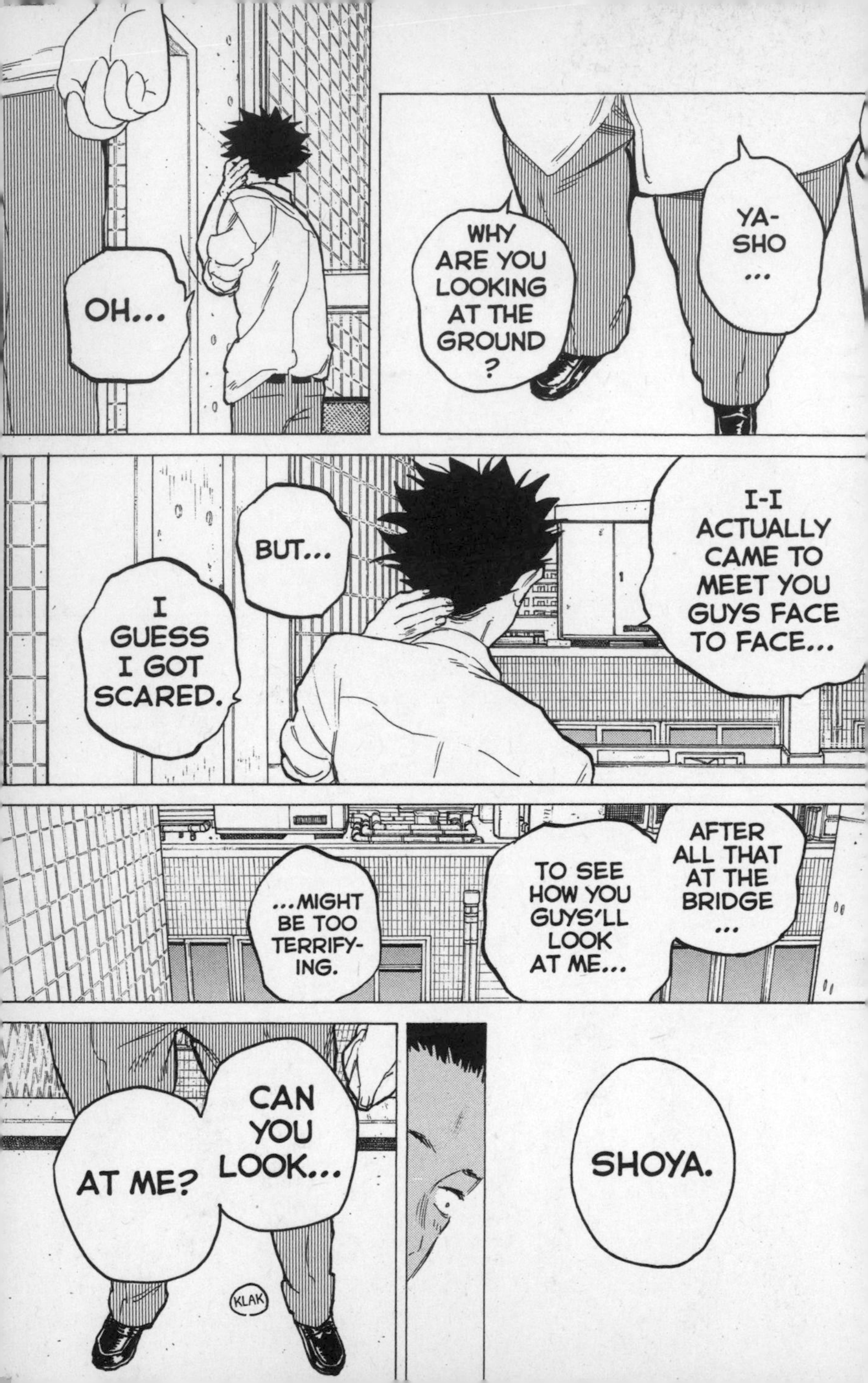
YA-SHO...
WHY ARE YOU LOOKING AT THE GROUND?
OH...
I-I ACTUALLY CAME TO MEET YOU GUYS FACE TO FACE...
BUT...
I GUESS I GOT SCARED.
AFTER ALL THAT AT THE BRIDGE...
TO SEE HOW YOU GUYS'LL LOOK AT ME...
...MIGHT BE TOO TERRIFY-ING.
SHOYA.
CAN YOU LOOK...
AT ME?
KLAK

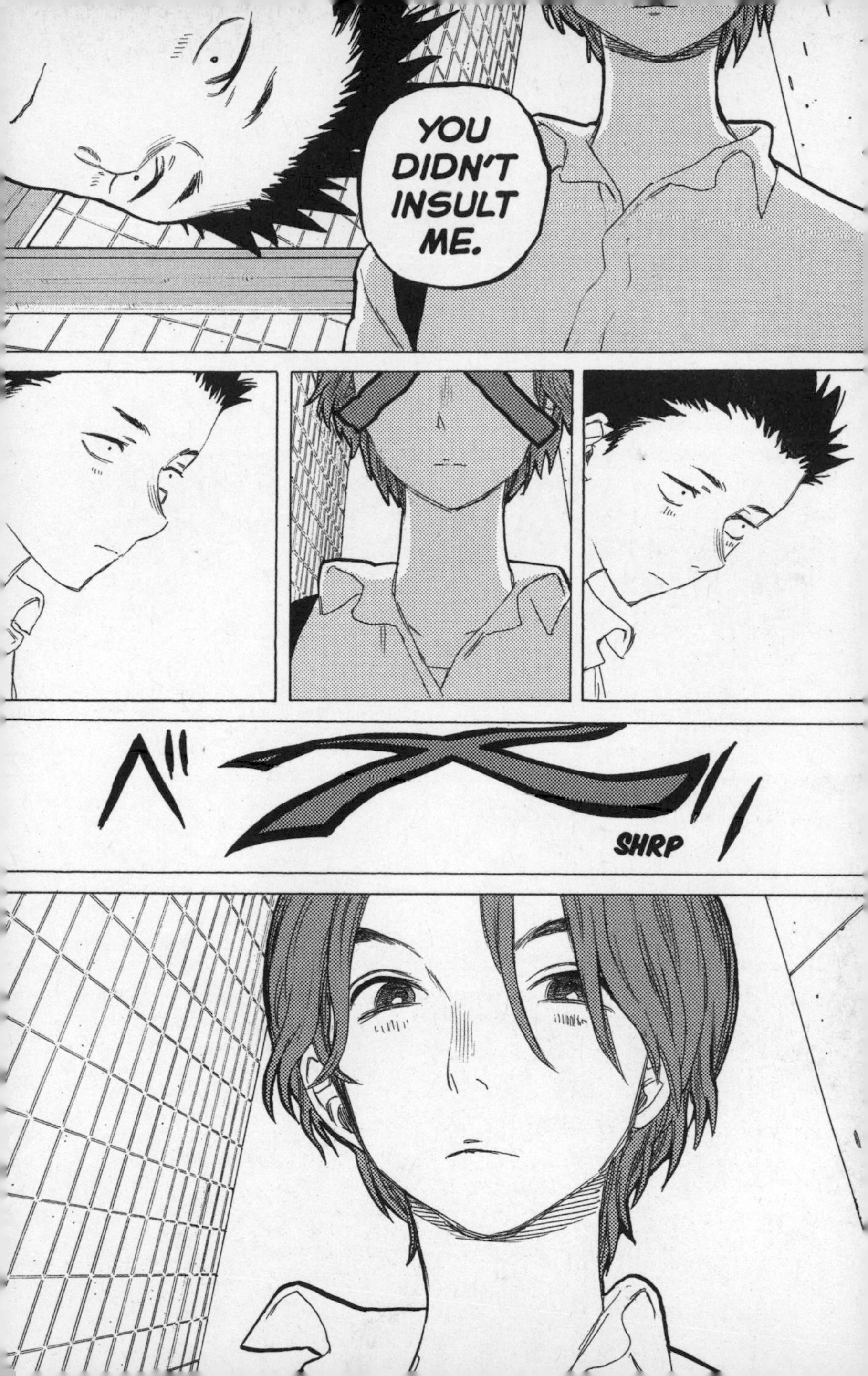
YOU DIDN'T INSULT ME.
SHRP

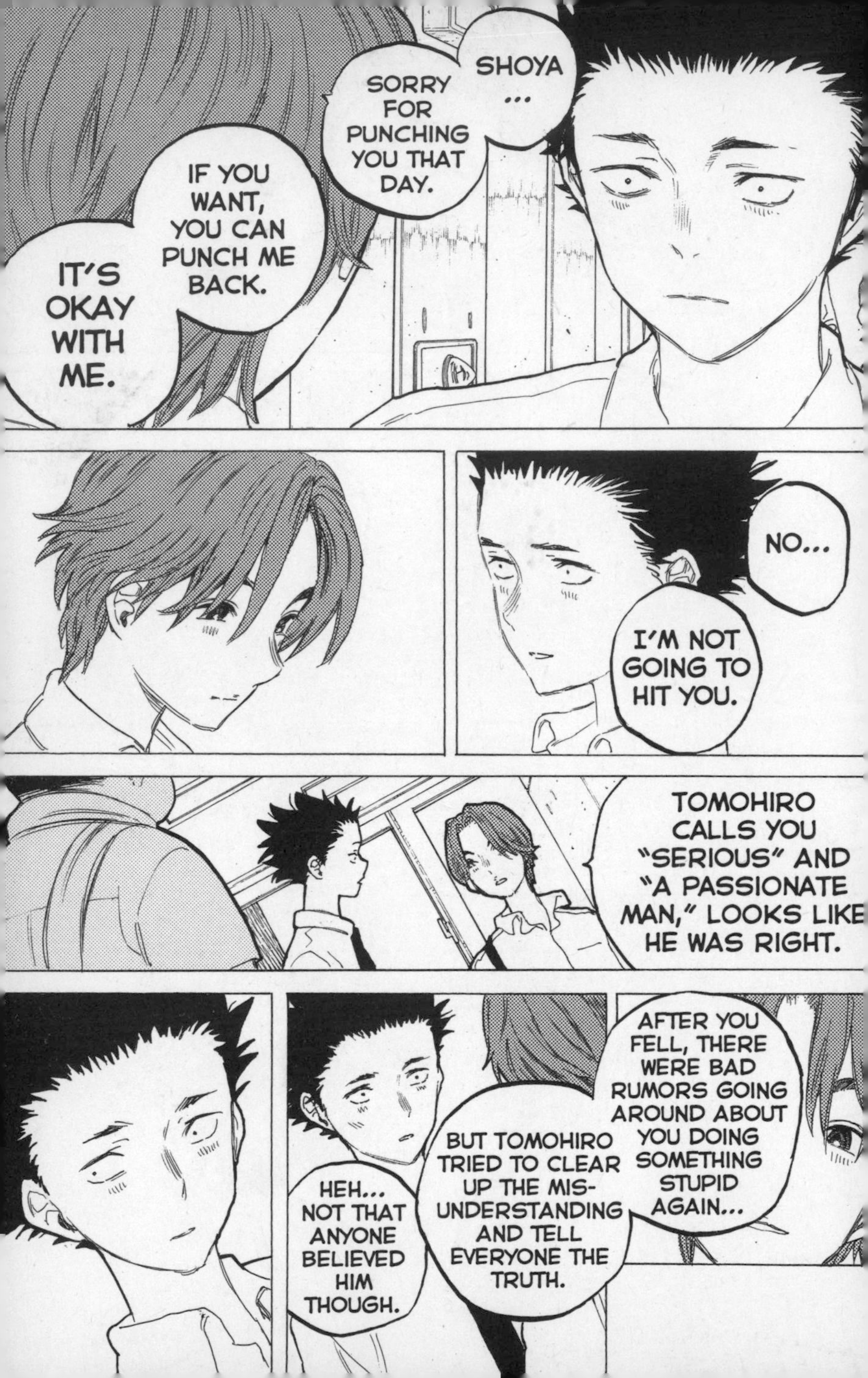
SHOYA...
SORRY FOR PUNCHING YOU THAT DAY.
IF YOU WANT, YOU CAN PUNCH ME BACK.
IT'S OKAY WITH ME.
NO...
I'M NOT GOING TO HIT YOU.
TOMOHIRO CALLS YOU "SERIOUS" AND "A PASSIONATE MAN," LOOKS LIKE HE WAS RIGHT.
AFTER YOU FELL, THERE WERE BAD RUMORS GOING AROUND ABOUT YOU DOING SOMETHING STUPID AGAIN...
BUT TOMOHIRO TRIED TO CLEAR UP THE MIS-UNDERSTANDING AND TELL EVERYONE THE TRUTH.
HEH... NOT THAT ANYONE BELIEVED HIM THOUGH.

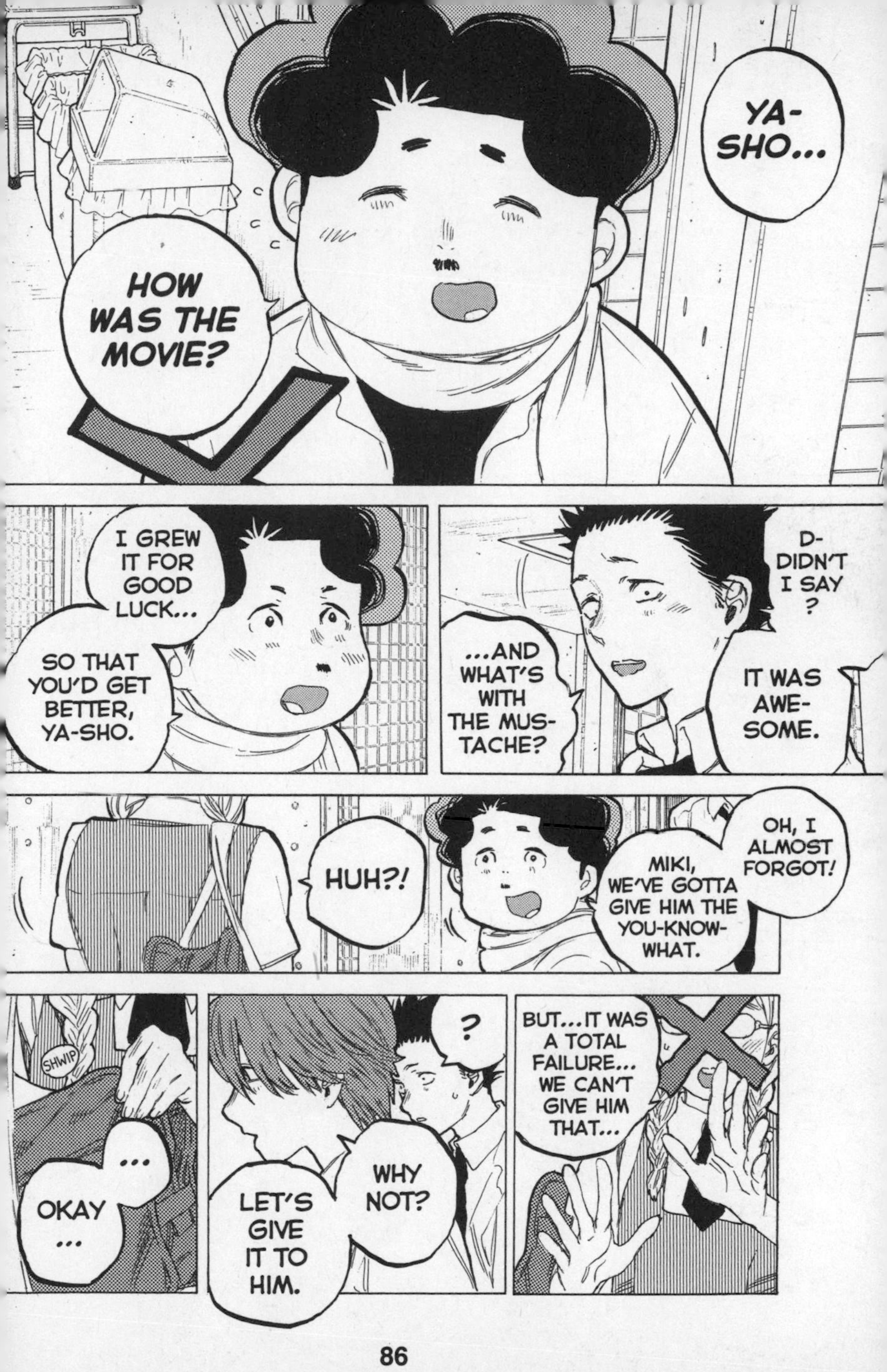
YA-SHO...
HOW WAS THE MOVIE?
D-DIDN'T I SAY?
IT WAS AWE-SOME.
...AND WHAT'S WITH THE MUS-TACHE?
I GREW IT FOR GOOD LUCK...
SO THAT YOU'D GET BETTER, YA-SHO.
OH, I ALMOST FORGOT!
MIKI, WE'VE GOTTA GIVE HIM THE YOU-KNOW-WHAT.
HUH?!
BUT...IT WAS A TOTAL FAILURE... WE CAN'T GIVE HIM THAT...
?
WHY NOT?
LET'S GIVE IT TO HIM.
SHWIP
... OKAY ...

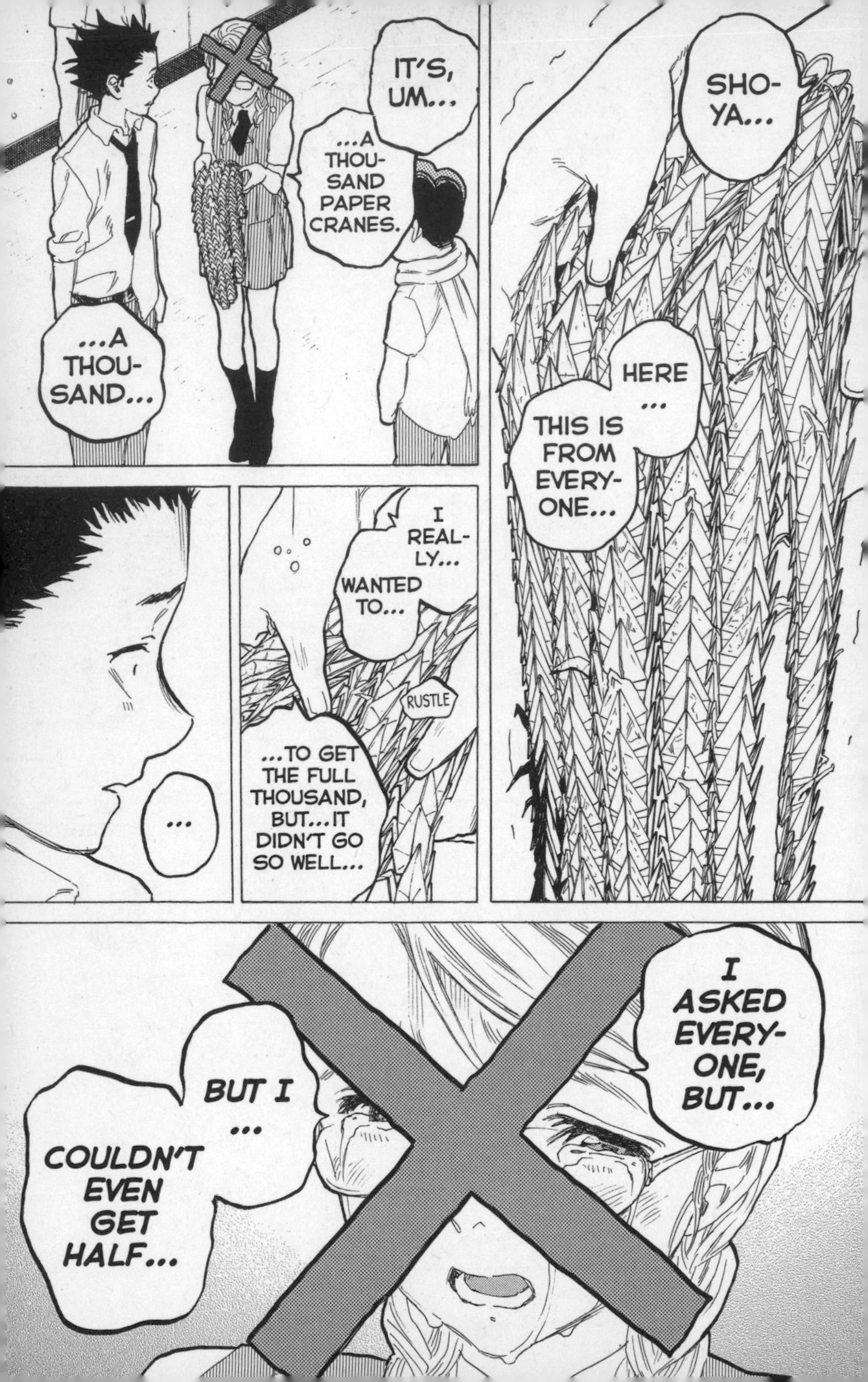
SHO-YA...
HERE...
THIS IS FROM EVERY-ONE...
IT'S, UM...
...A THOU-SAND PAPER CRANES.
...A THOU-SAND...
I REAL-LY...
WANTED TO...
RUSTLE
...TO GET THE FULL THOUSAND, BUT...IT DIDN'T GO SO WELL...
...
I ASKED EVERY-ONE, BUT...
BUT I...
COULDN'T EVEN GET HALF...

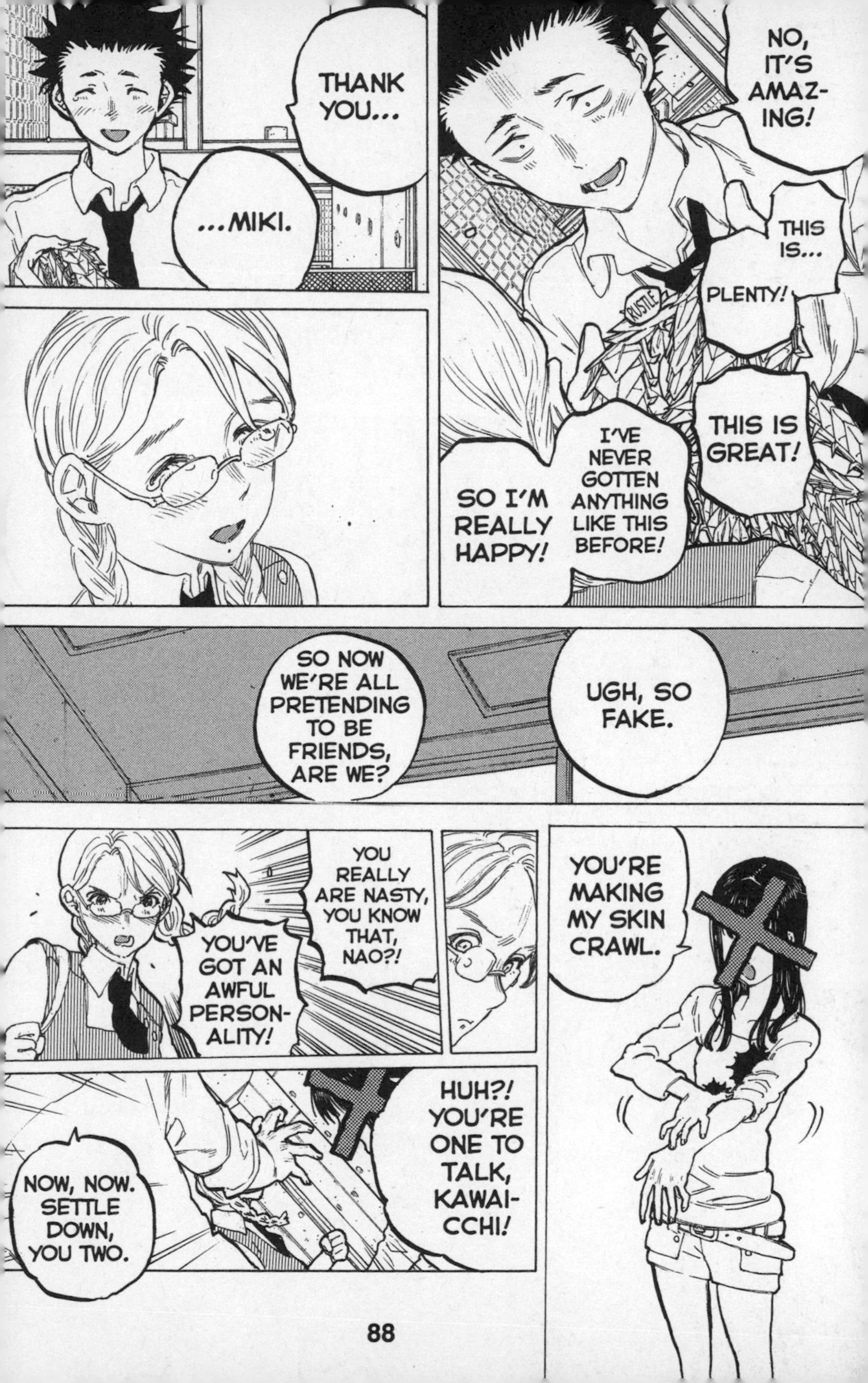
NO, IT'S AMAZ-ING!
THIS IS...
PLENTY!
RUSTLE
THIS IS GREAT!
I'VE NEVER GOTTEN ANYTHING LIKE THIS BEFORE!
SO I'M REALLY HAPPY!
THANK YOU...
...MIKI.
UGH, SO FAKE.
SO NOW WE'RE ALL PRETENDING TO BE FRIENDS, ARE WE?
YOU'RE MAKING MY SKIN CRAWL.
YOU REALLY ARE NASTY, YOU KNOW THAT, NAO?!
YOU'VE GOT AN AWFUL PERSON-ALITY!
HUH?! YOU'RE ONE TO TALK, KAWAI-CCHI!
NOW, NOW. SETTLE DOWN, YOU TWO.

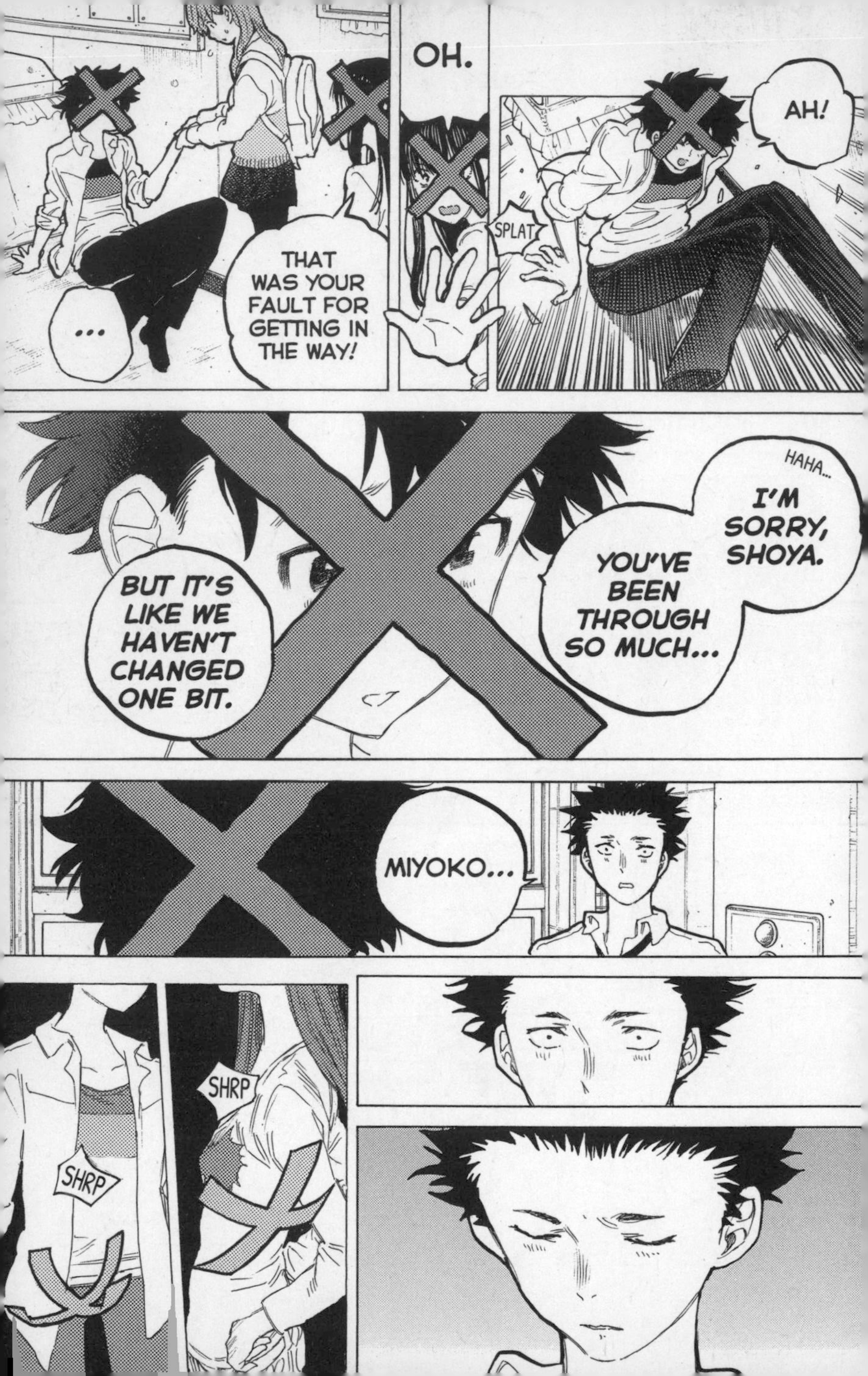
AH!
SPLAT
OH.
THAT WAS YOUR FAULT FOR GETTING IN THE WAY!
...
HAHA...
I'M SORRY, SHOYA.
YOU'VE BEEN THROUGH SO MUCH...
BUT IT'S LIKE WE HAVEN'T CHANGED ONE BIT.
MIYOKO...
SHRP
SHRP

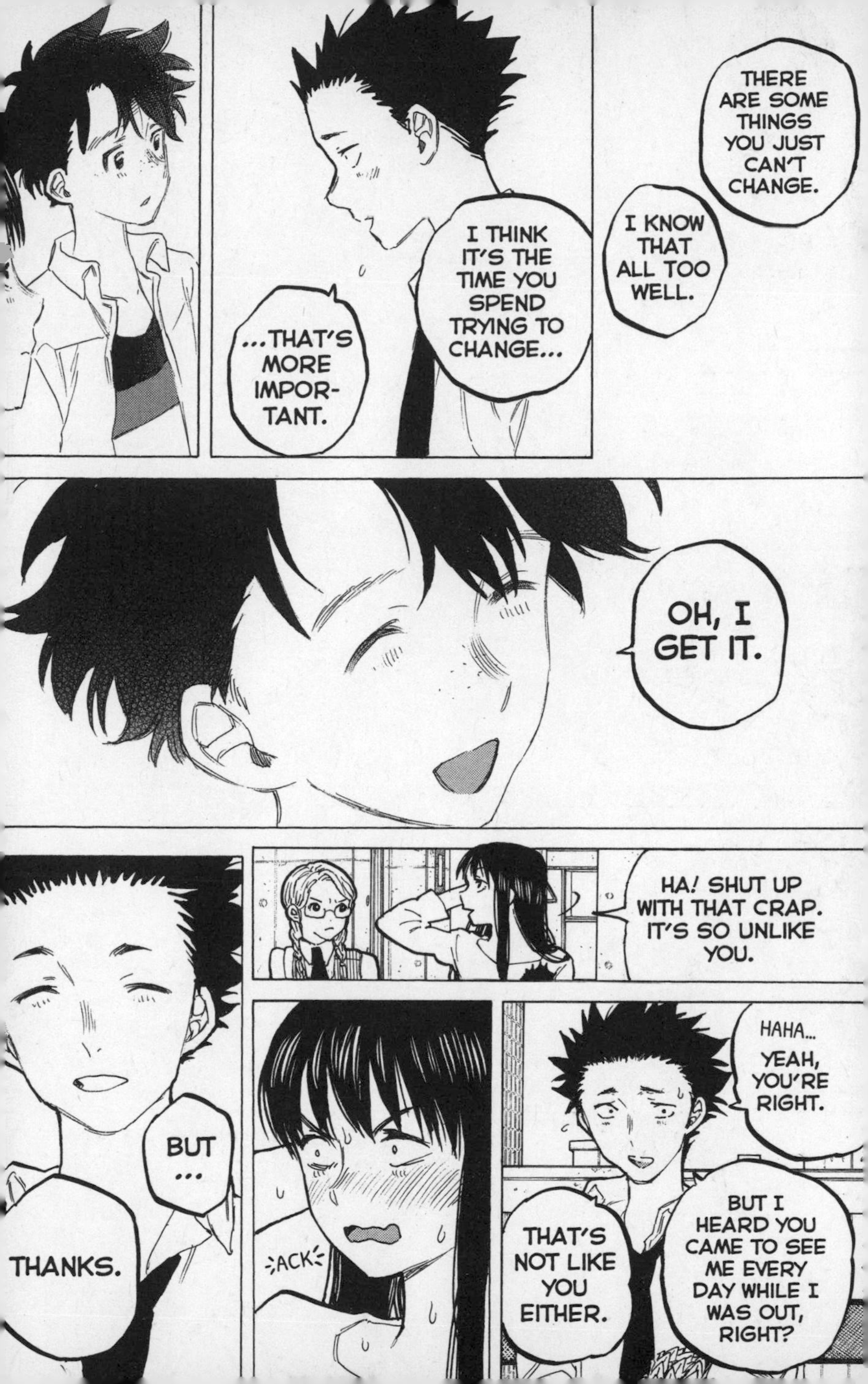
THERE ARE SOME THINGS YOU JUST CAN'T CHANGE.
I KNOW THAT ALL TOO WELL.
I THINK IT'S THE TIME YOU SPEND TRYING TO CHANGE...
...THAT'S MORE IMPORTANT.
OH, I GET IT.
HA! SHUT UP WITH THAT CRAP. IT'S SO UNLIKE YOU.
HAHA... YEAH, YOU'RE RIGHT.
BUT I HEARD YOU CAME TO SEE ME EVERY DAY WHILE I WAS OUT, RIGHT?
THAT'S NOT LIKE YOU EITHER.
ACK
BUT...
THANKS.

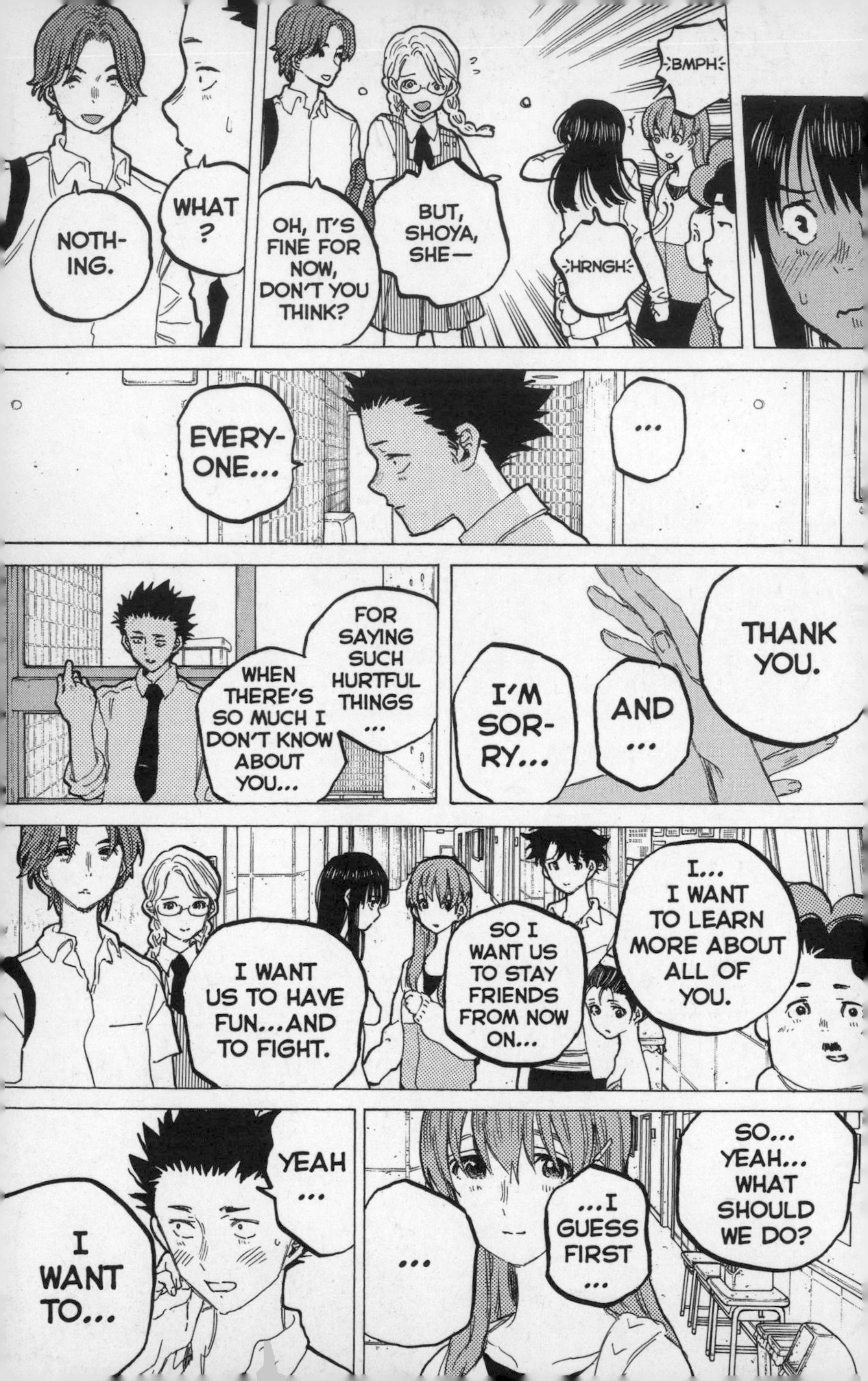
BMPH
HRNGH
BUT, SHOYA, SHE—
OH, IT'S FINE FOR NOW, DON'T YOU THINK?
WHAT?
NOTHING.
...
EVERYONE...
THANK YOU.
AND...
I'M SORRY...
FOR SAYING SUCH HURTFUL THINGS...
WHEN THERE'S SO MUCH I DON'T KNOW ABOUT YOU...
I... I WANT TO LEARN MORE ABOUT ALL OF YOU.
SO I WANT US TO STAY FRIENDS FROM NOW ON...
I WANT US TO HAVE FUN...AND TO FIGHT.
SO... YEAH... WHAT SHOULD WE DO?
...I GUESS FIRST...
...
YEAH...
I WANT TO...

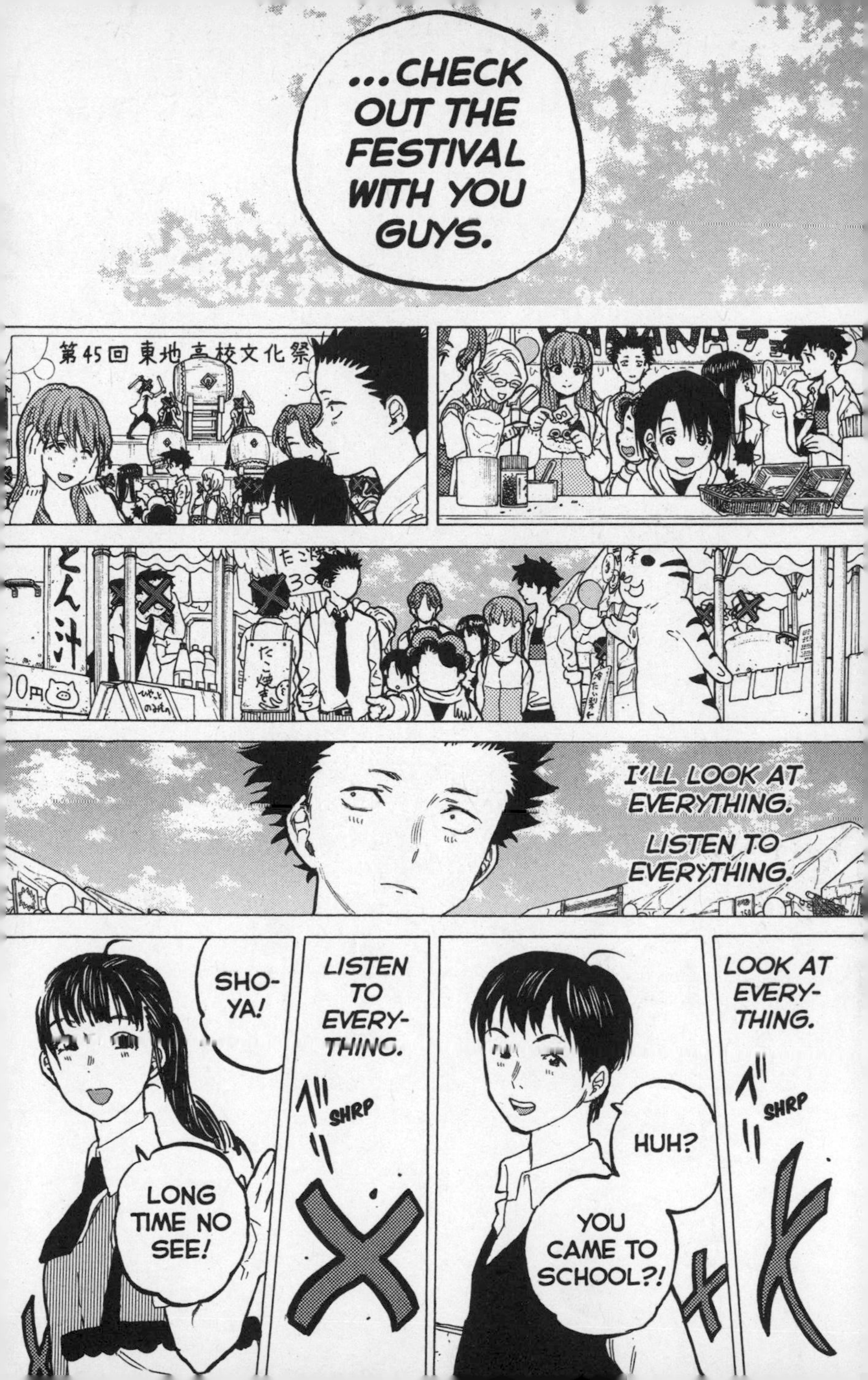
...CHECK OUT THE FESTIVAL WITH YOU GUYS.
第45回 東地高校文化祭
とん汁
I'LL LOOK AT EVERYTHING.
LISTEN TO EVERYTHING.
LOOK AT EVERY-THING.
SHRP
HUH?
YOU CAME TO SCHOOL?!
LISTEN TO EVERY-THING.
SHRP
SHO-YA!
LONG TIME NO SEE!

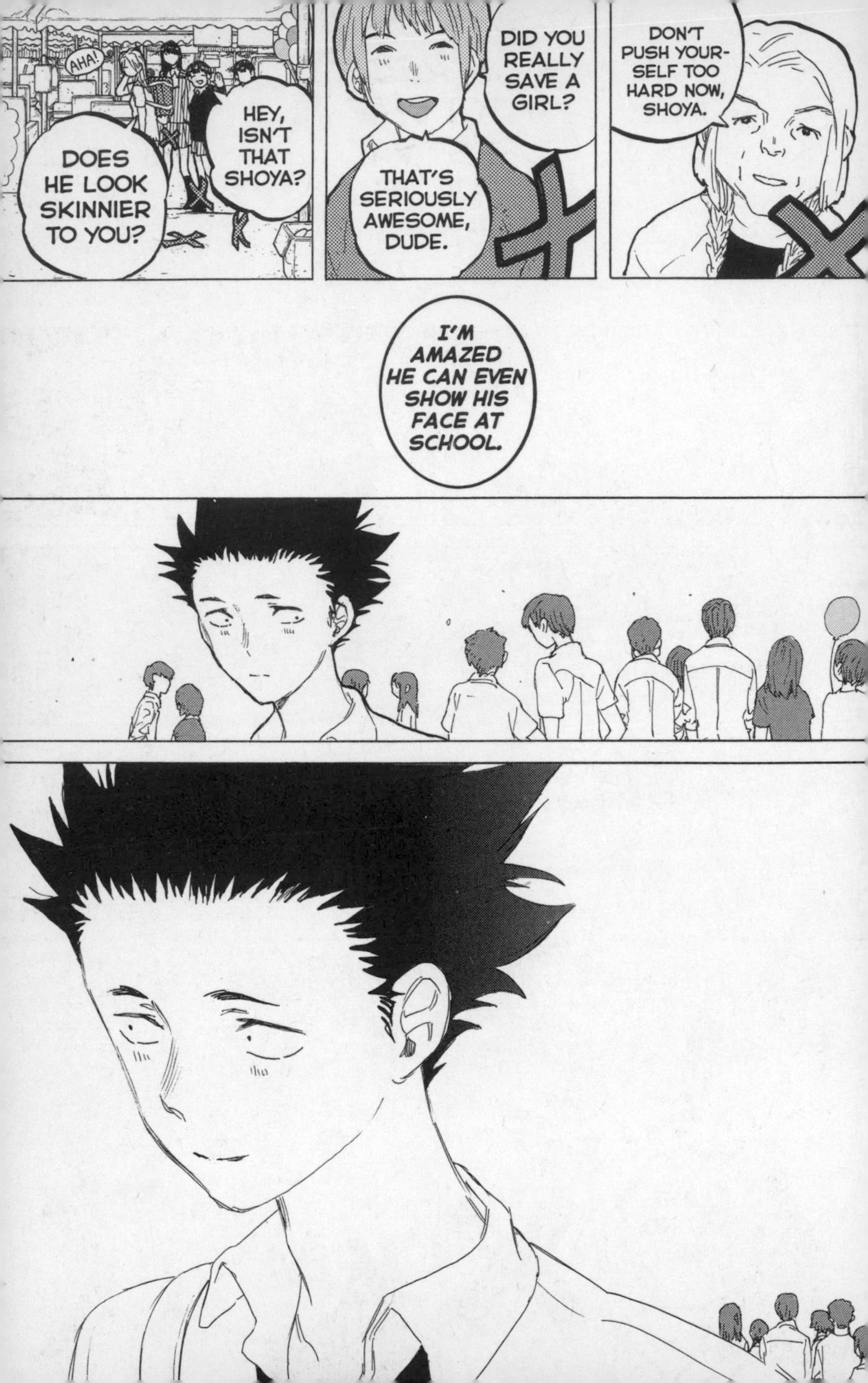
DON'T PUSH YOURSELF TOO HARD NOW, SHOYA.
DID YOU REALLY SAVE A GIRL?
THAT'S SERIOUSLY AWESOME, DUDE.
HEY, ISN'T THAT SHOYA?
AHA!
DOES HE LOOK SKINNIER TO YOU?
I'M AMAZED HE CAN EVEN SHOW HIS FACE AT SCHOOL.

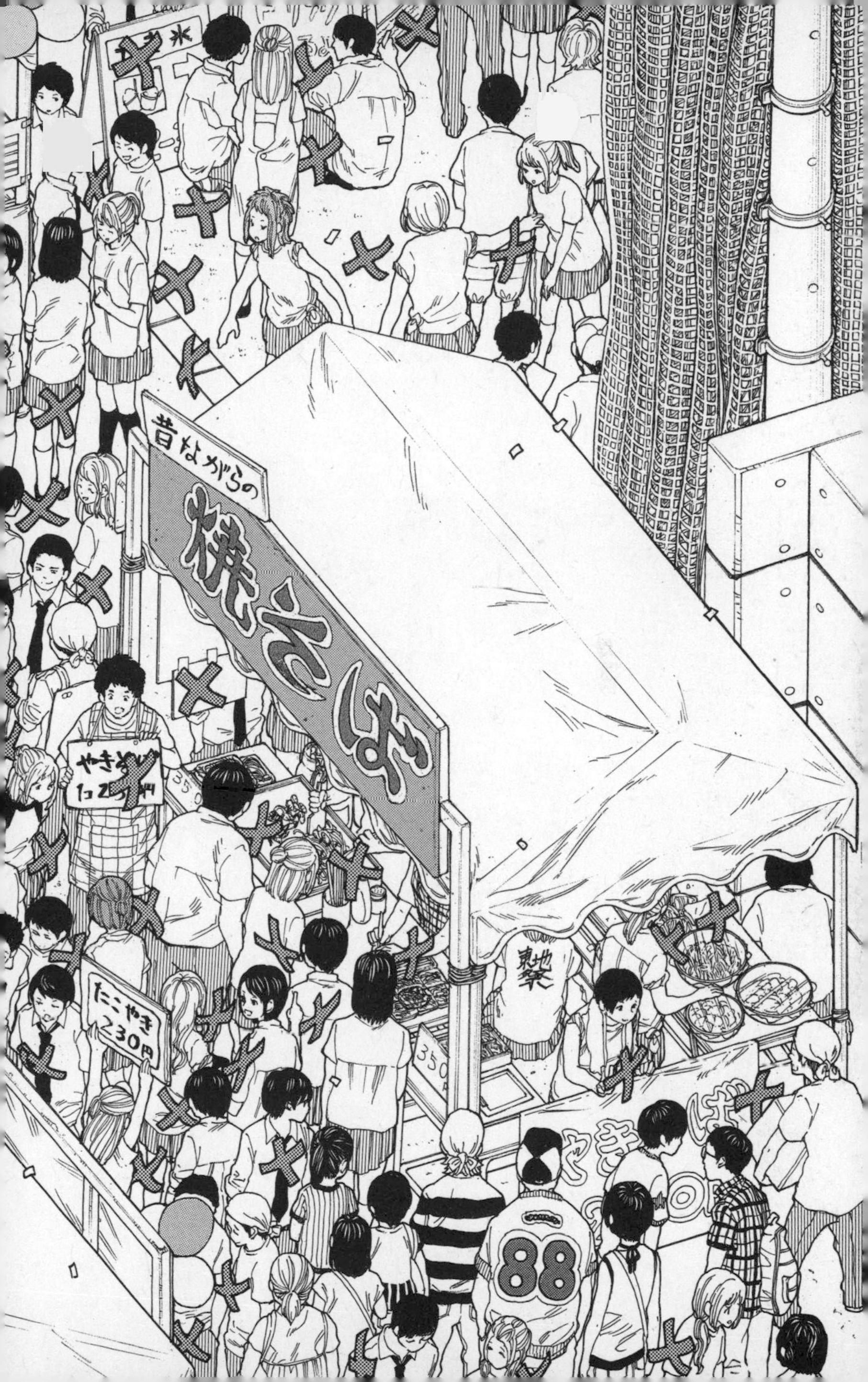
昔ながらの
焼そば
たこやき
230円
350
350
88

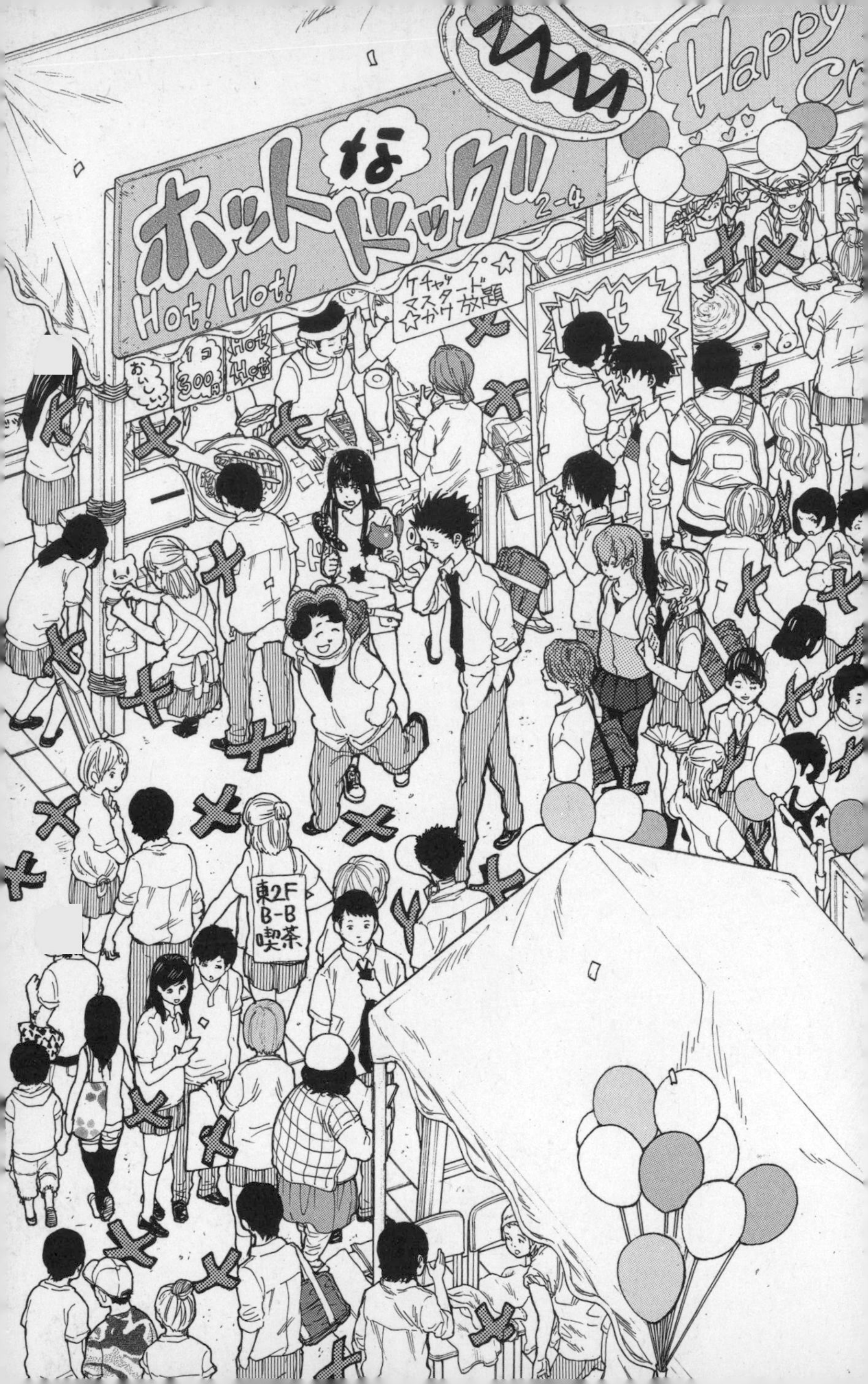
Happy
ホットなドッグ 2-4
Hot! Hot!
ケチャップ マスタード ☆かけ放題☆
Hot Hot
1コ 300円
おいしい
東2F B-B 喫茶

a Silent Voice

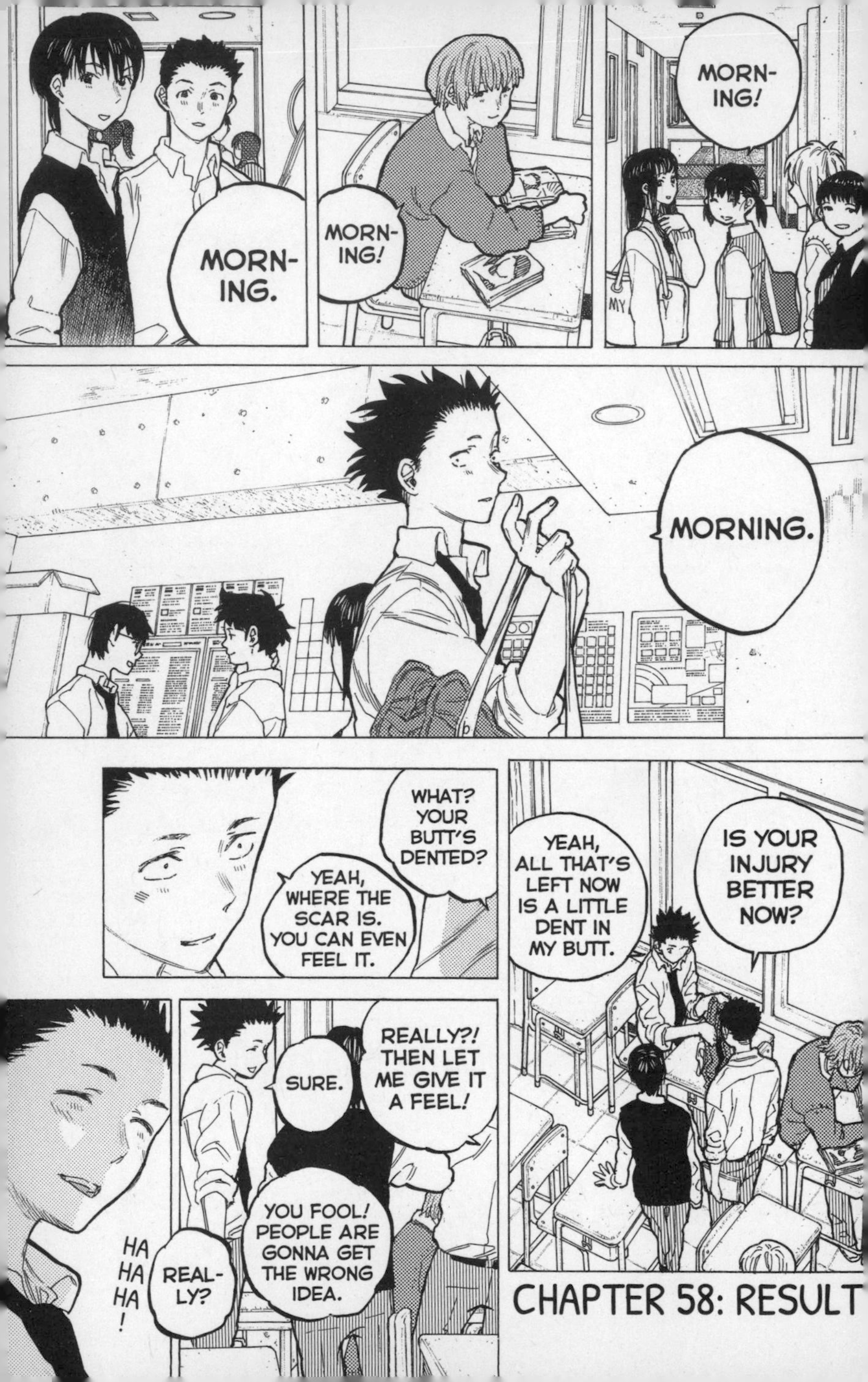
MORN-ING!
MORN-ING!
MORN-ING.
MORNING.
IS YOUR INJURY BETTER NOW?
YEAH, ALL THAT'S LEFT NOW IS A LITTLE DENT IN MY BUTT.
WHAT? YOUR BUTT'S DENTED?
YEAH, WHERE THE SCAR IS. YOU CAN EVEN FEEL IT.
REALLY?! THEN LET ME GIVE IT A FEEL!
SURE.
YOU FOOL! PEOPLE ARE GONNA GET THE WRONG IDEA.
REAL-LY?
HA HA HA!

CHAPTER 58: RESULT

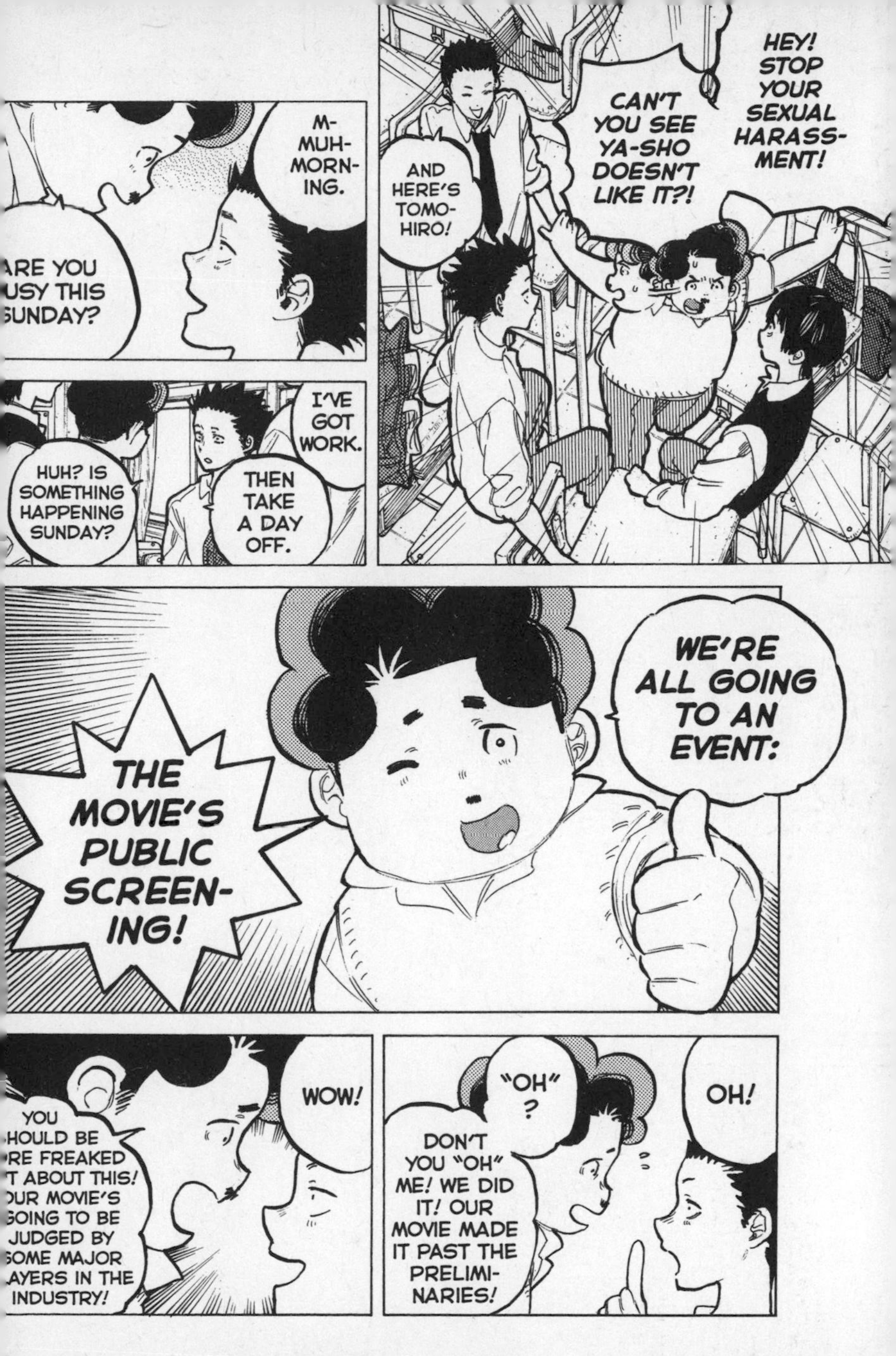
HEY! STOP YOUR SEXUAL HARASS-MENT!
CAN'T YOU SEE YA-SHO DOESN'T LIKE IT?!
AND HERE'S TOMO-HIRO!
M-MUH-MORN-ING.
ARE YOU USY THIS UNDAY?
I'VE GOT WORK.
THEN TAKE A DAY OFF.
HUH? IS SOMETHING HAPPENING SUNDAY?
WE'RE ALL GOING TO AN EVENT:
THE MOVIE'S PUBLIC SCREEN-ING!
OH!
"OH"?
DON'T YOU "OH" ME! WE DID IT! OUR MOVIE MADE IT PAST THE PRELIMI-NARIES!
WOW!
YOU HOULD BE RE FREAKED T ABOUT THIS! UR MOVIE'S OING TO BE JUDGED BY OME MAJOR AYERS IN THE INDUSTRY!

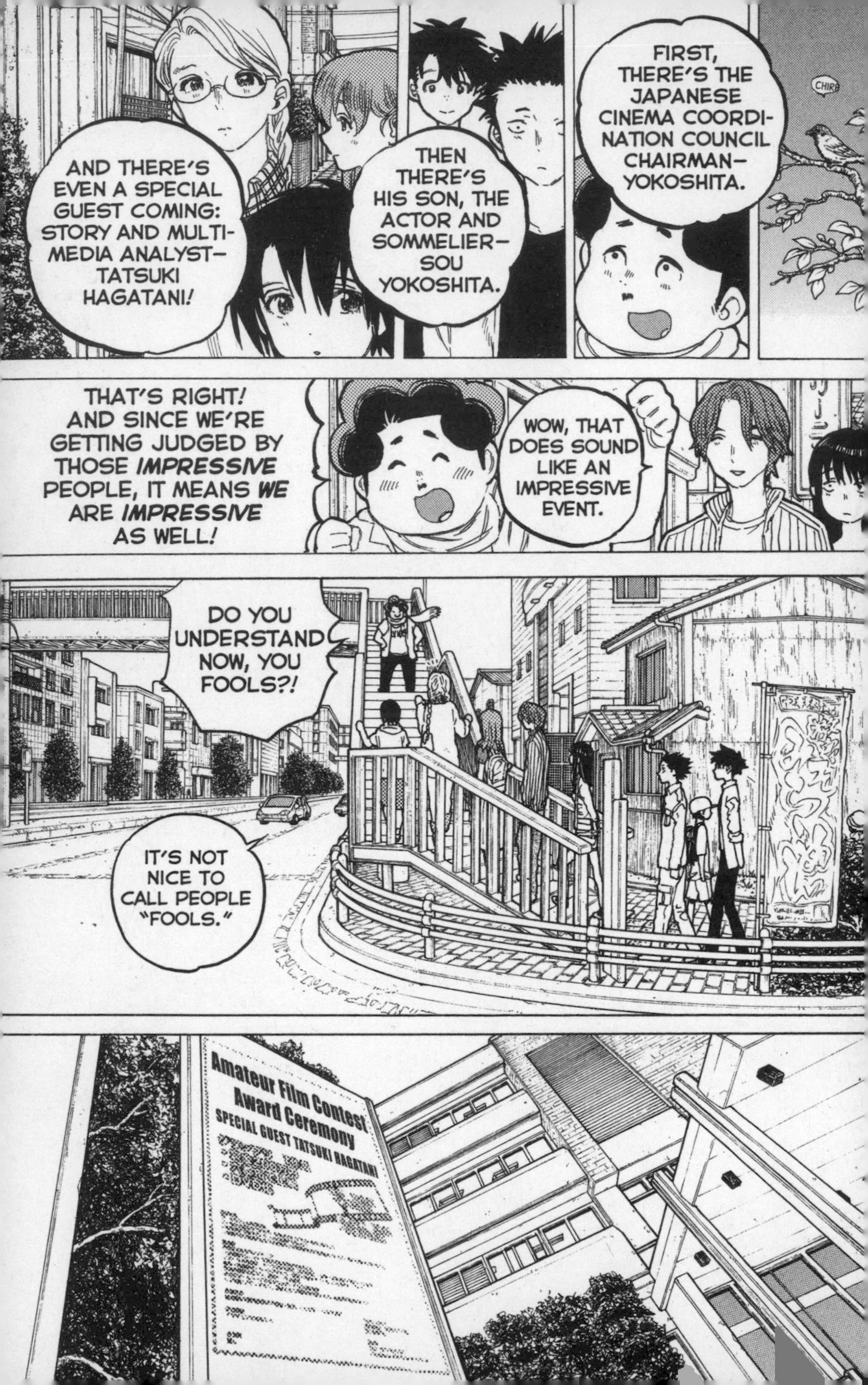
CHIRP
FIRST, THERE'S THE JAPANESE CINEMA COORDINATION COUNCIL CHAIRMAN—YOKOSHITA.
THEN THERE'S HIS SON, THE ACTOR AND SOMMELIER—SOU YOKOSHITA.
AND THERE'S EVEN A SPECIAL GUEST COMING: STORY AND MULTIMEDIA ANALYST—TATSUKI HAGATANI!
WOW, THAT DOES SOUND LIKE AN IMPRESSIVE EVENT.
THAT'S RIGHT! AND SINCE WE'RE GETTING JUDGED BY THOSE *IMPRESSIVE* PEOPLE, IT MEANS *WE* ARE *IMPRESSIVE* AS WELL!
DO YOU UNDERSTAND NOW, YOU FOOLS?!
IT'S NOT NICE TO CALL PEOPLE "FOOLS."
Amateur Film Contest
Award Ceremony
SPECIAL GUEST TATSUKI HAGATANI

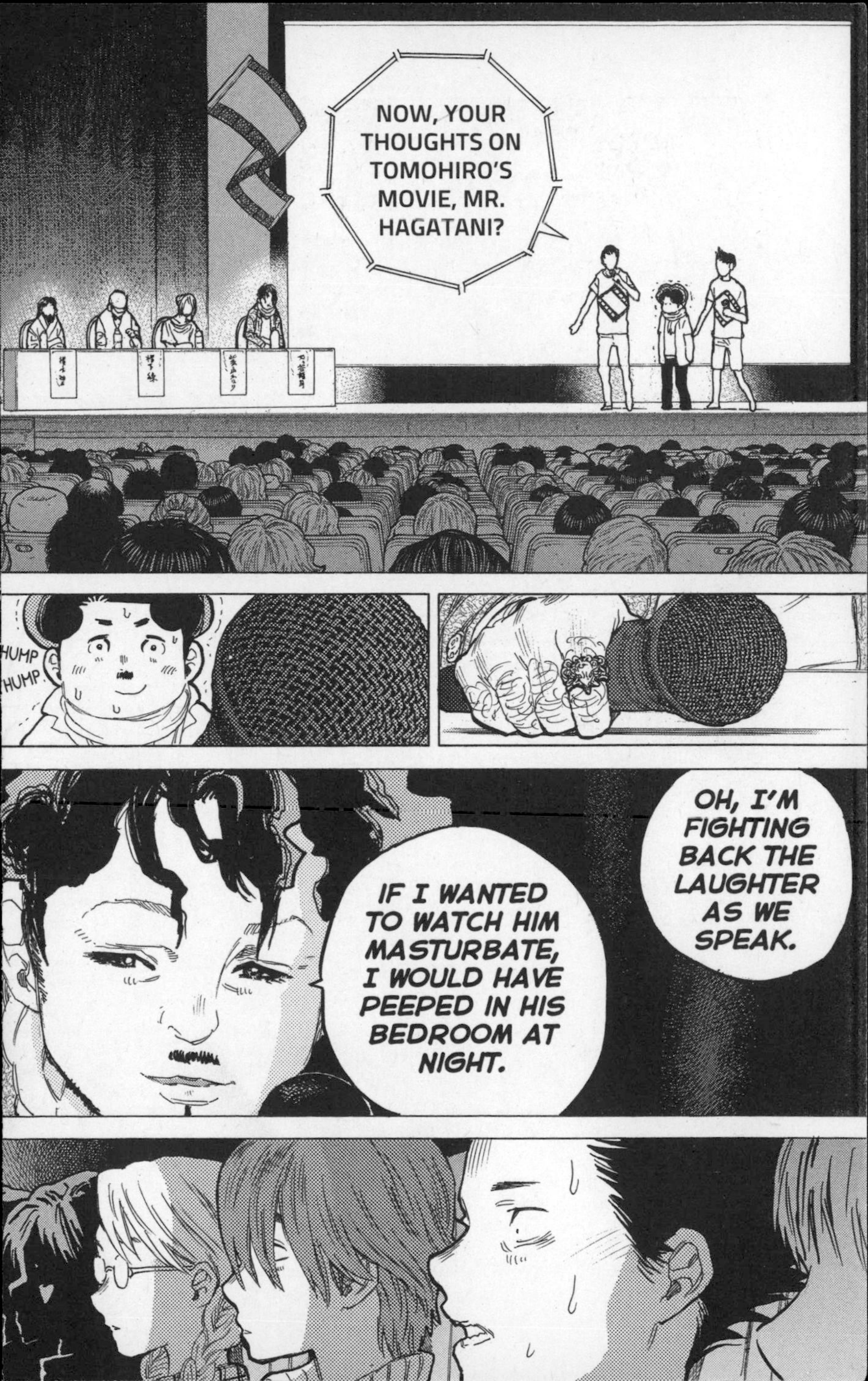
NOW, YOUR THOUGHTS ON TOMOHIRO'S MOVIE, MR. HAGATANI?
HUMP HUMP
OH, I'M FIGHTING BACK THE LAUGHTER AS WE SPEAK.
IF I WANTED TO WATCH HIM MASTURBATE, I WOULD HAVE PEEPED IN HIS BEDROOM AT NIGHT.

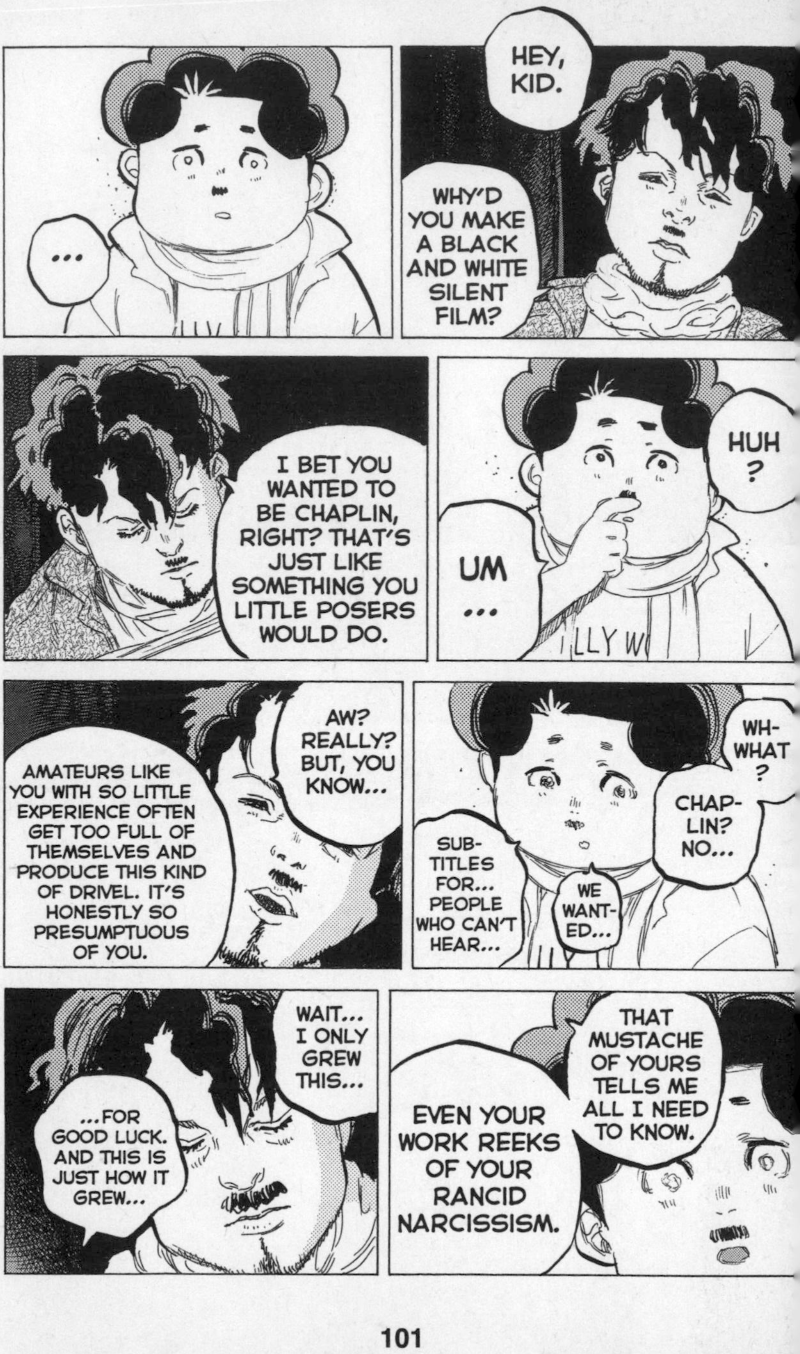
HEY, KID.
WHY'D YOU MAKE A BLACK AND WHITE SILENT FILM?
...
HUH?
UM...
I BET YOU WANTED TO BE CHAPLIN, RIGHT? THAT'S JUST LIKE SOMETHING YOU LITTLE POSERS WOULD DO.
WH-WHAT?
CHAP-LIN? NO...
WE WANT-ED...
SUB-TITLES FOR... PEOPLE WHO CAN'T HEAR...
AW? REALLY? BUT, YOU KNOW...
AMATEURS LIKE YOU WITH SO LITTLE EXPERIENCE OFTEN GET TOO FULL OF THEMSELVES AND PRODUCE THIS KIND OF DRIVEL. IT'S HONESTLY SO PRESUMPTUOUS OF YOU.
THAT MUSTACHE OF YOURS TELLS ME ALL I NEED TO KNOW.
EVEN YOUR WORK REEKS OF YOUR RANCID NARCISSISM.
WAIT... I ONLY GREW THIS...
...FOR GOOD LUCK. AND THIS IS JUST HOW IT GREW...

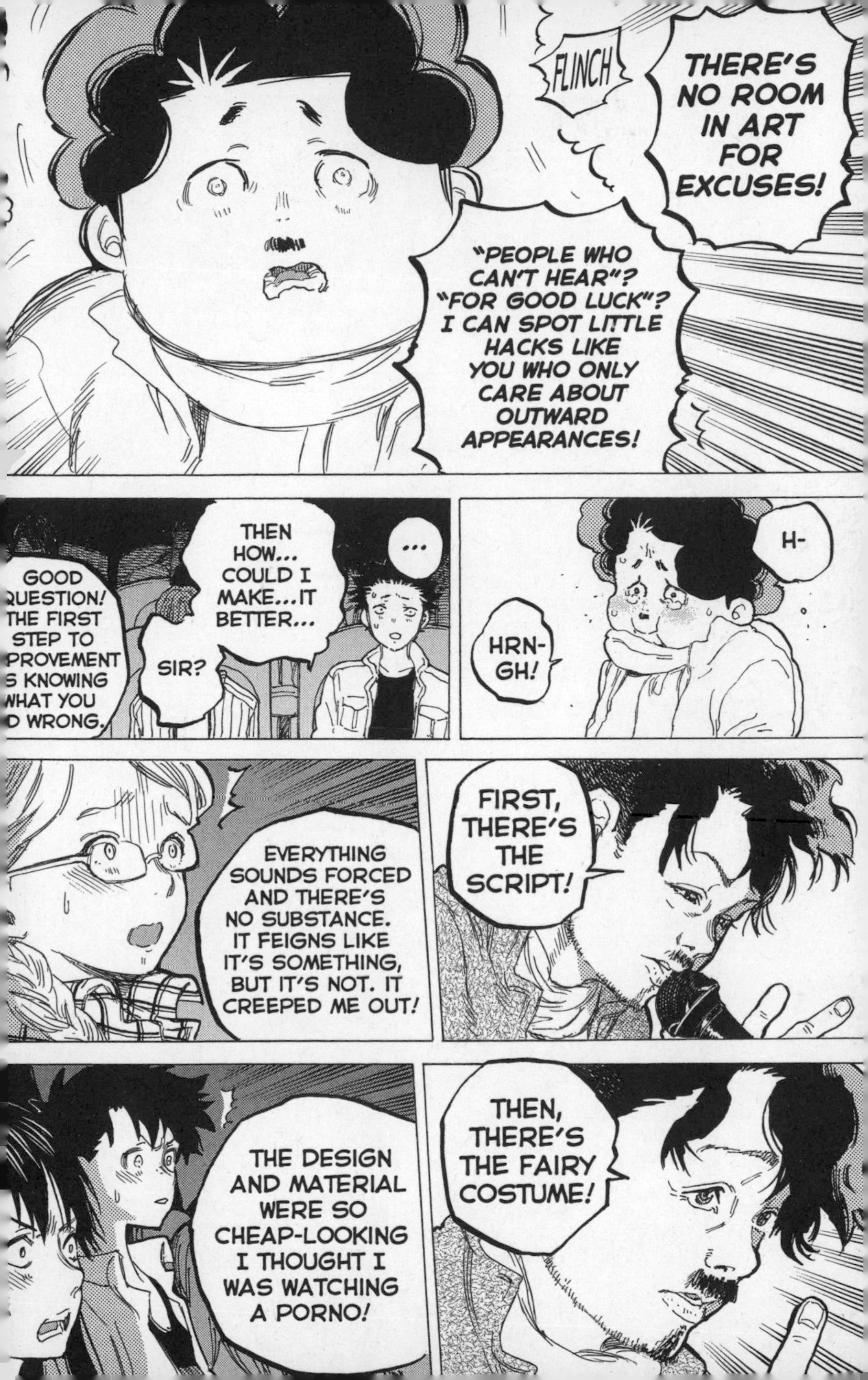
THERE'S NO ROOM IN ART FOR EXCUSES!
FLINCH
"PEOPLE WHO CAN'T HEAR"? "FOR GOOD LUCK"? I CAN SPOT LITTLE HACKS LIKE YOU WHO ONLY CARE ABOUT OUTWARD APPEARANCES!
H-
HRN-GH!
...
THEN HOW... COULD I MAKE...IT BETTER...
SIR?
GOOD QUESTION! THE FIRST STEP TO PROVEMENT S KNOWING WHAT YOU D WRONG.
FIRST, THERE'S THE SCRIPT!
EVERYTHING SOUNDS FORCED AND THERE'S NO SUBSTANCE. IT FEIGNS LIKE IT'S SOMETHING, BUT IT'S NOT. IT CREEPED ME OUT!
THEN, THERE'S THE FAIRY COSTUME!
THE DESIGN AND MATERIAL WERE SO CHEAP-LOOKING I THOUGHT I WAS WATCHING A PORNO!

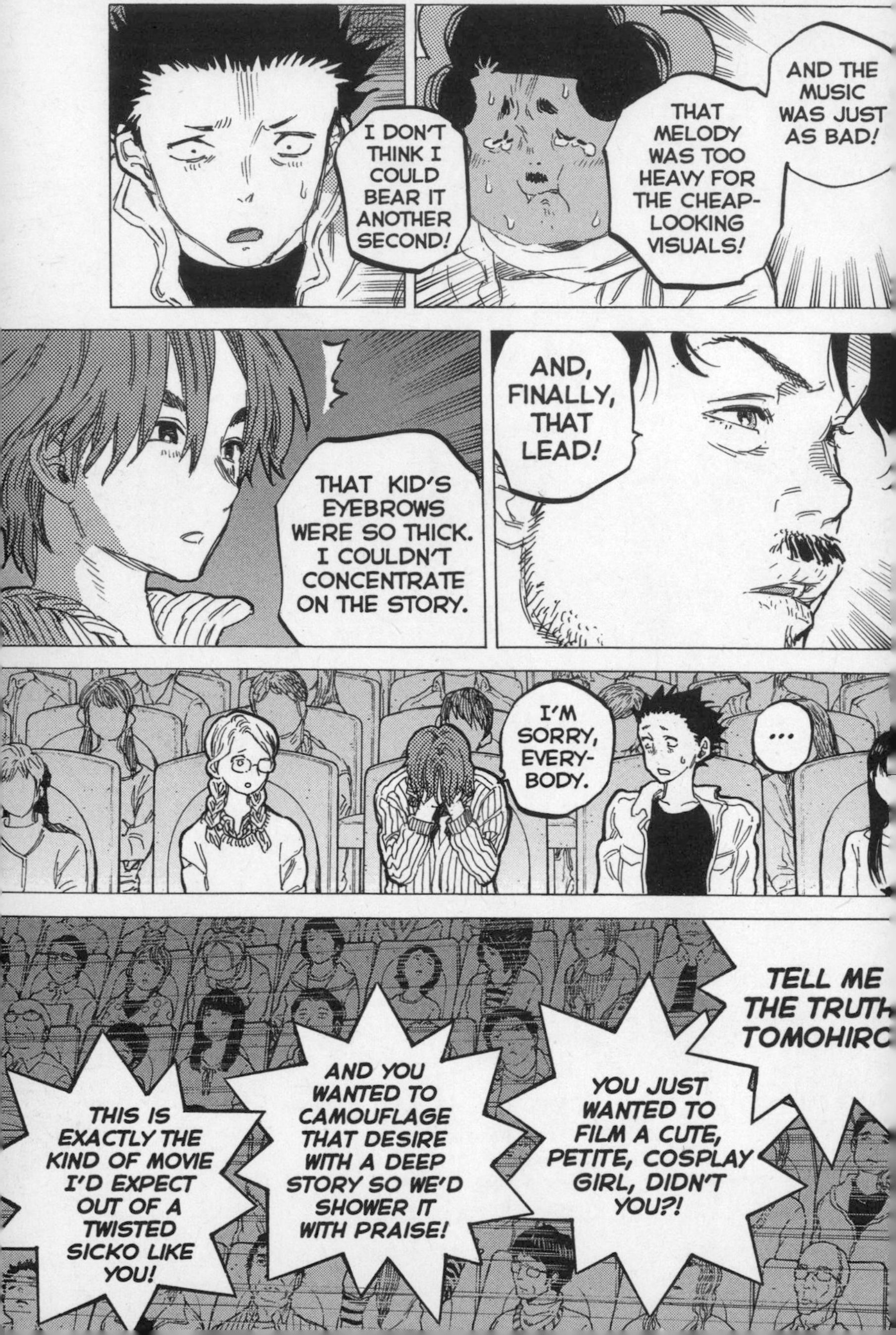
AND THE MUSIC WAS JUST AS BAD!
THAT MELODY WAS TOO HEAVY FOR THE CHEAP-LOOKING VISUALS!
I DON'T THINK I COULD BEAR IT ANOTHER SECOND!
AND, FINALLY, THAT LEAD!
THAT KID'S EYEBROWS WERE SO THICK. I COULDN'T CONCENTRATE ON THE STORY.
...
I'M SORRY, EVERYBODY.
TELL ME THE TRUTH TOMOHIRO
YOU JUST WANTED TO FILM A CUTE, PETITE, COSPLAY GIRL, DIDN'T YOU?!
AND YOU WANTED TO CAMOUFLAGE THAT DESIRE WITH A DEEP STORY SO WE'D SHOWER IT WITH PRAISE!
THIS IS EXACTLY THE KIND OF MOVIE I'D EXPECT OUT OF A TWISTED SICKO LIKE YOU!

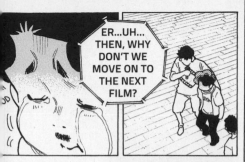

ER...UH... THEN, WHY DON'T WE MOVE ON TO THE NEXT FILM?

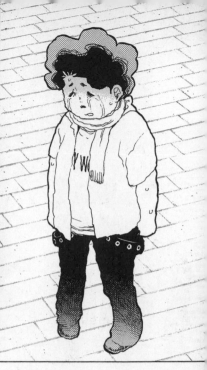

THANK YOU, TOMO-HIRO.

CLAP CLAP CLAP CLAP CLAP

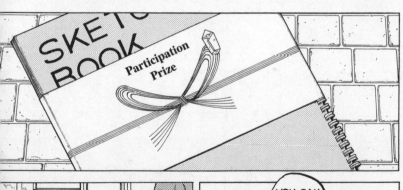

SKETCH BOOK

Participation Prize

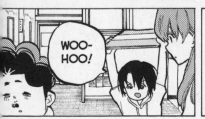

WOO-HOO!

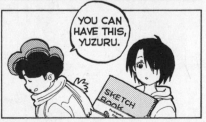

YOU CAN HAVE THIS, YUZURU.

SKETCH BOOK

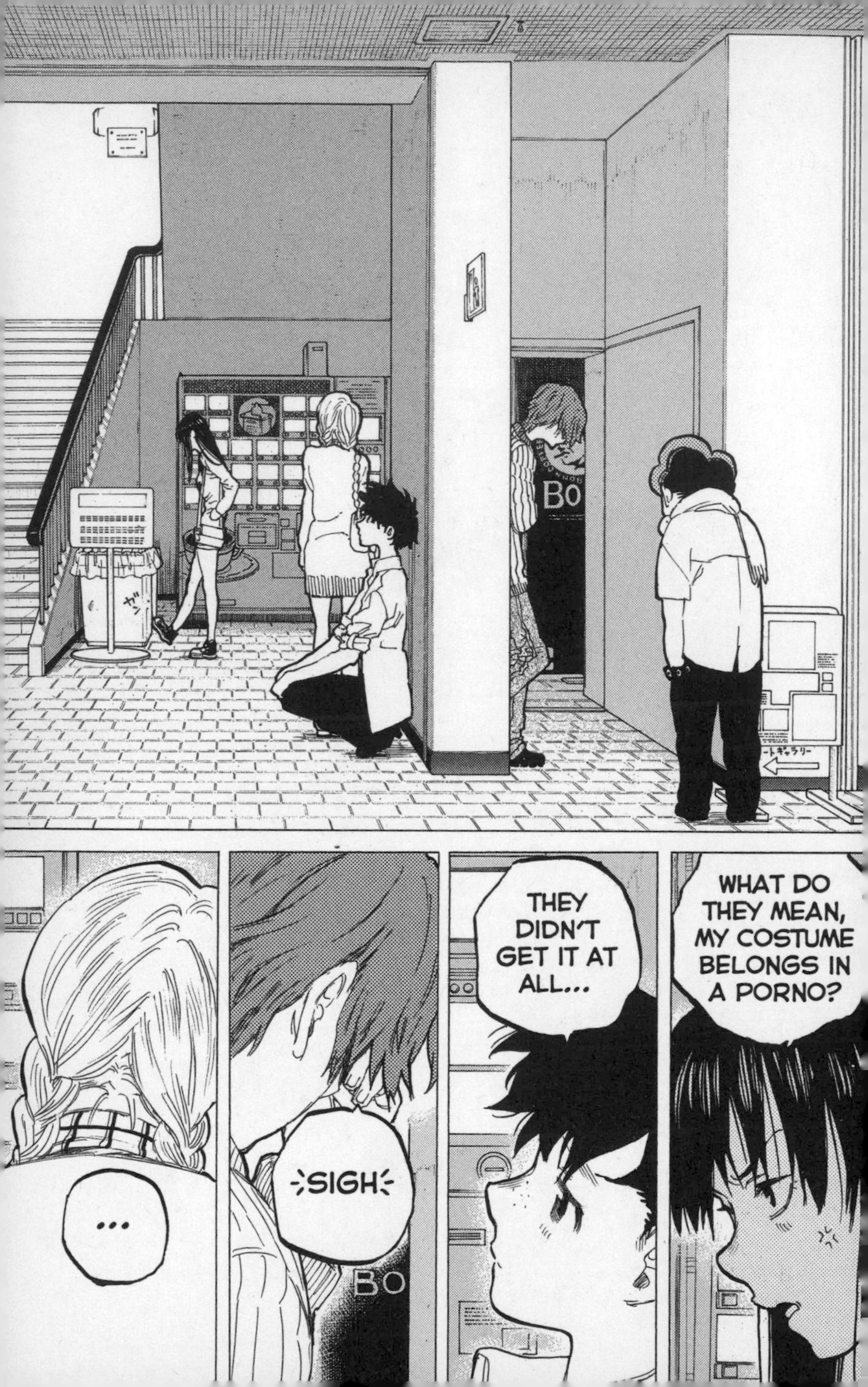
WHAT DO THEY MEAN, MY COSTUME BELONGS IN A PORNO?
THEY DIDN'T GET IT AT ALL...
SIGH
...

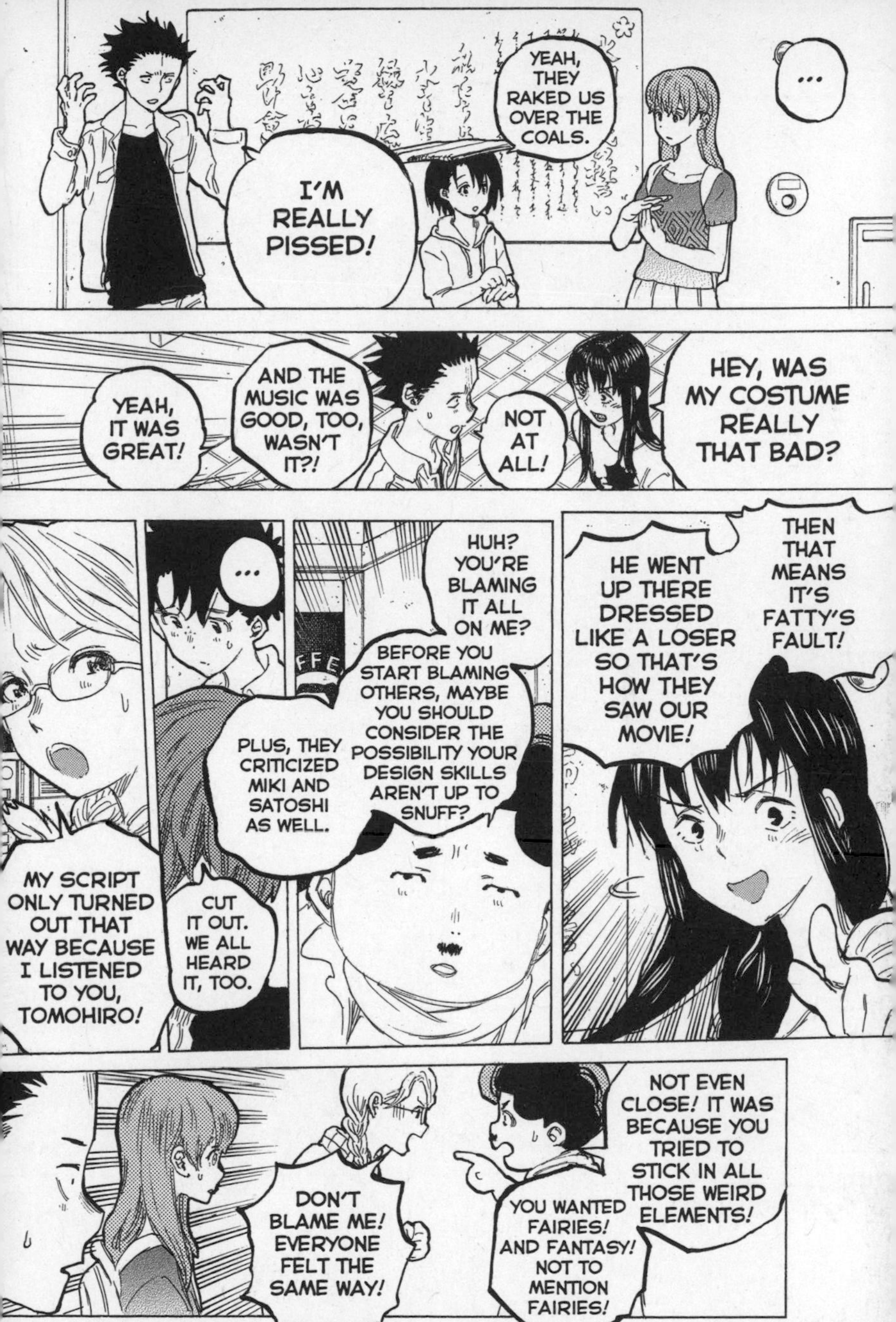
...
YEAH, THEY RAKED US OVER THE COALS.
I'M REALLY PISSED!
HEY, WAS MY COSTUME REALLY THAT BAD?
NOT AT ALL!
AND THE MUSIC WAS GOOD, TOO, WASN'T IT?!
YEAH, IT WAS GREAT!
THEN THAT MEANS IT'S FATTY'S FAULT!
HE WENT UP THERE DRESSED LIKE A LOSER SO THAT'S HOW THEY SAW OUR MOVIE!
HUH? YOU'RE BLAMING IT ALL ON ME?
BEFORE YOU START BLAMING OTHERS, MAYBE YOU SHOULD CONSIDER THE POSSIBILITY YOUR DESIGN SKILLS AREN'T UP TO SNUFF?
PLUS, THEY CRITICIZED MIKI AND SATOSHI AS WELL.
...
CUT IT OUT. WE ALL HEARD IT, TOO.
MY SCRIPT ONLY TURNED OUT THAT WAY BECAUSE I LISTENED TO YOU, TOMOHIRO!
NOT EVEN CLOSE! IT WAS BECAUSE YOU TRIED TO STICK IN ALL THOSE WEIRD ELEMENTS!
YOU WANTED FAIRIES! AND FANTASY! NOT TO MENTION FAIRIES!
DON'T BLAME ME! EVERYONE FELT THE SAME WAY!

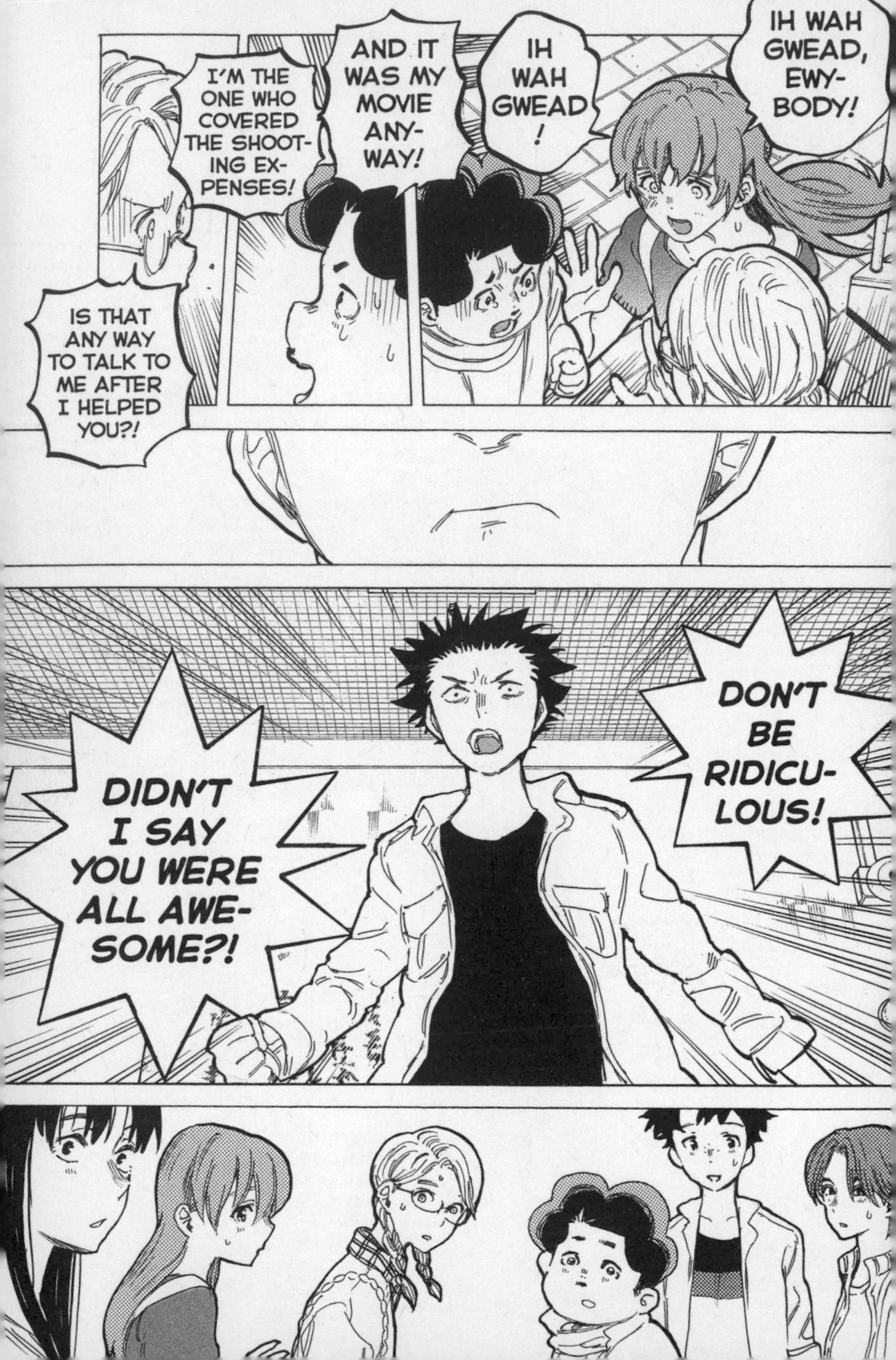
IH WAH GWEAD, EWY-BODY!
IH WAH GWEAD!
AND IT WAS MY MOVIE ANY-WAY!
I'M THE ONE WHO COVERED THE SHOOT-ING EX-PENSES!
IS THAT ANY WAY TO TALK TO ME AFTER I HELPED YOU?!
DON'T BE RIDICU-LOUS!
DIDN'T I SAY YOU WERE ALL AWE-SOME?!

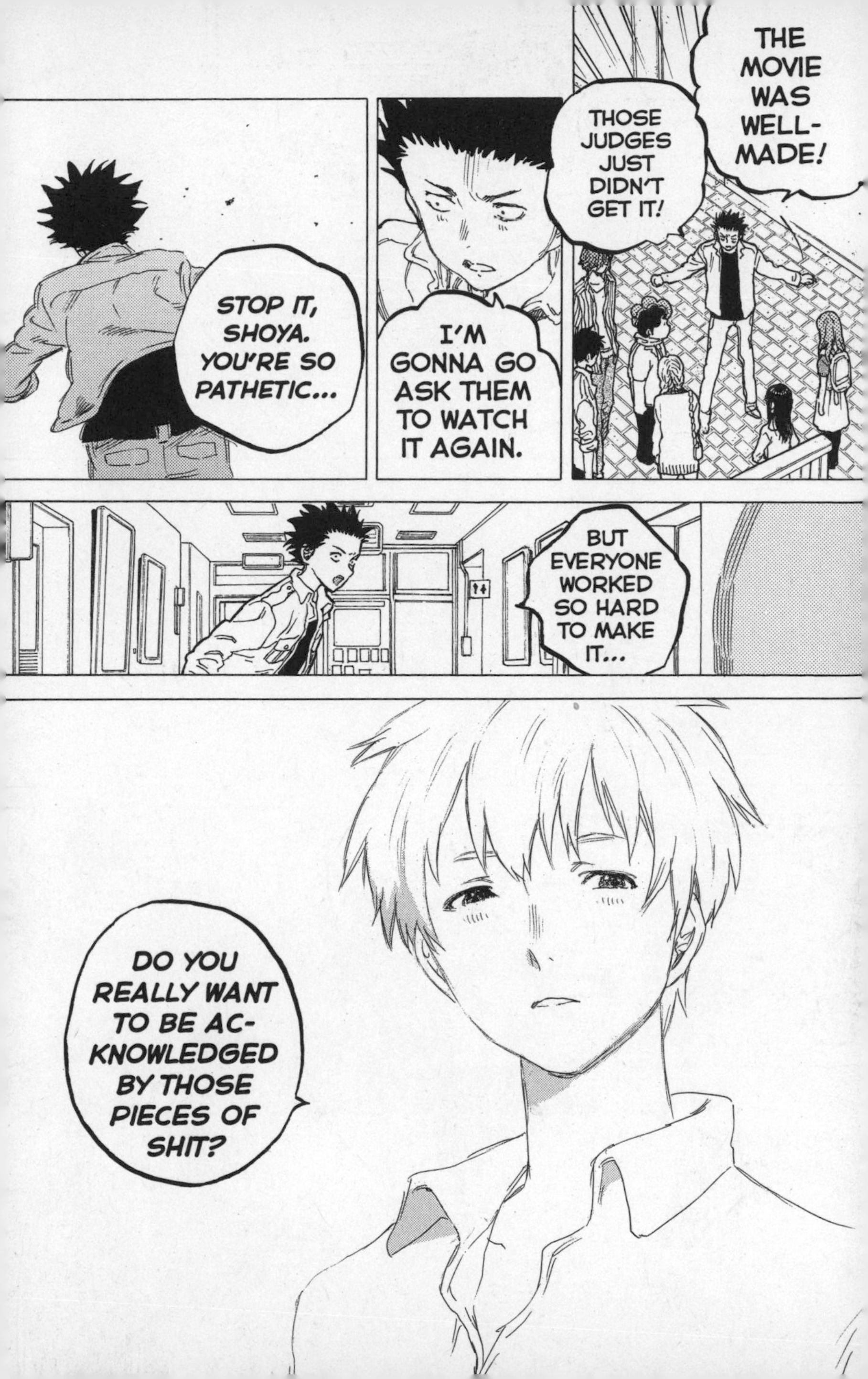
THE MOVIE WAS WELL-MADE!
THOSE JUDGES JUST DIDN'T GET IT!
I'M GONNA GO ASK THEM TO WATCH IT AGAIN.
STOP IT, SHOYA. YOU'RE SO PATHETIC...
BUT EVERYONE WORKED SO HARD TO MAKE IT...
DO YOU REALLY WANT TO BE AC-KNOWLEDGED BY THOSE PIECES OF SHIT?

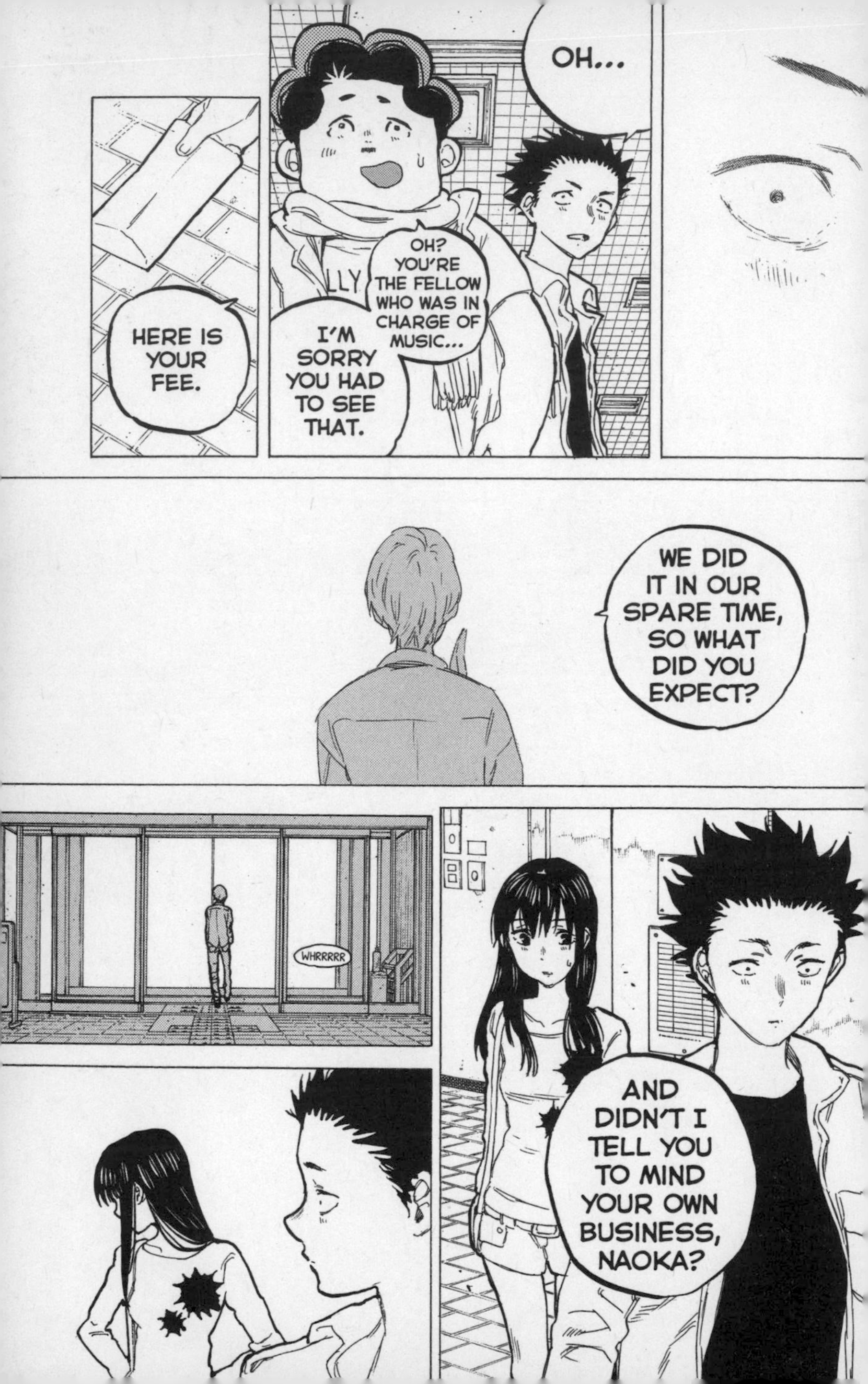
OH...
OH? YOU'RE THE FELLOW WHO WAS IN CHARGE OF MUSIC...
I'M SORRY YOU HAD TO SEE THAT.
HERE IS YOUR FEE.
WE DID IT IN OUR SPARE TIME, SO WHAT DID YOU EXPECT?
AND DIDN'T I TELL YOU TO MIND YOUR OWN BUSINESS, NAOKA?
WHRRRRR

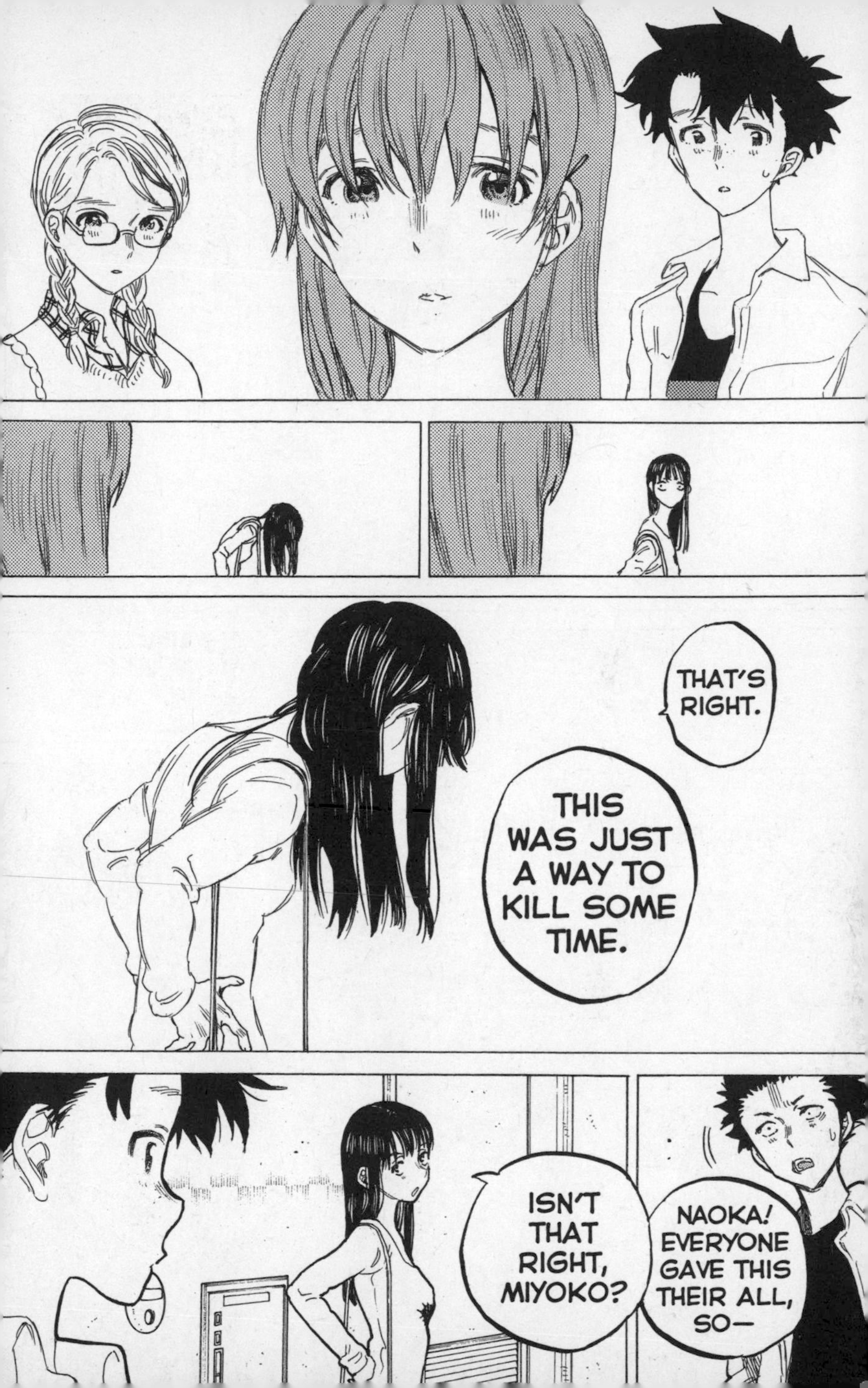
THAT'S RIGHT.
THIS WAS JUST A WAY TO KILL SOME TIME.
NAOKA! EVERYONE GAVE THIS THEIR ALL, SO—
ISN'T THAT RIGHT, MIYOKO?

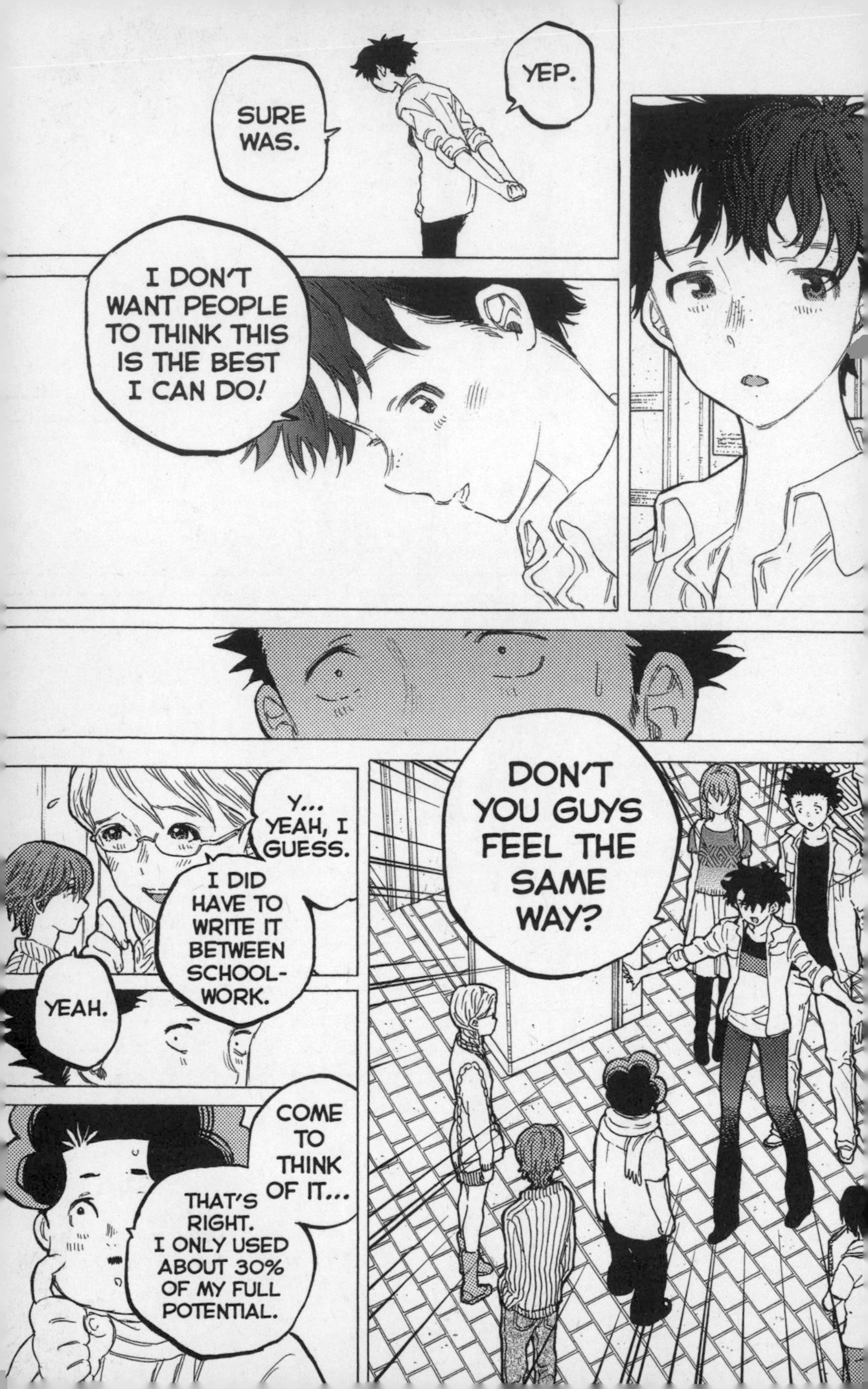
YEP.
SURE WAS.
I DON'T WANT PEOPLE TO THINK THIS IS THE BEST I CAN DO!
DON'T YOU GUYS FEEL THE SAME WAY?
Y... YEAH, I GUESS.
I DID HAVE TO WRITE IT BETWEEN SCHOOL-WORK.
YEAH.
COME TO THINK OF IT...
THAT'S RIGHT. I ONLY USED ABOUT 30% OF MY FULL POTENTIAL.

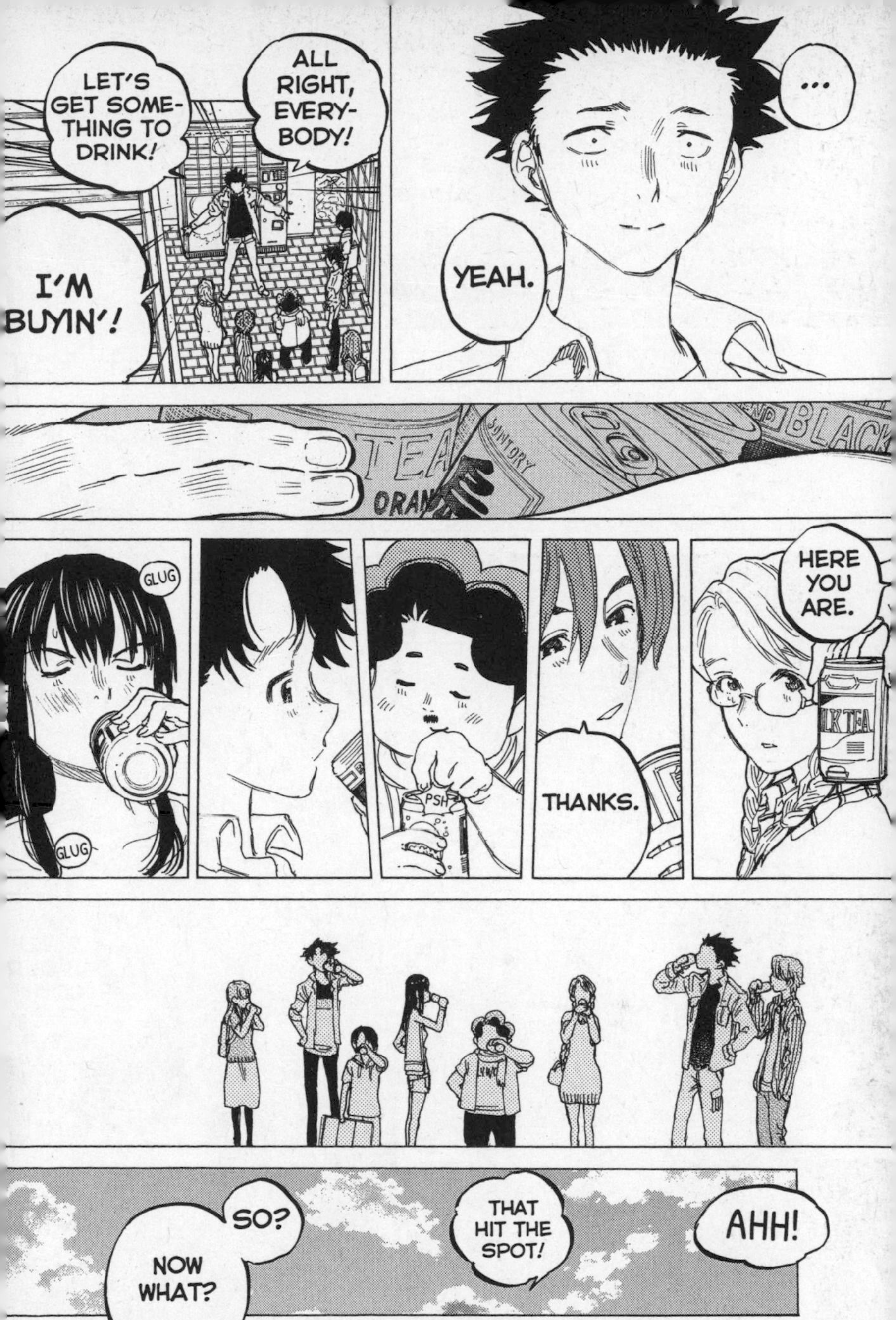
...
YEAH.
ALL RIGHT, EVERYBODY!
LET'S GET SOMETHING TO DRINK!
I'M BUYIN'!
SUNTORY
TEA
HERE YOU ARE.
THANKS.
PSH
GLUG
GLUG
AHH!
THAT HIT THE SPOT!
SO?
NOW WHAT?

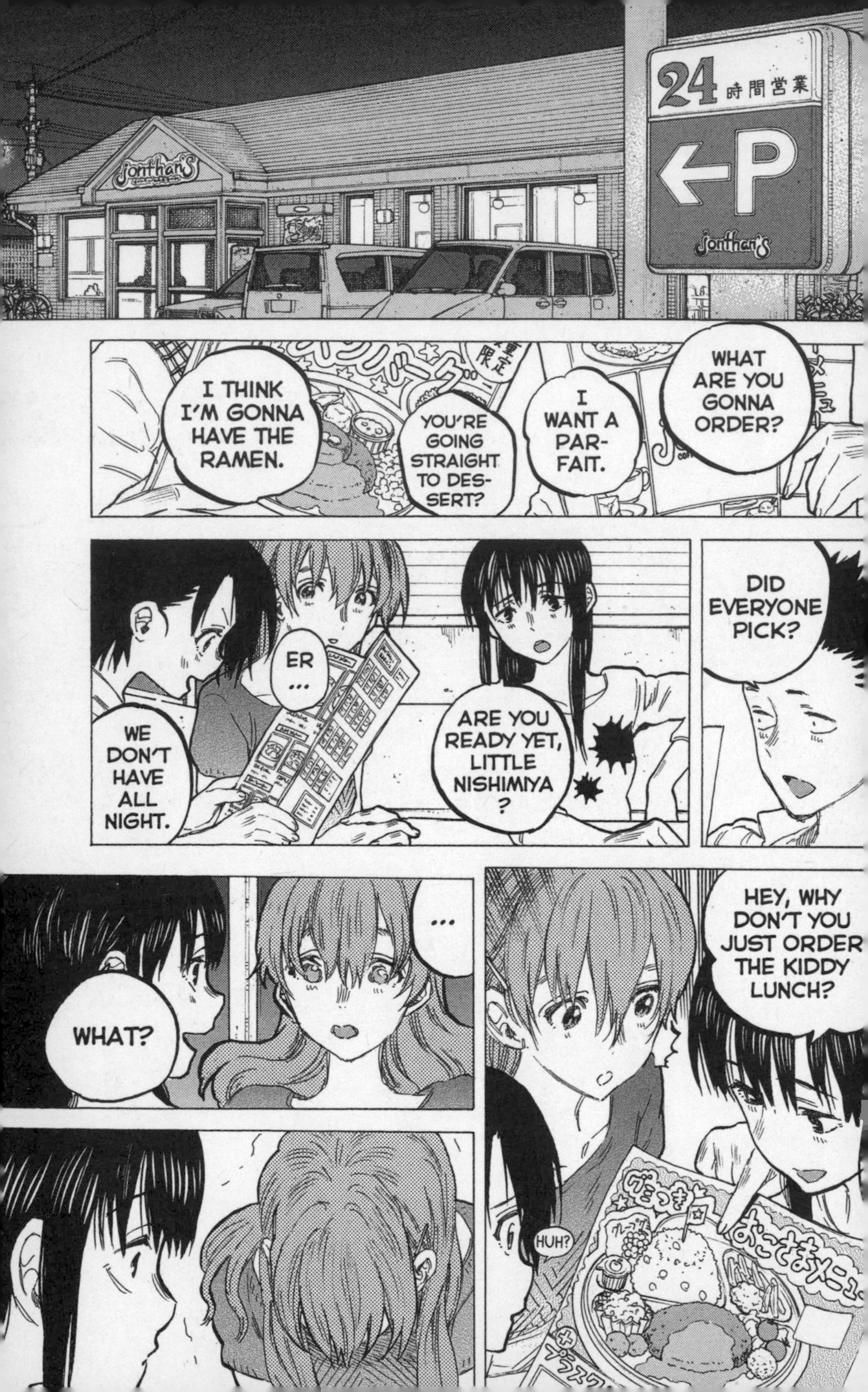

24 時間営業
P
jonthan's
jonthan's
WHAT ARE YOU GONNA ORDER?
I WANT A PARFAIT.
YOU'RE GOING STRAIGHT TO DESSERT?
I THINK I'M GONNA HAVE THE RAMEN.
DID EVERYONE PICK?
ARE YOU READY YET, LITTLE NISHIMIYA?
ER...
WE DON'T HAVE ALL NIGHT.
HEY, WHY DON'T YOU JUST ORDER THE KIDDY LUNCH?
HUH?
...
WHAT?

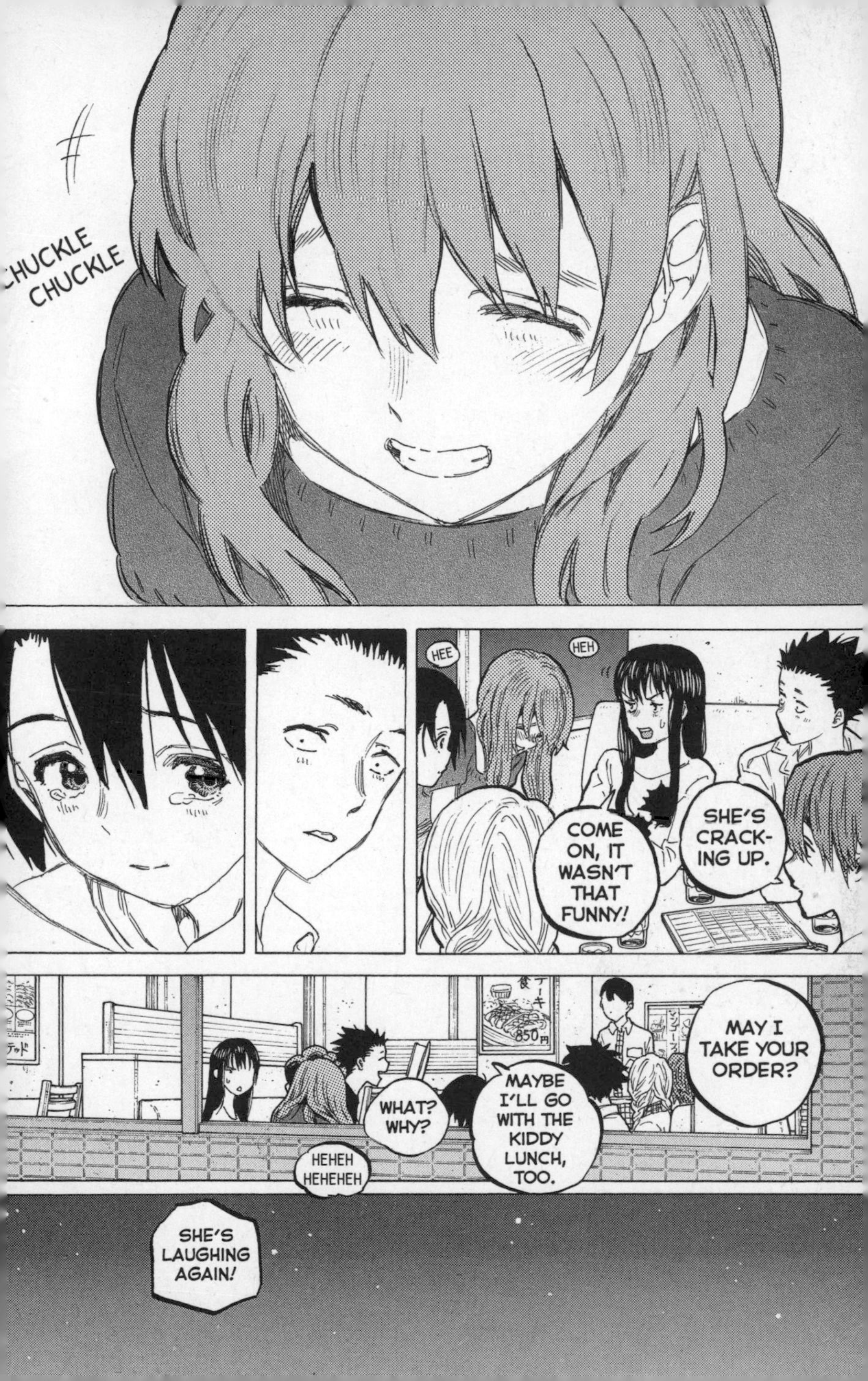
CHUCKLE CHUCKLE
HEH
HEE
SHE'S CRACKING UP.
COME ON, IT WASN'T THAT FUNNY!
MAY I TAKE YOUR ORDER?
MAYBE I'LL GO WITH THE KIDDY LUNCH, TOO.
WHAT? WHY?
HEHEH HEHEHEH
SHE'S LAUGHING AGAIN!

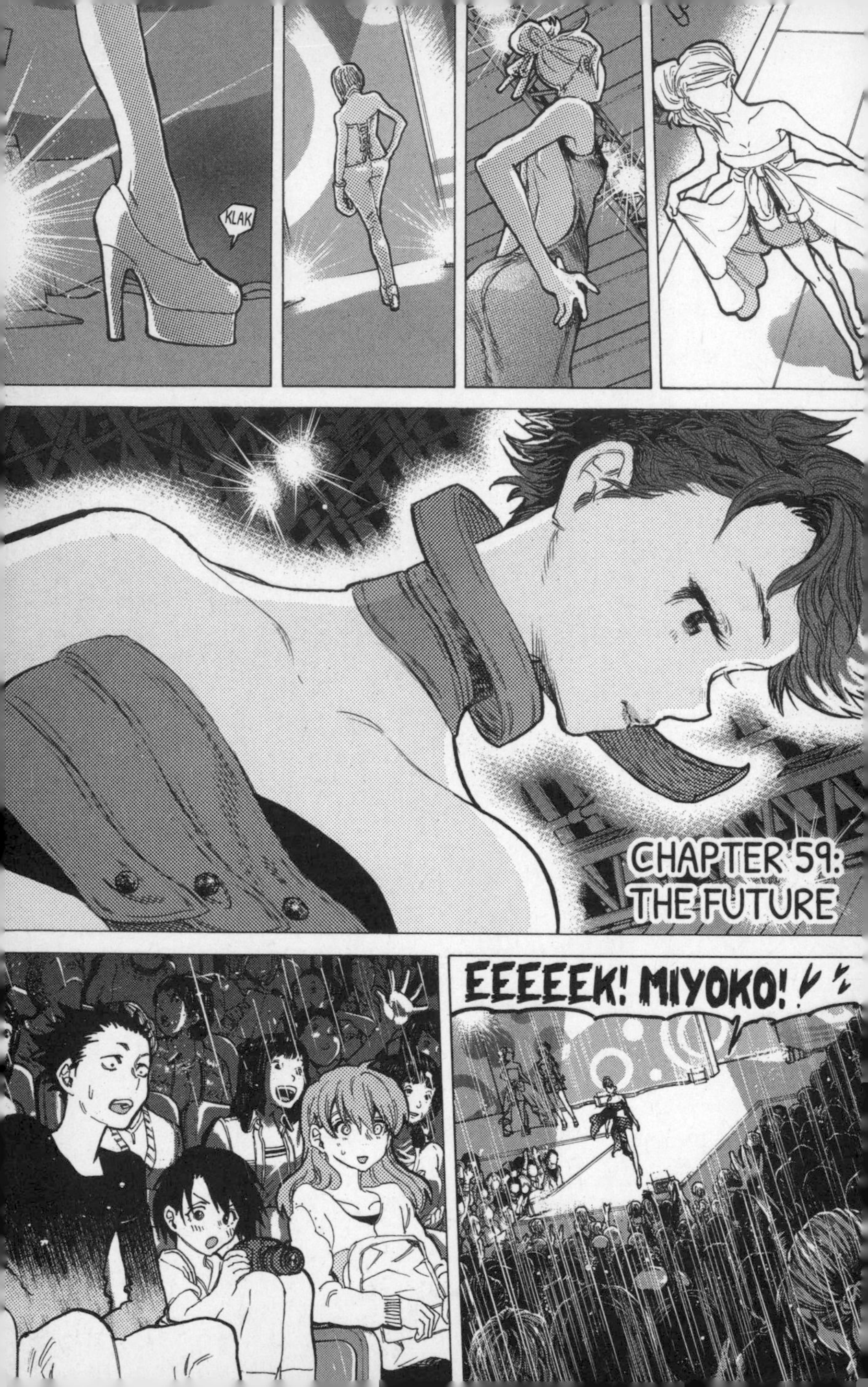
KLAK
CHAPTER 59:
THE FUTURE
EEEEEK! MIYOKO!

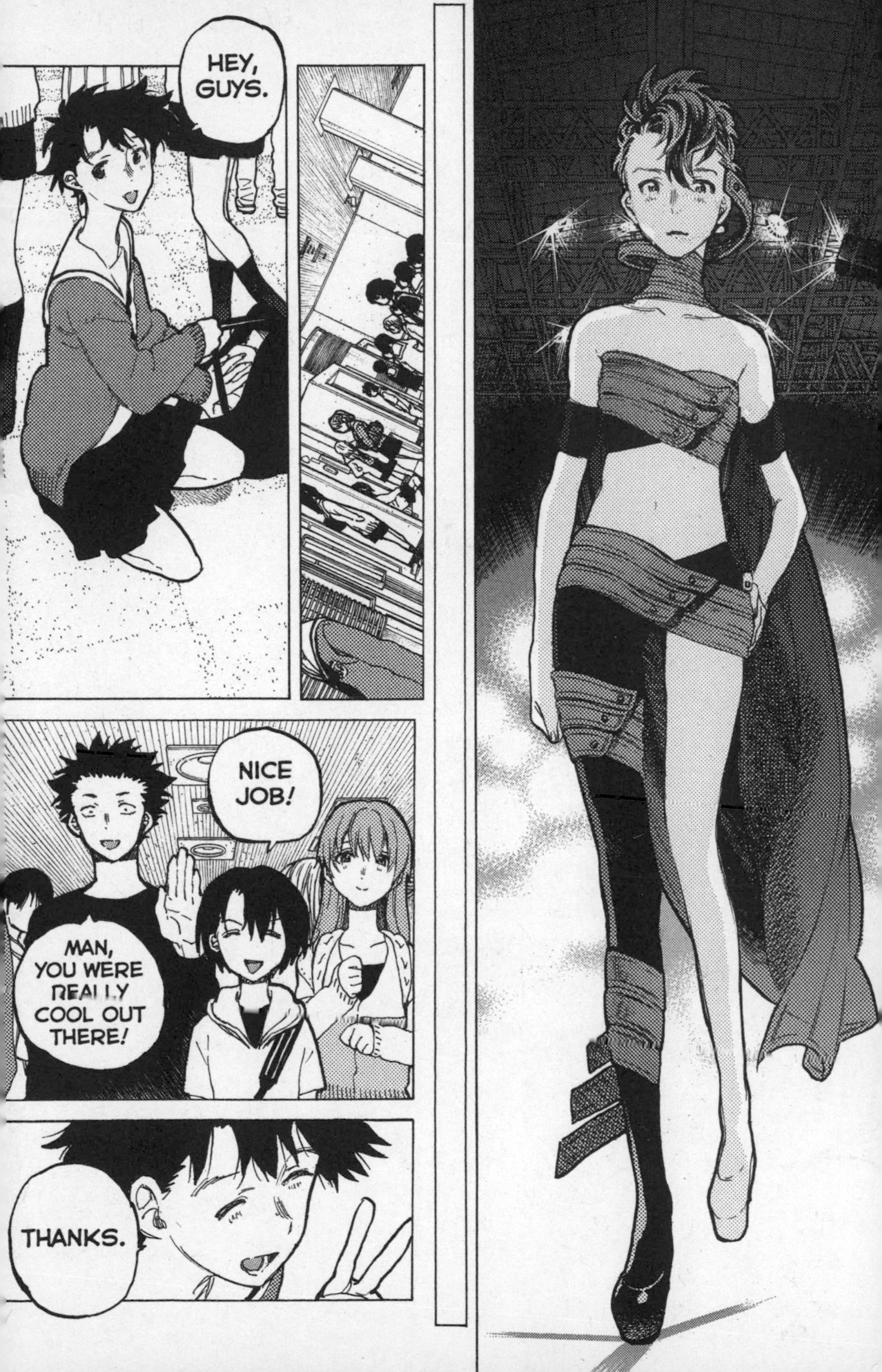
HEY, GUYS.
NICE JOB!
MAN, YOU WERE REALLY COOL OUT THERE!
THANKS.

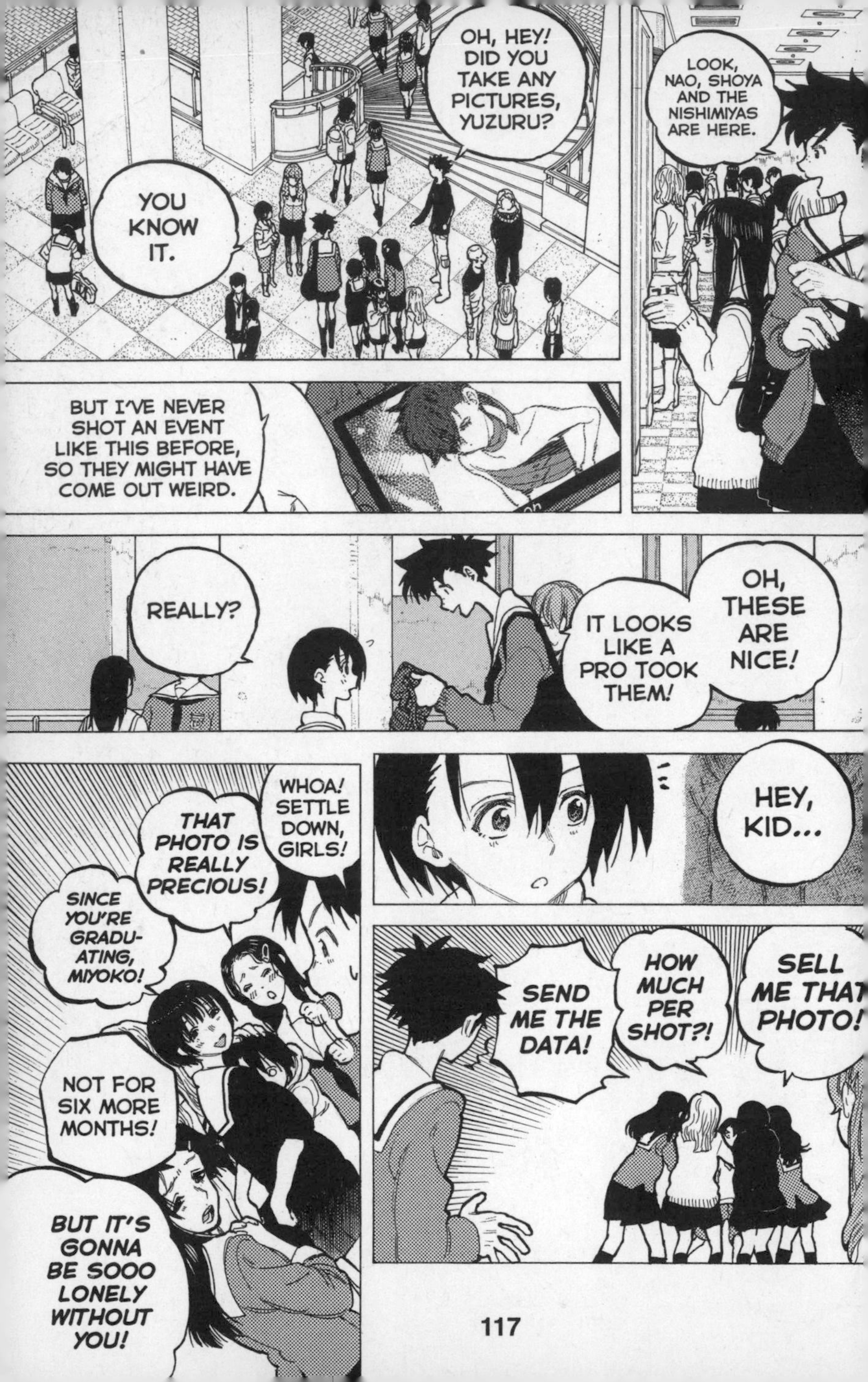
LOOK, NAO, SHOYA AND THE NISHIMIYAS ARE HERE.
OH, HEY! DID YOU TAKE ANY PICTURES, YUZURU?
YOU KNOW IT.
BUT I'VE NEVER SHOT AN EVENT LIKE THIS BEFORE, SO THEY MIGHT HAVE COME OUT WEIRD.
OH, THESE ARE NICE!
IT LOOKS LIKE A PRO TOOK THEM!
REALLY?
HEY, KID...
SELL ME THAT PHOTO!
HOW MUCH PER SHOT?!
SEND ME THE DATA!
WHOA! SETTLE DOWN, GIRLS!
THAT PHOTO IS REALLY PRECIOUS!
SINCE YOU'RE GRADU-ATING, MIYOKO!
NOT FOR SIX MORE MONTHS!
BUT IT'S GONNA BE SOOO LONELY WITHOUT YOU!

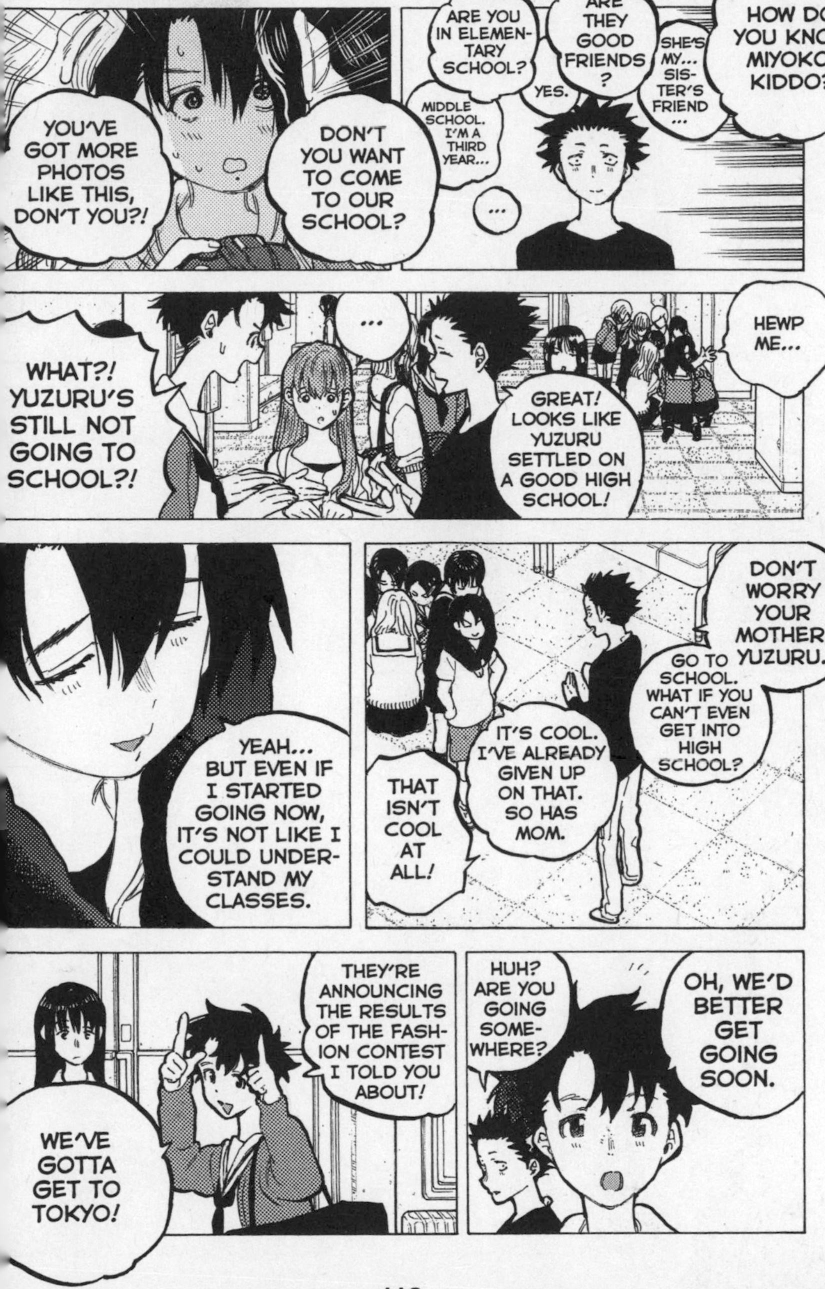
HOW DO YOU KNOW MIYOKO, KIDDO?
SHE'S MY... SISTER'S FRIEND...
ARE THEY GOOD FRIENDS?
YES.
ARE YOU IN ELEMENTARY SCHOOL?
MIDDLE SCHOOL. I'M A THIRD YEAR...
...
DON'T YOU WANT TO COME TO OUR SCHOOL?
YOU'VE GOT MORE PHOTOS LIKE THIS, DON'T YOU?!
HEWP ME...
GREAT! LOOKS LIKE YUZURU SETTLED ON A GOOD HIGH SCHOOL!
...
WHAT?! YUZURU'S STILL NOT GOING TO SCHOOL?!
DON'T WORRY YOUR MOTHER, YUZURU.
GO TO SCHOOL. WHAT IF YOU CAN'T EVEN GET INTO HIGH SCHOOL?
IT'S COOL. I'VE ALREADY GIVEN UP ON THAT. SO HAS MOM.
THAT ISN'T COOL AT ALL!
YEAH... BUT EVEN IF I STARTED GOING NOW, IT'S NOT LIKE I COULD UNDERSTAND MY CLASSES.
OH, WE'D BETTER GET GOING SOON.
HUH? ARE YOU GOING SOMEWHERE?
THEY'RE ANNOUNCING THE RESULTS OF THE FASHION CONTEST I TOLD YOU ABOUT!
WE'VE GOTTA GET TO TOKYO!

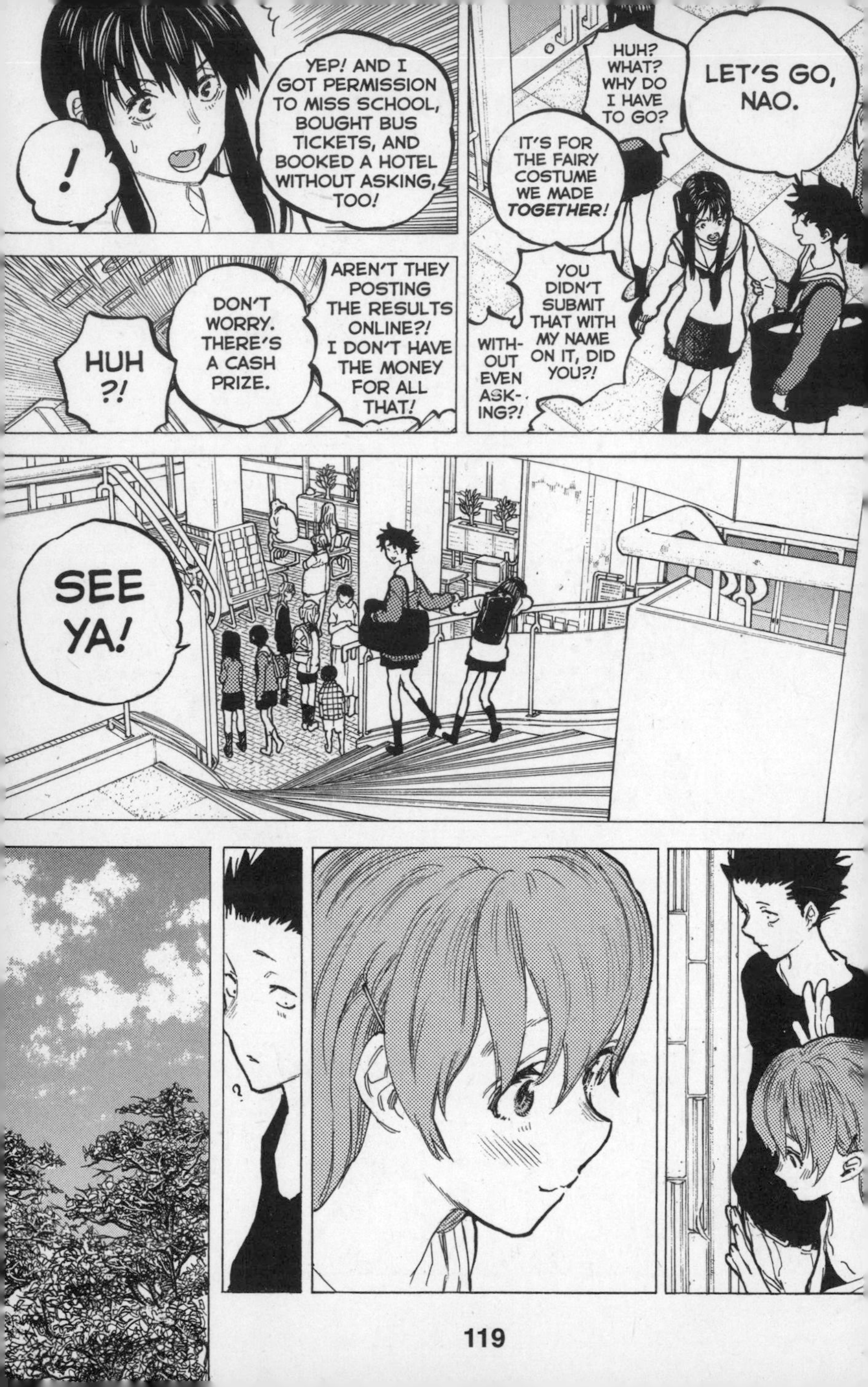
LET'S GO, NAO.
HUH? WHAT? WHY DO I HAVE TO GO?
IT'S FOR THE FAIRY COSTUME WE MADE *TOGETHER*!
YOU DIDN'T SUBMIT THAT WITH MY NAME ON IT, DID YOU?!
WITH-OUT EVEN ASK-ING?!
YEP! AND I GOT PERMISSION TO MISS SCHOOL, BOUGHT BUS TICKETS, AND BOOKED A HOTEL WITHOUT ASKING, TOO!
!
AREN'T THEY POSTING THE RESULTS ONLINE?! I DON'T HAVE THE MONEY FOR ALL THAT!
DON'T WORRY. THERE'S A CASH PRIZE.
HUH ?!
SEE YA!
?

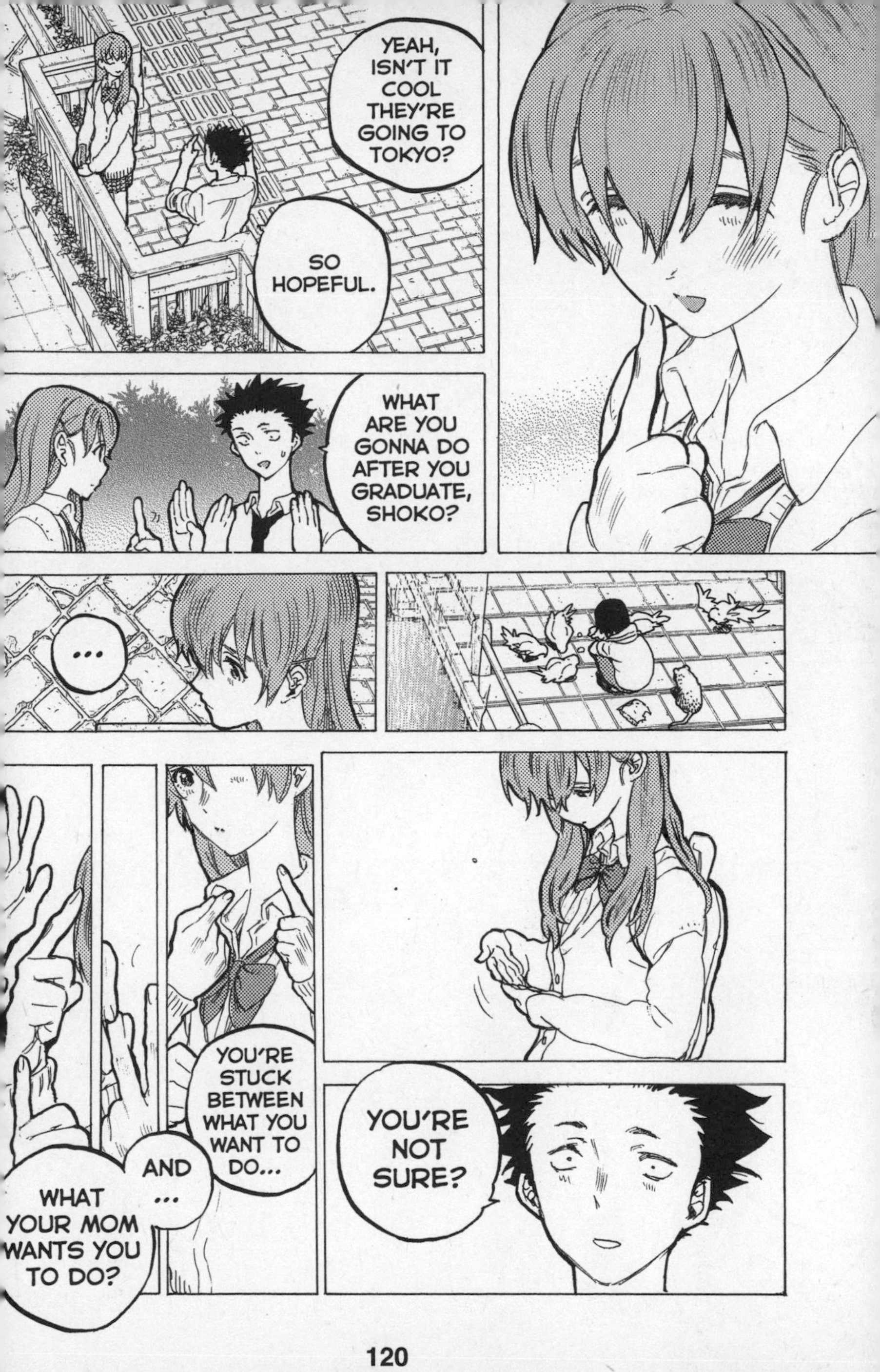
YEAH, ISN'T IT COOL THEY'RE GOING TO TOKYO?
SO HOPEFUL.
WHAT ARE YOU GONNA DO AFTER YOU GRADUATE, SHOKO?
...
YOU'RE NOT SURE?
YOU'RE STUCK BETWEEN WHAT YOU WANT TO DO...
AND ...
WHAT YOUR MOM WANTS YOU TO DO?

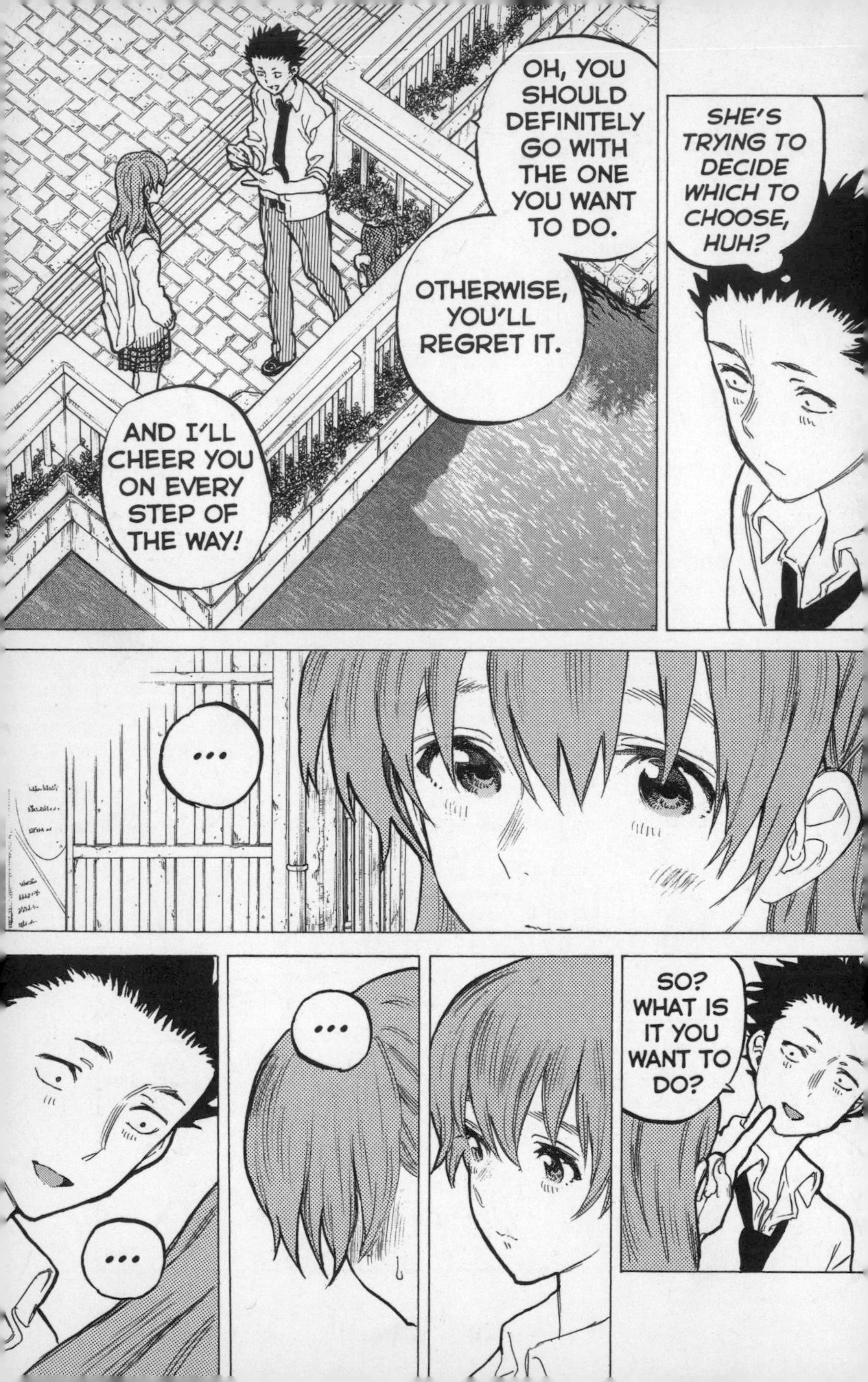
SHE'S TRYING TO DECIDE WHICH TO CHOOSE, HUH?
OH, YOU SHOULD DEFINITELY GO WITH THE ONE YOU WANT TO DO.
OTHERWISE, YOU'LL REGRET IT.
AND I'LL CHEER YOU ON EVERY STEP OF THE WAY!
...
SO? WHAT IS IT YOU WANT TO DO?
...
...

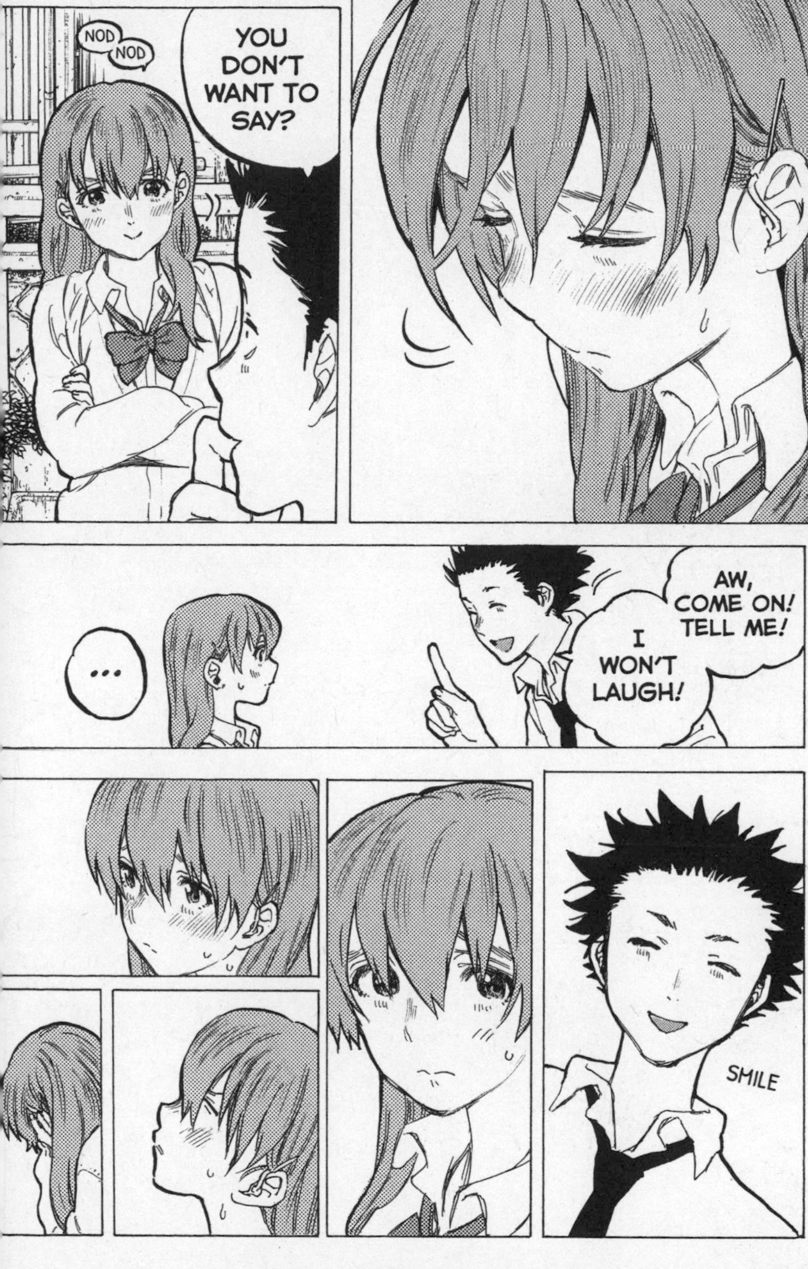
YOU DON'T WANT TO SAY?
NOD NOD
AW, COME ON! TELL ME!
I WON'T LAUGH!
...
SMILE

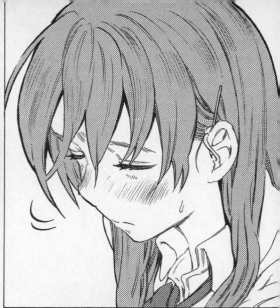

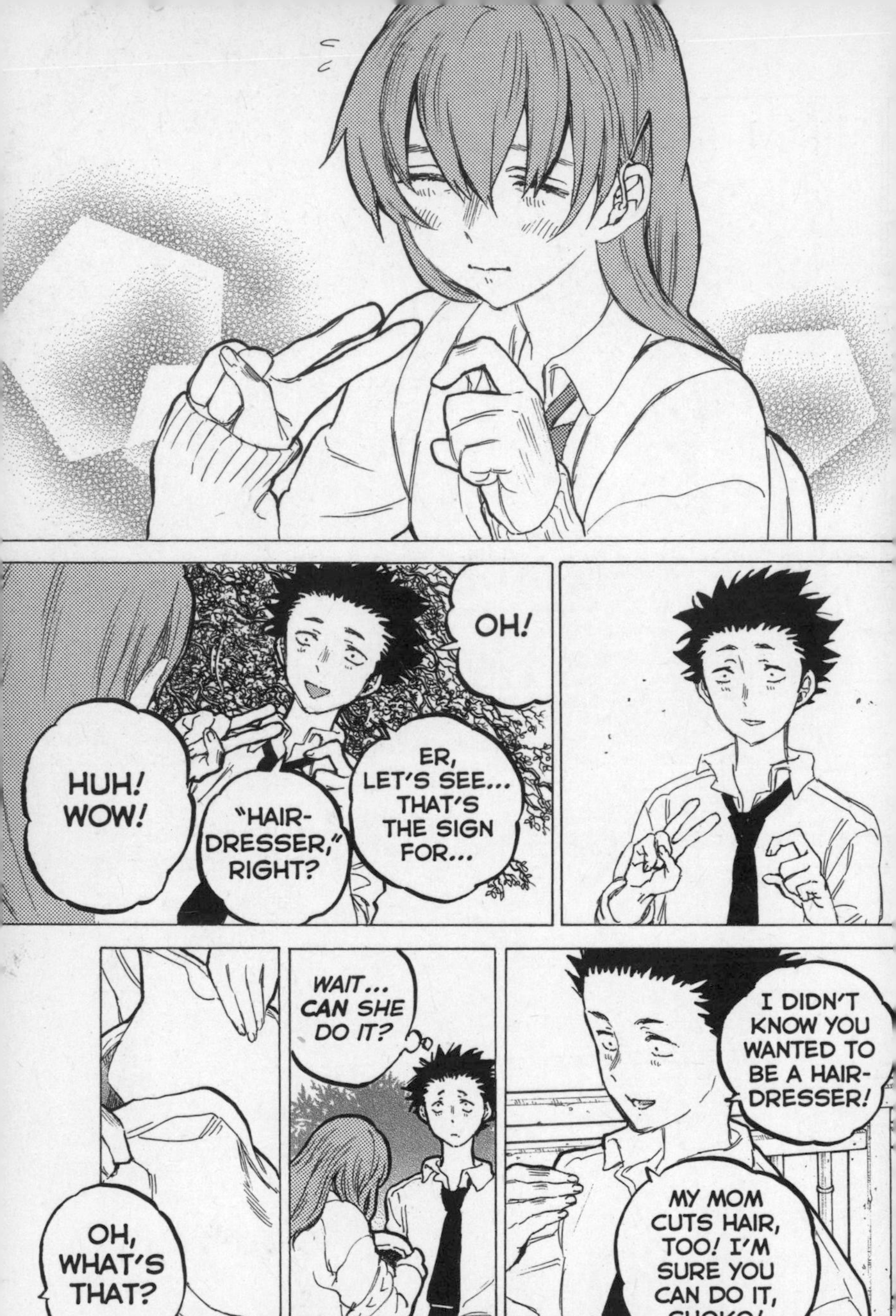
OH!
ER, LET'S SEE... THAT'S THE SIGN FOR...
"HAIR-DRESSER," RIGHT?
HUH! WOW!
I DIDN'T KNOW YOU WANTED TO BE A HAIR-DRESSER!
MY MOM CUTS HAIR, TOO! I'M SURE YOU CAN DO IT, SHOKO!
WAIT... CAN SHE DO IT?
OH, WHAT'S THAT?

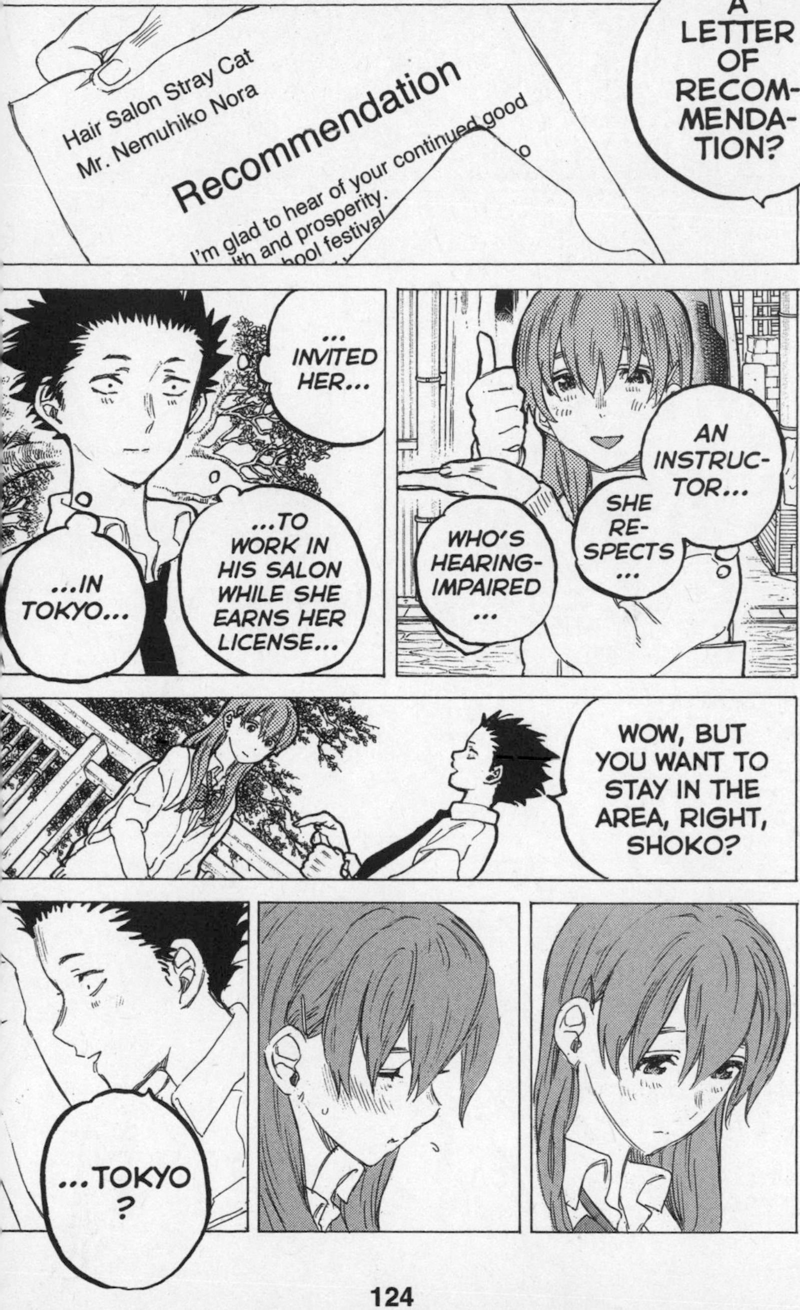
A LETTER OF RECOMMENDATION?
Hair Salon Stray Cat
Mr. Nemuhiko Nora
Recommendation
I'm glad to hear of your continued good
lth and prosperity.
hool festival
AN INSTRUCTOR...
SHE RESPECTS...
WHO'S HEARING-IMPAIRED...
...INVITED HER...
...TO WORK IN HIS SALON WHILE SHE EARNS HER LICENSE...
...IN TOKYO...
WOW, BUT YOU WANT TO STAY IN THE AREA, RIGHT, SHOKO?
...TOKYO?

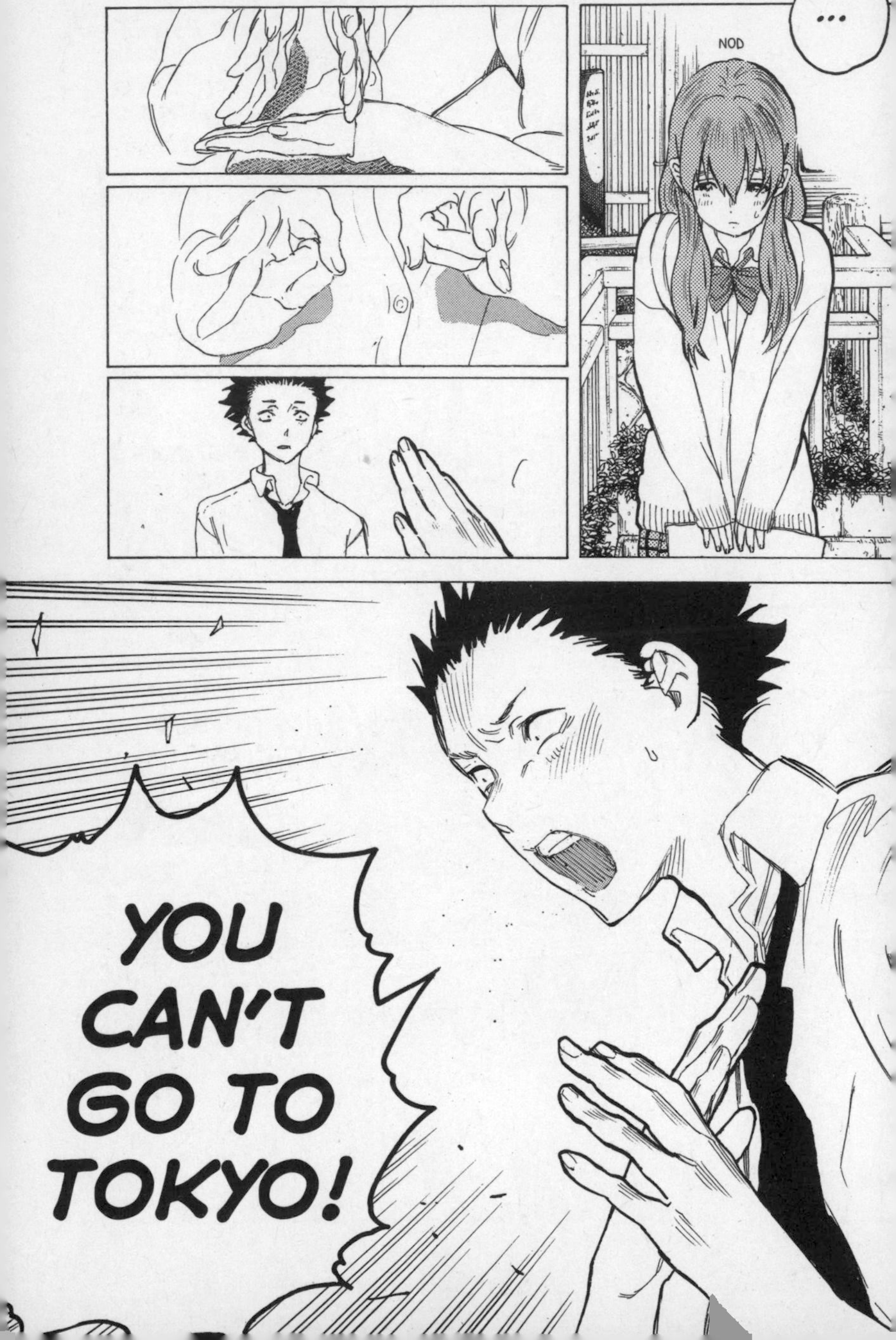
...
NOD
YOU CAN'T GO TO TOKYO!

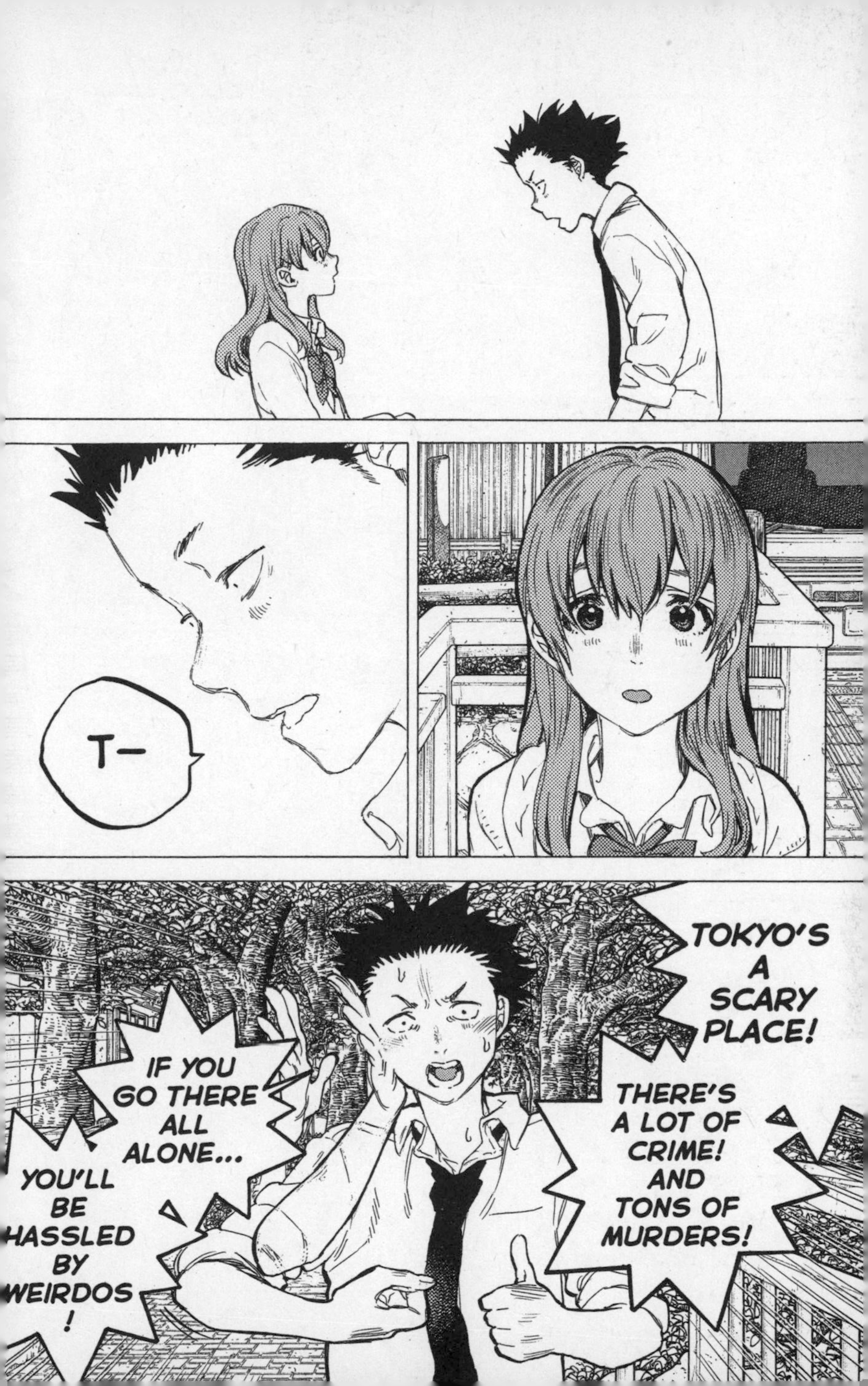
T–
TOKYO'S A SCARY PLACE!
THERE'S A LOT OF CRIME! AND TONS OF MURDERS!
IF YOU GO THERE ALL ALONE...
YOU'LL BE HASSLED BY WEIRDOS!

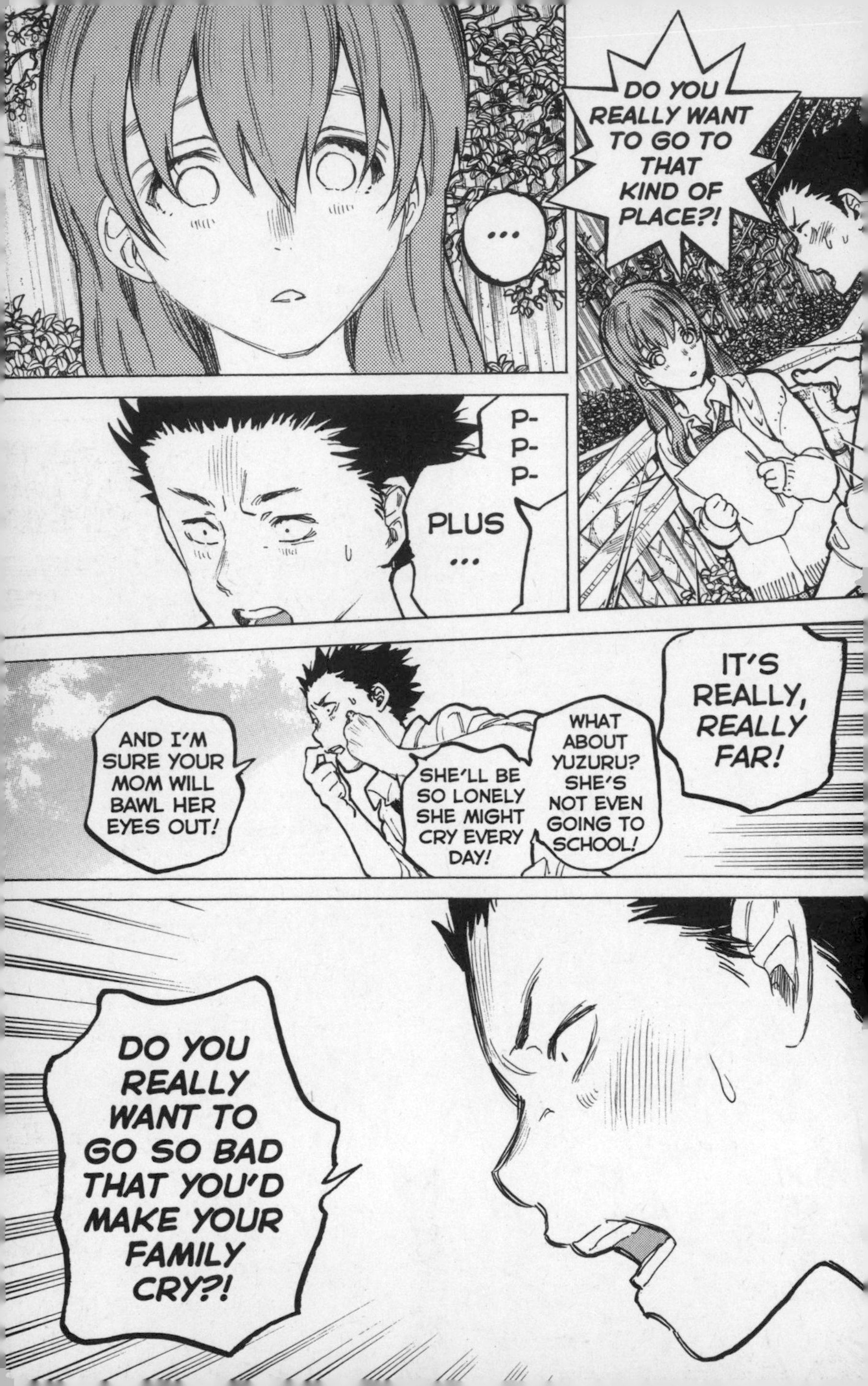
DO YOU REALLY WANT TO GO TO THAT KIND OF PLACE?!
...
P- P- P- PLUS ...
IT'S REALLY, *REALLY* FAR!
WHAT ABOUT YUZURU? SHE'S NOT EVEN GOING TO SCHOOL!
SHE'LL BE SO LONELY SHE MIGHT CRY EVERY DAY!
AND I'M SURE YOUR MOM WILL BAWL HER EYES OUT!
DO YOU REALLY WANT TO GO SO BAD THAT YOU'D MAKE YOUR FAMILY CRY?!

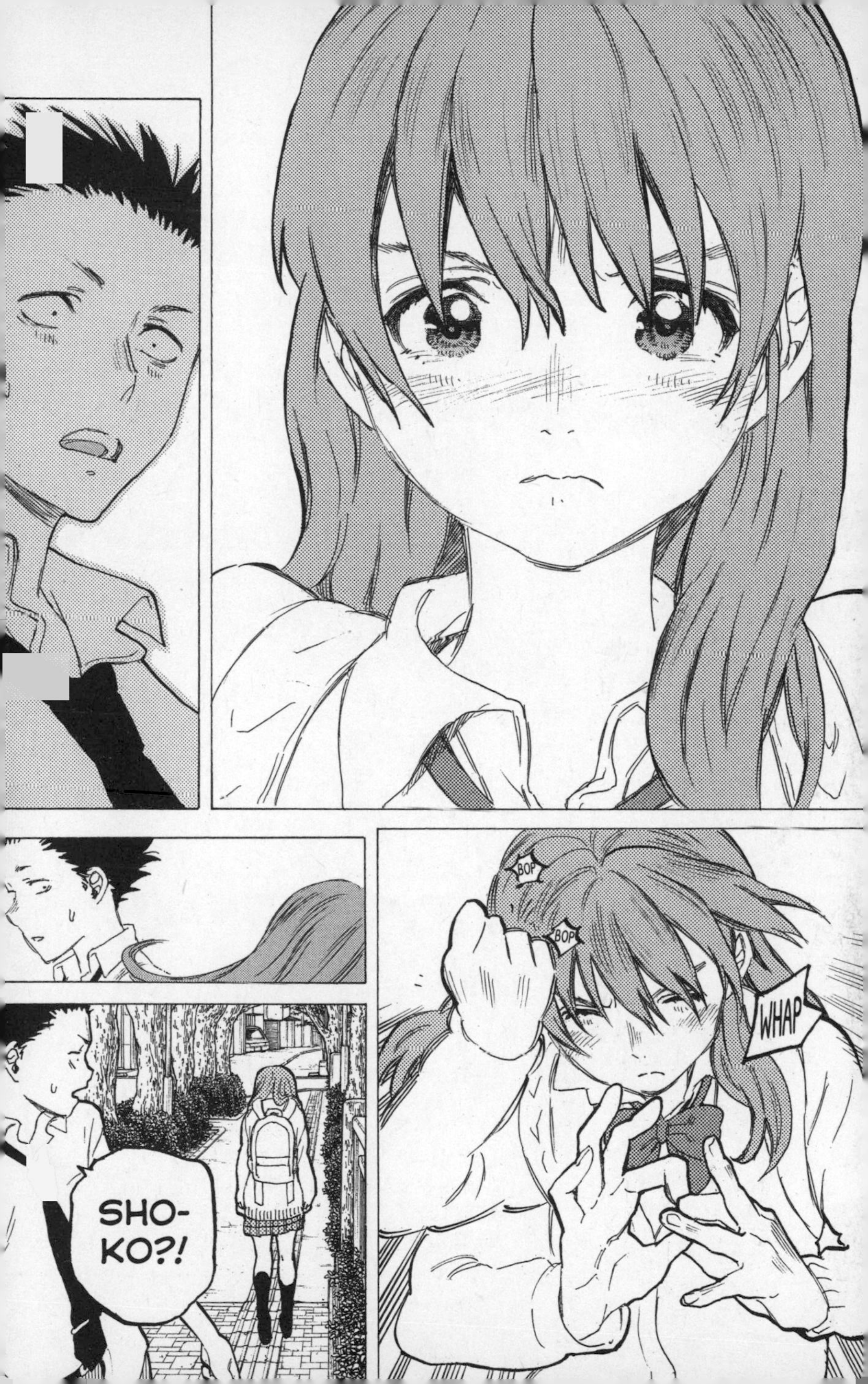
BOP
BOP
WHAP
SHO-KO?!

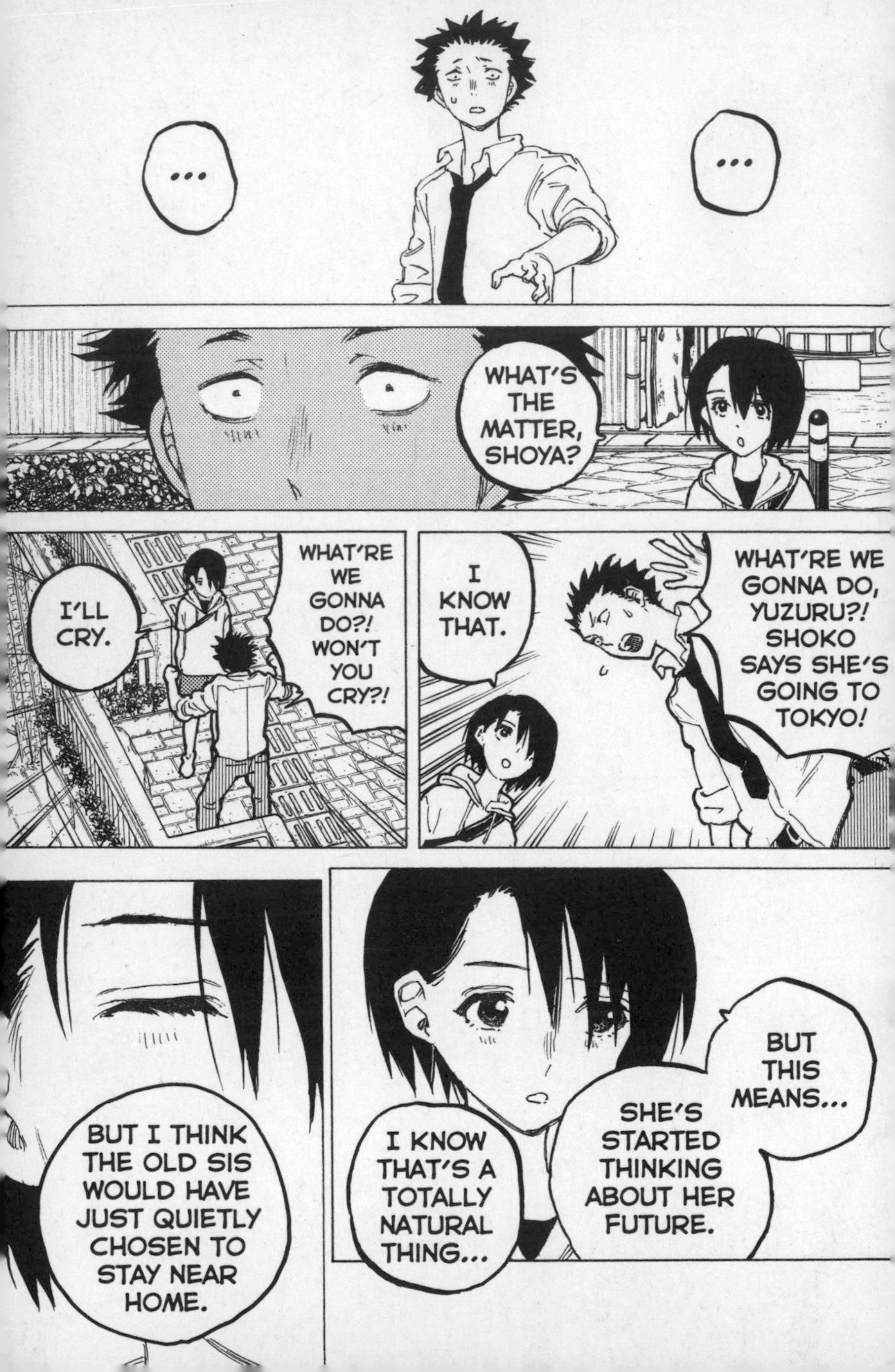
...
...
WHAT'S THE MATTER, SHOYA?
WHAT'RE WE GONNA DO, YUZURU?! SHOKO SAYS SHE'S GOING TO TOKYO!
I KNOW THAT.
WHAT'RE WE GONNA DO?! WON'T YOU CRY?!
I'LL CRY.
BUT THIS MEANS...
SHE'S STARTED THINKING ABOUT HER FUTURE.
I KNOW THAT'S A TOTALLY NATURAL THING...
BUT I THINK THE OLD SIS WOULD HAVE JUST QUIETLY CHOSEN TO STAY NEAR HOME.

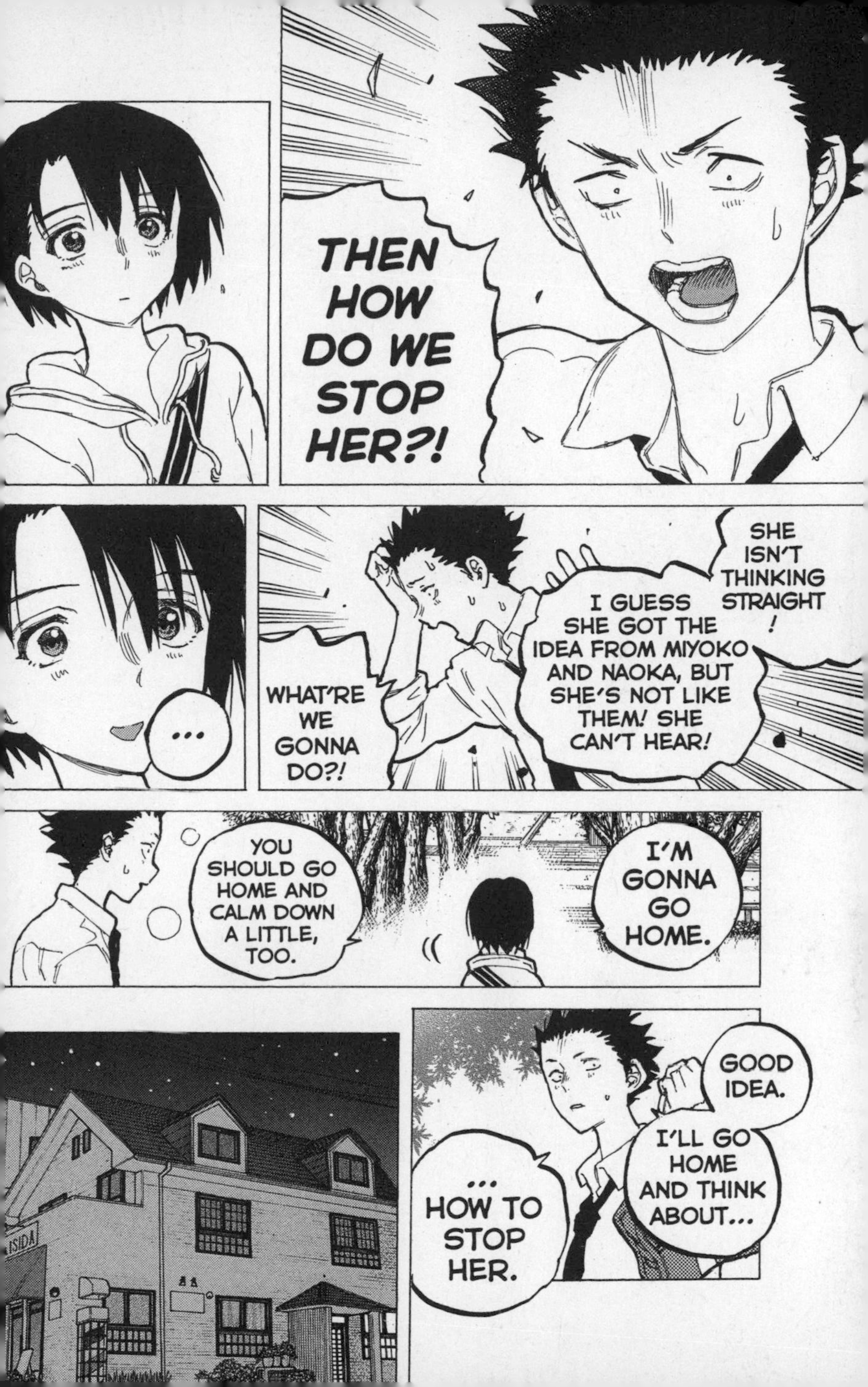
THEN HOW DO WE STOP HER?!
SHE ISN'T THINKING STRAIGHT!
I GUESS SHE GOT THE IDEA FROM MIYOKO AND NAOKA, BUT SHE'S NOT LIKE THEM! SHE CAN'T HEAR!
WHAT'RE WE GONNA DO?!
...
I'M GONNA GO HOME.
YOU SHOULD GO HOME AND CALM DOWN A LITTLE, TOO.
GOOD IDEA.
I'LL GO HOME AND THINK ABOUT...
... HOW TO STOP HER.
ISIDA

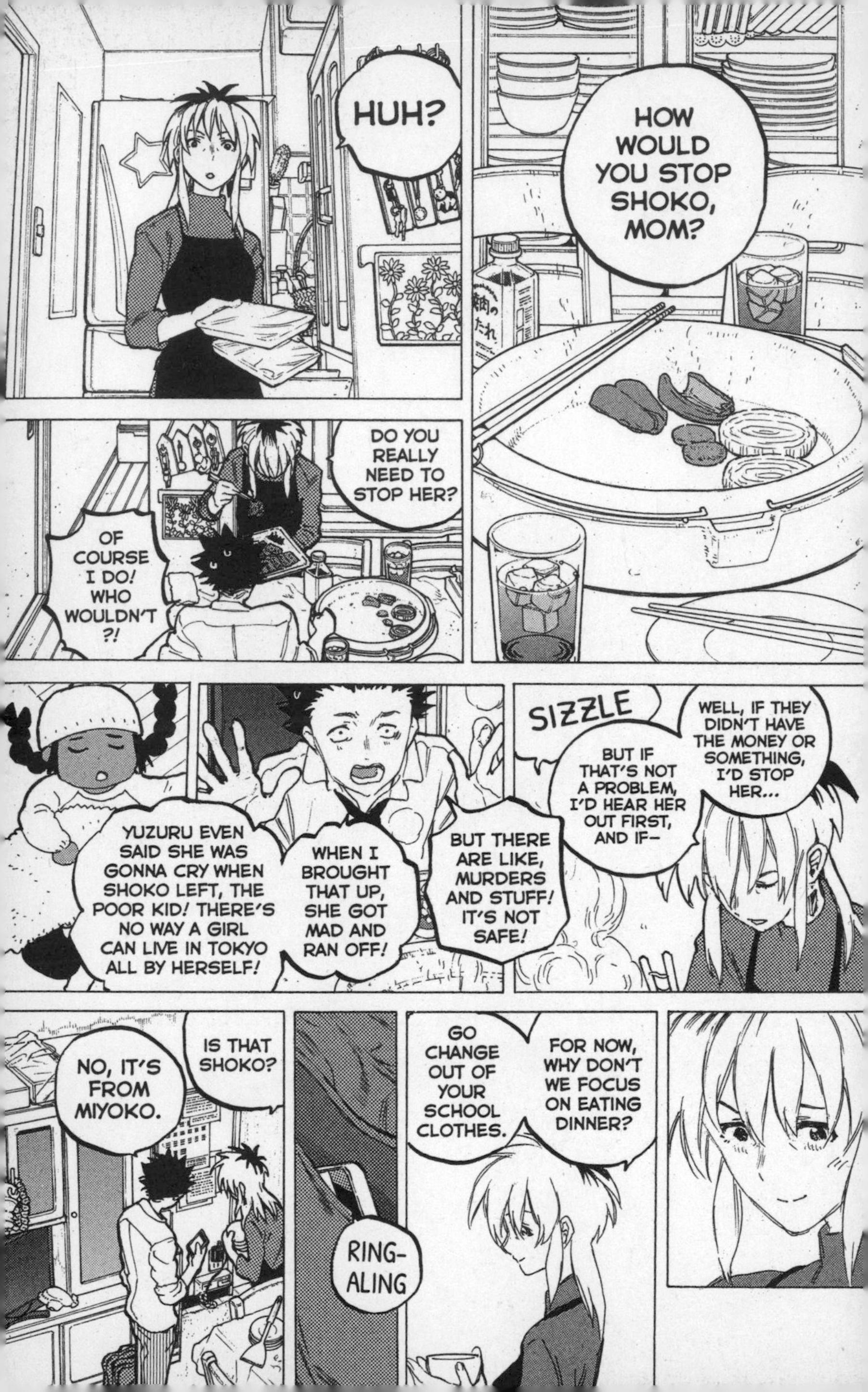
HOW WOULD YOU STOP SHOKO, MOM?
HUH?
DO YOU REALLY NEED TO STOP HER?
OF COURSE I DO! WHO WOULDN'T ?!
SIZZLE
WELL, IF THEY DIDN'T HAVE THE MONEY OR SOMETHING, I'D STOP HER...
BUT IF THAT'S NOT A PROBLEM, I'D HEAR HER OUT FIRST, AND IF–
BUT THERE ARE LIKE, MURDERS AND STUFF! IT'S NOT SAFE!
WHEN I BROUGHT THAT UP, SHE GOT MAD AND RAN OFF!
YUZURU EVEN SAID SHE WAS GONNA CRY WHEN SHOKO LEFT, THE POOR KID! THERE'S NO WAY A GIRL CAN LIVE IN TOKYO ALL BY HERSELF!
FOR NOW, WHY DON'T WE FOCUS ON EATING DINNER?
GO CHANGE OUT OF YOUR SCHOOL CLOTHES.
RING-ALING
IS THAT SHOKO?
NO, IT'S FROM MIYOKO.

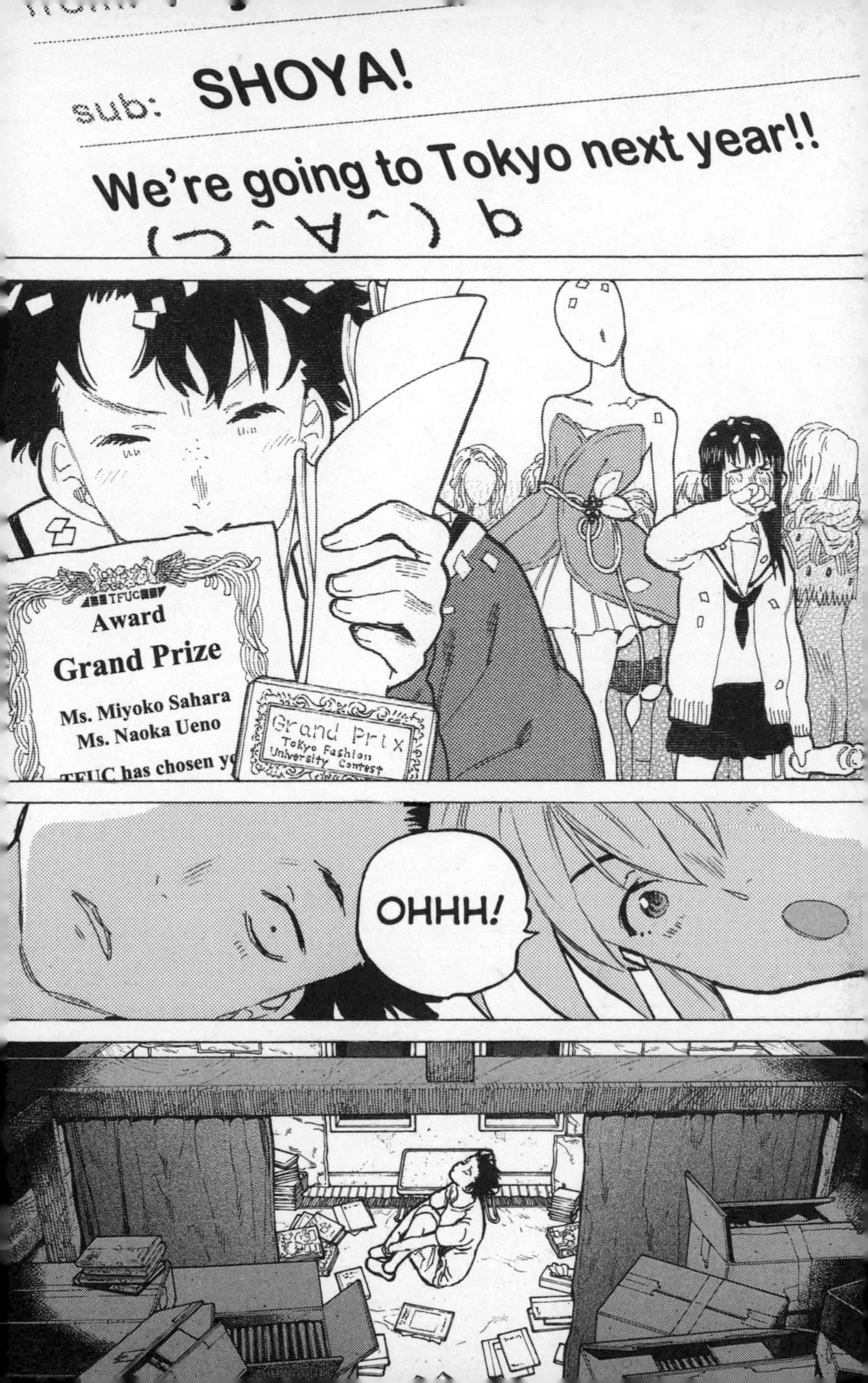
sub: SHOYA!
We're going to Tokyo next year!!
TFUC
Award
Grand Prize
Ms. Miyoko Sahara
Ms. Naoka Ueno
Grand Prix
Tokyo Fashion University Contest
OHHH!

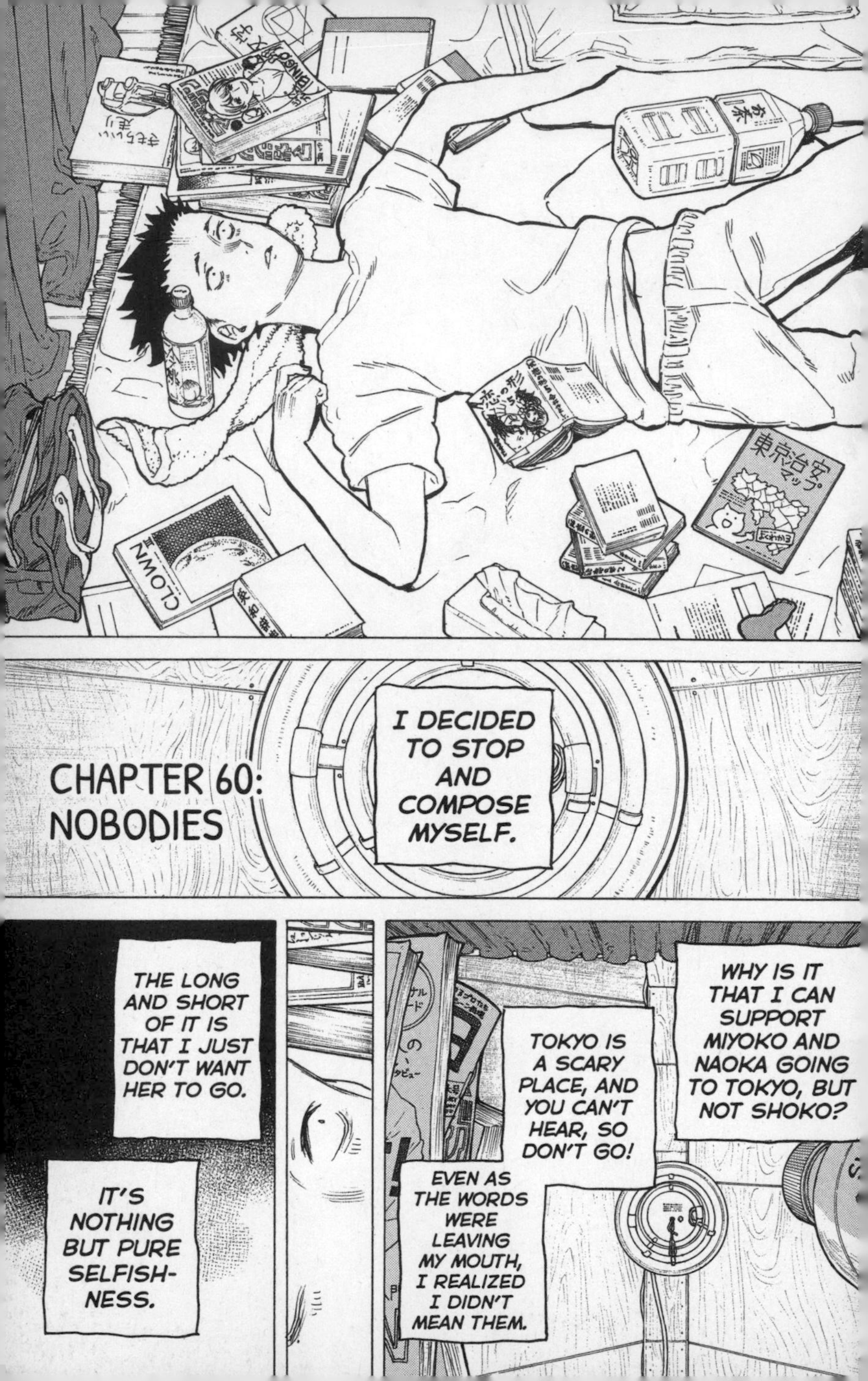
CLOWN
東京治安マップ
I DECIDED TO STOP AND COMPOSE MYSELF.
CHAPTER 60: NOBODIES
WHY IS IT THAT I CAN SUPPORT MIYOKO AND NAOKA GOING TO TOKYO, BUT NOT SHOKO?
TOKYO IS A SCARY PLACE, AND YOU CAN'T HEAR, SO DON'T GO!
EVEN AS THE WORDS WERE LEAVING MY MOUTH, I REALIZED I DIDN'T MEAN THEM.
THE LONG AND SHORT OF IT IS THAT I JUST DON'T WANT HER TO GO.
IT'S NOTHING BUT PURE SELFISH-NESS.

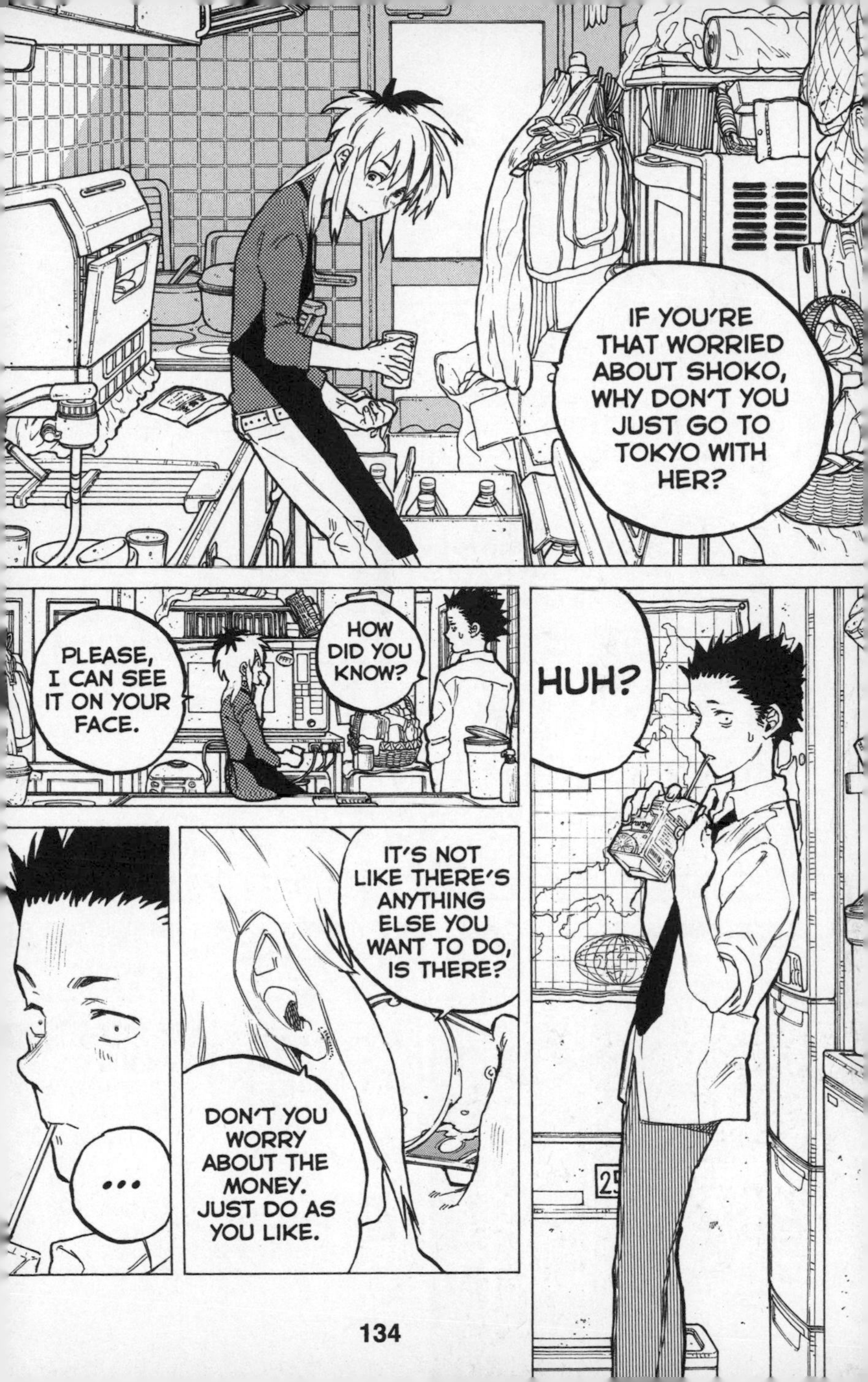
IF YOU'RE THAT WORRIED ABOUT SHOKO, WHY DON'T YOU JUST GO TO TOKYO WITH HER?
HUH?
HOW DID YOU KNOW?
PLEASE, I CAN SEE IT ON YOUR FACE.
IT'S NOT LIKE THERE'S ANYTHING ELSE YOU WANT TO DO, IS THERE?
DON'T YOU WORRY ABOUT THE MONEY. JUST DO AS YOU LIKE.
...

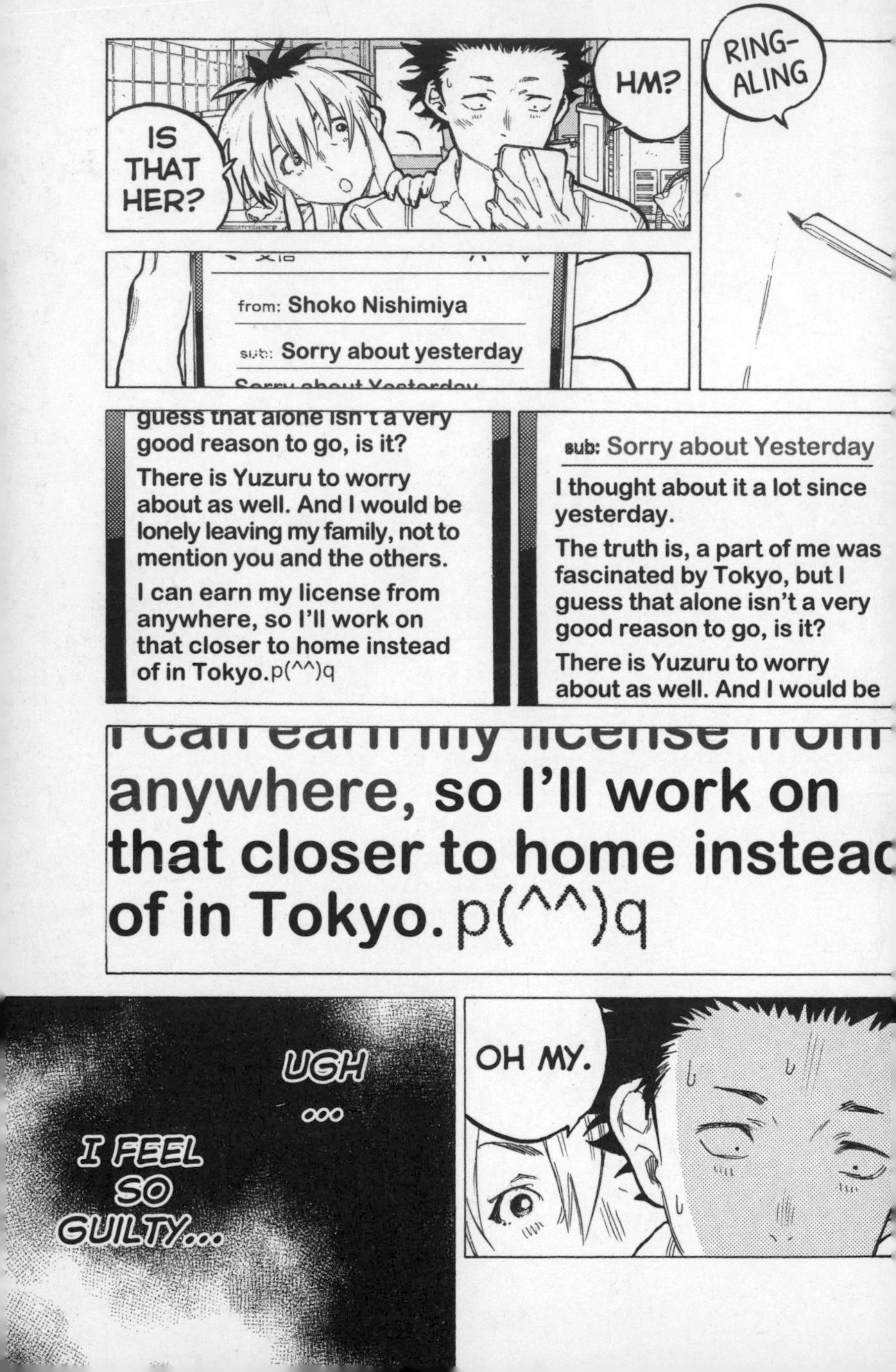

RING-ALING
HM?
IS THAT HER?
from: Shoko Nishimiya
sub: Sorry about yesterday
sub: Sorry about Yesterday
I thought about it a lot since yesterday.
The truth is, a part of me was fascinated by Tokyo, but I guess that alone isn't a very good reason to go, is it?
There is Yuzuru to worry about as well. And I would be
guess that alone isn't a very good reason to go, is it?
There is Yuzuru to worry about as well. And I would be lonely leaving my family, not to mention you and the others.
I can earn my license from anywhere, so I'll work on that closer to home instead of in Tokyo. p(^^)q
anywhere, so I'll work on that closer to home instead of in Tokyo. p(^^)q
OH MY.
UGH ...
I FEEL SO GUILTY...

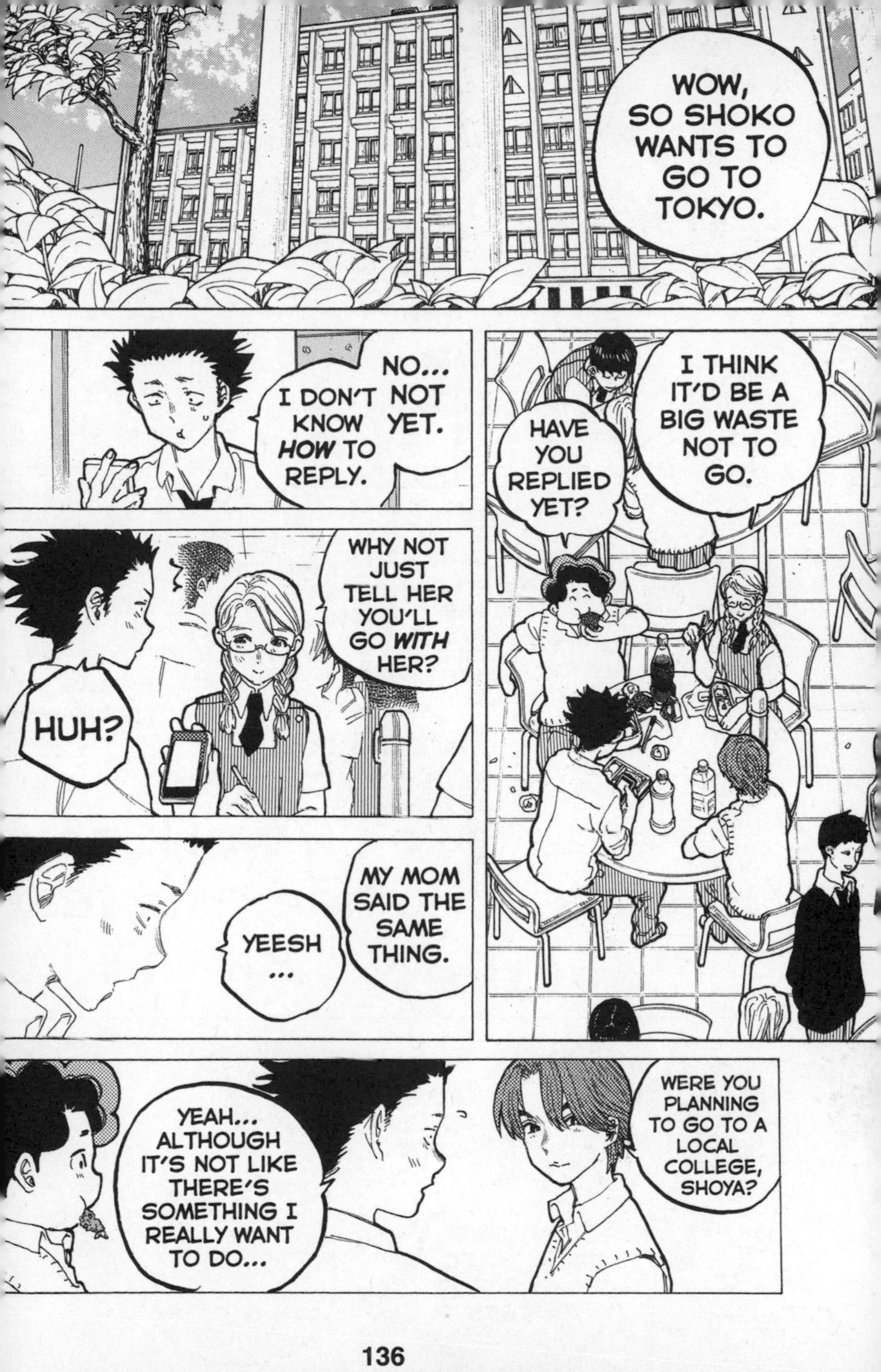
WOW, SO SHOKO WANTS TO GO TO TOKYO.
I THINK IT'D BE A BIG WASTE NOT TO GO.
HAVE YOU REPLIED YET?
NO... NOT YET.
I DON'T KNOW *HOW* TO REPLY.
WHY NOT JUST TELL HER YOU'LL GO *WITH* HER?
HUH?
MY MOM SAID THE SAME THING.
YEESH...
WERE YOU PLANNING TO GO TO A LOCAL COLLEGE, SHOYA?
YEAH... ALTHOUGH IT'S NOT LIKE THERE'S SOMETHING I REALLY WANT TO DO...

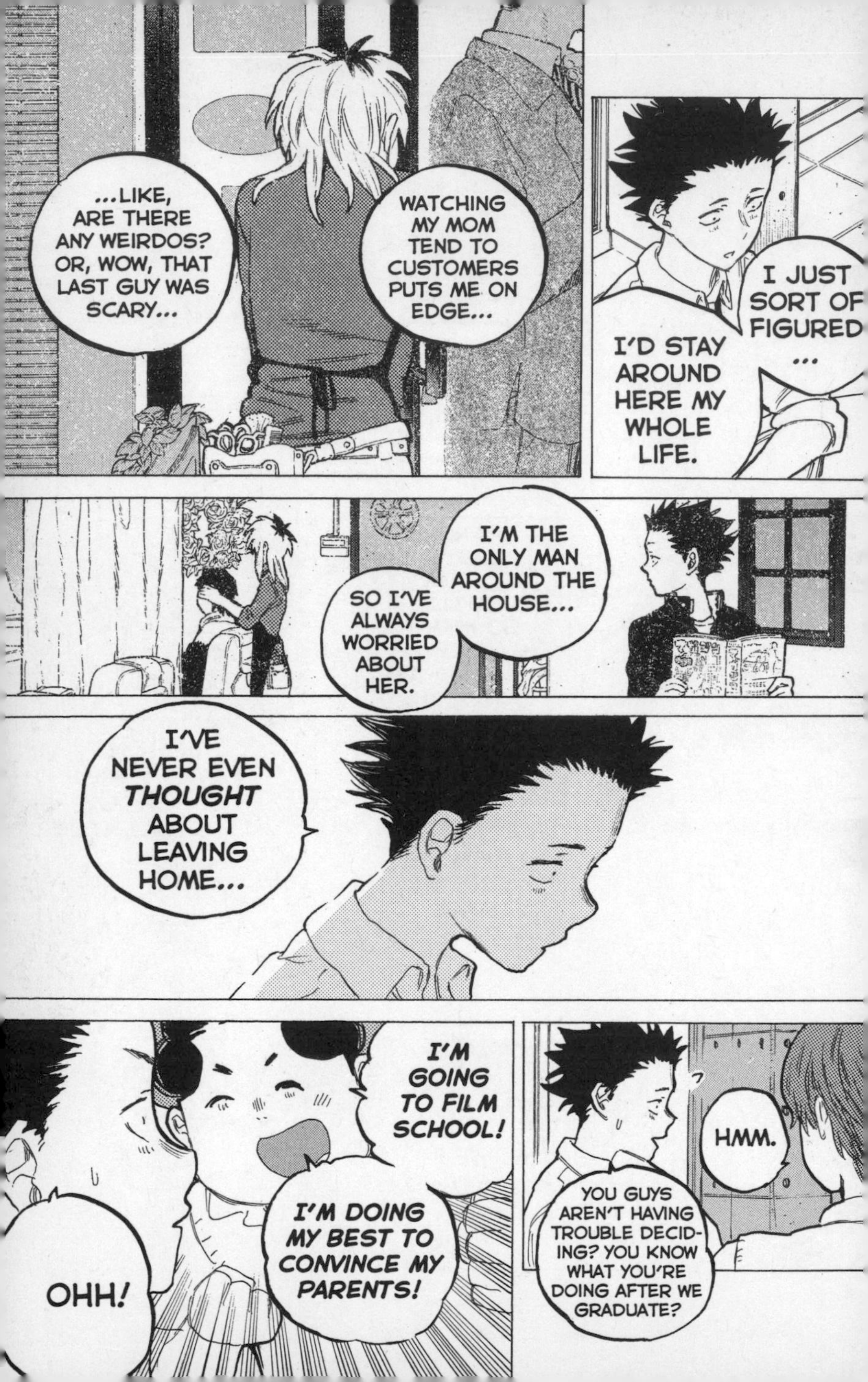
I JUST SORT OF FIGURED...
I'D STAY AROUND HERE MY WHOLE LIFE.
WATCHING MY MOM TEND TO CUSTOMERS PUTS ME ON EDGE...
...LIKE, ARE THERE ANY WEIRDOS? OR, WOW, THAT LAST GUY WAS SCARY...
I'M THE ONLY MAN AROUND THE HOUSE...
SO I'VE ALWAYS WORRIED ABOUT HER.
I'VE NEVER EVEN *THOUGHT* ABOUT LEAVING HOME...
HMM.
YOU GUYS AREN'T HAVING TROUBLE DECIDING? YOU KNOW WHAT YOU'RE DOING AFTER WE GRADUATE?
I'M GOING TO FILM SCHOOL!
I'M DOING MY BEST TO CONVINCE MY PARENTS!
OHH!

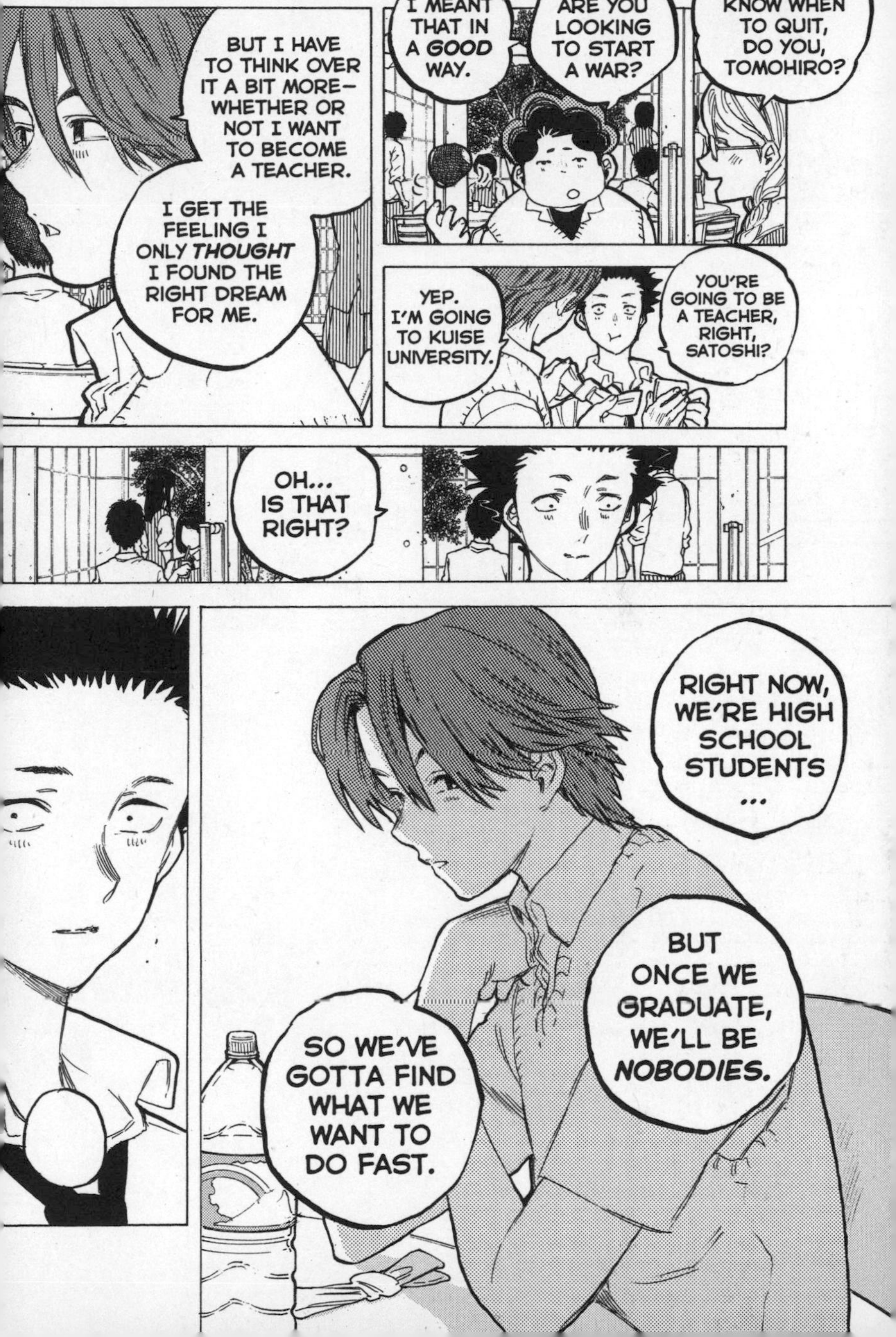
HEHEH! YOU DON'T KNOW WHEN TO QUIT, DO YOU, TOMOHIRO?
WHAT? ARE YOU LOOKING TO START A WAR?
I MEANT THAT IN A *GOOD* WAY.
YOU'RE GOING TO BE A TEACHER, RIGHT, SATOSHI?
YEP. I'M GOING TO KUISE UNIVERSITY.
BUT I HAVE TO THINK OVER IT A BIT MORE— WHETHER OR NOT I WANT TO BECOME A TEACHER.
I GET THE FEELING I ONLY *THOUGHT* I FOUND THE RIGHT DREAM FOR ME.
OH... IS THAT RIGHT?
RIGHT NOW, WE'RE HIGH SCHOOL STUDENTS ...
BUT ONCE WE GRADUATE, WE'LL BE *NOBODIES.*
SO WE'VE GOTTA FIND WHAT WE WANT TO DO FAST.

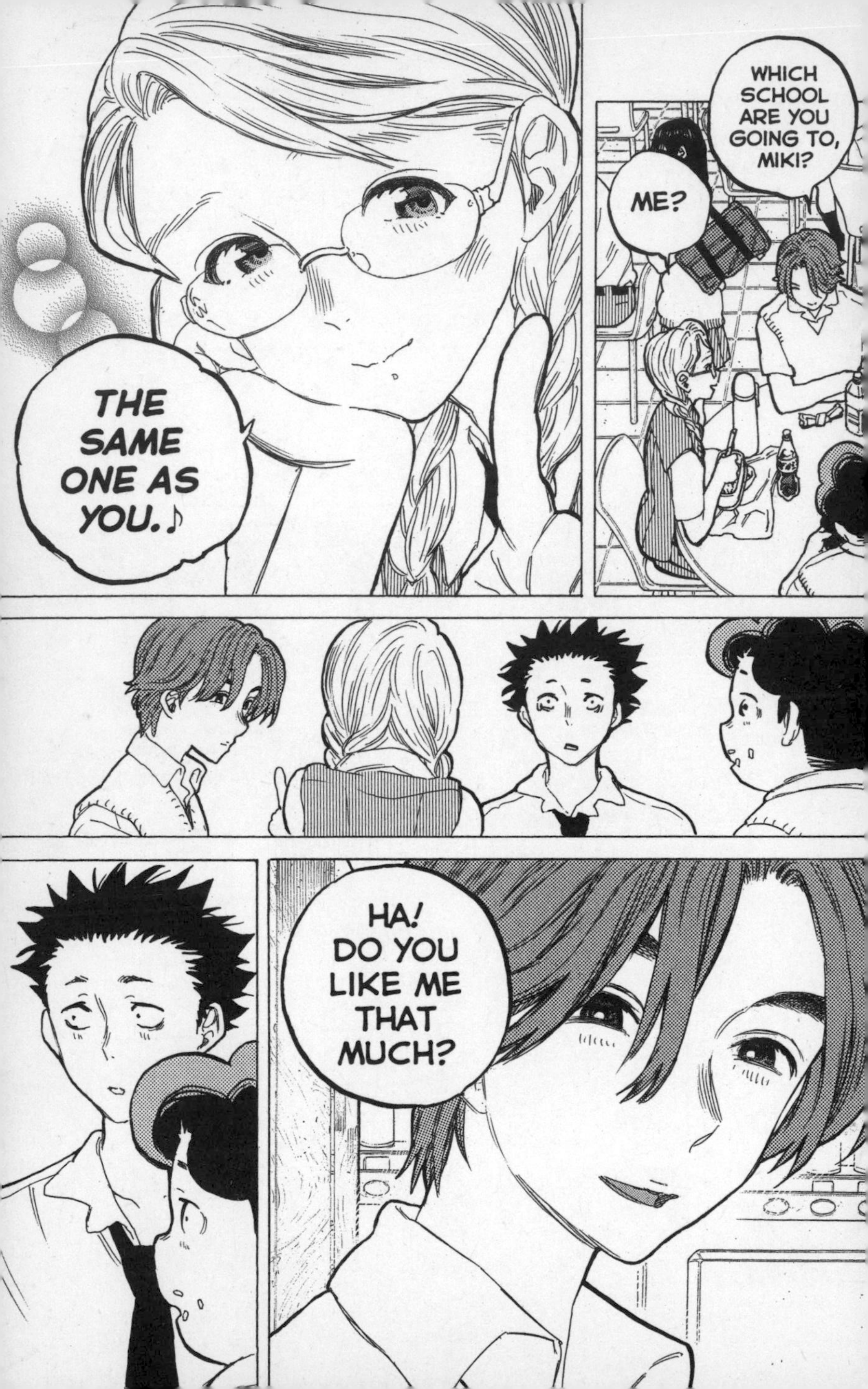
WHICH SCHOOL ARE YOU GOING TO, MIKI?
ME?
THE SAME ONE AS YOU.♪
HA! DO YOU LIKE ME THAT MUCH?

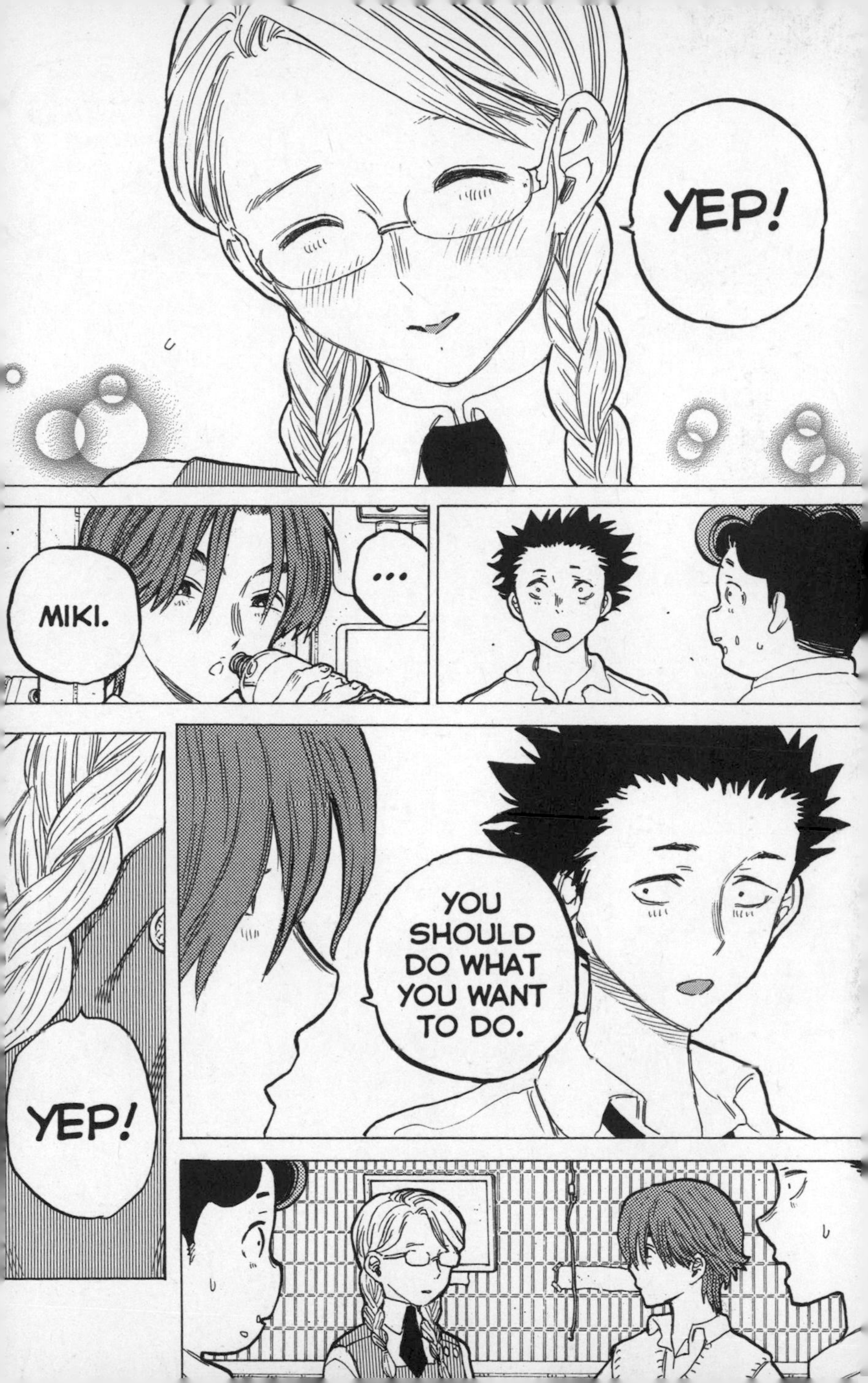
YEP!
...
MIKI.
YOU SHOULD DO WHAT YOU WANT TO DO.
YEP!

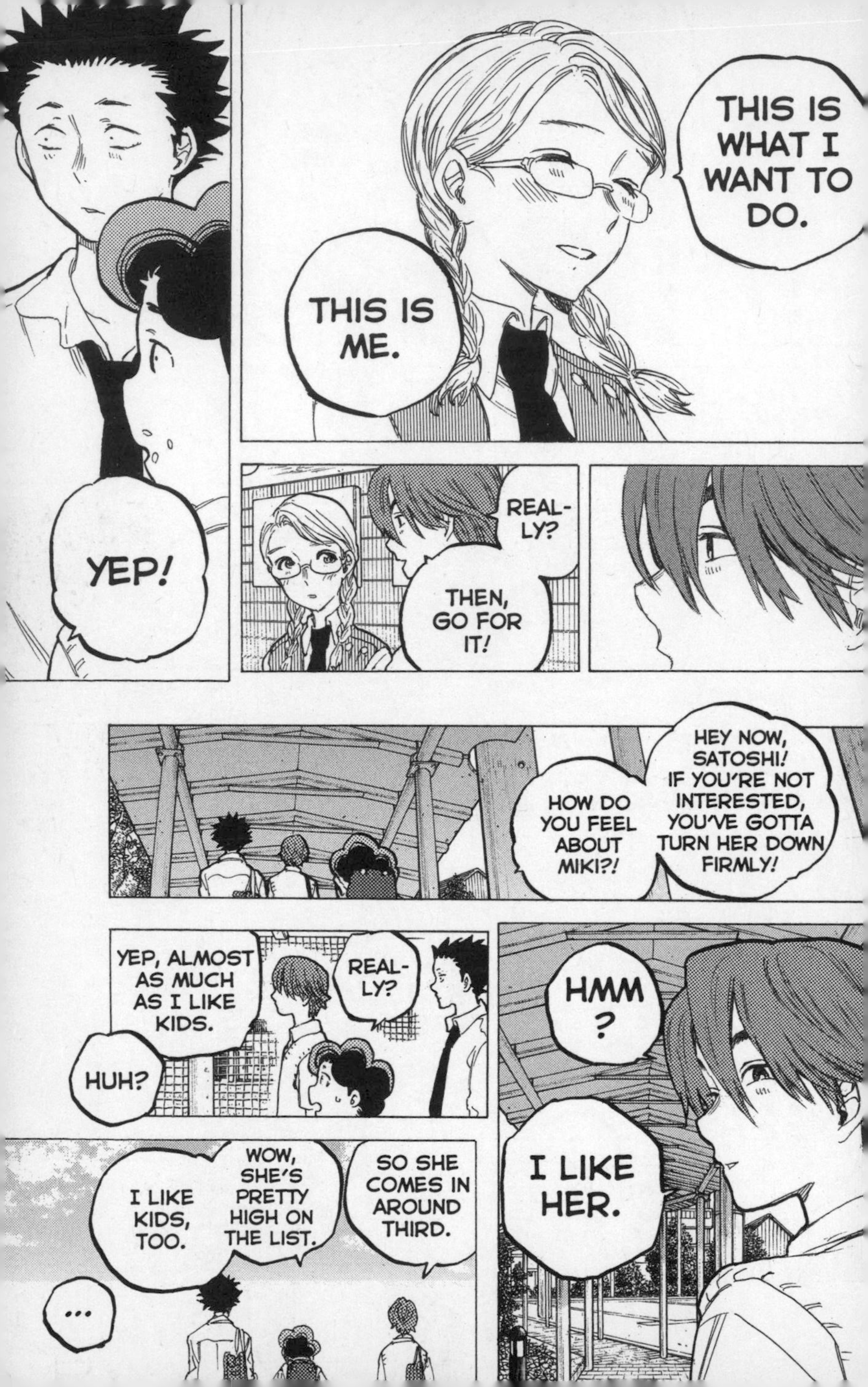
THIS IS WHAT I WANT TO DO.
THIS IS ME.
REAL-LY?
THEN, GO FOR IT!
YEP!
HEY NOW, SATOSHI! IF YOU'RE NOT INTERESTED, YOU'VE GOTTA TURN HER DOWN FIRMLY!
HOW DO YOU FEEL ABOUT MIKI?!
HMM?
I LIKE HER.
REAL-LY?
YEP, ALMOST AS MUCH AS I LIKE KIDS.
HUH?
SO SHE COMES IN AROUND THIRD.
WOW, SHE'S PRETTY HIGH ON THE LIST.
I LIKE KIDS, TOO.
...

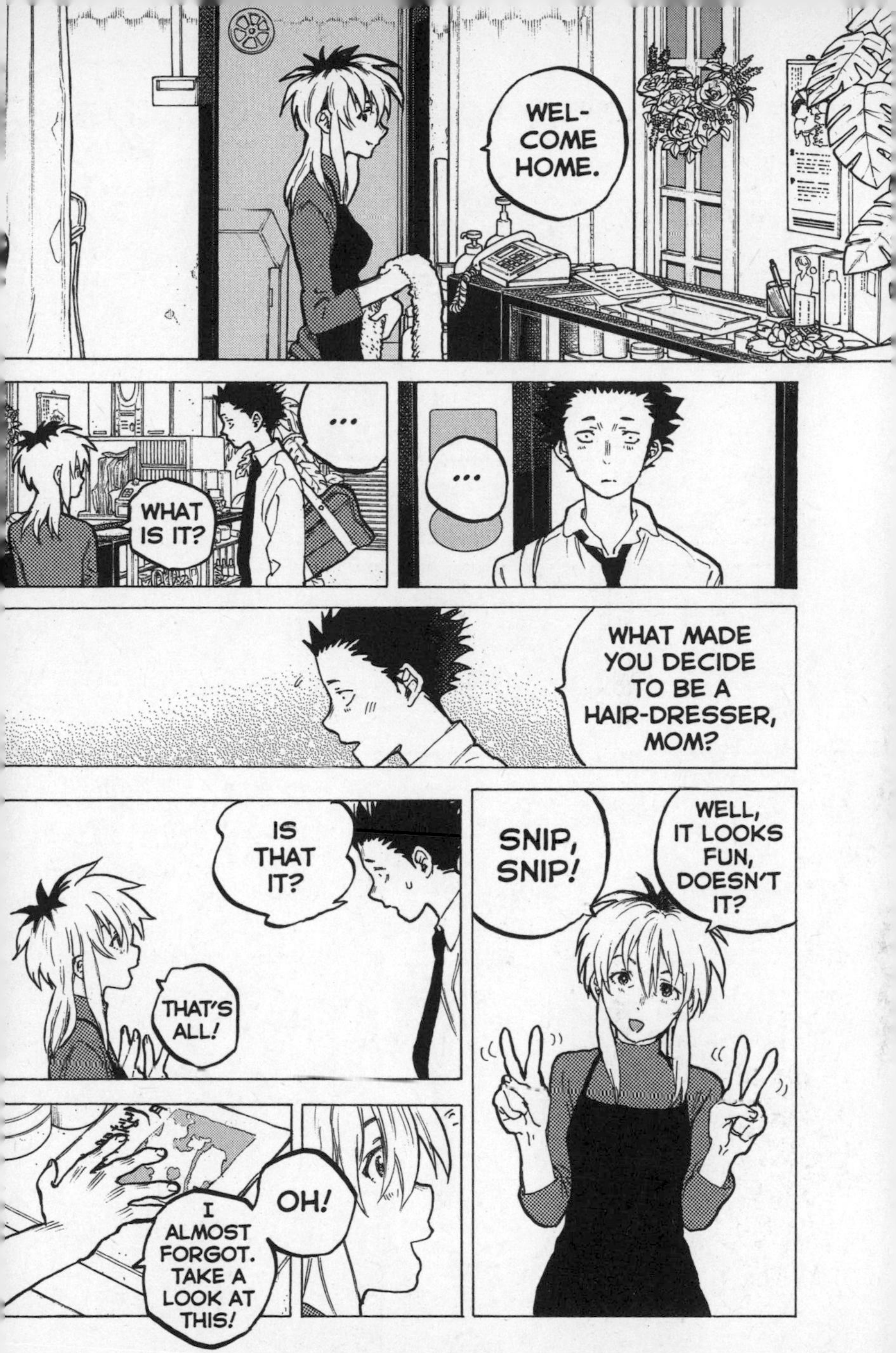
WEL-COME HOME.
...
...
WHAT IS IT?
WHAT MADE YOU DECIDE TO BE A HAIR-DRESSER, MOM?
WELL, IT LOOKS FUN, DOESN'T IT?
SNIP, SNIP!
IS THAT IT?
THAT'S ALL!
OH!
I ALMOST FORGOT. TAKE A LOOK AT THIS!

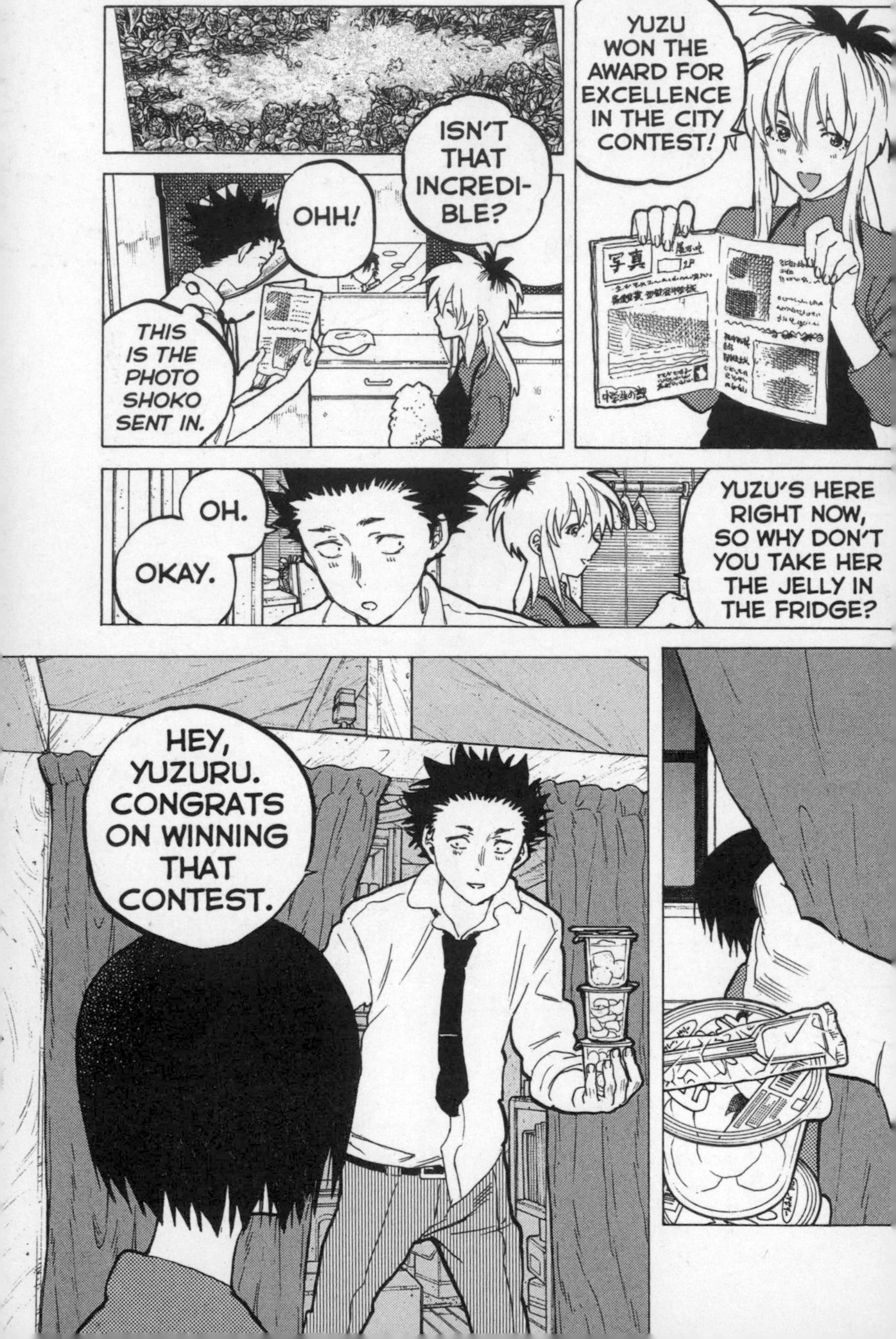
YUZU WON THE AWARD FOR EXCELLENCE IN THE CITY CONTEST!
写真
ISN'T THAT INCREDIBLE?
OHH!
THIS IS THE PHOTO SHOKO SENT IN.
YUZU'S HERE RIGHT NOW, SO WHY DON'T YOU TAKE HER THE JELLY IN THE FRIDGE?
OH.
OKAY.
HEY, YUZURU. CONGRATS ON WINNING THAT CONTEST.

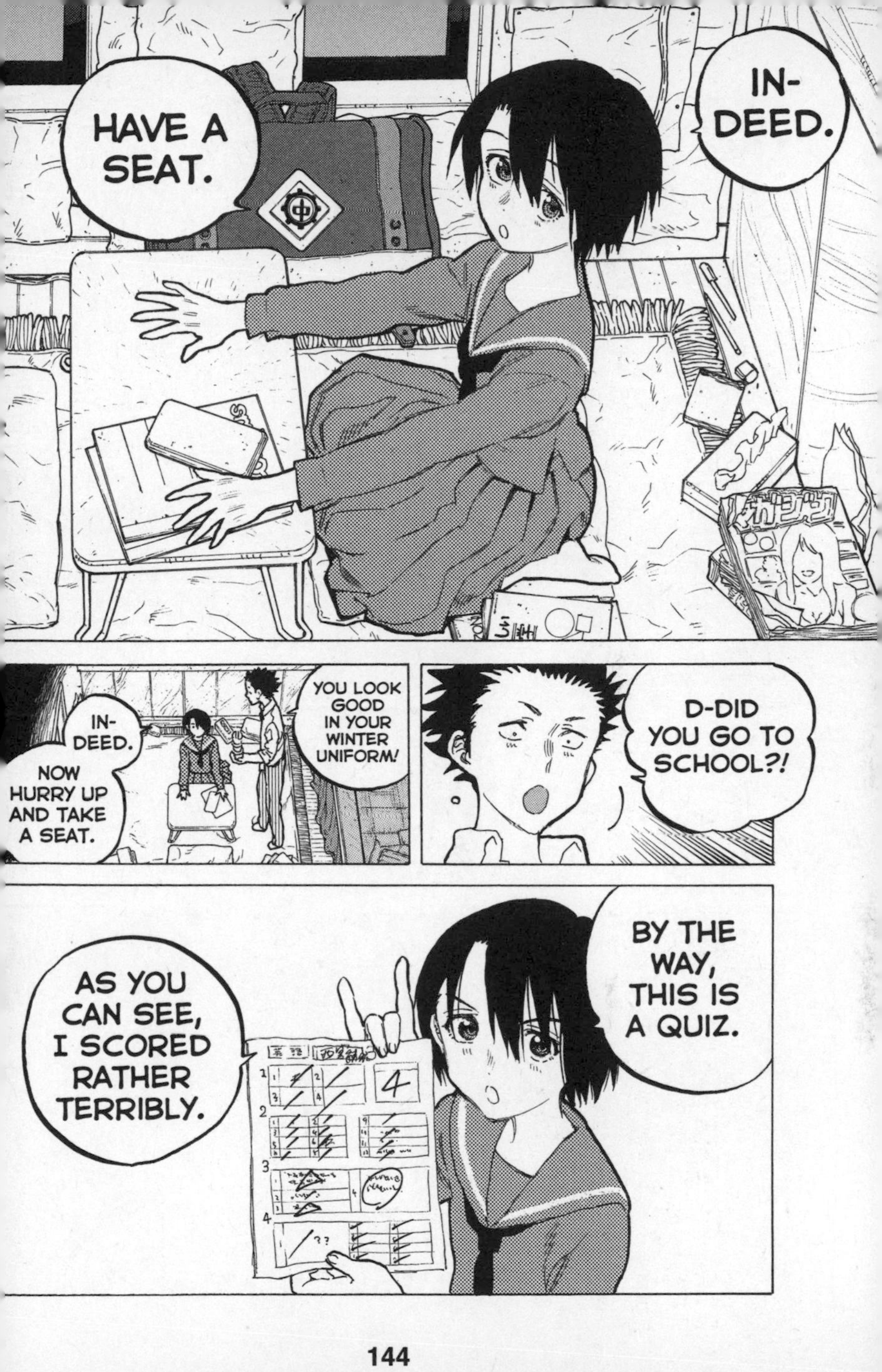
IN-DEED.
HAVE A SEAT.
D-DID YOU GO TO SCHOOL?!
YOU LOOK GOOD IN YOUR WINTER UNIFORM!
IN-DEED.
NOW HURRY UP AND TAKE A SEAT.
BY THE WAY, THIS IS A QUIZ.
AS YOU CAN SEE, I SCORED RATHER TERRIBLY.

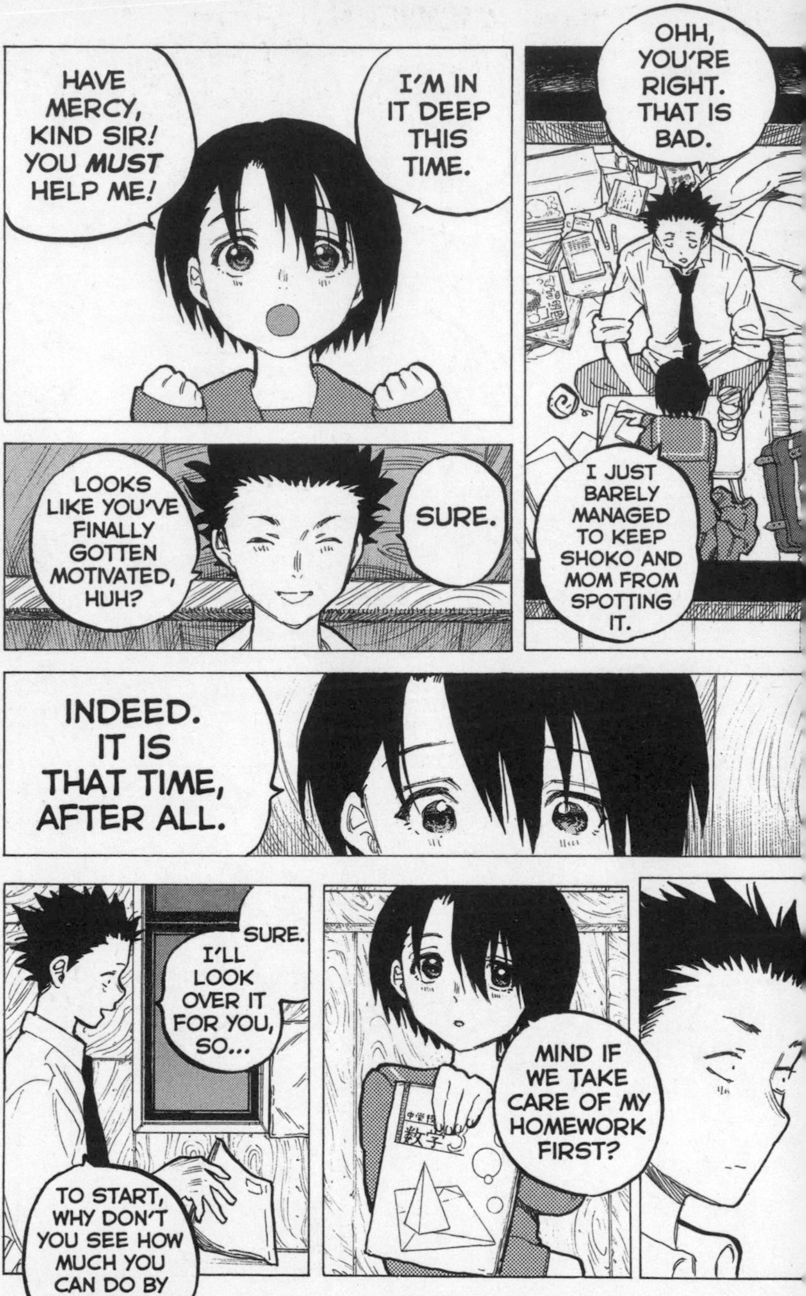
OHH, YOU'RE RIGHT. THAT IS BAD.
I JUST BARELY MANAGED TO KEEP SHOKO AND MOM FROM SPOTTING IT.
I'M IN IT DEEP THIS TIME.
HAVE MERCY, KIND SIR! YOU *MUST* HELP ME!
SURE.
LOOKS LIKE YOU'VE FINALLY GOTTEN MOTIVATED, HUH?
INDEED. IT IS THAT TIME, AFTER ALL.
MIND IF WE TAKE CARE OF MY HOMEWORK FIRST?
SURE. I'LL LOOK OVER IT FOR YOU, SO...
TO START, WHY DON'T YOU SEE HOW MUCH YOU CAN DO BY YOURSELF?

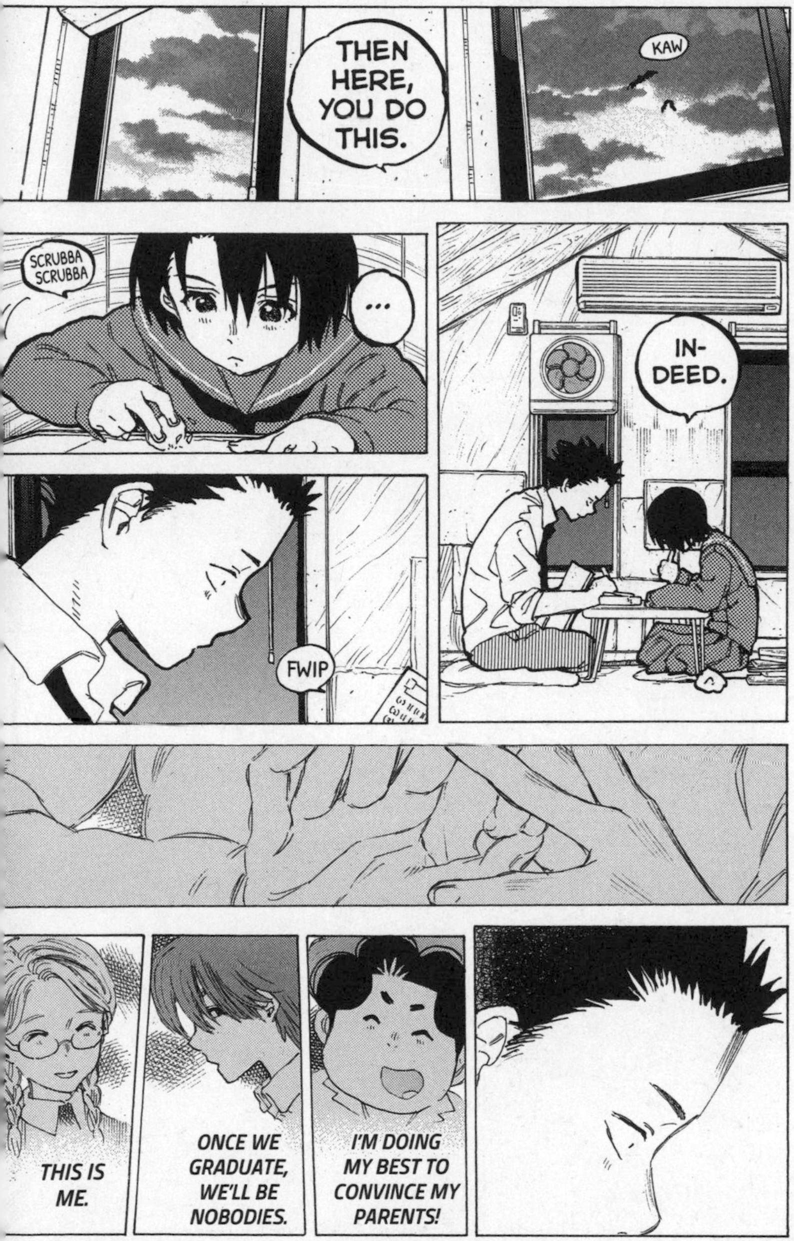
KAW
THEN HERE, YOU DO THIS.
IN-DEED.
...
SCRUBBA SCRUBBA
FWIP
I'M DOING MY BEST TO CONVINCE MY PARENTS!
ONCE WE GRADUATE, WE'LL BE NOBODIES.
THIS IS ME.

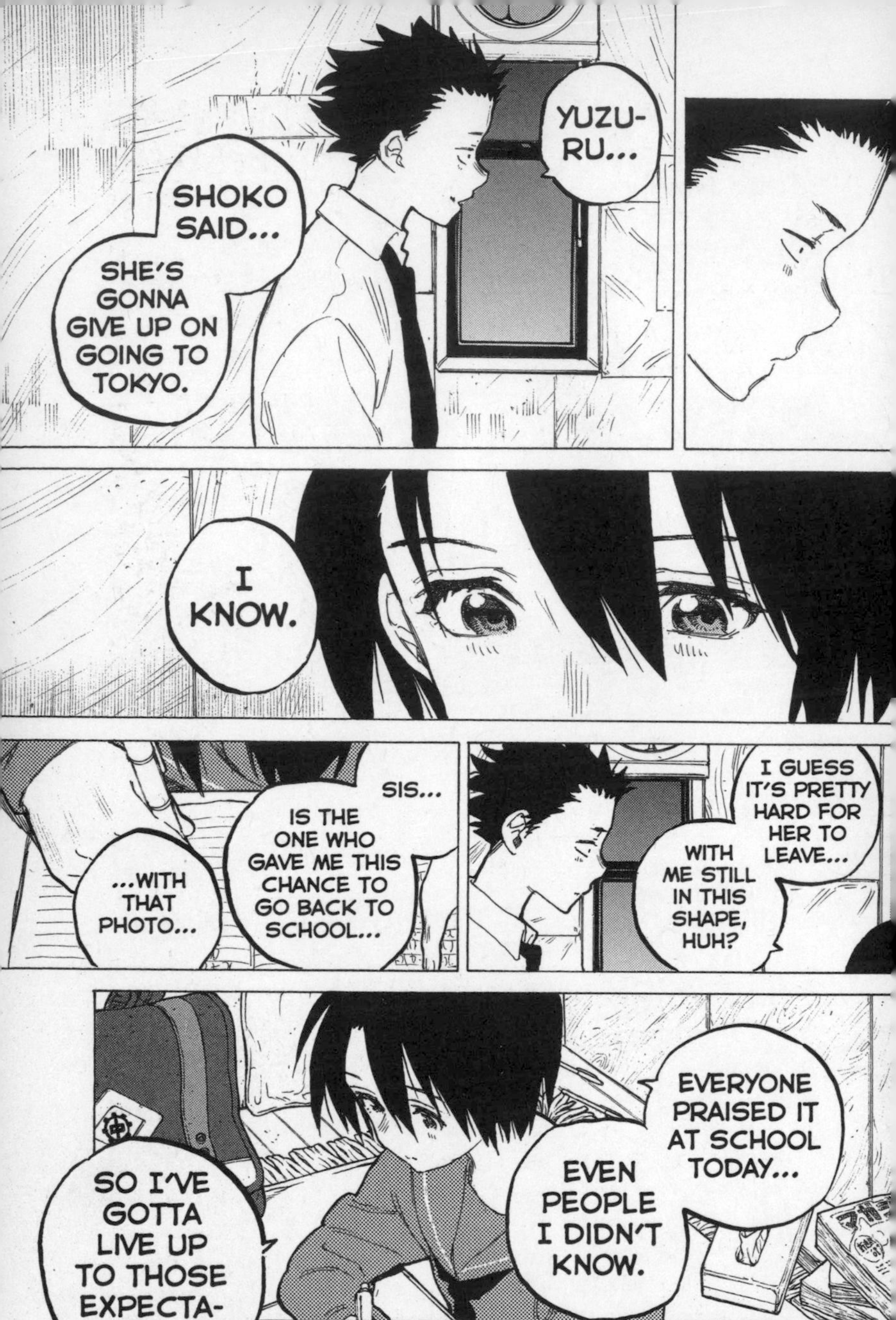
YUZU-RU...
SHOKO SAID...
SHE'S GONNA GIVE UP ON GOING TO TOKYO.
I KNOW.
I GUESS IT'S PRETTY HARD FOR HER TO LEAVE...
WITH ME STILL IN THIS SHAPE, HUH?
SIS...
IS THE ONE WHO GAVE ME THIS CHANCE TO GO BACK TO SCHOOL...
...WITH THAT PHOTO...
EVERYONE PRAISED IT AT SCHOOL TODAY...
EVEN PEOPLE I DIDN'T KNOW.
SO I'VE GOTTA LIVE UP TO THOSE EXPECTATIONS.

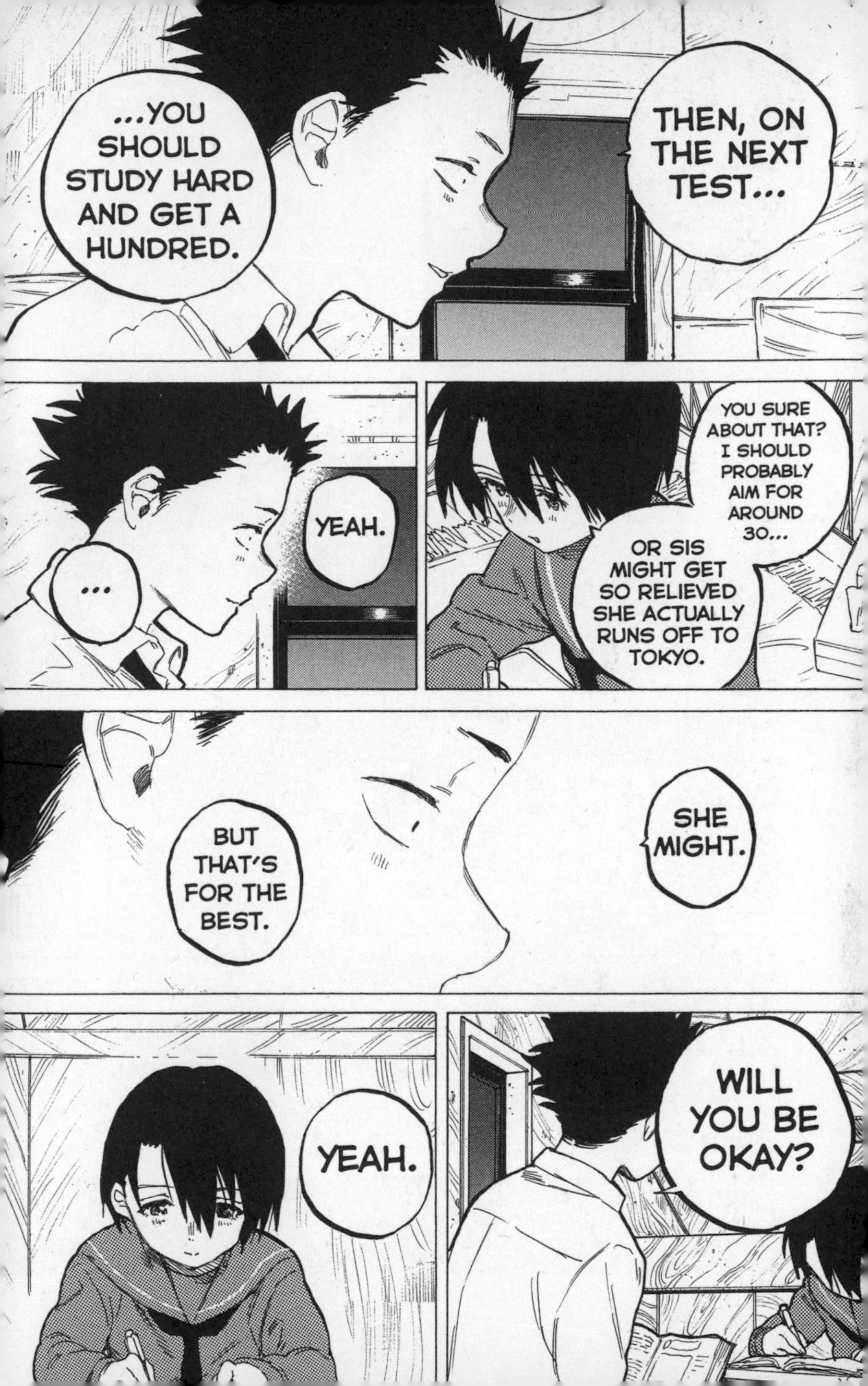
THEN, ON THE NEXT TEST...
...YOU SHOULD STUDY HARD AND GET A HUNDRED.
YOU SURE ABOUT THAT? I SHOULD PROBABLY AIM FOR AROUND 30...
OR SIS MIGHT GET SO RELIEVED SHE ACTUALLY RUNS OFF TO TOKYO.
YEAH.
...
SHE MIGHT.
BUT THAT'S FOR THE BEST.
WILL YOU BE OKAY?
YEAH.

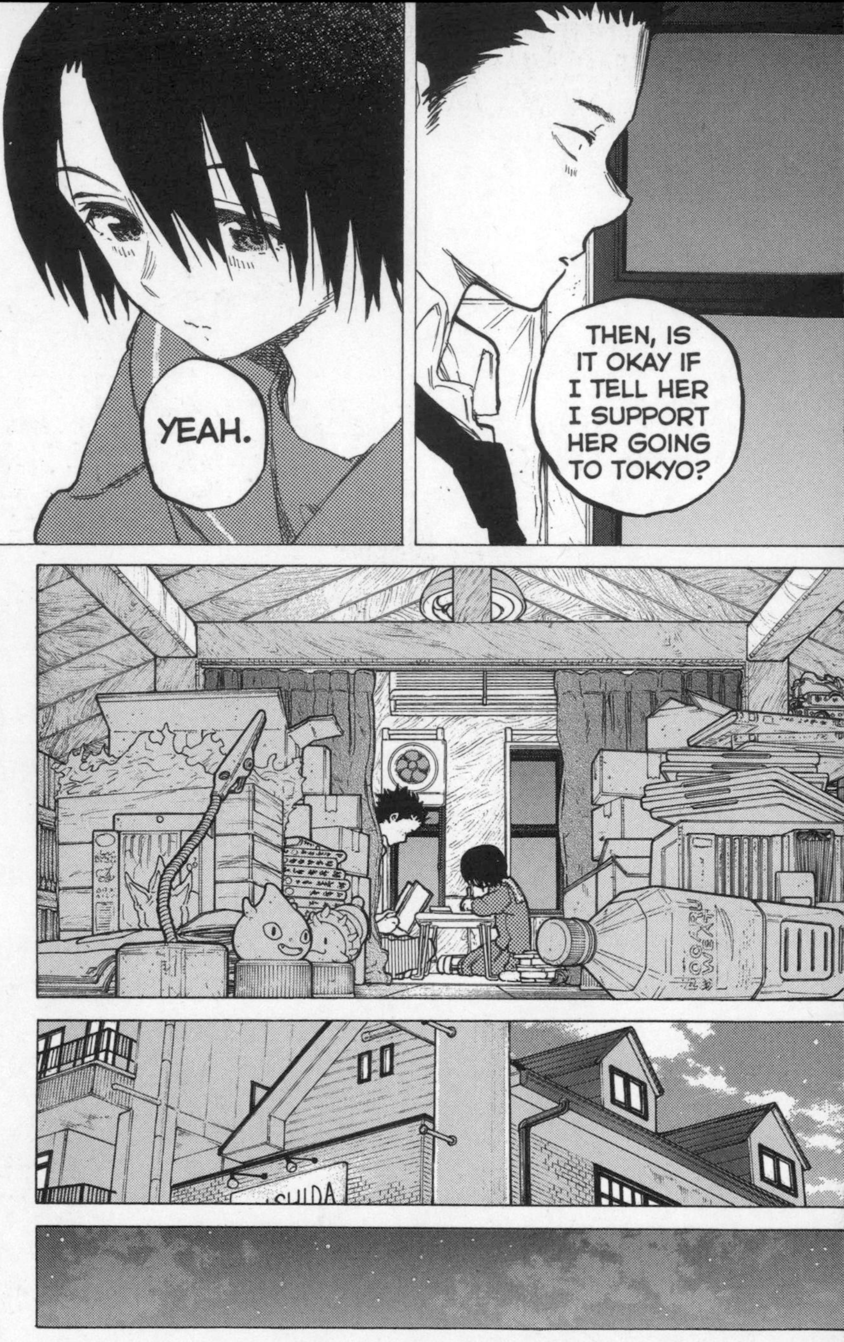
THEN, IS IT OKAY IF I TELL HER I SUPPORT HER GOING TO TOKYO?
YEAH.

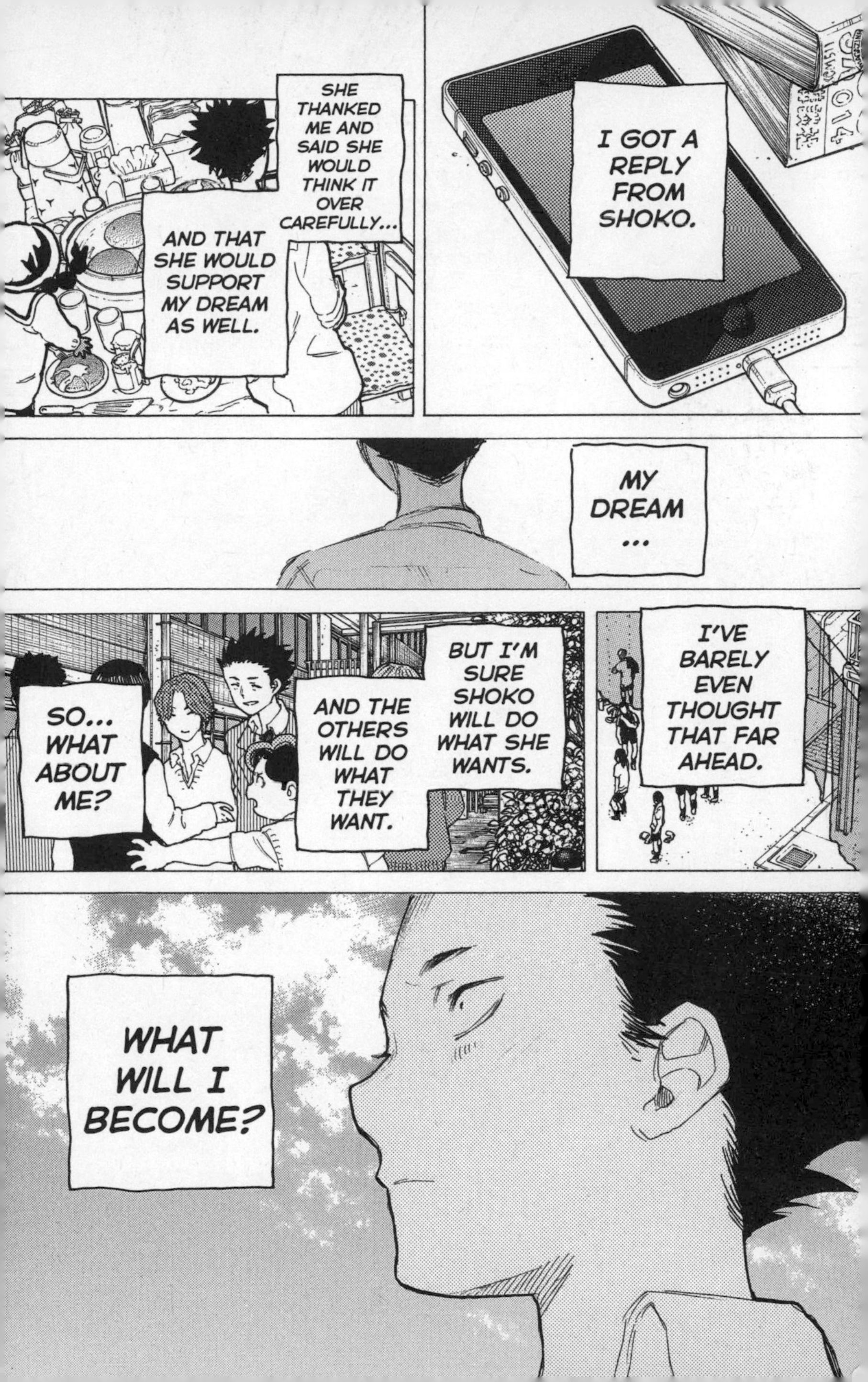
I GOT A REPLY FROM SHOKO.
SHE THANKED ME AND SAID SHE WOULD THINK IT OVER CAREFULLY...
AND THAT SHE WOULD SUPPORT MY DREAM AS WELL.
MY DREAM ...
I'VE BARELY EVEN THOUGHT THAT FAR AHEAD.
BUT I'M SURE SHOKO WILL DO WHAT SHE WANTS.
AND THE OTHERS WILL DO WHAT THEY WANT.
SO... WHAT ABOUT ME?
WHAT WILL I BECOME?

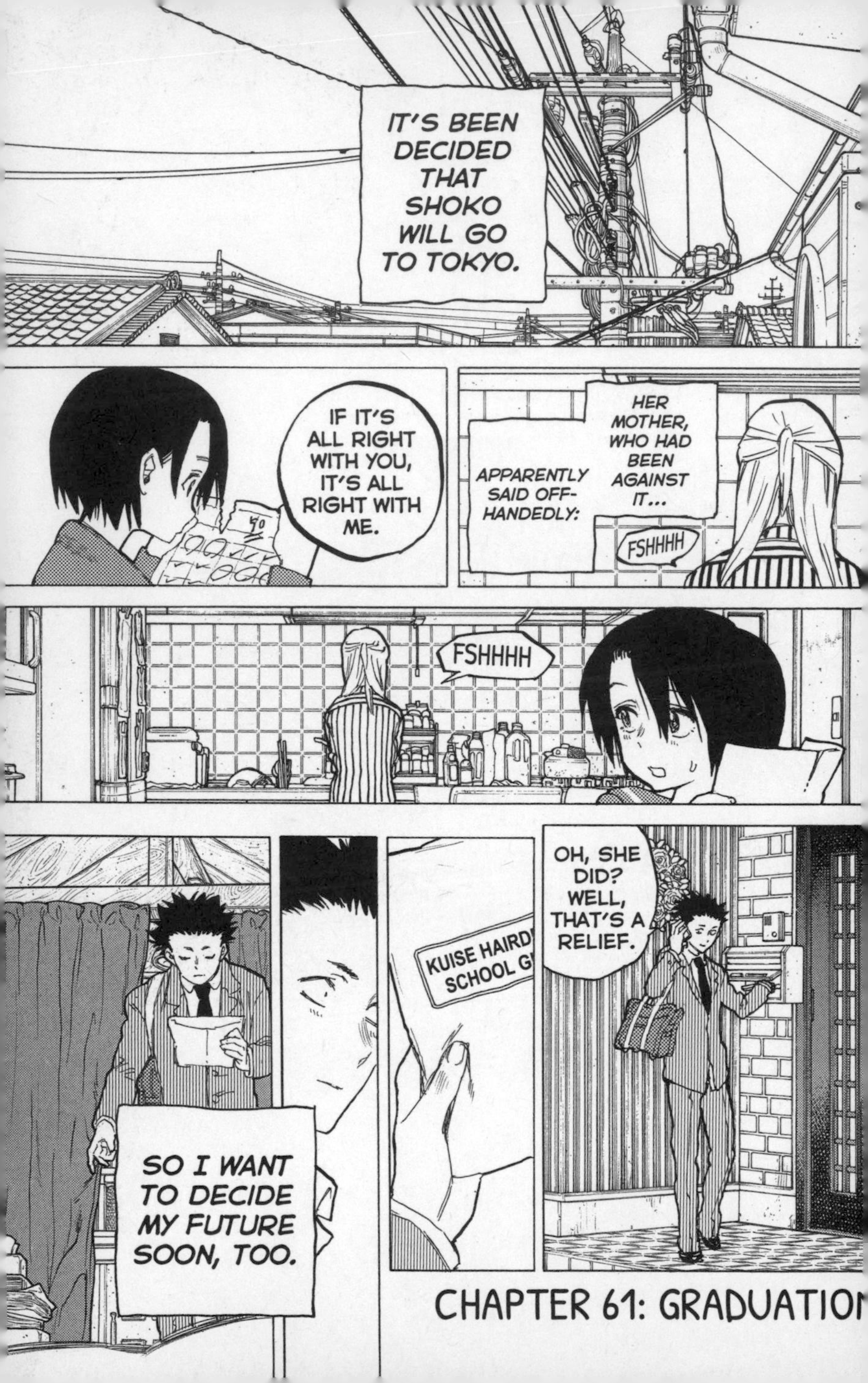
IT'S BEEN DECIDED THAT SHOKO WILL GO TO TOKYO.
HER MOTHER, WHO HAD BEEN AGAINST IT...
APPARENTLY SAID OFF-HANDEDLY:
FSHHHH
IF IT'S ALL RIGHT WITH YOU, IT'S ALL RIGHT WITH ME.
FSHHHH
OH, SHE DID? WELL, THAT'S A RELIEF.
KUISE HAIRD
SCHOOL G
SO I WANT TO DECIDE MY FUTURE SOON, TOO.

CHAPTER 61: GRADUATION

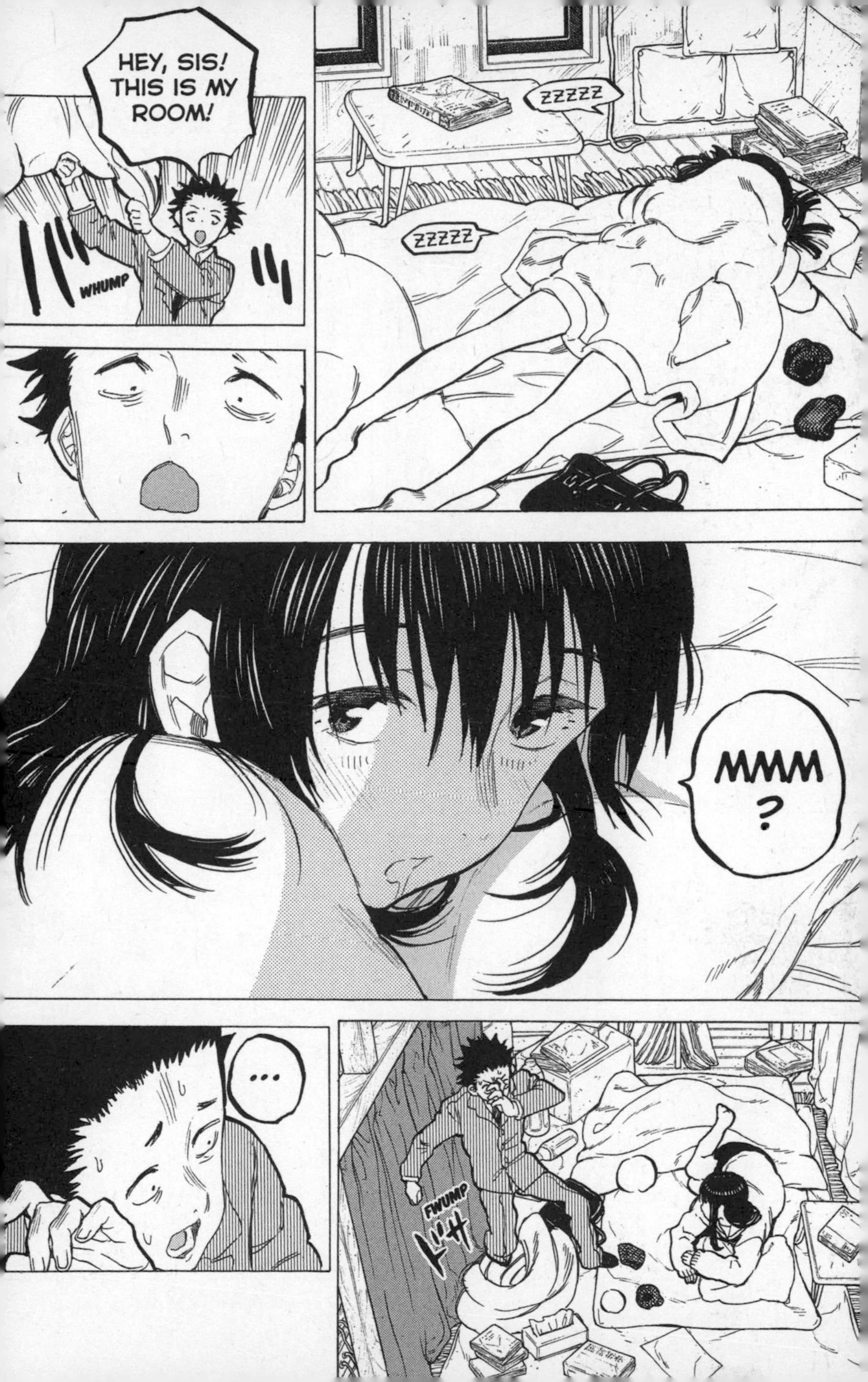
ZZZZZ
ZZZZZ
HEY, SIS! THIS IS MY ROOM!
WHUMP
MMM ?
FWUMP
...

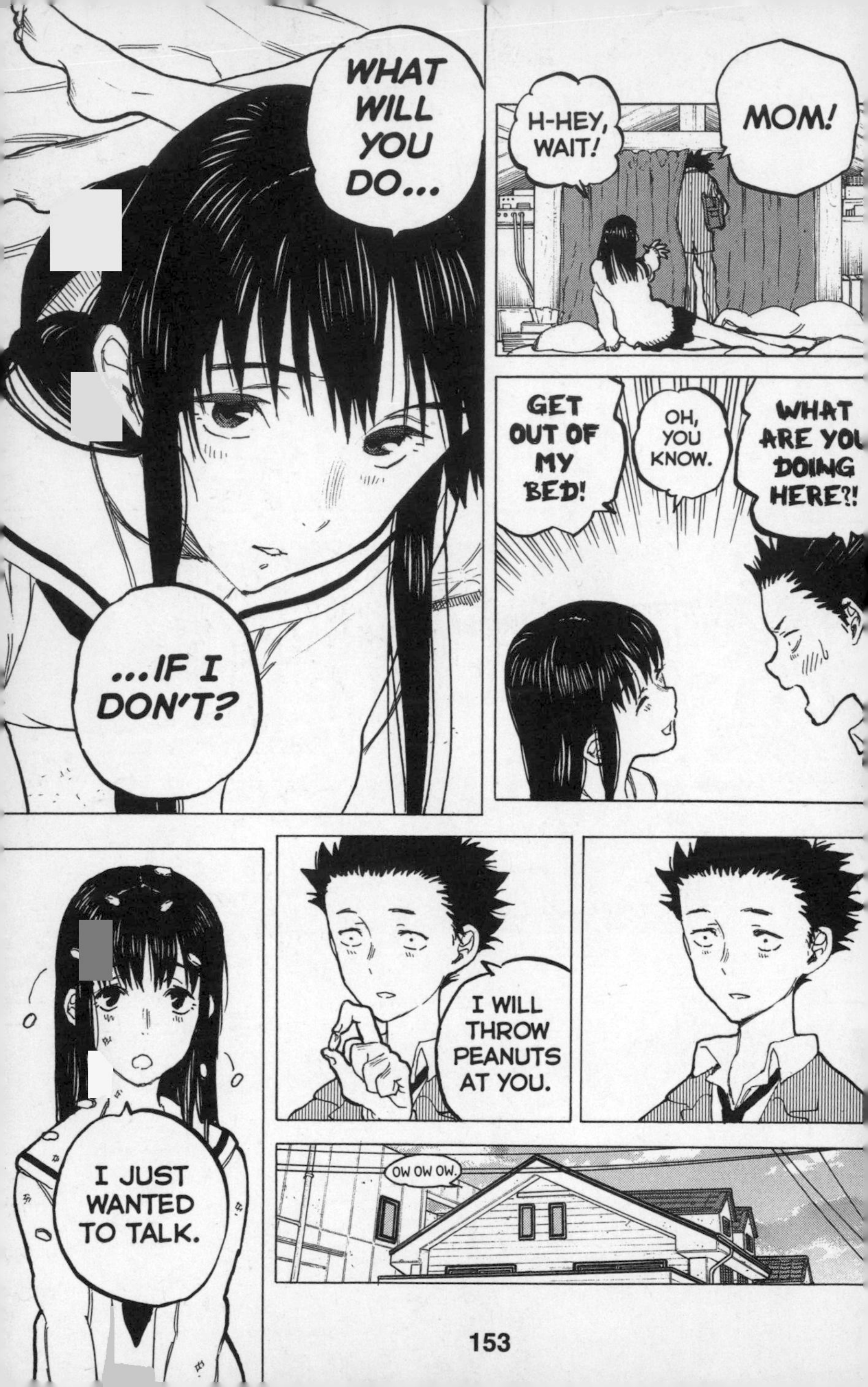
MOM!
H-HEY, WAIT!
WHAT ARE YOU DOING HERE?!
OH, YOU KNOW.
GET OUT OF MY BED!
WHAT WILL YOU DO...
...IF I DON'T?
I WILL THROW PEANUTS AT YOU.
OW OW OW.
I JUST WANTED TO TALK.

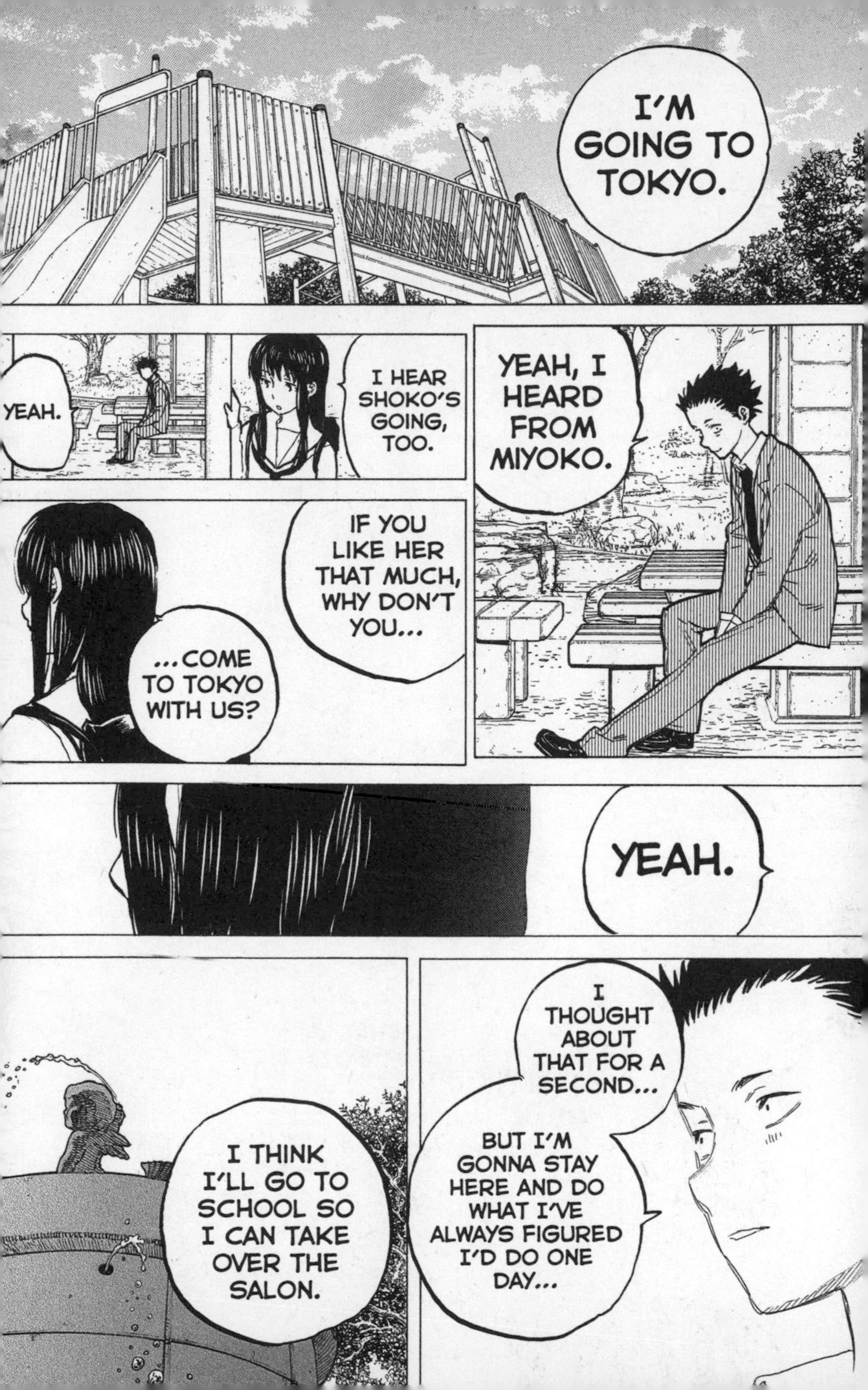
I'M GOING TO TOKYO.
YEAH, I HEARD FROM MIYOKO.
I HEAR SHOKO'S GOING, TOO.
YEAH.
IF YOU LIKE HER THAT MUCH, WHY DON'T YOU...
...COME TO TOKYO WITH US?
YEAH.
I THOUGHT ABOUT THAT FOR A SECOND...
BUT I'M GONNA STAY HERE AND DO WHAT I'VE ALWAYS FIGURED I'D DO ONE DAY...
I THINK I'LL GO TO SCHOOL SO I CAN TAKE OVER THE SALON.

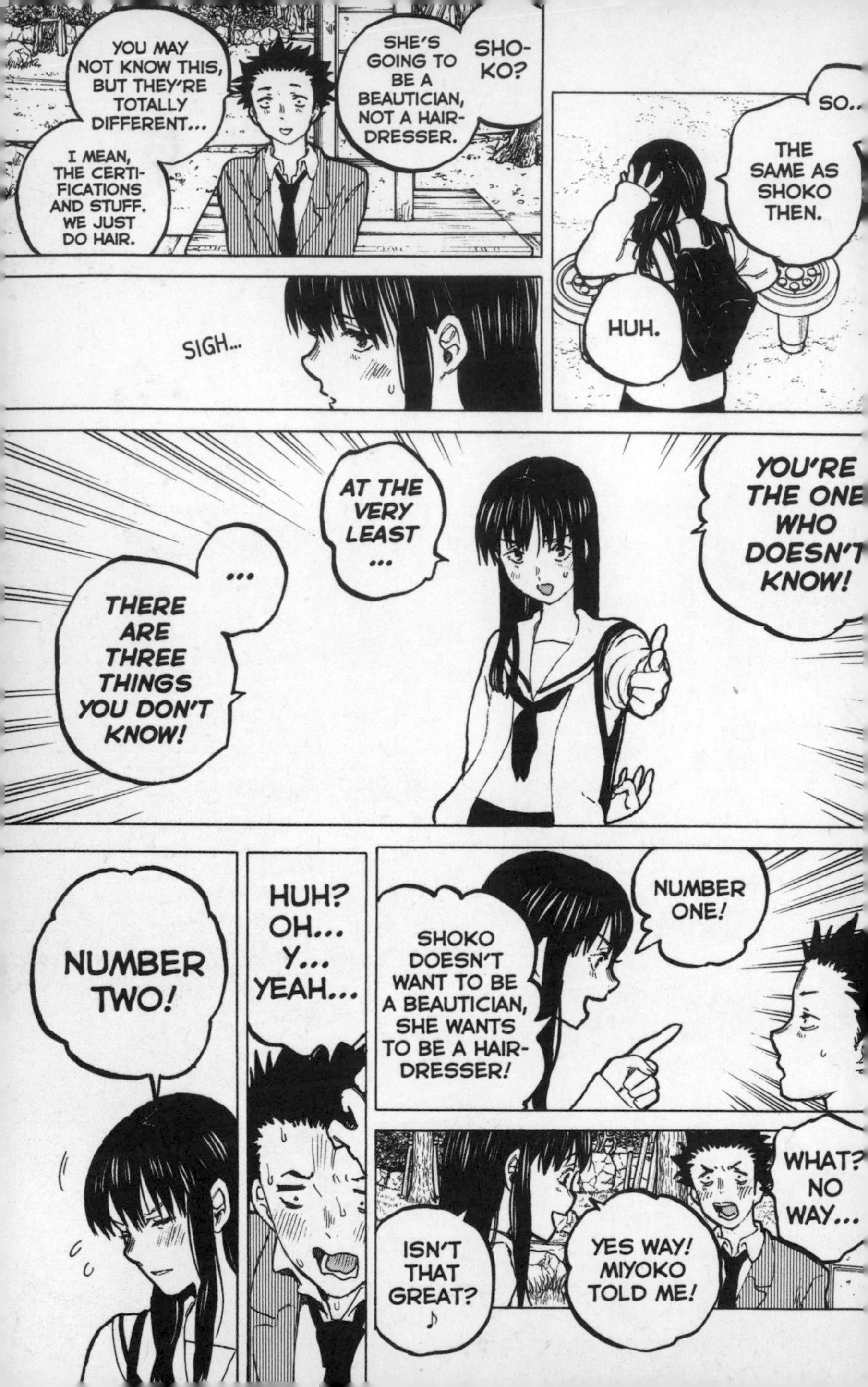
SO...
THE SAME AS SHOKO THEN.
HUH.
SHO-KO?
SHE'S GOING TO BE A BEAUTICIAN, NOT A HAIR-DRESSER.
YOU MAY NOT KNOW THIS, BUT THEY'RE TOTALLY DIFFERENT...
I MEAN, THE CERTI-FICATIONS AND STUFF. WE JUST DO HAIR.
SIGH...
YOU'RE THE ONE WHO DOESN'T KNOW!
AT THE VERY LEAST ...
... THERE ARE THREE THINGS YOU DON'T KNOW!
NUMBER ONE!
SHOKO DOESN'T WANT TO BE A BEAUTICIAN, SHE WANTS TO BE A HAIR-DRESSER!
WHAT? NO WAY...
YES WAY! MIYOKO TOLD ME!
ISN'T THAT GREAT? ♪
HUH? OH... Y... YEAH...
NUMBER TWO!

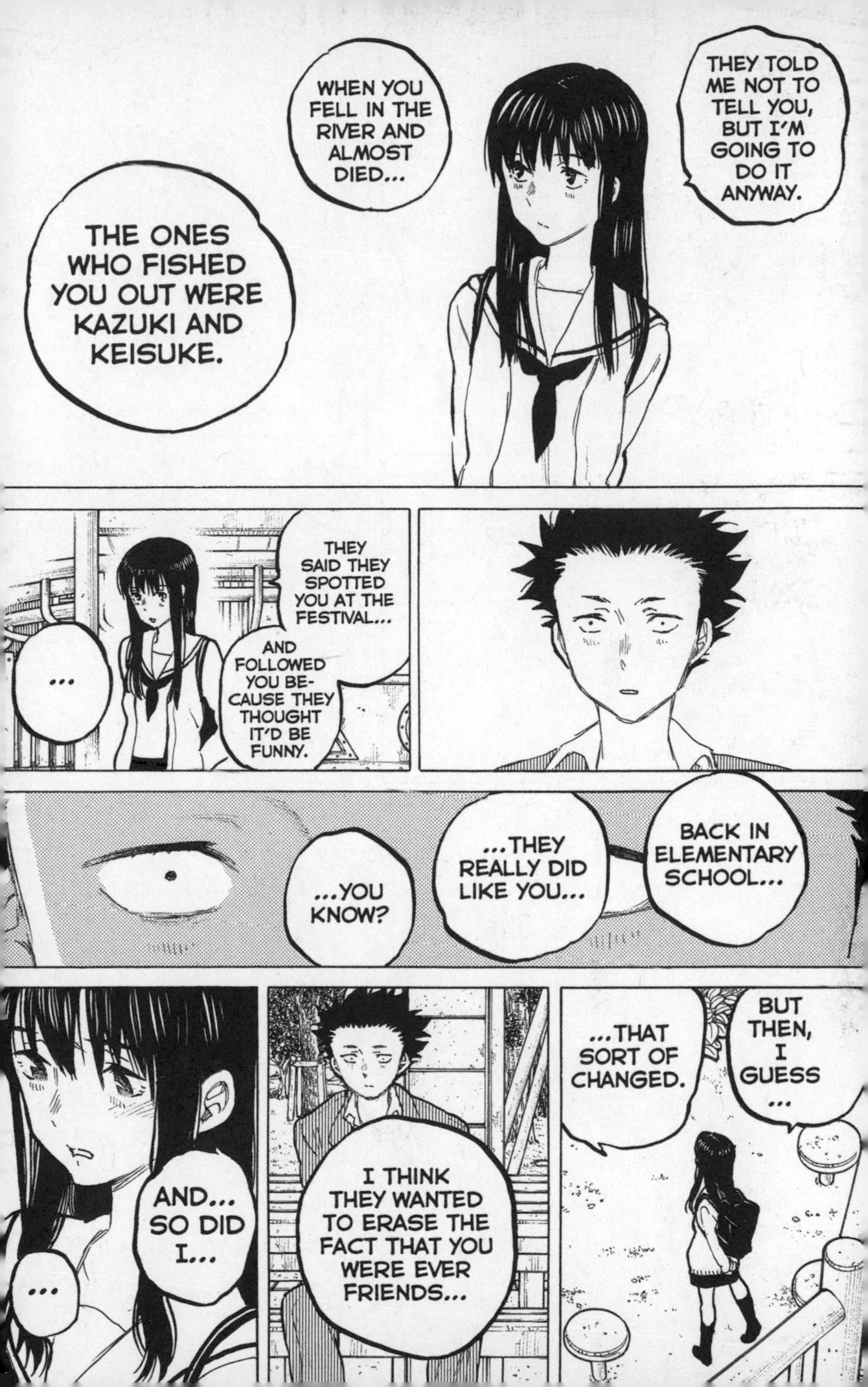
THEY TOLD ME NOT TO TELL YOU, BUT I'M GOING TO DO IT ANYWAY.
WHEN YOU FELL IN THE RIVER AND ALMOST DIED...
THE ONES WHO FISHED YOU OUT WERE KAZUKI AND KEISUKE.
THEY SAID THEY SPOTTED YOU AT THE FESTIVAL...
AND FOLLOWED YOU BE-CAUSE THEY THOUGHT IT'D BE FUNNY.
...
BACK IN ELEMENTARY SCHOOL...
...THEY REALLY DID LIKE YOU...
...YOU KNOW?
BUT THEN, I GUESS ...
...THAT SORT OF CHANGED.
I THINK THEY WANTED TO ERASE THE FACT THAT YOU WERE EVER FRIENDS...
AND... SO DID I...
...

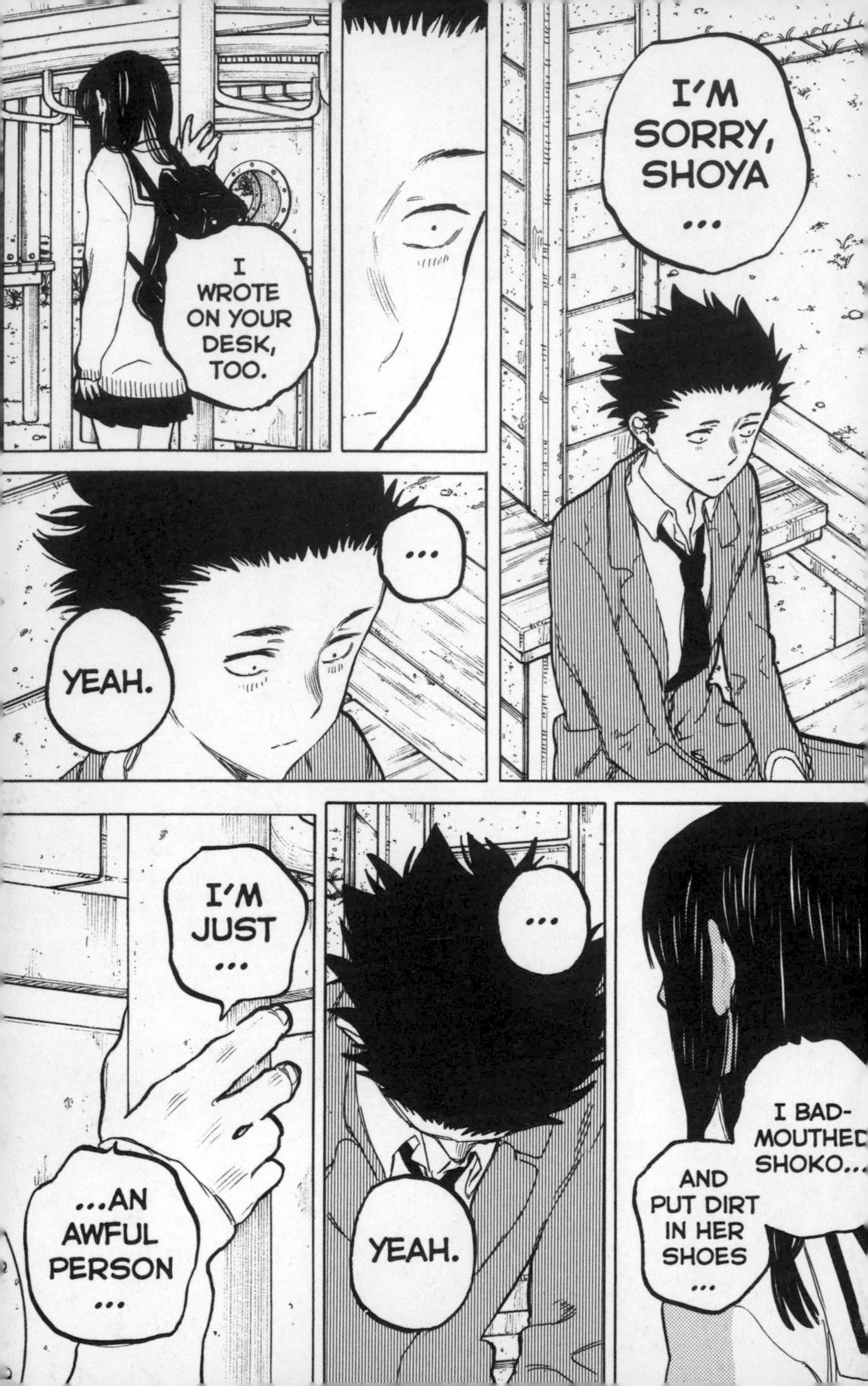
I'M SORRY, SHOYA ...
I WROTE ON YOUR DESK, TOO.
...
YEAH.
I BAD-MOUTHED SHOKO...
AND PUT DIRT IN HER SHOES ...
...
YEAH.
I'M JUST ...
...AN AWFUL PERSON ...

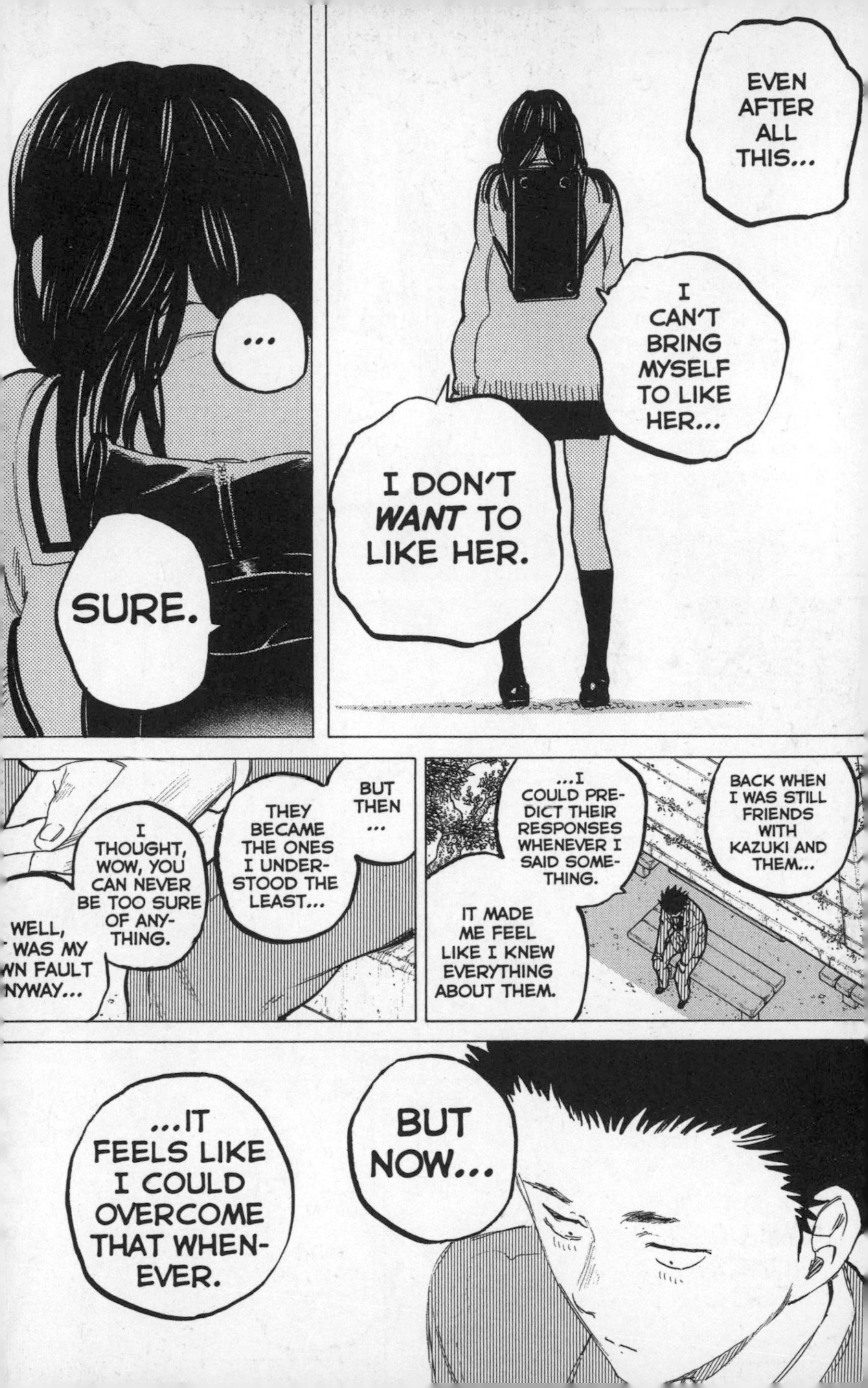
EVEN AFTER ALL THIS...
I CAN'T BRING MYSELF TO LIKE HER...
I DON'T *WANT* TO LIKE HER.
...
SURE.
BACK WHEN I WAS STILL FRIENDS WITH KAZUKI AND THEM...
...I COULD PREDICT THEIR RESPONSES WHENEVER I SAID SOMETHING.
IT MADE ME FEEL LIKE I KNEW EVERYTHING ABOUT THEM.
BUT THEN...
THEY BECAME THE ONES I UNDERSTOOD THE LEAST...
I THOUGHT, WOW, YOU CAN NEVER BE TOO SURE OF ANYTHING.
WELL, T WAS MY WN FAULT NYWAY...
BUT NOW...
...IT FEELS LIKE I COULD OVERCOME THAT WHENEVER.

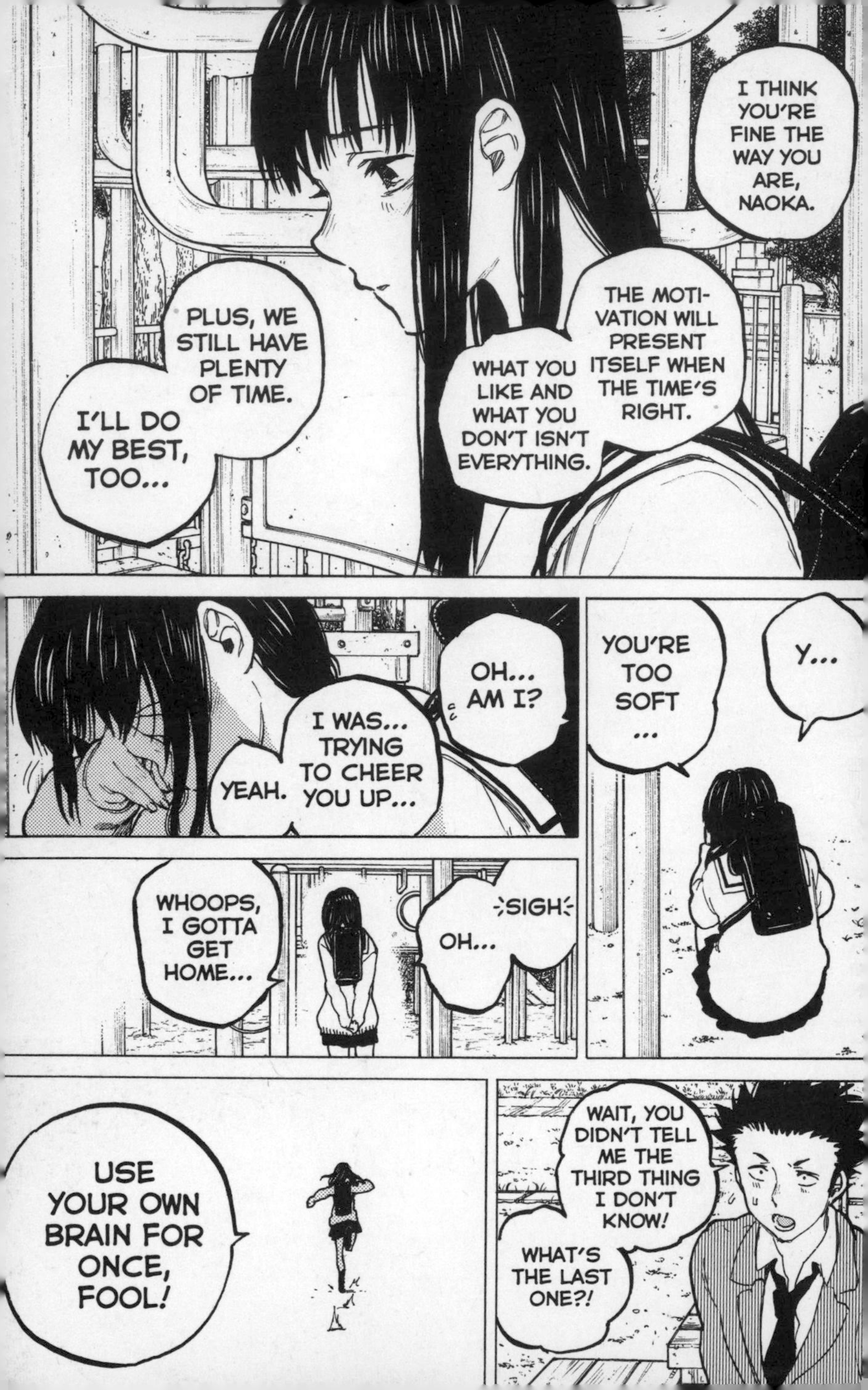
I THINK YOU'RE FINE THE WAY YOU ARE, NAOKA.
THE MOTIVATION WILL PRESENT ITSELF WHEN THE TIME'S RIGHT.
WHAT YOU LIKE AND WHAT YOU DON'T ISN'T EVERYTHING.
PLUS, WE STILL HAVE PLENTY OF TIME.
I'LL DO MY BEST, TOO...
Y...
YOU'RE TOO SOFT ...
OH... AM I?
I WAS... TRYING TO CHEER YOU UP...
YEAH.
SIGH
OH...
WHOOPS, I GOTTA GET HOME...
WAIT, YOU DIDN'T TELL ME THE THIRD THING I DON'T KNOW!
WHAT'S THE LAST ONE?!
USE YOUR OWN BRAIN FOR ONCE, FOOL!

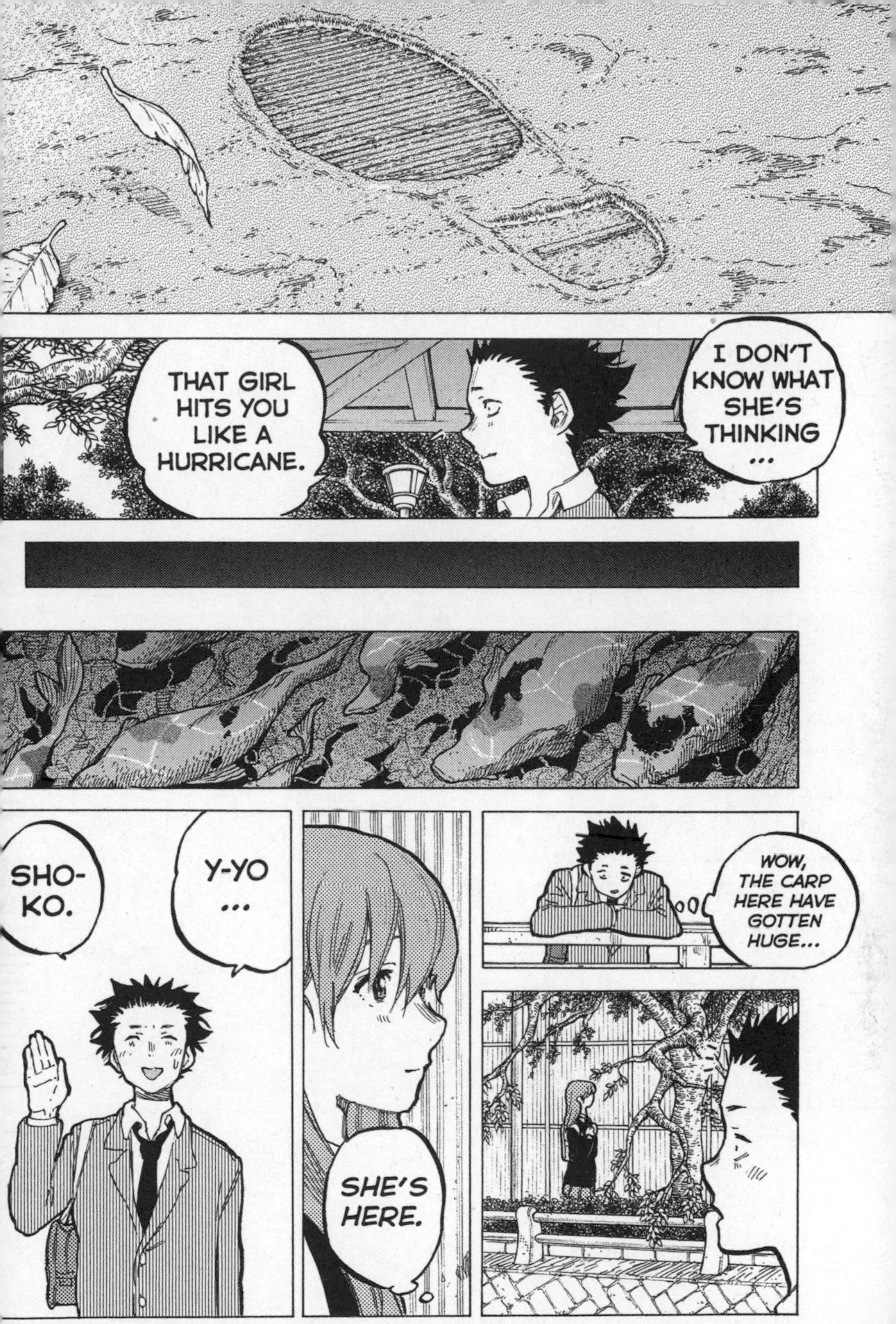
I DON'T KNOW WHAT SHE'S THINKING ...
THAT GIRL HITS YOU LIKE A HURRICANE.
WOW, THE CARP HERE HAVE GOTTEN HUGE...
SHE'S HERE.
Y-YO ...
SHO-KO.

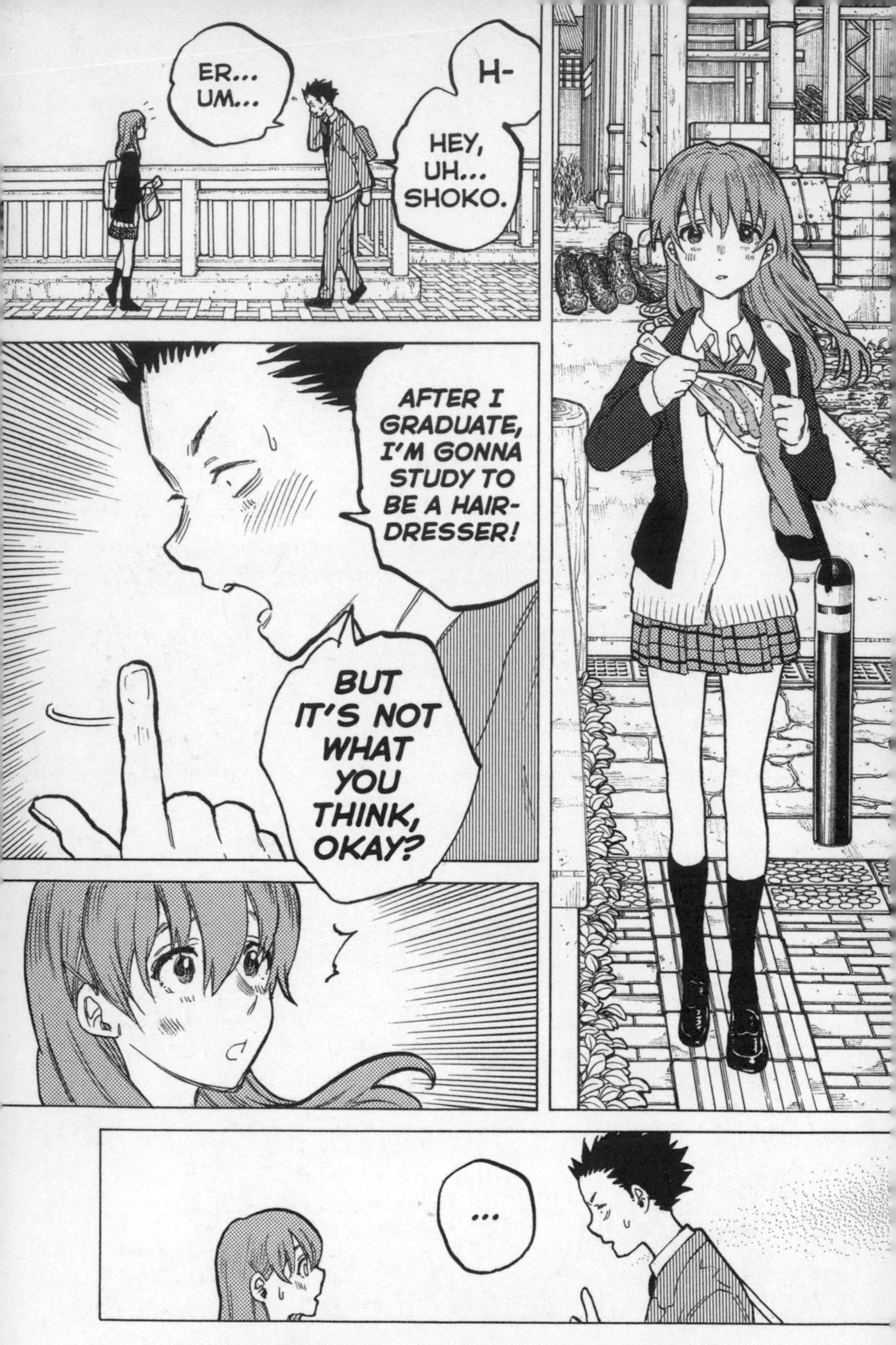
H-
HEY, UH... SHOKO.
ER... UM...
AFTER I GRADUATE, I'M GONNA STUDY TO BE A HAIR-DRESSER!
BUT IT'S NOT WHAT YOU THINK, OKAY?
...

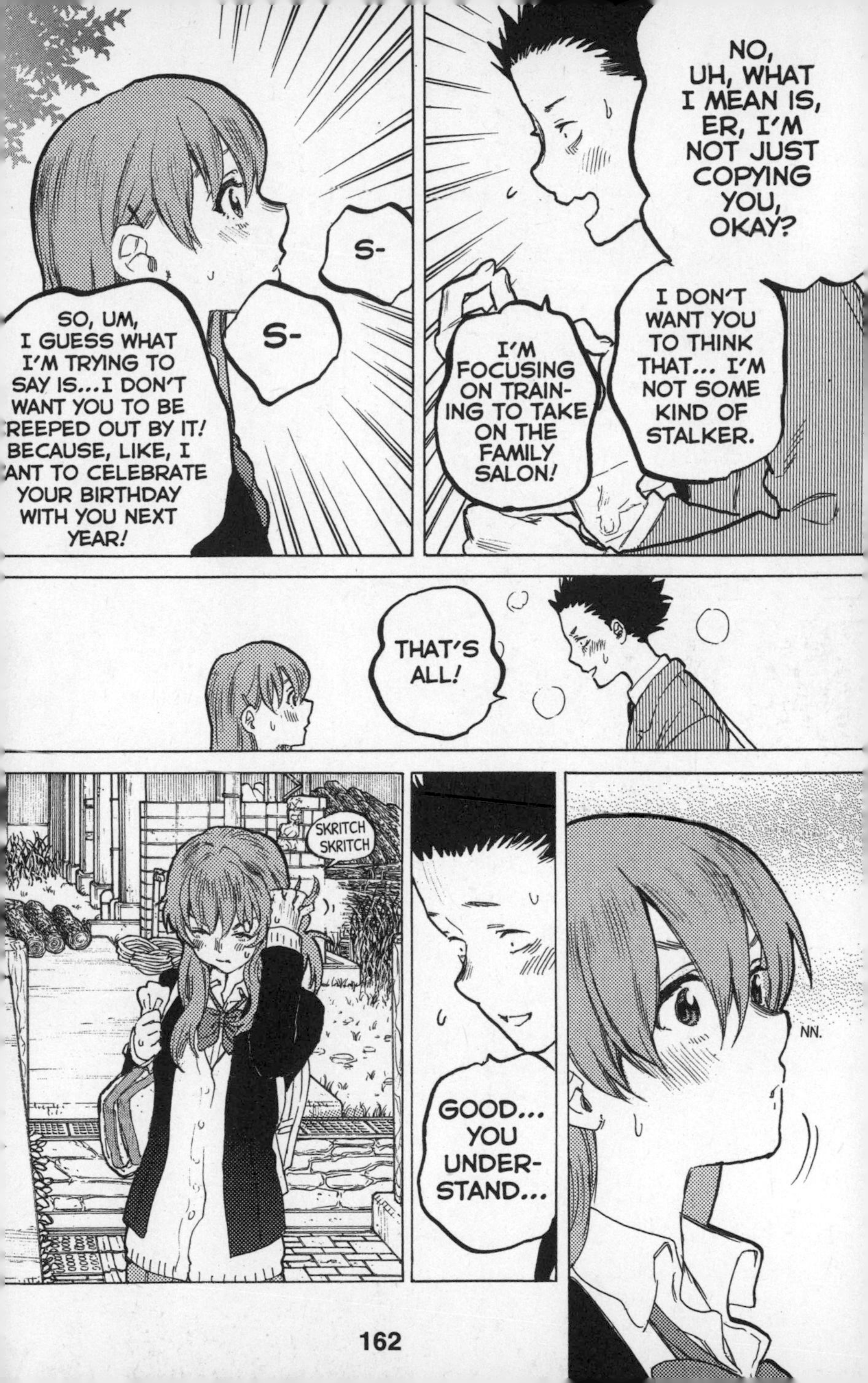
NO, UH, WHAT I MEAN IS, ER, I'M NOT JUST COPYING YOU, OKAY?
I DON'T WANT YOU TO THINK THAT... I'M NOT SOME KIND OF STALKER.
I'M FOCUSING ON TRAIN-ING TO TAKE ON THE FAMILY SALON!
S-
S-
SO, UM, I GUESS WHAT I'M TRYING TO SAY IS...I DON'T WANT YOU TO BE REEPED OUT BY IT! BECAUSE, LIKE, I ANT TO CELEBRATE YOUR BIRTHDAY WITH YOU NEXT YEAR!
THAT'S ALL!
NN.
GOOD... YOU UNDER-STAND...
SKRITCH SKRITCH

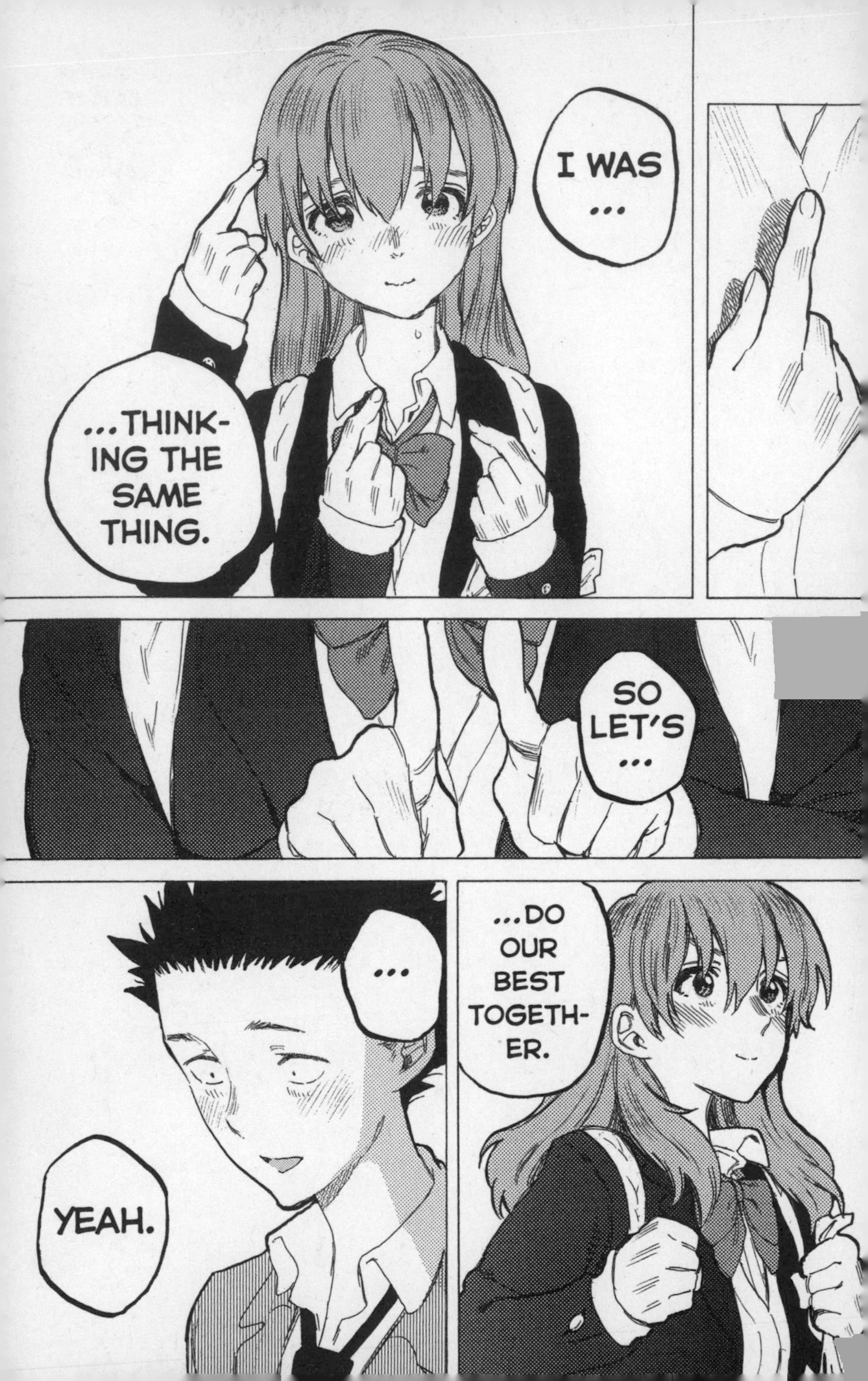
I WAS ...
...THINKING THE SAME THING.
SO LET'S ...
...DO OUR BEST TOGETHER.
...
YEAH.

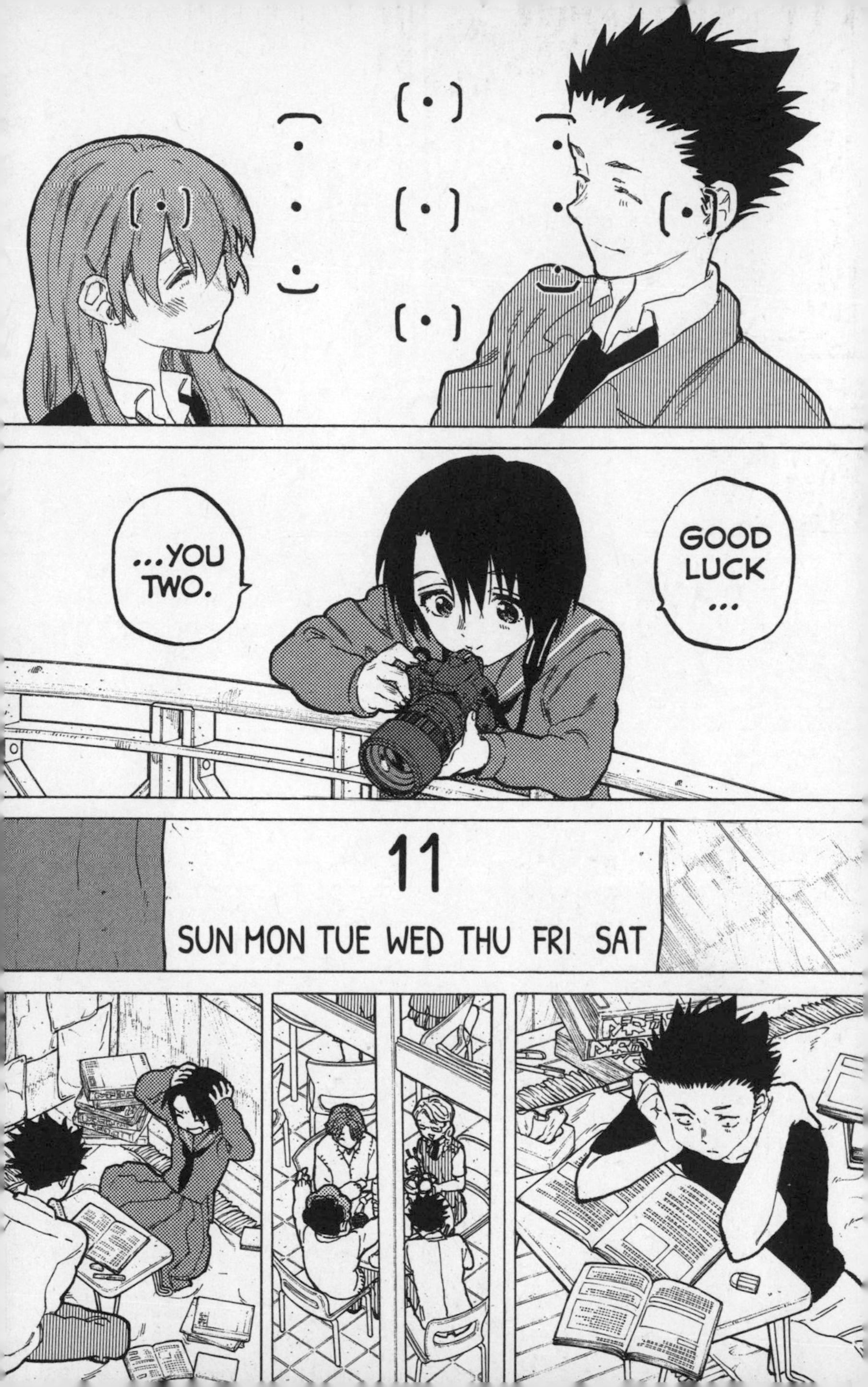
GOOD LUCK ...
...YOU TWO.
11
SUN MON TUE WED THU FRI SAT

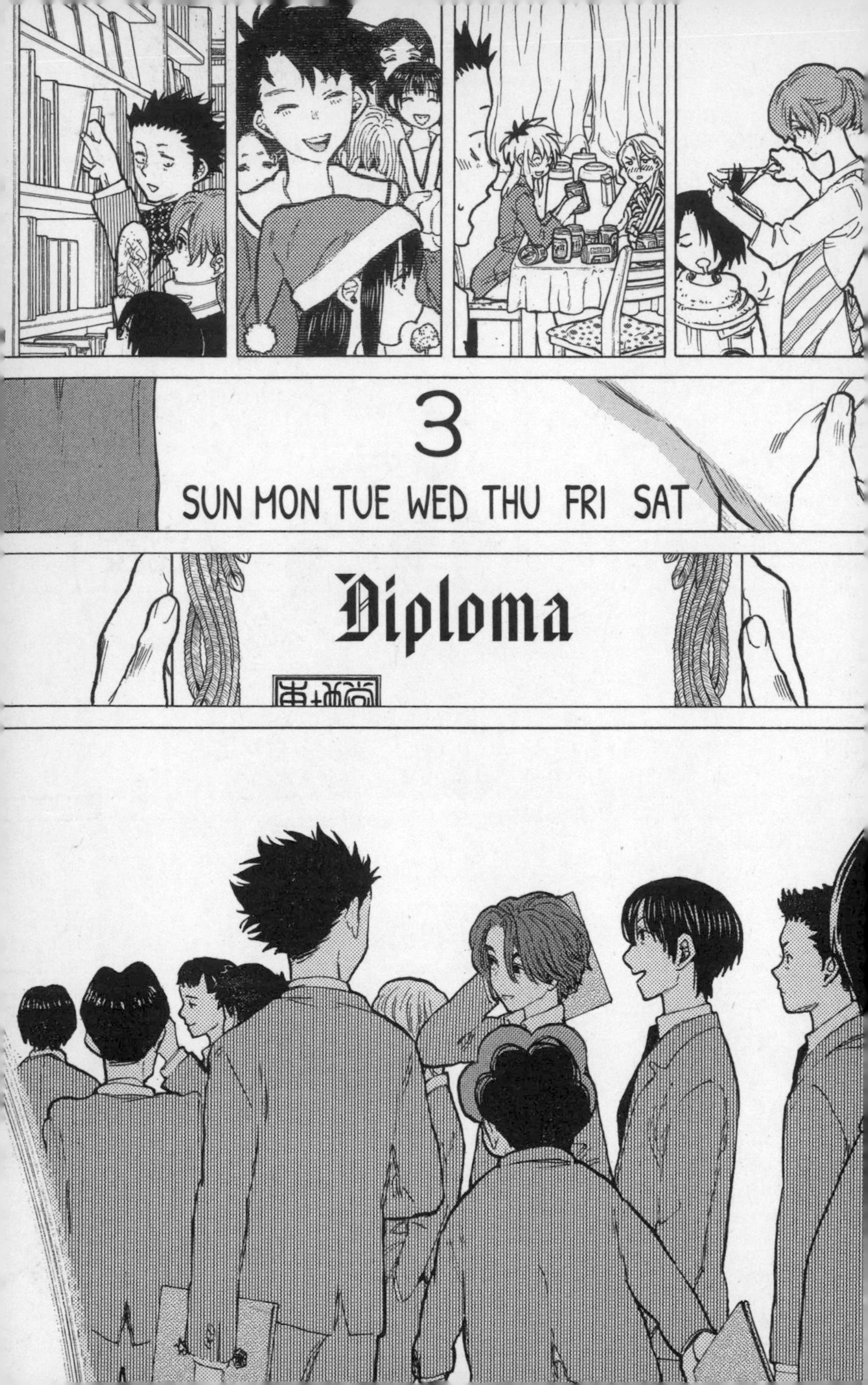
3
SUN MON TUE WED THU FRI SAT
Diploma

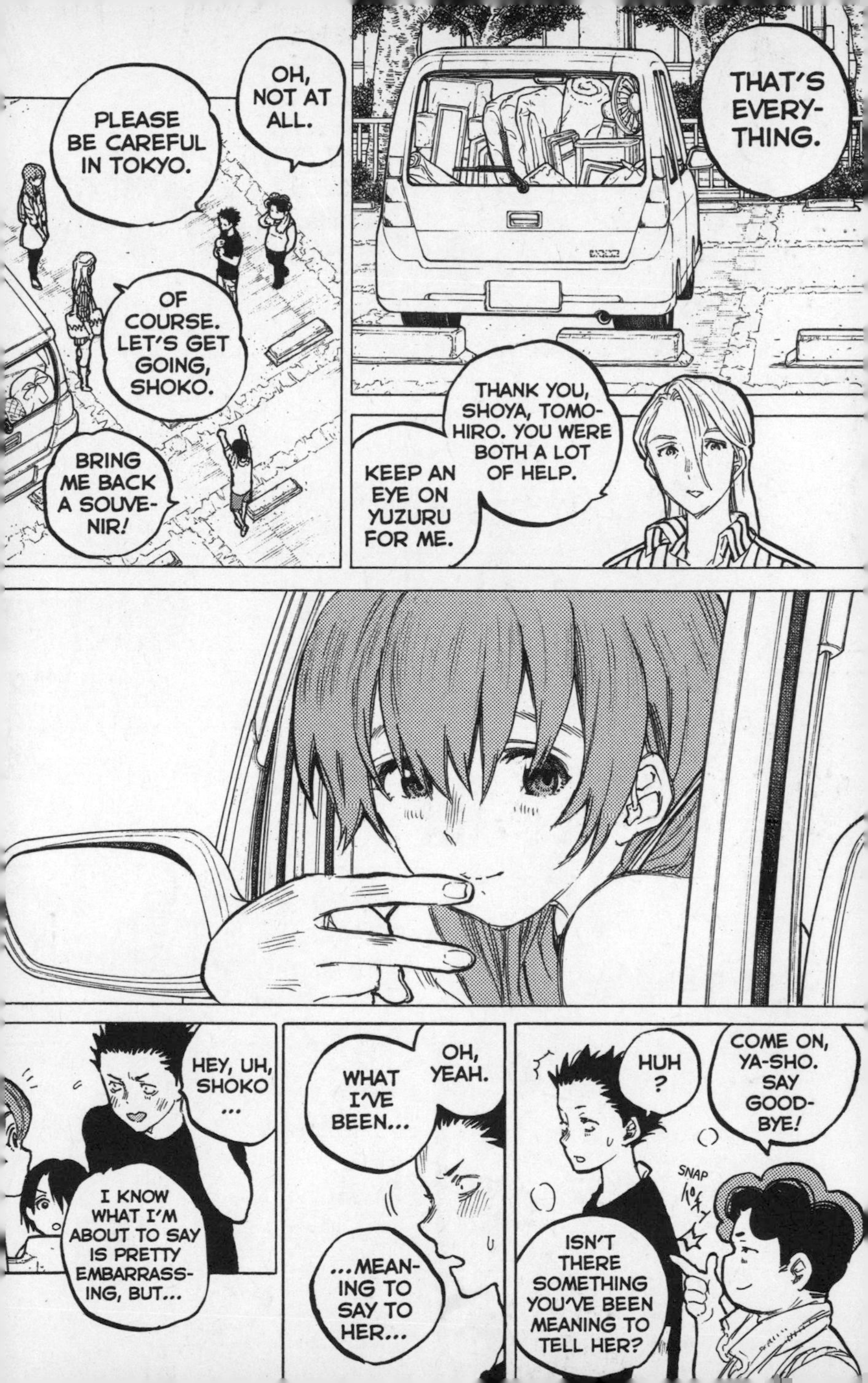
THAT'S EVERYTHING.
THANK YOU, SHOYA, TOMOHIRO. YOU WERE BOTH A LOT OF HELP.
KEEP AN EYE ON YUZURU FOR ME.
OH, NOT AT ALL.
PLEASE BE CAREFUL IN TOKYO.
OF COURSE. LET'S GET GOING, SHOKO.
BRING ME BACK A SOUVENIR!
COME ON, YA-SHO. SAY GOOD-BYE!
HUH ?
SNAP
ISN'T THERE SOMETHING YOU'VE BEEN MEANING TO TELL HER?
OH, YEAH.
WHAT I'VE BEEN...
...MEANING TO SAY TO HER...
HEY, UH, SHOKO ...
I KNOW WHAT I'M ABOUT TO SAY IS PRETTY EMBARRASSING, BUT...

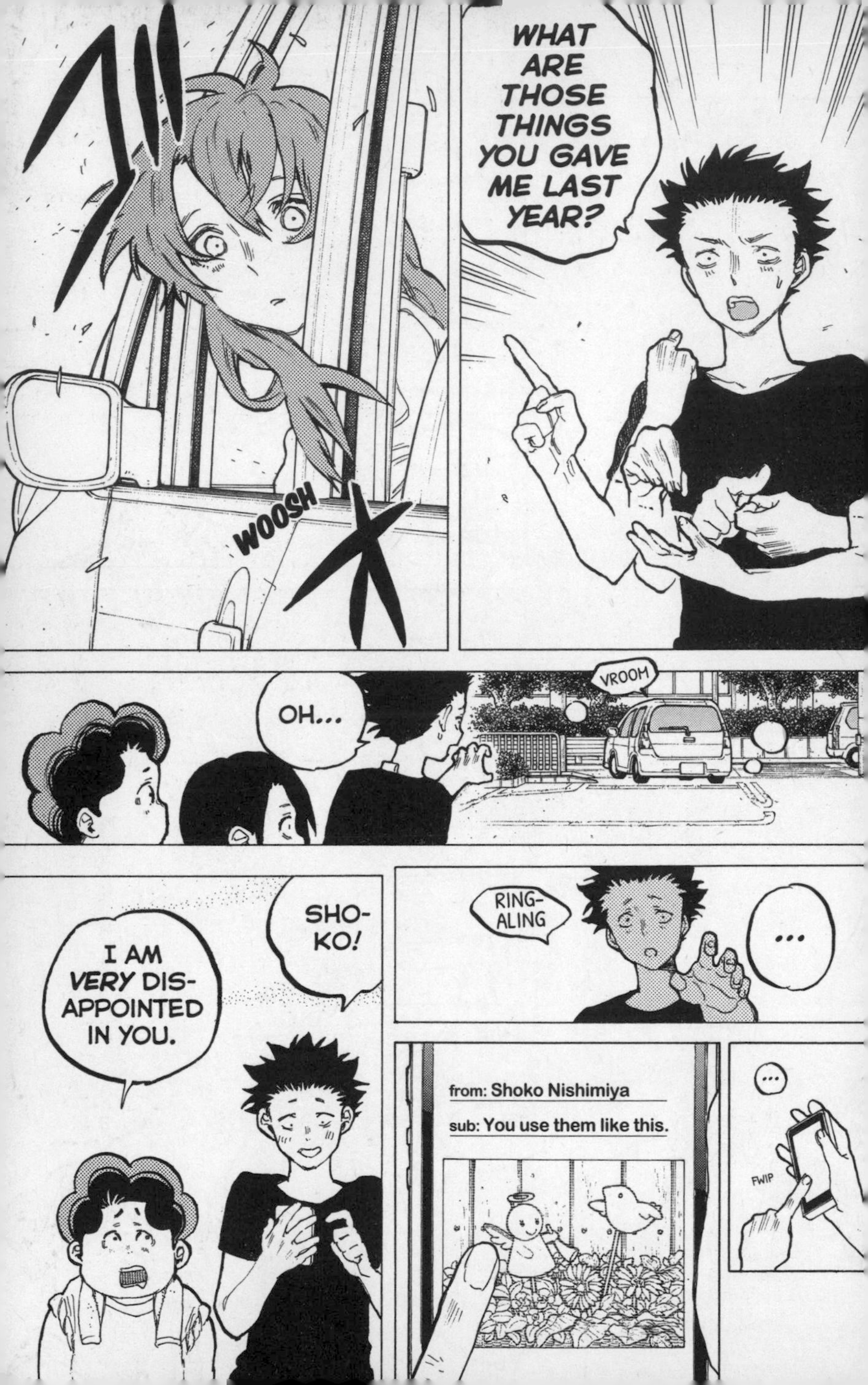
WHAT ARE THOSE THINGS YOU GAVE ME LAST YEAR?
WOOSH
VROOM
OH...
...
RING-ALING
...
FWIP
from: Shoko Nishimiya
sub: You use them like this.
SHO-KO!
I AM *VERY* DIS-APPOINTED IN YOU.

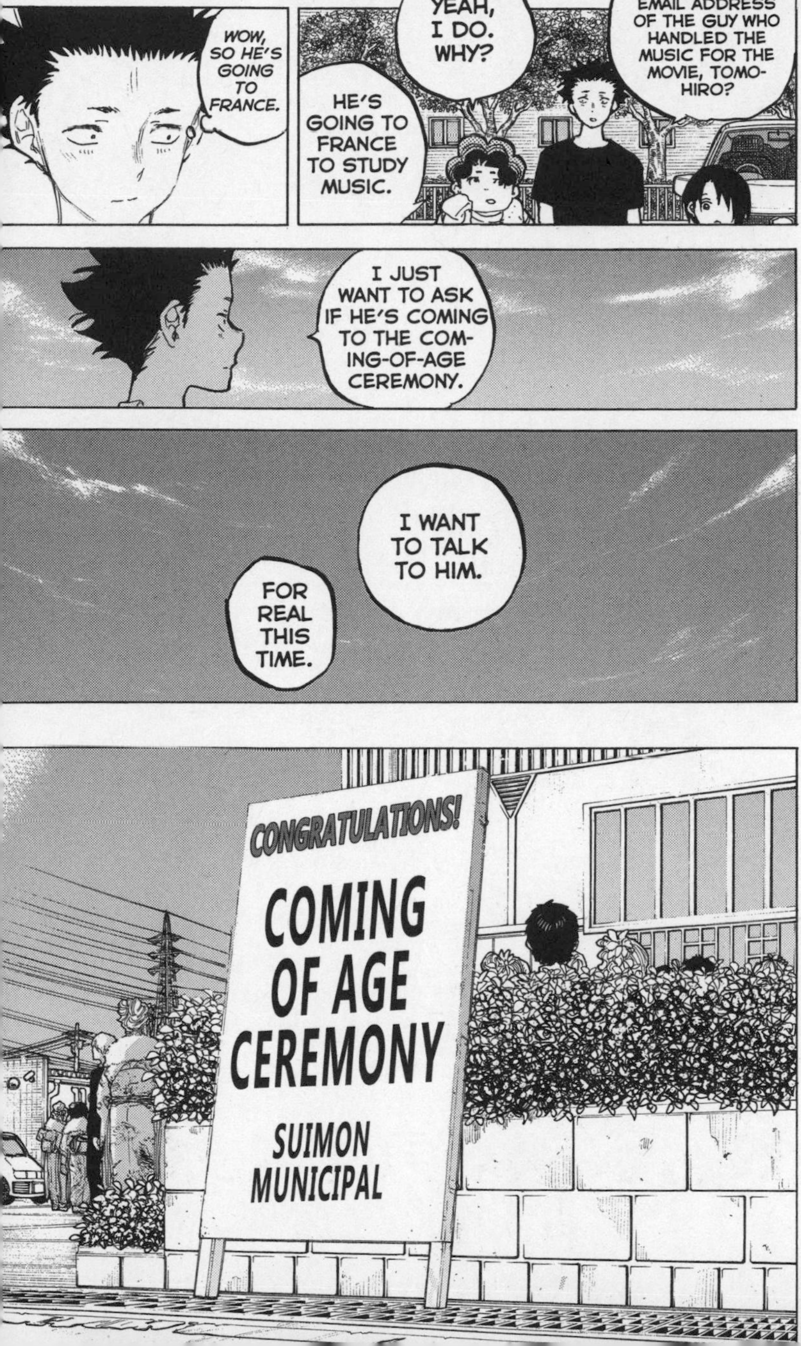
OH, COME TO THINK OF IT, DO YOU HAVE THE EMAIL ADDRESS OF THE GUY WHO HANDLED THE MUSIC FOR THE MOVIE, TOMOHIRO?
YEAH, I DO. WHY?
HE'S GOING TO FRANCE TO STUDY MUSIC.
WOW, SO HE'S GOING TO FRANCE.
I JUST WANT TO ASK IF HE'S COMING TO THE COMING-OF-AGE CEREMONY.
I WANT TO TALK TO HIM.
FOR REAL THIS TIME.
CONGRATULATIONS!
COMING OF AGE CEREMONY
SUIMON MUNICIPAL

a Silent Voice

a Silent Voice

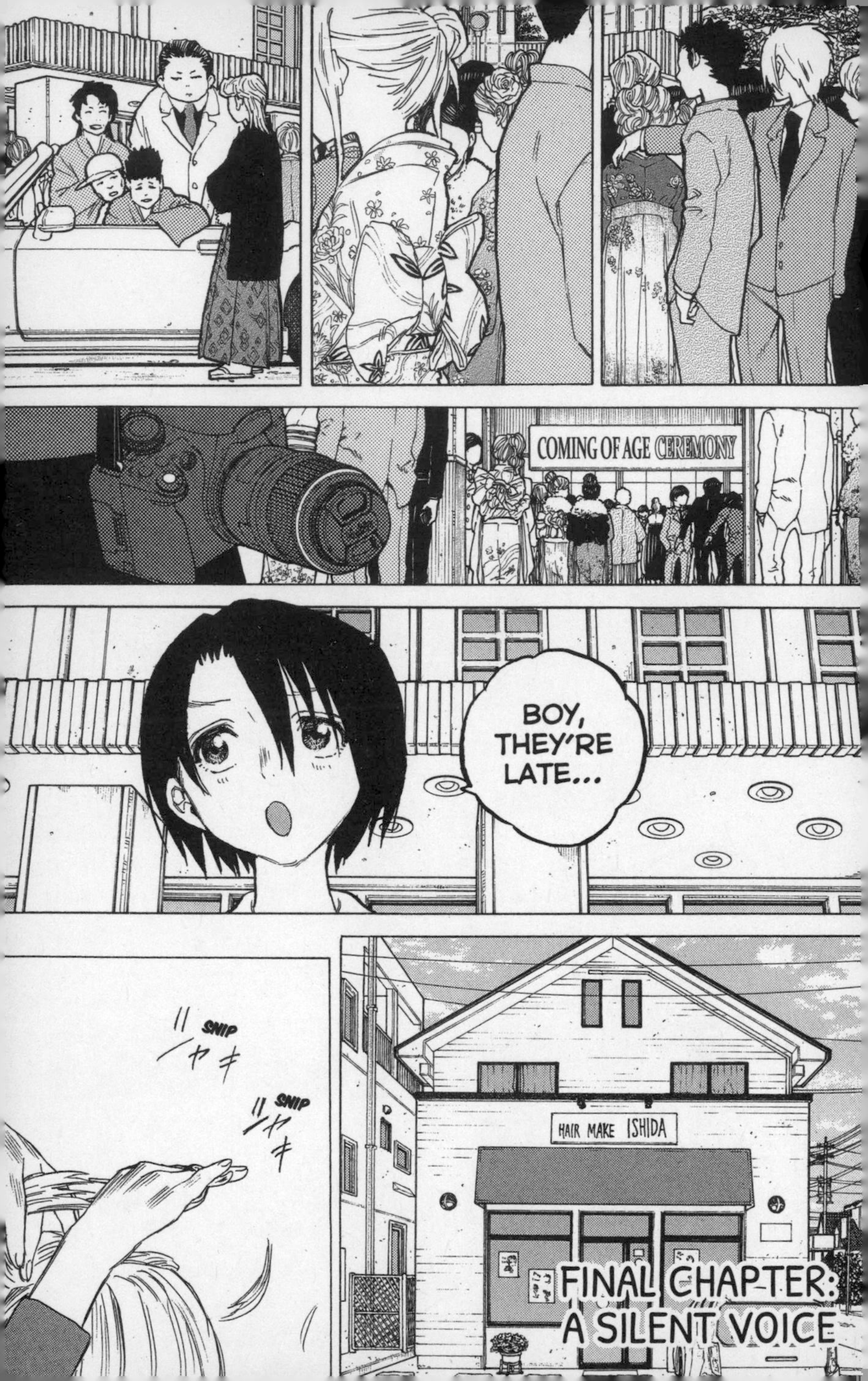
COMING OF AGE CEREMONY
BOY, THEY'RE LATE...
HAIR MAKE ISHIDA
FINAL CHAPTER: A SILENT VOICE
SNIP
SNIP

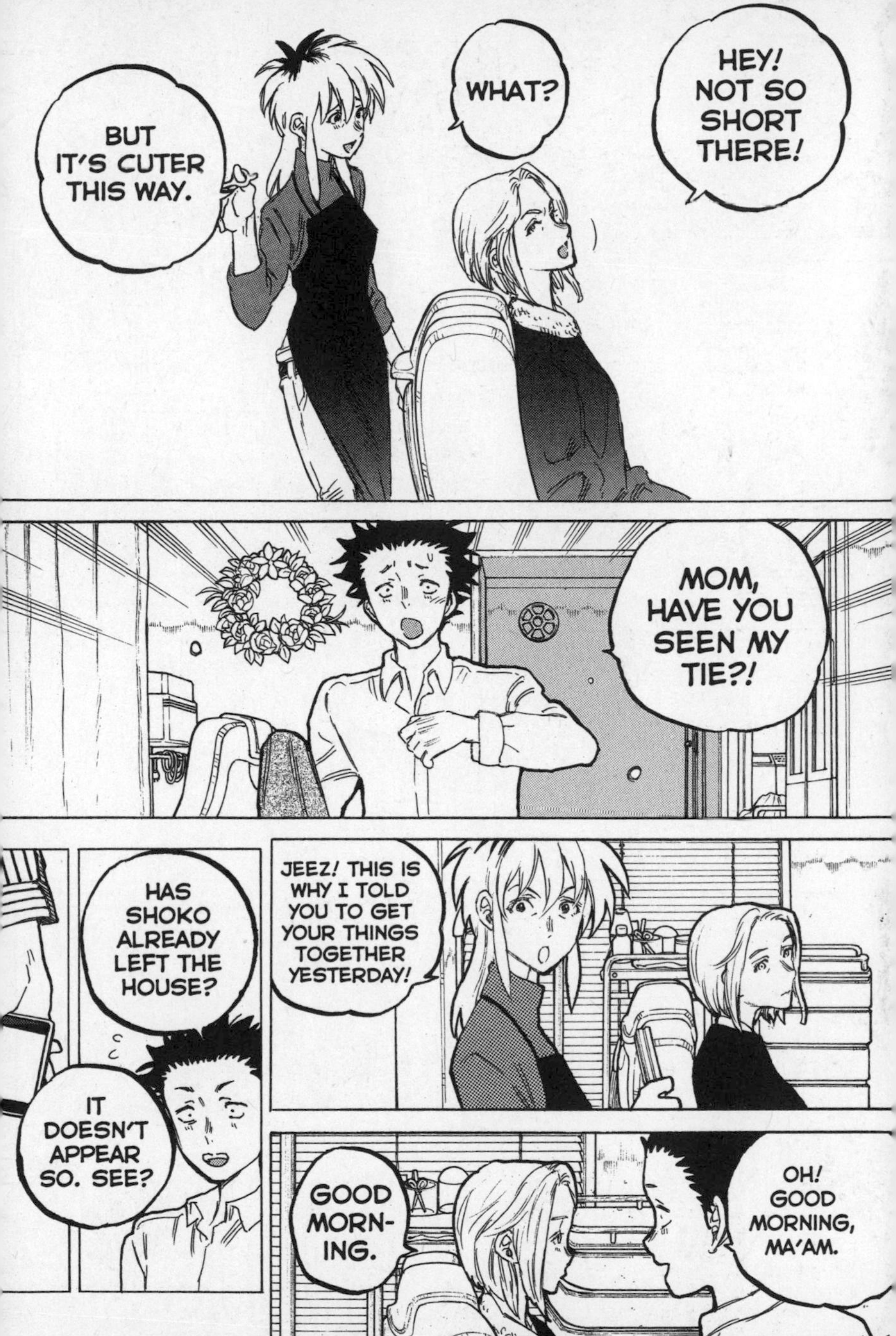
HEY! NOT SO SHORT THERE!
WHAT?
BUT IT'S CUTER THIS WAY.
MOM, HAVE YOU SEEN MY TIE?!
JEEZ! THIS IS WHY I TOLD YOU TO GET YOUR THINGS TOGETHER YESTERDAY!
OH! GOOD MORNING, MA'AM.
GOOD MORN-ING.
HAS SHOKO ALREADY LEFT THE HOUSE?
IT DOESN'T APPEAR SO. SEE?

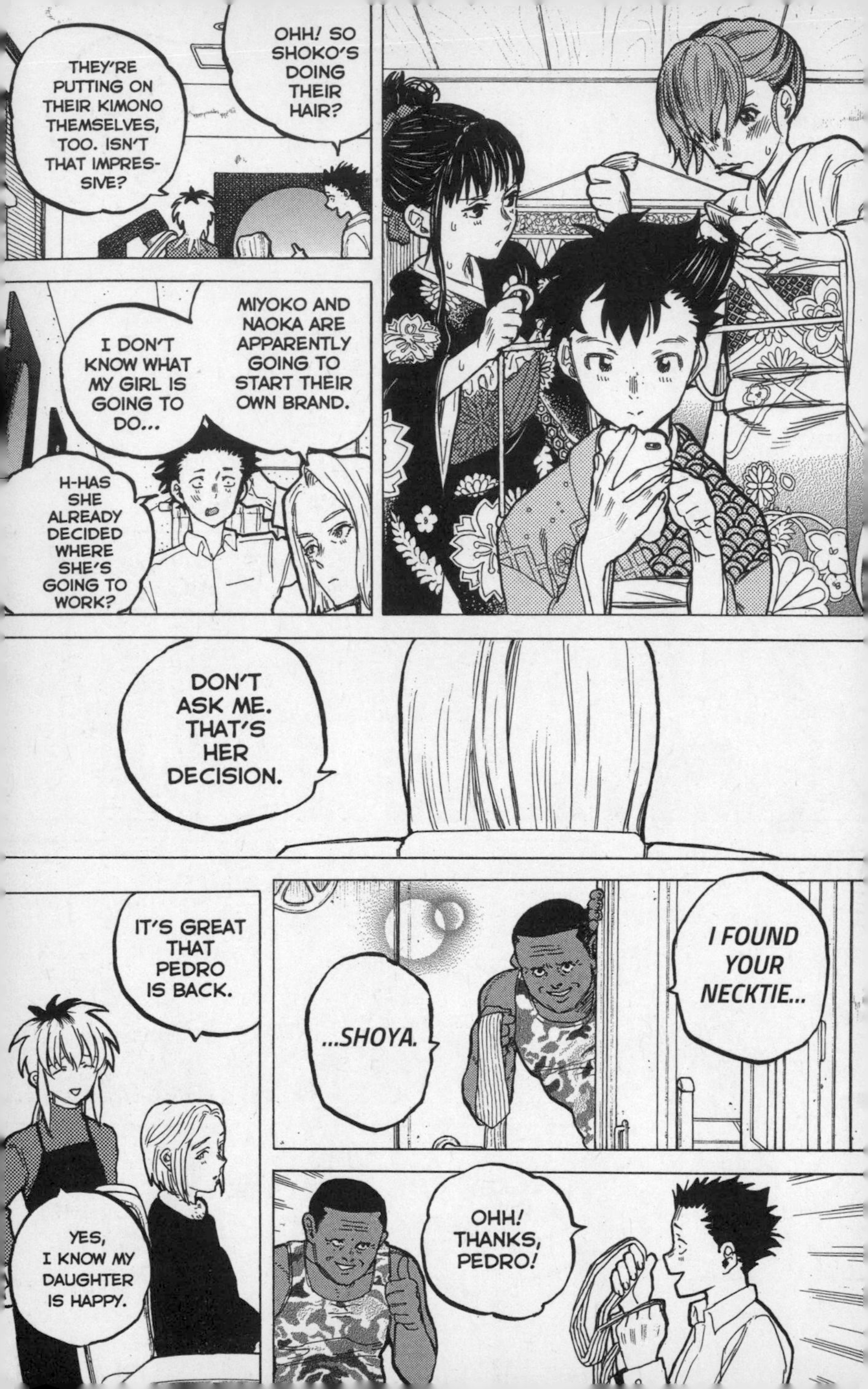
OHH! SO SHOKO'S DOING THEIR HAIR?
THEY'RE PUTTING ON THEIR KIMONO THEMSELVES, TOO. ISN'T THAT IMPRESSIVE?
MIYOKO AND NAOKA ARE APPARENTLY GOING TO START THEIR OWN BRAND.
I DON'T KNOW WHAT MY GIRL IS GOING TO DO...
H-HAS SHE ALREADY DECIDED WHERE SHE'S GOING TO WORK?
DON'T ASK ME. THAT'S HER DECISION.
I FOUND YOUR NECKTIE...
...SHOYA.
OHH! THANKS, PEDRO!
IT'S GREAT THAT PEDRO IS BACK.
YES, I KNOW MY DAUGHTER IS HAPPY.

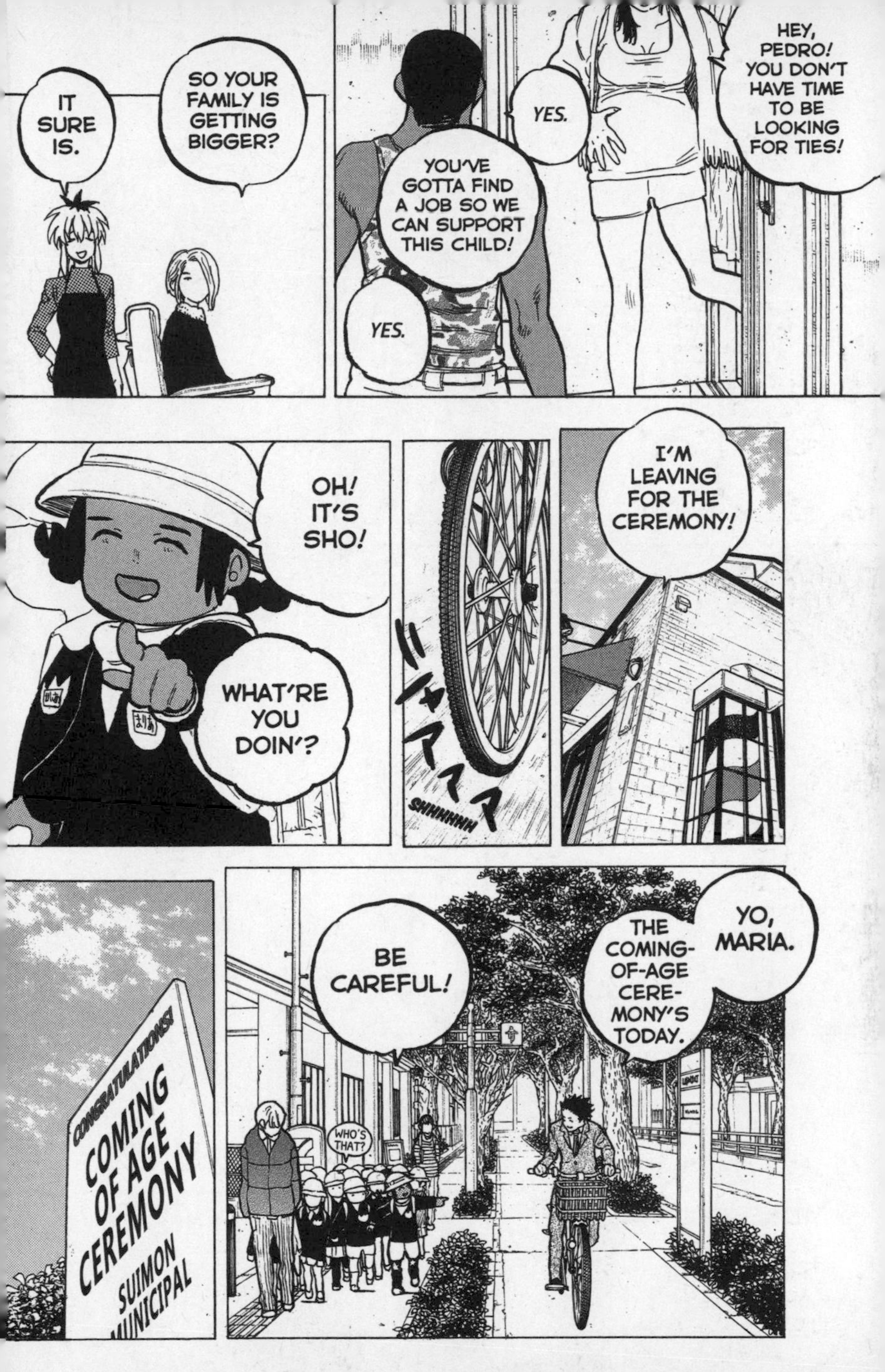
HEY, PEDRO! YOU DON'T HAVE TIME TO BE LOOKING FOR TIES!
YES.
YOU'VE GOTTA FIND A JOB SO WE CAN SUPPORT THIS CHILD!
YES.
SO YOUR FAMILY IS GETTING BIGGER?
IT SURE IS.
I'M LEAVING FOR THE CEREMONY!
シャアアア
SHHHHHH
OH! IT'S SHO!
WHAT'RE YOU DOIN'?
YO, MARIA.
THE COMING-OF-AGE CEREMONY'S TODAY.
BE CAREFUL!
WHO'S THAT?
CONGRATULATIONS!
COMING OF AGE CEREMONY
SUIMON MUNICIPAL

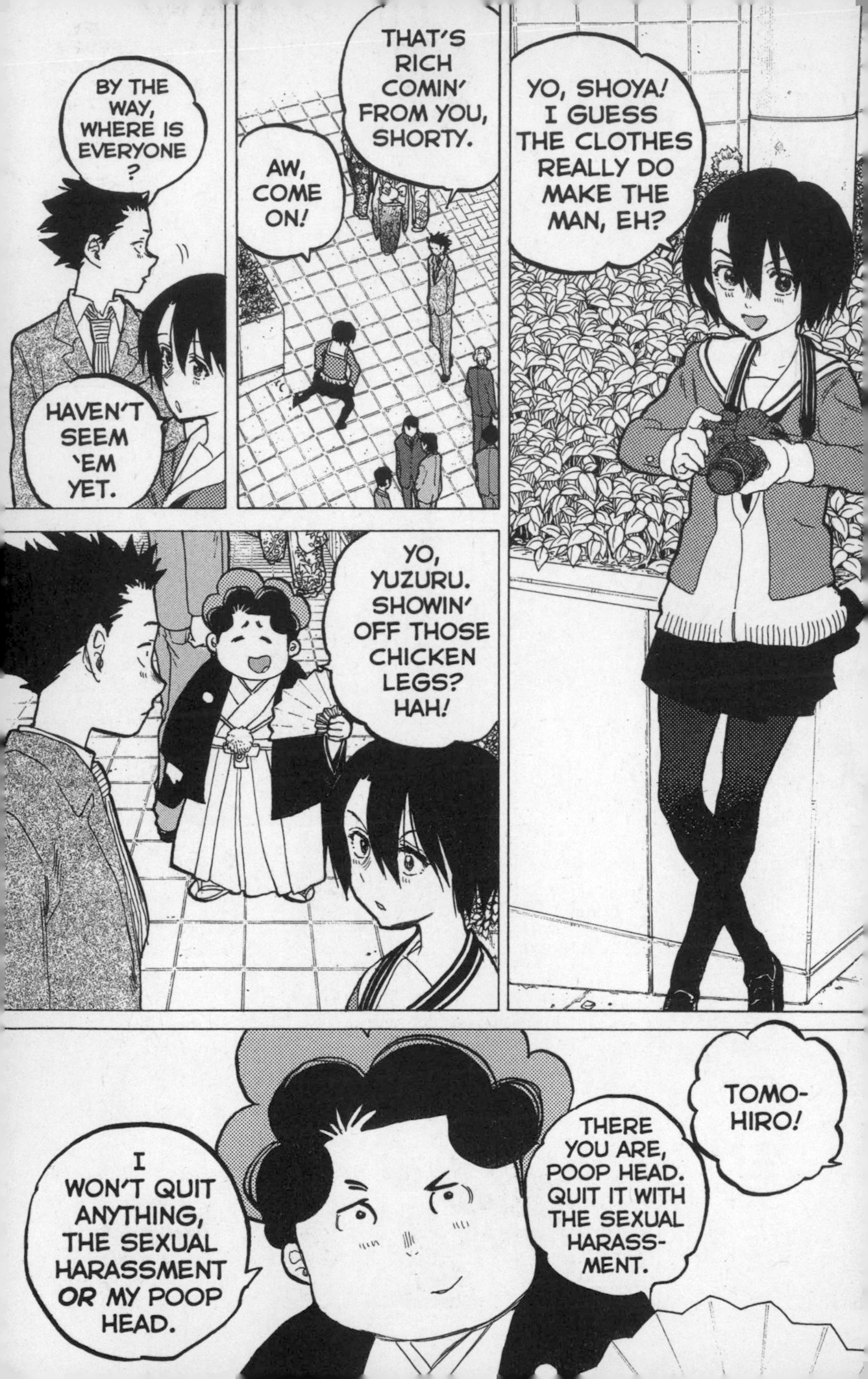
YO, SHOYA! I GUESS THE CLOTHES REALLY DO MAKE THE MAN, EH?
THAT'S RICH COMIN' FROM YOU, SHORTY.
AW, COME ON!
BY THE WAY, WHERE IS EVERYONE?
HAVEN'T SEEM 'EM YET.
YO, YUZURU. SHOWIN' OFF THOSE CHICKEN LEGS? HAH!
TOMO-HIRO!
THERE YOU ARE, POOP HEAD. QUIT IT WITH THE SEXUAL HARASS-MENT.
I WON'T QUIT ANYTHING, THE SEXUAL HARASSMENT OR MY POOP HEAD.

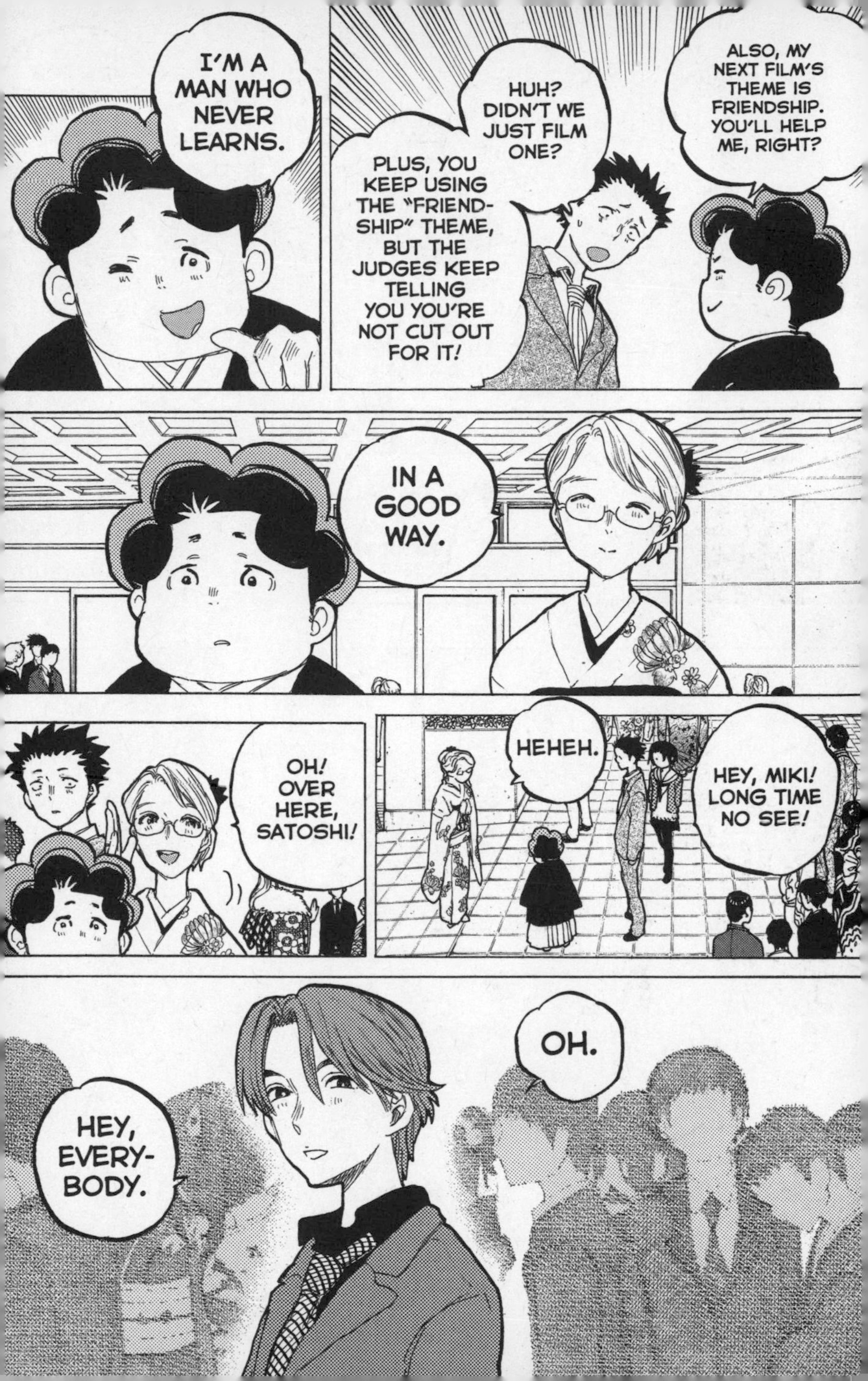
ALSO, MY NEXT FILM'S THEME IS FRIENDSHIP. YOU'LL HELP ME, RIGHT?
HUH? DIDN'T WE JUST FILM ONE?
PLUS, YOU KEEP USING THE "FRIENDSHIP" THEME, BUT THE JUDGES KEEP TELLING YOU YOU'RE NOT CUT OUT FOR IT!
I'M A MAN WHO NEVER LEARNS.
IN A GOOD WAY.
HEY, MIKI! LONG TIME NO SEE!
HEHEH.
OH! OVER HERE, SATOSHI!
OH.
HEY, EVERYBODY.

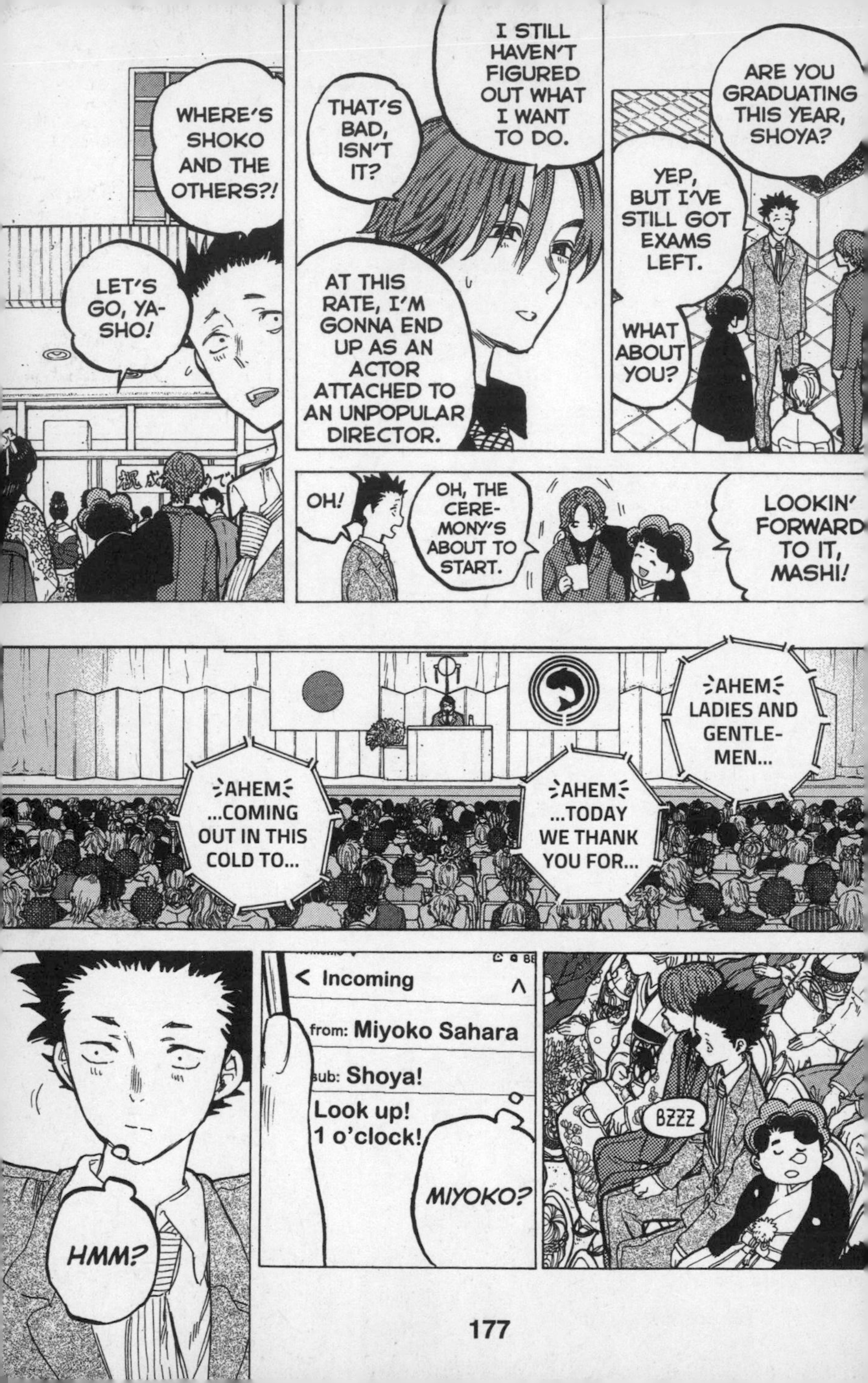
ARE YOU GRADUATING THIS YEAR, SHOYA?
YEP, BUT I'VE STILL GOT EXAMS LEFT.
WHAT ABOUT YOU?
I STILL HAVEN'T FIGURED OUT WHAT I WANT TO DO.
THAT'S BAD, ISN'T IT?
AT THIS RATE, I'M GONNA END UP AS AN ACTOR ATTACHED TO AN UNPOPULAR DIRECTOR.
LOOKIN' FORWARD TO IT, MASHI!
OH, THE CERE-MONY'S ABOUT TO START.
OH!
WHERE'S SHOKO AND THE OTHERS?!
LET'S GO, YA-SHO!
AHEM LADIES AND GENTLE-MEN...
AHEM ...TODAY WE THANK YOU FOR...
AHEM ...COMING OUT IN THIS COLD TO...
BZZZ
< Incoming
from: Miyoko Sahara
sub: Shoya!
Look up! 1 o'clock!
MIYOKO?
HMM?

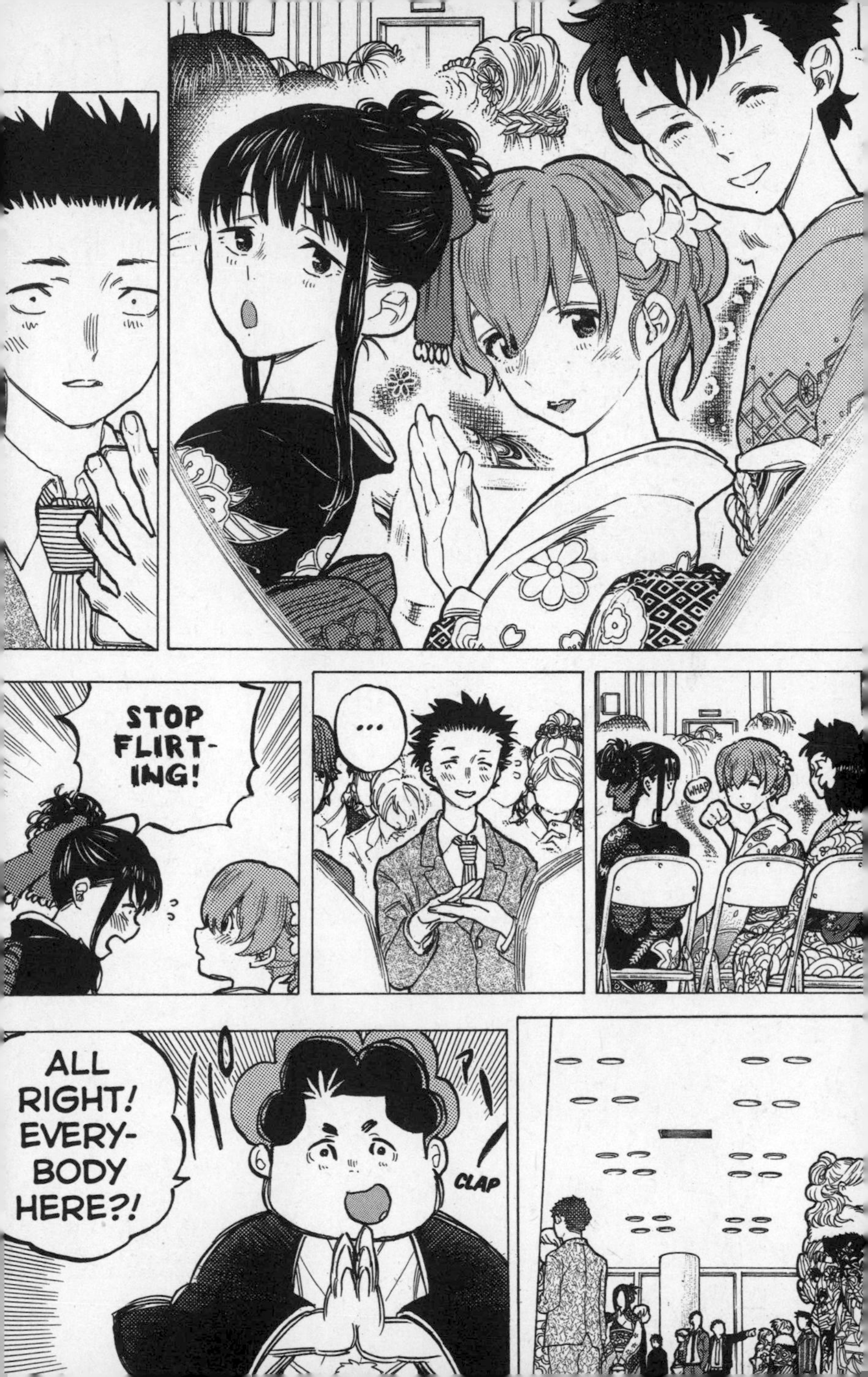
WHAP
...
STOP FLIRT-ING!
ALL RIGHT! EVERY-BODY HERE?!
CLAP

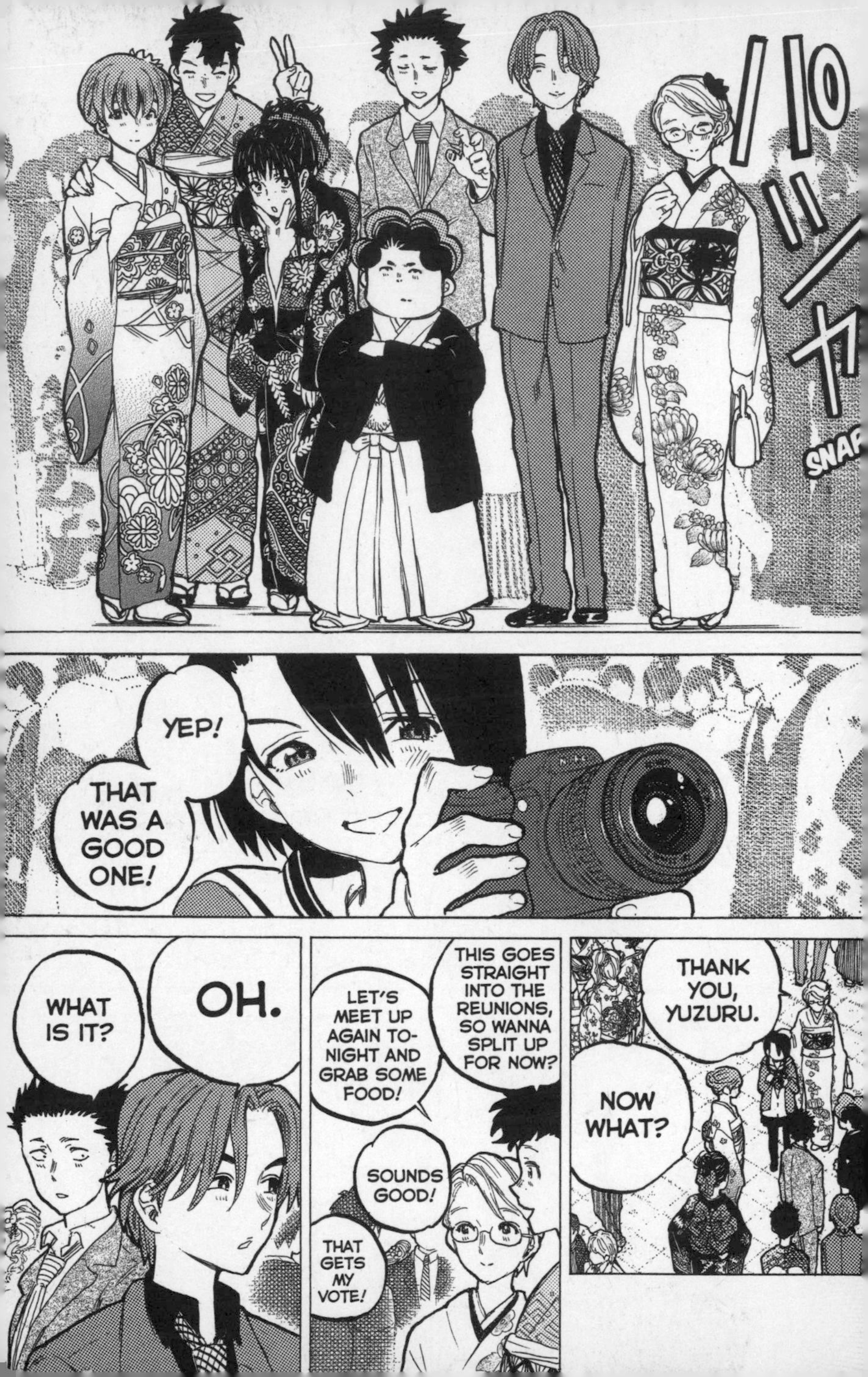
パシャ
SNAP
YEP!
THAT WAS A GOOD ONE!
THANK YOU, YUZURU.
NOW WHAT?
THIS GOES STRAIGHT INTO THE REUNIONS, SO WANNA SPLIT UP FOR NOW?
LET'S MEET UP AGAIN TO-NIGHT AND GRAB SOME FOOD!
SOUNDS GOOD!
THAT GETS MY VOTE!
OH.
WHAT IS IT?

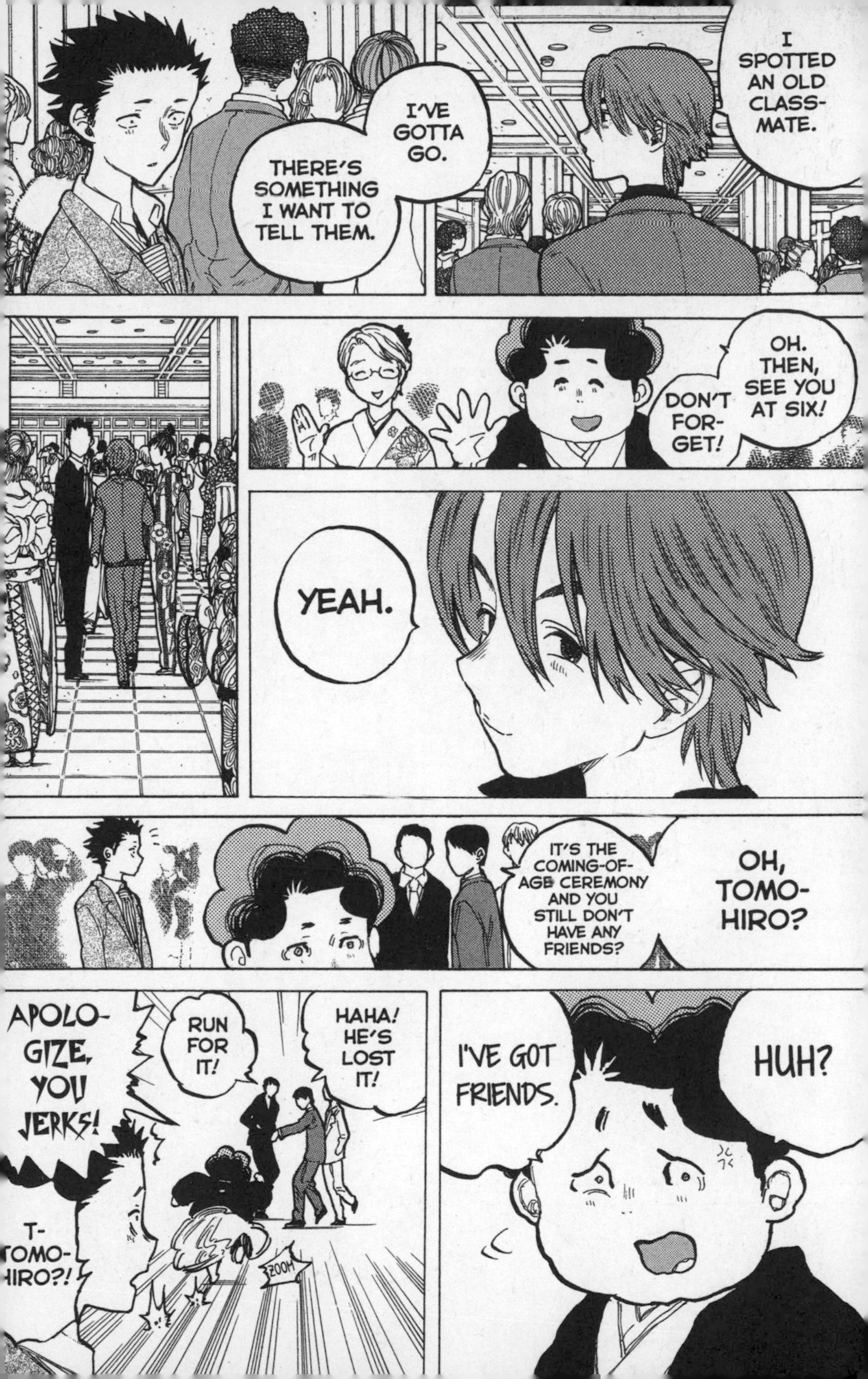
I SPOTTED AN OLD CLASSMATE.
I'VE GOTTA GO.
THERE'S SOMETHING I WANT TO TELL THEM.
OH. THEN, SEE YOU AT SIX!
DON'T FORGET!
YEAH.
OH, TOMO-HIRO?
IT'S THE COMING-OF-AGE CEREMONY AND YOU STILL DON'T HAVE ANY FRIENDS?
HUH?
I'VE GOT FRIENDS.
HAHA! HE'S LOST IT!
RUN FOR IT!
APOLO-GIZE, YOU JERKS!
ZOOM
T-TOMO-HIRO?!

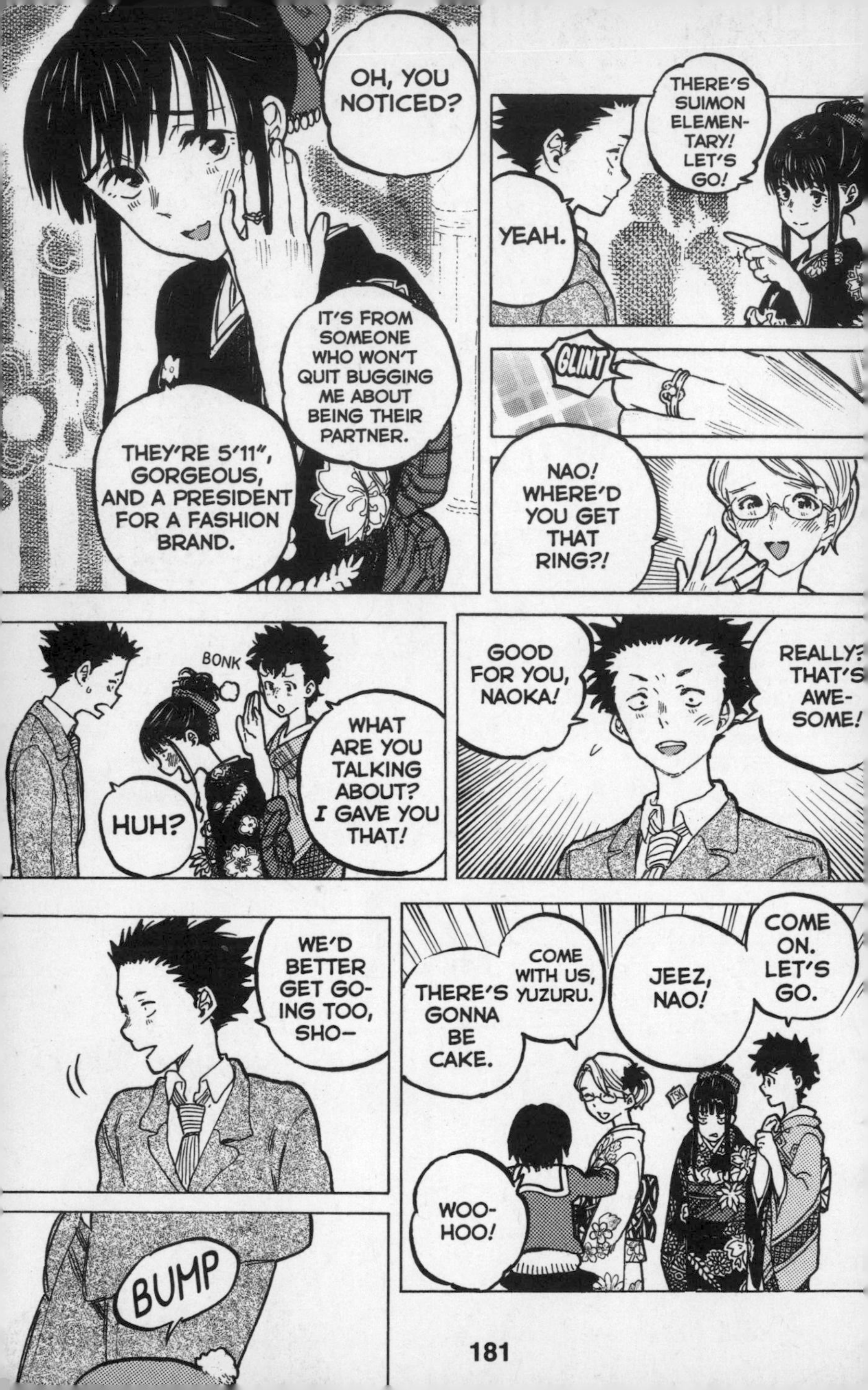
THERE'S SUIMON ELEMENTARY! LET'S GO!
YEAH.
GLINT
NAO! WHERE'D YOU GET THAT RING?!
OH, YOU NOTICED?
IT'S FROM SOMEONE WHO WON'T QUIT BUGGING ME ABOUT BEING THEIR PARTNER.
THEY'RE 5'11", GORGEOUS, AND A PRESIDENT FOR A FASHION BRAND.
REALLY? THAT'S AWESOME!
GOOD FOR YOU, NAOKA!
BONK
WHAT ARE YOU TALKING ABOUT? *I* GAVE YOU THAT!
HUH?
COME ON. LET'S GO.
JEEZ, NAO!
COME WITH US, YUZURU.
THERE'S GONNA BE CAKE.
TSK
WOO-HOO!
WE'D BETTER GET GOING TOO, SHO—
BUMP

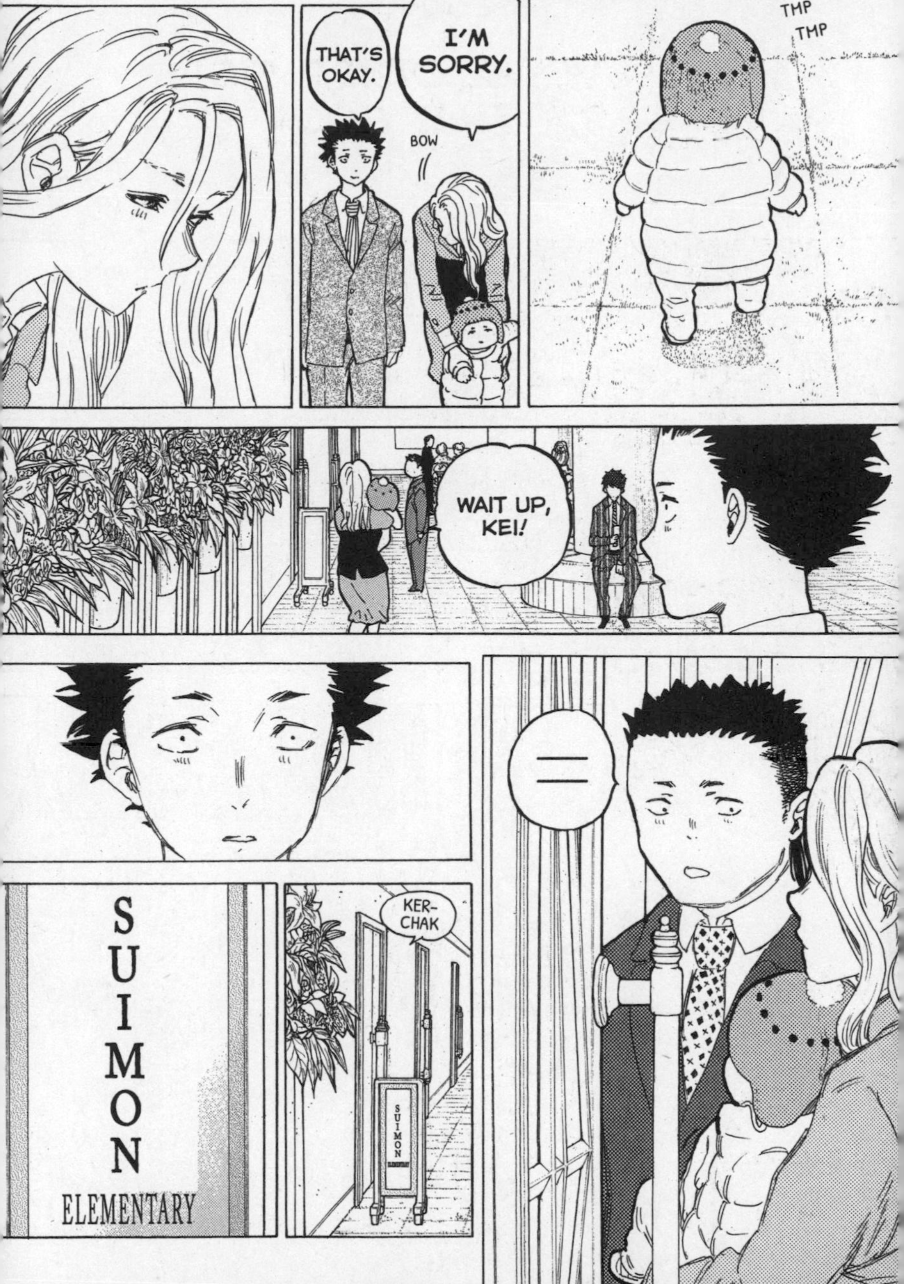

TMP
TMP
I'M SORRY.
THAT'S OKAY.
BOW
WAIT UP, KEI!
KER-CHAK
SUIMON
SUIMON ELEMENTARY

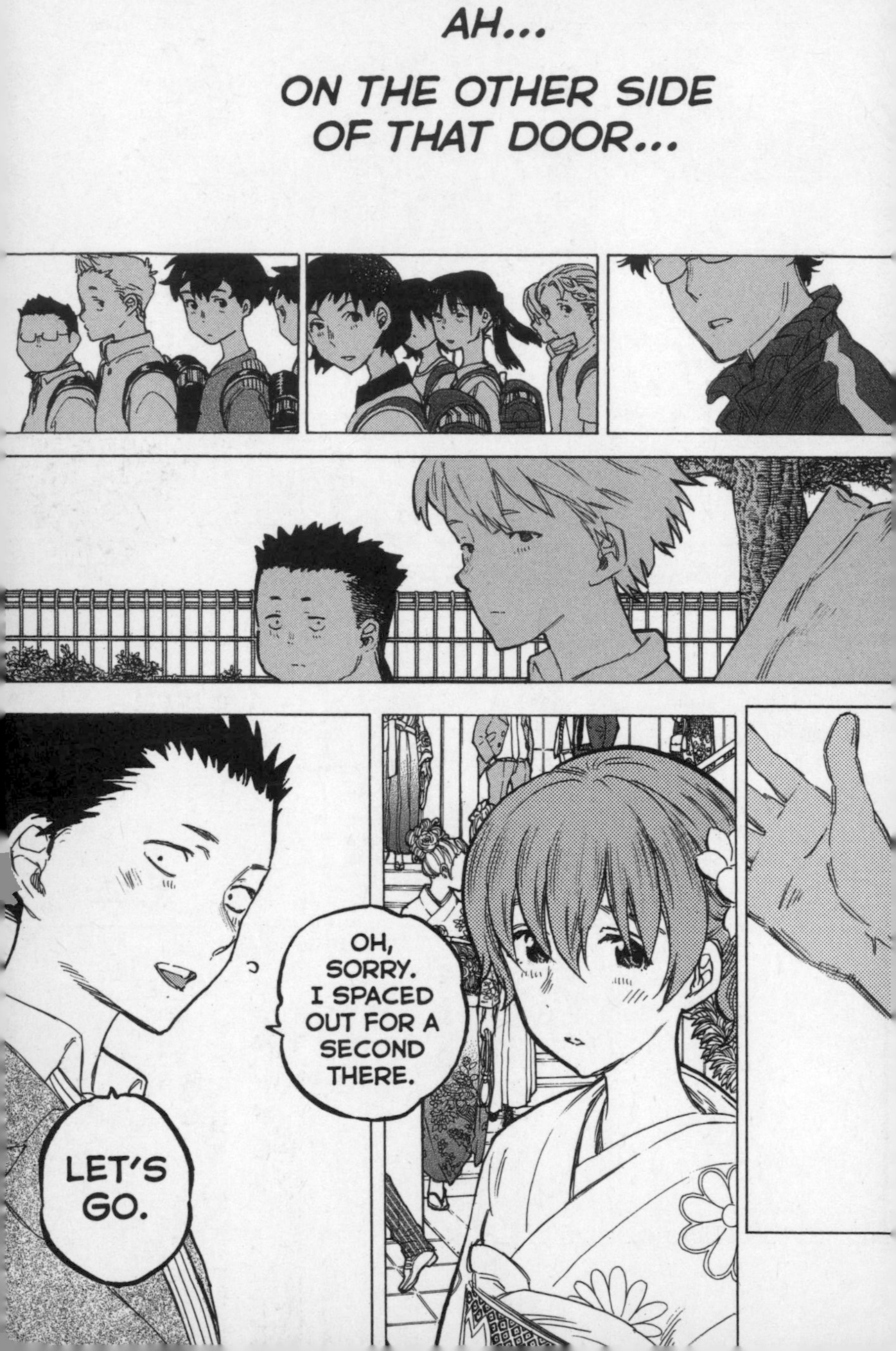
AH...
ON THE OTHER SIDE OF THAT DOOR...
OH, SORRY. I SPACED OUT FOR A SECOND THERE.
LET'S GO.

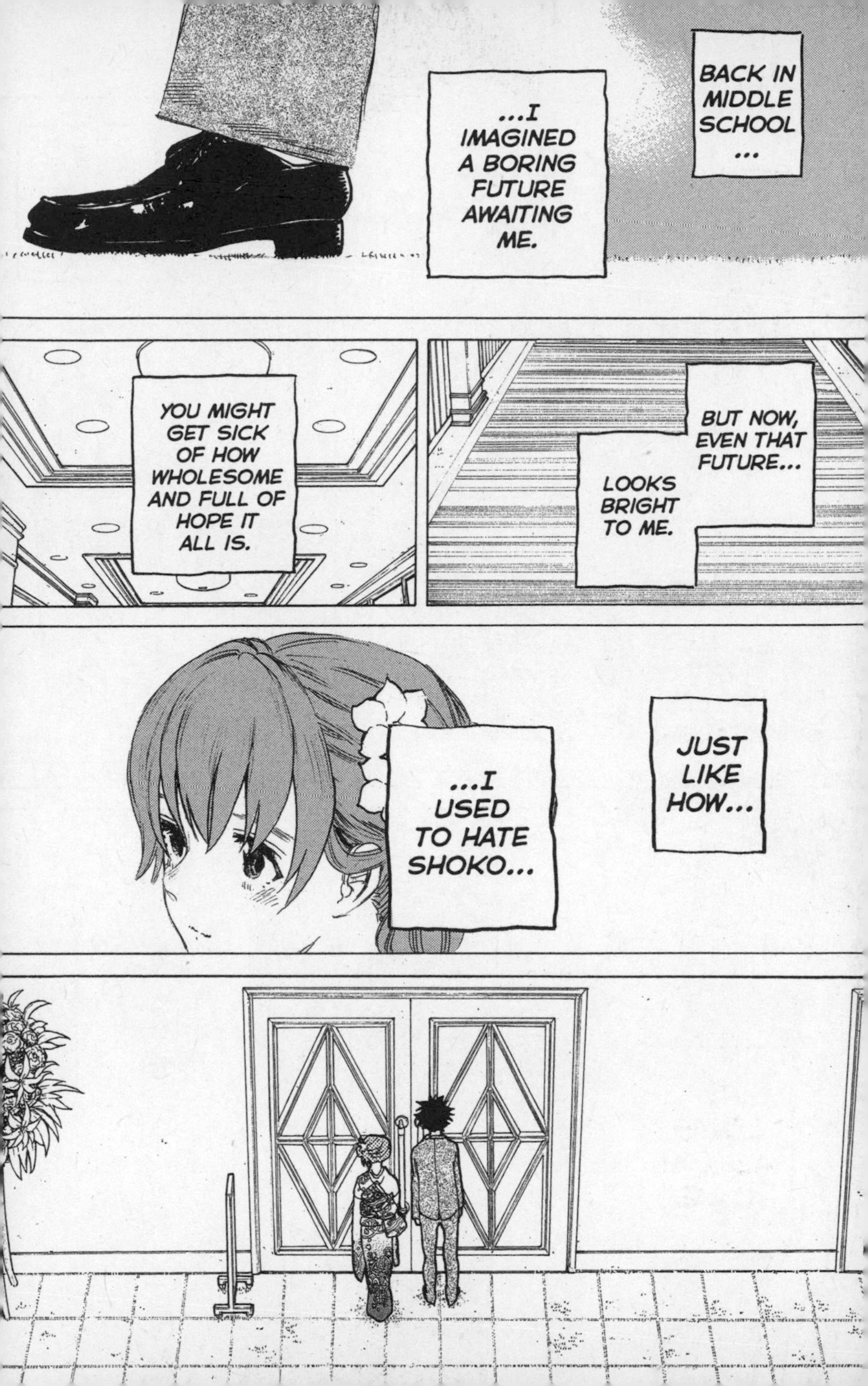
BACK IN MIDDLE SCHOOL...
...I IMAGINED A BORING FUTURE AWAITING ME.
BUT NOW, EVEN THAT FUTURE...
LOOKS BRIGHT TO ME.
YOU MIGHT GET SICK OF HOW WHOLESOME AND FULL OF HOPE IT ALL IS.
JUST LIKE HOW...
...I USED TO HATE SHOKO...

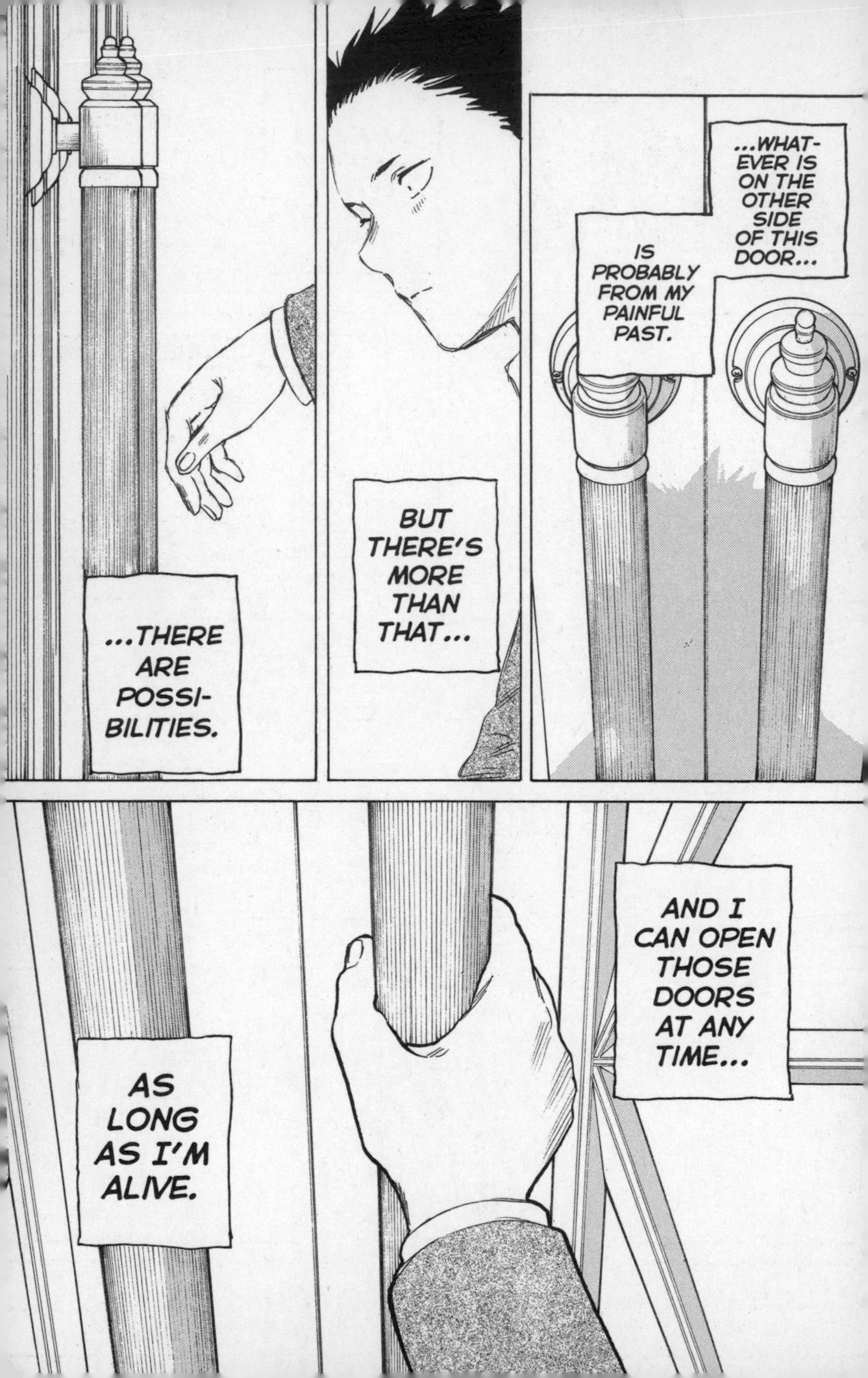
...WHATEVER IS ON THE OTHER SIDE OF THIS DOOR...
IS PROBABLY FROM MY PAINFUL PAST.
BUT THERE'S MORE THAN THAT...
...THERE ARE POSSIBILITIES.
AND I CAN OPEN THOSE DOORS AT ANY TIME...
AS LONG AS I'M ALIVE.

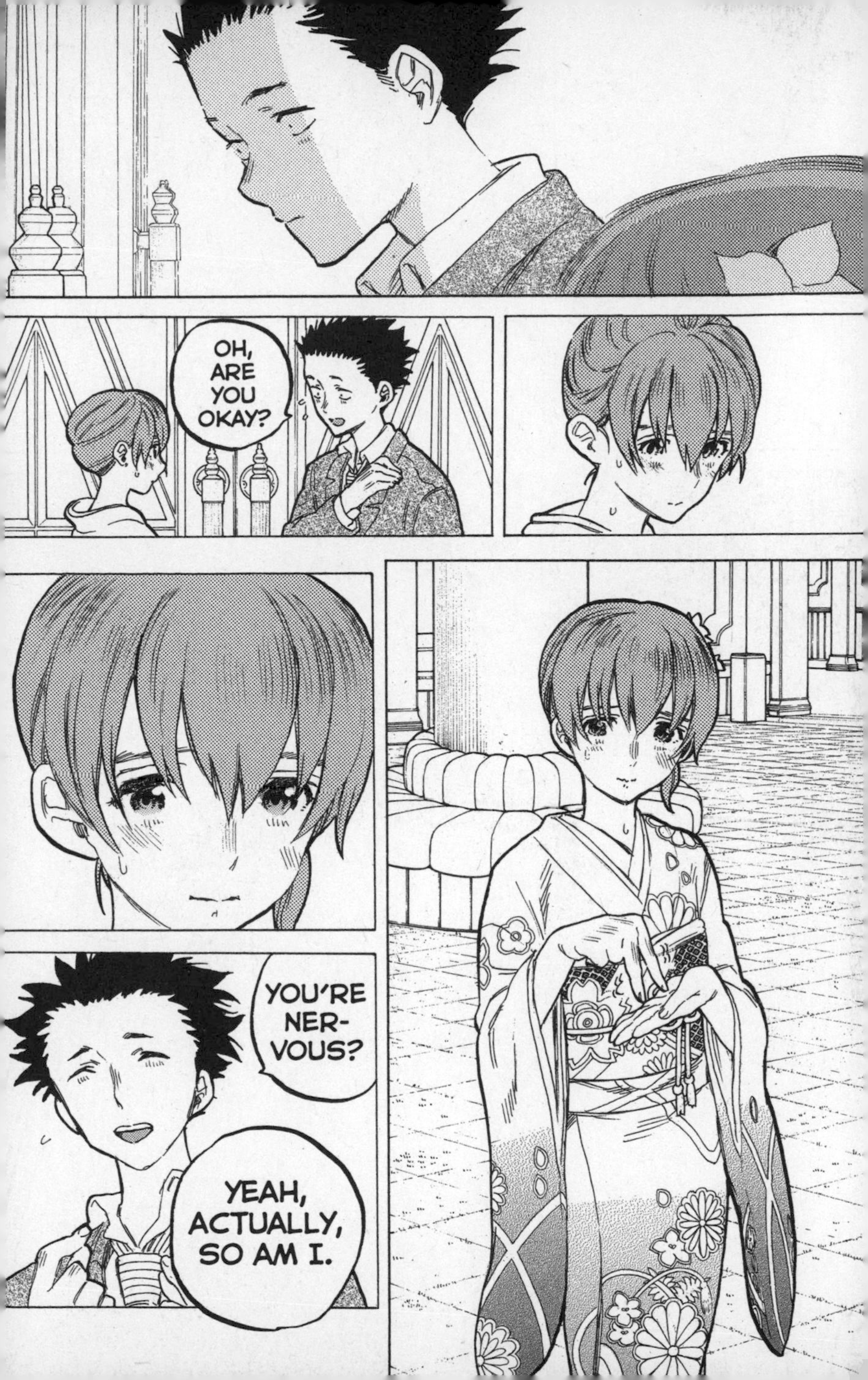
OH, ARE YOU OKAY?
YOU'RE NER-VOUS?
YEAH, ACTUALLY, SO AM I.

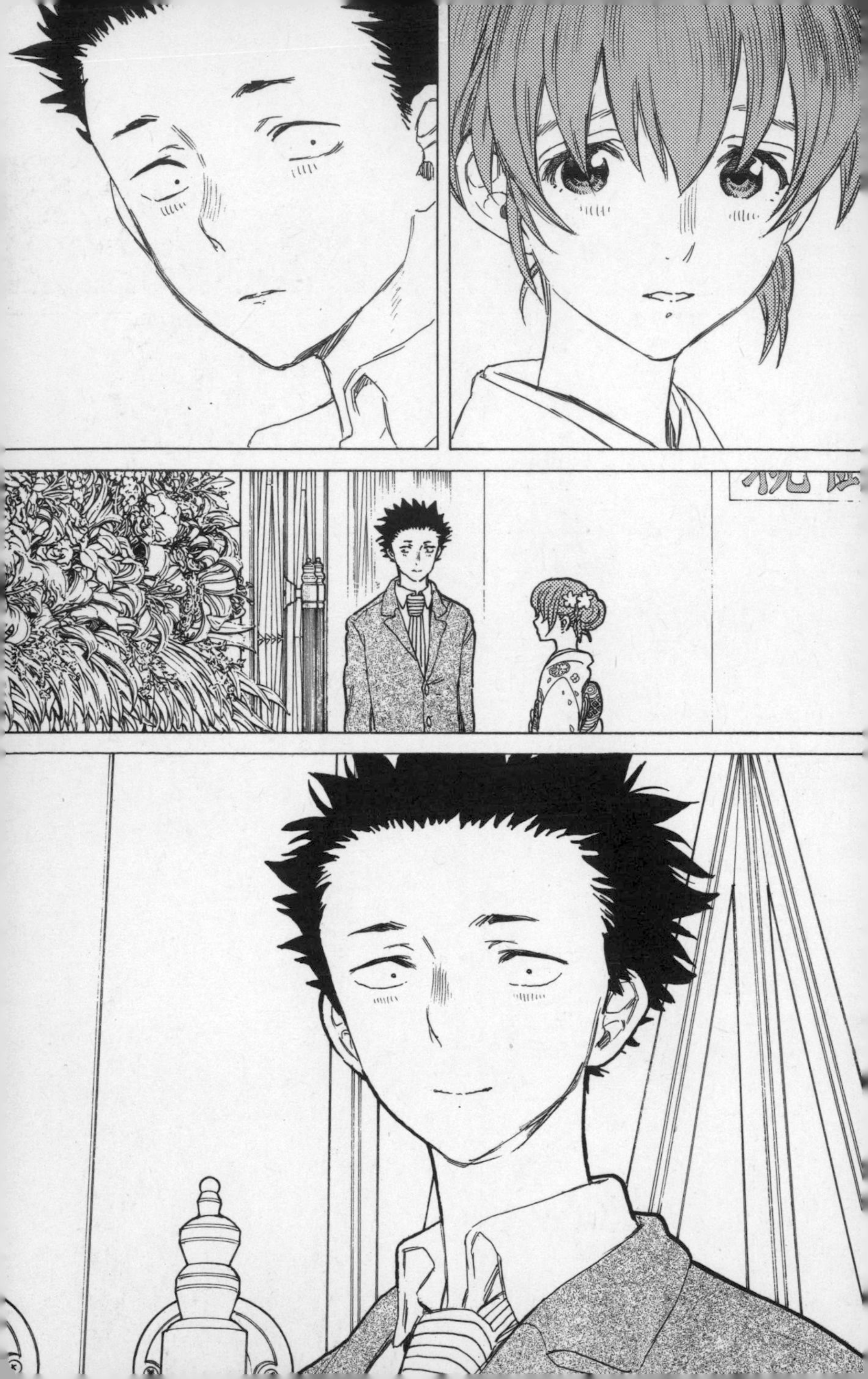

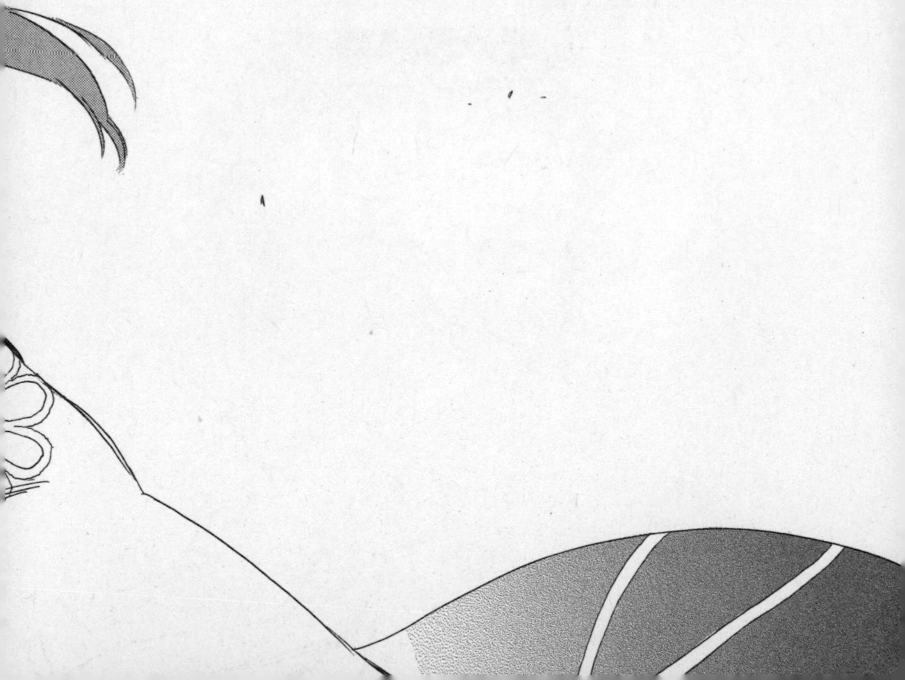

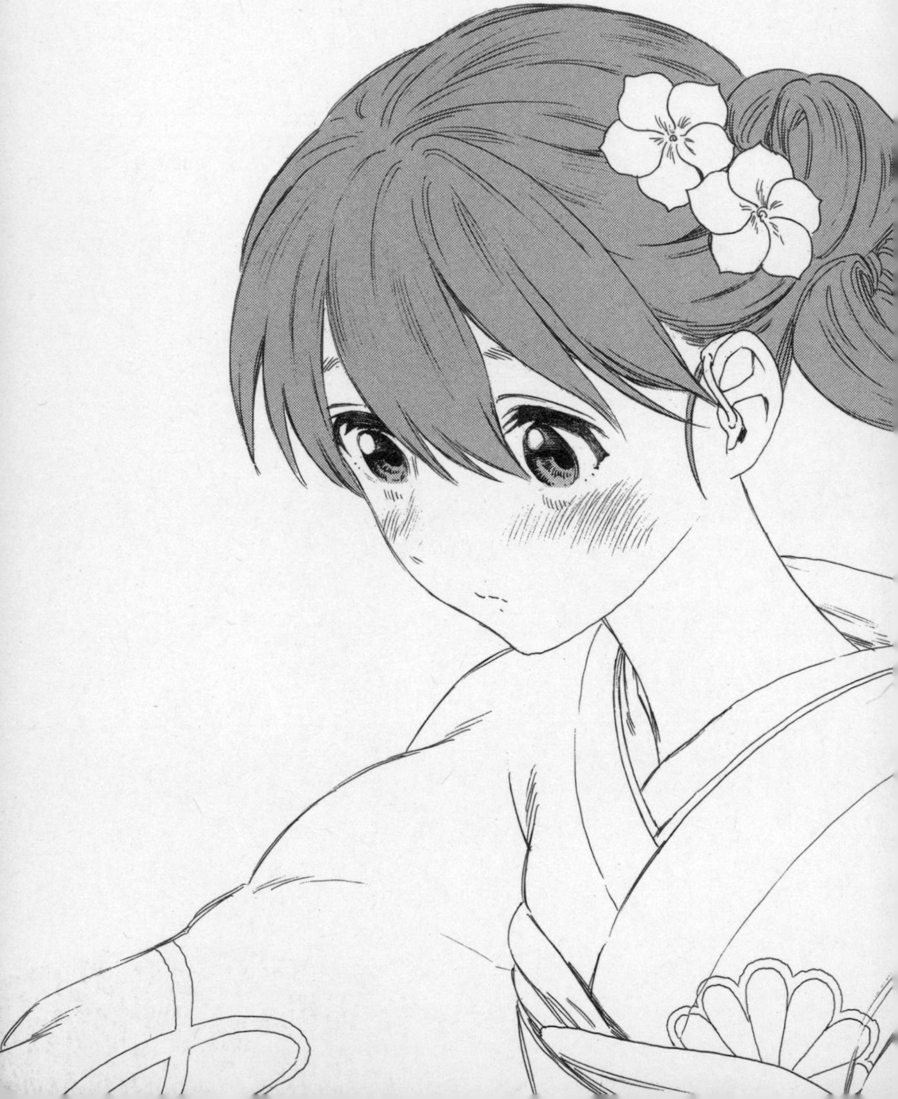

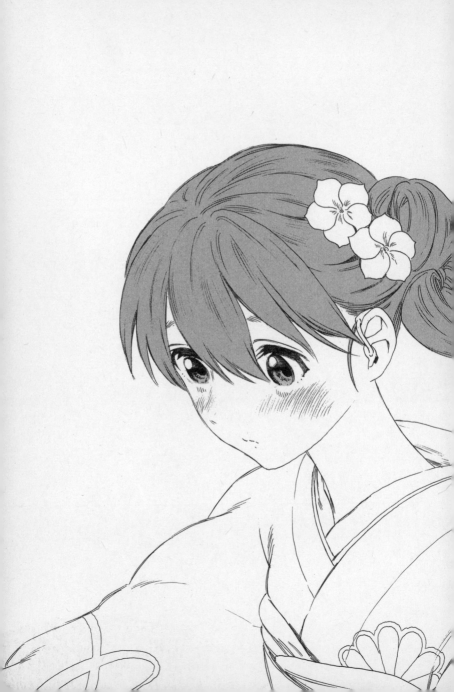

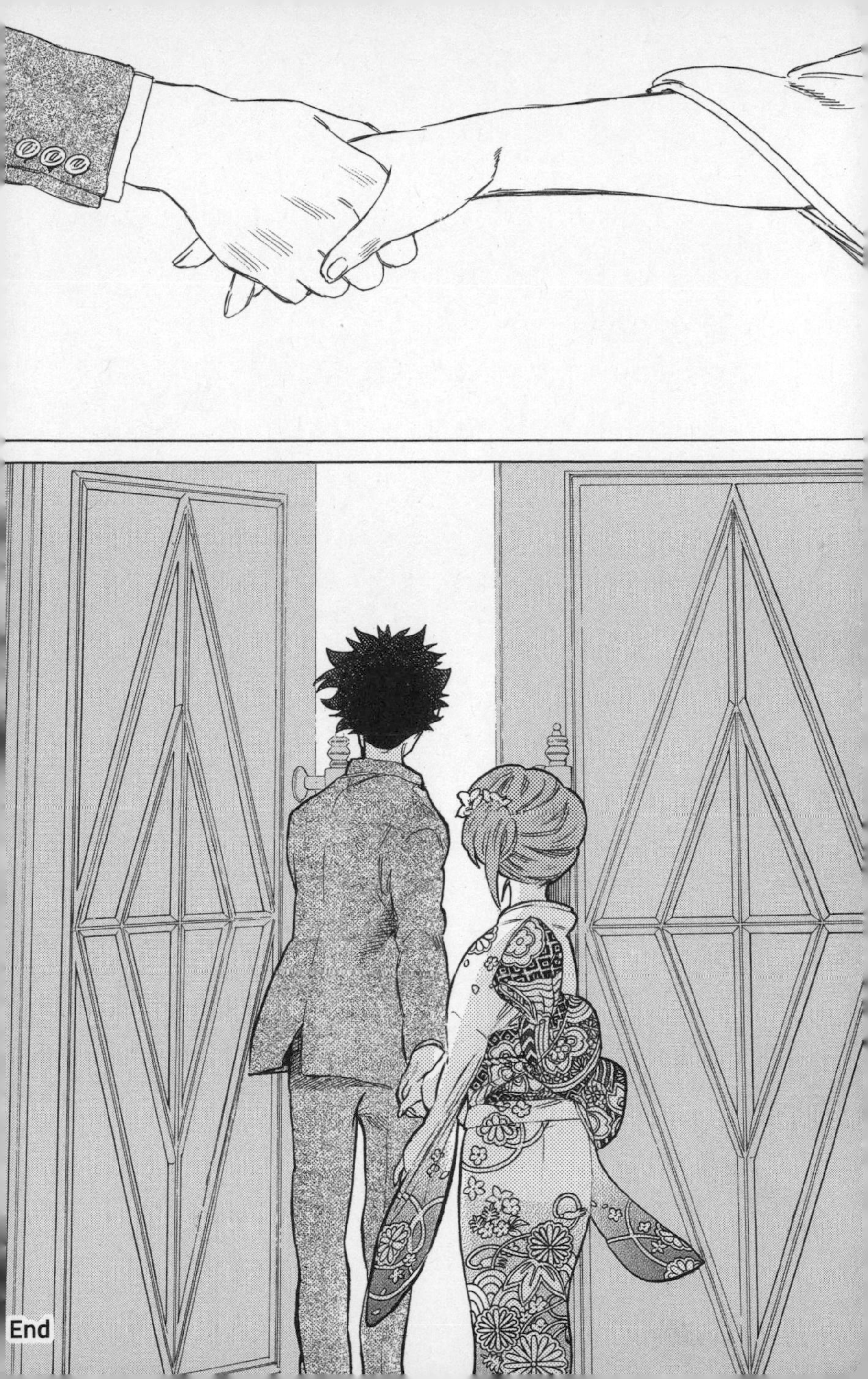
End

a Silent Voice

Translation Notes

Japanese can be a difficult language for some readers, and translation is often more art than science. For your edification and reading pleasure, here are notes on some of the places where we could have gone in a different direction with our translation, or where a Japanese cultural reference is used.

A Thousand Paper Cranes, p.87

The *senbazuru* is made up of a thousand origami cranes held together by string. It is often given to the sick or injured as a get-well gift. This is because in Japanese, *-zuru* means crane. There is a saying that goes, "a crane lives a thousand years; a turtle ten-thousand." Thus, cranes are lucky symbols; the thousand cranes bring good fortune and health for a long life.

Coming of Age Day, p.168

The Japanese holiday, *Seijin no Hi*, or Coming of Age Day falls on the second Monday of January every year. It is a day to recognize a 20-year-old as an adult and celebrate them. All those who have turned 20 in the past year, or are about to, are invited to the ceremony. It is usually held locally, or broken up by prefectures. Attendees dress formally, and traditional Japanese attire is still common. This is also an opportunity for the young women to wear a special kimono called *furisode*. Shoko and the girls are wearing *furisode* (see p.179), which are distinguishable by their very long sleeves.

MARDOCK

マルドゥック・スクランブル

SCRAMBLE

**Created by
Tow Ubukata** ✕ **Manga by
Yoshitoki Oima**

"I'd rather be dead."

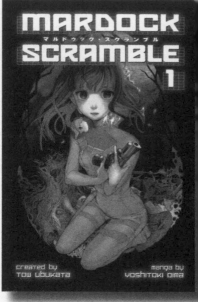

Rune Balot was a lost girl with nothing to live for. A man named Shell took her in and cared for her...until he tried to murder her. Standing at the precipice of death, Rune is saved by Dr. Easter, a private investigator. He uses an experimental procedure known as "Mardock Scramble 09" on Rune, and it grants her extraordinary abilities. Now, Rune must decide whether or not to use her new powers to help Dr. Easter bring Shell to justice. But, does she even have the will to keep living a life that's been broken so badly?

Ages: 16+

VISIT KODANSHACOMICS.COM TO:
- View release date calendars for upcoming volumes
- Find out the latest about upcoming Kodansha Comics series

A Kodansha Comics Trade Paperback Original.

A Silent Voice volume 7 copyright © 2014 Yoshitoki Oima
English translation copyright © 2016 Yoshitoki Oima

Published in the United States by Kodansha Comics, an imprint of Kodansha USA Publishing, LLC, New York.

Publication rights for this English edition arranged through Kodansha Ltd., Tokyo.

First published in Japan in 2014 by Kodansha Ltd., Tokyo, as Koe no katachi volume 7.

ISBN 978-1-63236-222-3

Printed in the United States of America.

www.kodanshacomics.com

9 8 7 6 5 4 3 2

Translation: Steven LeCroy
Lettering: Steven LeCroy & Hiroko Mizuno
Additional Touch-up: James Dashiell
Editing: Haruko Hashimoto
Kodansha Comics edition cover design by Phil Balsman